DIVERGE

To Christian BROOK
from Yakob K Adhana,
06.07.17

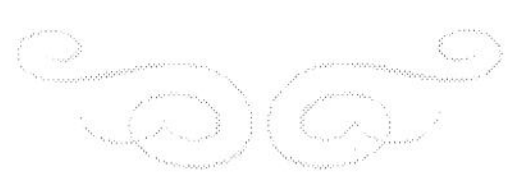

DIVERGE

Wake Up to the Purposeful Life you are Meant to Live

Based on true stories

YAKOB KIDANE ADHANOM

ISBN-13: 9781537007793
ISBN-10: 1537007793
Library of Congress Control Number: 2016916126
CreateSpace Independent Publishing Platform
North Charleston, South Carolina

To

… … … … … … … … … … … … … …

From

… … … … … … … … … … … … … …

Occasion

… … … … … … … … … … … … … …

AUTHOR'S NOTE

There is not greater agony than an untold story inside you.

— *Dr. Maya Angelo*

Life is full of adventurous good versus bad choices, with rewards as well as consequences for each.

There is a good choice to make; there is a bad choice. There is a long way to have life's journey; there is a short way to have fulfillment once one diverges. *Diverge* tells about learning life's choices, struggles, the quest for identity, fairness, justice, and honest service at a time when apathy in the face of urgency destroys human value. *Diverge* also informs how one can find purpose in one's personal existence once one diverges from self-destructive ways to self-mastering.

A few decades back, the author received the word "Diverge" in a dream. He felt that it was the last warning or face the consequence. Hence, he diverged and turned out to be like never before. The scripts throughout the manuscript are the tallied up bits and pieces of lots of true accounts of trials, temptations, and hurts that contributed to making the author who he is today.

All biblical quotations come from Kenneth Baker (ed.), *The New International Version Study Bible*, Grand Rapids, MI: Zondervan Publishing House, 1995.

When you were born, you cried and the world rejoiced. live your life so that when you die, the world cries and you rejoice.

— CHEROKEE EXPRESSION

This is a tribute to my father. He heard of the completion of this project yet did not see the published book.

Rev. Kidane Adhanom Hagos
November 27, 1927-August 2, 2013

What a man of God my father was: what a theologian, what a historian, what a linguist, what a genealogist, what an anthropologist, what a husband, what a father, and much, much more. His parental wisdom flows throughout this book.

He was an Orthodox priest. An American soldier, Rev. Don Taws, who became a believer in the field of duty, gave him a New Testament Bible. Later, when the Old Testament Bible was printed, he worked and received it as an exchange for his labor. "On one occasion, Priest Kidane spoke to missionary Rev. Francis Mahaffy of his desire to have a Bible in Tigrigna, but was short of funds. In order to test his sincerity (many people want Bibles but do not wish to do anything to earn them) Mr. Mahaffy offered him one in return for four days of work—a Bible costs U.S. $1.60 and the wage for common labor in this land is less than 40 cents per day. He willingly did this and avidly studied the Scriptures.

During the spring of 1958, Kidane asked to be examined by Mr. Mahaffy and missionary Rev. Clarence Duff for public confession of faith. This was done and he gave public testimony to his faith in Christ in the market places of *Senafe* and *Adi Caieh*."

(The Orthodox Presbyterian Messenger, February, 1959.)

DEDICATION

When the righteous thrive, the people rejoice; when the wicked rule, the people groan.

— *Proverbs 29:2*

To My Lord and God, who represented my cases in all the places that I've been, silencing every voice that rose up against me. He has been and continues to be my champion, my provider, my refuge, my strength and my strong tower where I go to be safe. Abba, I'm unworthy to hear your voice, that you spoke to me several times, and undeserving of your mercy, gracious love, your faithfulness, and all that you have done for me. Lord, may you use the message of this project for your glory!

My father, Rev. Kidane Adhanom Hagos, and my mother, Letebrhan Tekie, thank you for the sacrifices you made for your children.

Dr. William Macharia, Dr. Eustace, Dr. and Mrs. Agnes Karo, Alice Mortlock, and Mrs. Ruth Crum: thank you for your unconditional love and service.

Rev. Bruno Tron and Rev. Sture Normark of Swedish Evangelical Mission, thank you for opening the educational and employment door for my father.

Rev. Clarence and Dora Duff, Rev. Donald and Jeanette Taws, Rev. Francis and Arlena Mahaffy, Rev. Herbert and Mary Bird, Rev. Charles and Fern Stanton, and Anna

Strikwerda of The Orthodox Presbyterian Church missionaries, who served as American Evangelical Mission. Your labor in the Lord is not in vain. Thank you for your service.

The United States of America- "For I was hungry and you gave me something to eat. I was thirsty and you gave me a drink. I was a stranger and you invited me in. I needed clothes, and you clothed me, I was sick, and you looked after me."

Annie Hellstrom, a Swedish Saint who influenced my life and showed me Christ and Christianity more than any human being ever could.

Annie, the practical Christian living of trust that I saw in you inspired me to walk through the wilderness in the life journey. You served humanity wholeheartedly. That is, giving food to the hungry, drink to the thirsty, welcoming strangers to your home, clothing the naked, taking care of the sick, visiting prisoners, and weeping with the bereaved. As the perfect example of a Christian that people can follow, your kindness without racial or religious discrimination motivates us to give the same love onto others. Had you been from the Catholic Church, the Pope would have declared you a 'Saint' just as he did with Mother Teresa. However, that does not worry me because, the God, whom the Pope himself serves, has declared you a Saint. Annie, thank you for your service, and we thank God for you.

ACKNOWLEDGMENTS

In acknowledging a few of the many people who have influenced the writing of this book, I would first like to address the greatest debt that I owe, which is to my family. All of them believed in my ability.

Thank you also to CNN for initiating the birth of this book.

Finally, yet importantly, I would like to acknowledge my readers. Thank you all for trusting me and purchasing my book.

DISCLAIMER NOTICE

The book to read is not the one, which thinks for you, but the one that makes you think. no book in the world equals the bible for that.

— *Harper Lee*

The content of this publication is based on a lot of true stories that happened in life. However, the characters' names and the names of institutions mentioned throughout are fictitious. Any resemblance to actual events, places, or persons living or dead is unintended. The author reserves the right not to be responsible for the accuracy and completeness of this publication. Liability claims regarding damage caused using any information provided in this publication, including information that is incomplete or incorrect will, therefore, be rejected. All matters discussed in this publication are the author's creation and do not represent the views of the author's family or any organization, are not binding, and are without obligation. Readers that are younger than ten years old will need parental guidance.

Thank you and God bless you, Yakob Kidane Adhanom

PREFACE

God will use whatever he wants to display his glory. heavens and stars. history and nations. people and problems.

— *Max Lucado*

Behold, a woman in the East African nation of Eritrea is giving birth to a motivated and tenacious son, who would fall into the chasm of tolerance, apathy, and faithlessness, costing him three decades until he chose to diverge out of foolishness by himself.

It is a rainy and windy summer night in the Highlands. The cold is so intense at times; it feels as if one can reach out and touch it. The brisk night breeze blows the mint-scented eucalyptus and olive tree leaves.

A blanket of misty clouds lurks through the mountainous lands to nearly eight thousand feet above sea level. The city of Asmara is on the edge of a long, steep slope.

The cries of a woman in labor cut through the hazy sky like a sword. The shrieks of pain emanate from a small, rundown shack. Suddenly, the woman's voice quiets and the sound of a baby's cry echoes over the hills. Shouts of joy and happiness rouse the neighbors from their beds. Cheerful women dance and chant "*E-Leal-ta*" seven times. The loud and melodious chant surpasses and silences the night racket of crickets and bleating of frogs. The women's joyful *E-Leal-ta* declare to the villagers the birth of a baby.

"Did you hear seven times *E-Leal-ta*? It is a boy," announces the good news teller, who has long braided hair. If it were the birth of a girl, the *E-Leal-ta* would be three times. The newborn is an African, a Semitic by tribe, born between the months of August and September in the early 1970s. This happens in a country where each month has thirty days. The child's name is HAYET AFRICA, the son of SHEDEN AFRICA. One may pronounce Hayet as "hyat," or as "ha-yet," and Sheden is pronounced "she-den." Hayet means a cub and Sheden a lion, the leader of the pride. The mother's name is WA-EURO, meaning lioness, pronounced as "Wa and Euro."

Hayet grows to hate some aspects of the temporal earthly dwelling that would determine his personhood and fate. As a youth, he hates spending Sundays and holidays as well as dinnertime without his father. As a young man, he will despise seeing the unfair or unjust treatment of the defenseless using religious faith, the control of money, power, and gender as manipulative means of intimidation. He will hate systems or governments that mislead, exploit, and enslave their helpless citizens. He will come to hate being a loser in life, with every door shut in his face. Hate having been expelled from a prestigious university and the thought of dying without seeing the fulfillment of his father's dreams and his mother's wishes. Hate his grandparents' unwavering faith that God has destined him for greatness. Yet, Hayet allows fear and uncertainty to overwhelm him. He hates seeing people drift away from a purposeful living. More than anything else, he hates the innate feeling that had told him there was a seed of greatness in his life. He longs for someone to reveal to him what that feeling was saying and how to achieve it. As for now, Hayet is content with being an infant, fresh from his mother's womb.

Hayet spends his formative years in Africa, embracing the values that would shape him for the rest of his life. Africa is a naturally beautiful, rich, and lovely continent where a leader, a president, or a king is always right and above the law, mostly stays in power for life, until one gets overthrown or gets killed, where chubbiness is an exception for the rich.

Hayet's society measures the impeccable beauty of a woman to the likeness of Saint Mary. The community measures the handsomeness of a man in the likeness of the Saint Angel Michael. Hayet personifies Michael-like handsomeness because his mother prayed for such children.

The women of Eritrea are extremely beautiful, a few inches shorter than the men. They have skinny, slim bodies endowed with a head-turning curviness. Their hair is kinky, and when it is not braided back, it is left free to bounce in the wind.

Often, during the day, the sky is filled with a sporadic scene of stars, eagles, and jet fighters that consistently hover at a low altitude. At twilight under dimly lit streetlights that obscure the moonlight and starlight shimmers Asmara, which is perhaps one of the safest capital city in the world, with near zero records of robbery, vandalism, or gun related crimes. Local and foreign men, women and children can socialize anytime, as much as they want, whenever they want without any fear of being kidnapped or other disturbances.

Cold, foggy air blows over the pantile and zinc-roofed houses coming from the mountain chains of the Red Sea, creating at nightfall a lovely and sensational utopia. In the evenings, elegant jewelry-adorned pedestrians promenade to meet or be seen by others of the same interest. That is when even the president leisurely strolls without bodyguards through the columns of date fruit–bearing palm trees, along the white, burgundy, magenta, orange, pink, and purple bougainvillea decorated with black stone– fenced gated compounds. Perhaps it would not be an exaggeration to say most of the houses in the city and all the residential places in the villages are gated.

The indoor and outdoor pavement café's striking pastry aromas entice passersby to stop for a hot cappuccino, red tea from a traditional small glass cup, bottled alcoholic drinks, or food for the rich, listening and singing along the action evoking audio social, revolutionary, and love songs. The poor also joyfully enjoy the panoramic view of the city, which was not allowed during the

Italian colonial days, purchasing warm roasted red-skin peanuts from illegal vendors that come to the street to sell after the city council patrols end their day duty. Hayet's father, Mr. Sheden, a graceful and intelligent man, works out of town. Consequently, Hayet lives without the daily presence of his affectionate father, who shows his love practically.

In most African cultures, men eat spicy, salty, smoky, and roasted meals, specifically prepared in an unglazed and natural clay cooking pots intended for the man of the house. At mealtime, if there are remnants when the man finishes eating, the wife adds more water to the stew and then gives it to the children. Plenty of families cook chickens or, rarely, hens. When they do, the better section is given per one's importance in the family. In some families, the only boy in the family might receive bigger, as well as better, portions of the leg and breast meat.

The favoritism reveals that a son is superior to the older daughters, while the favored girls may get a neck or a wing. Sometimes the father may allow the boy to dine with him while the girls eat watery stew and the remnants of the males' dinner with their mother in the kitchen. However, Mr. Sheden treats all his children equally. Although his wife desires to prepare a special meal for him alone, he insists, "I will eat whatever my children eat." He drinks from the same enamel tin cup and eats at the one dinner table with his family members.

Regardless of his father's frequent absence due to work, Hayet has the constant presence of his gracious and nurturing mother. Mrs. Sheden never went to school because she is a female. In addition, education was rare, even for males, who have a higher possibility of going to school. Nevertheless, Mrs. Sheden knows the value of education and ensures that her children take advantage of it. Regularly, she looks over their exercise books. Whenever she finds a wrong mark, she questions her children, "Why did you receive an 'X' sign?" and insists each child answer honestly.

The value of having sincere friendships and serving humanity in truth and fairness without personal interest, meaning 'what is in there for me' is important to the family. Maintaining unbreakable and loyal friendships with whomever the family knows is a no-brainer. Hayet's parents have instilled in the children the significance of having unwavering biblical principles as a guide for life. From his earliest years, Hayet chooses to live by their standards until some new insights test his precepts. Sadly, the community has disowned Hayet's parents for their newly adopted evangelical beliefs that would have a significant effect on his life journey.

Chapter 1

It is so much easier to tell people what they want to hear instead of what they need to hear.

— Dr. Phil McGraw

Have you ever seen an achievable task that should have been short unreasonably stretch out into decades due to failure to identify a fixable wrong life choice? If so, then you know how irritating it can be to drag out a task for longer than the allotted period.

It took three decades for Hayet to complete a three-year accelerated or four years' regular college studies. How long will it take you to achieve a task that you must complete? It all depends on the individual. Acquiring knowledge from Hayet's experience could save one from doing the same wrong all over again. Because in the end, after wasting resources and years of one's life, eventually, one would do what is right. That is to say, if you lost a key, money, a friend, a spouse, a child, health, purpose, and so forth, go to where you lost find what you lost, hold what you lost, embrace what you lost never to lose it for the second time and start all over again.

Just like anybody else, Hayet is God's workmanship, his own master's handmade creation, regenerated from above—spiritually transformed, well matched and equipped to be used for good works. God prepared a way for him beforehand, taking a course that He set, so that he would walk in it enjoying rest and peace that He predestined. However, Hayet makes poor choices and deviates from purposeful living. His internal destiny directing whisper voice and loved ones give him lectures about what he needed to do and how an intentional living could get him to his promised land without taking an unnecessary detour of life journey. Yet he fails to perceive that more often, what he need to hear is what he does not want to hear, and how hard it is for him to kick against the merciless pricks of life.

Learning from others who rebelled against their destiny could save him from learning life the hard way, which he would not be fond of, repeating the same mistakes of others. In the future for the very speech that he hates his intolerant critics for correcting him, he will love them. Eventually, Hayet chooses to jaywalk by the wide entryway that many enter through, ignoring the small entryway of destiny that only a few find at a cost of time and resources to himself and others that could have benefited from his services.

Late on a Tuesday night toward the end of January, an adventurous journey of Hayet's life comes to completion. The long-awaited passenger airplane lands on American soil, carrying an unknown young man with an untapped potential that would influence the nations of the world for good.

The heat from an unknown source that Hayet has never seen or felt before in Africa warms Chicago O'Hare International Airport. As he gazes out of the airport lounge windows, the wind just picks up a little. There should be only a legitimate work-related reason to be outside in the face of the 35 mph wind. The blizzard is expected to last for several more hours.

The wind consistently blows the red and white–striped cones away from where they have been placed for direction and safety. The short marshal chases the windblown cones, minding his steps in the freezing and slippery snow while awaiting the aircraft that has reached an exit ramp. The tall employee equipped with a helmet, reflecting wands and reflecting safety vest signals for a direction and the pilot turns and slows, following the aircraft marshal's signaling to an assigned parking bay between two huge airplanes. Hayet's big brown eyes are heavy, forcing themselves to shut up, needing some sleep. He has not slept for over twenty-four hours.

With apprehension, nervousness, and an audible heartbeat, he anticipates exiting the airport. He is dressed in layers of coats and sweaters as he panics; at the same time, he wants to see for himself how the cold feels, walk out on the cotton-like churning feathery snowflakes that blanket the earth and scoop some snow without a glove. Most important to Hayet is to see how his adoptive parents accept him at his destination in New York.

Hayet is a handsome teenager. Long before he was born, during the ten years of barrenness, "Lord, bless me with beautiful and handsome children, also make them twin sets so that I may catch up with my peers," his mother prayed and God heard her prayers.

His height is average, about five feet tall; he is well built with stocky arms and legs, having a neatly trimmed Afro that covers his entire head as well as most of his ears. He has some enhanced cheekbones, a strong, defined jawline with a beard and mustache just starting to grow. He is gifted with large light brown eyes; his snub nose and mouth are symmetrically perfect and add to the effect of his face, giving him an adorable look.

Due to his Semitic heritage, he has complex skin color, which is light, like a caramel coating. He is not as dark as most of the dark Africans, neither is he white. He has a loving, trusting, lovable, and favorable appearance and facial disposition that portrays innocence of the heart that gives him an unmerited kindness even before merciless people. One more personality trait that others do not take note of about Hayet is that he is shy, a man of few words, an underdog, having a positive attitude that never gives up no matter what, which gives him an unthought-of victory that catches his opponents by surprise.

The forecast on the airport television screen calls for colder gusty weather conditions that are expected to generate heavier snow and freezing rain late into the evening and continue through the morning hours. Frost covers the edge of the thick double-pane windows, and snow falls from the hazy universe of the sky. As far as Hayet can see, the ground outside the airport is covered with a thick cotton-like blanket of snow. Yet the airplanes after intensive deicing are taking off and landing, unhindered by the adverse weather, thanks to the snow-clearing crew working diligently; their trucks with flashing yellow lights make the airport functional.

From the first step out of the airplane cabin, Hayet learns that the passengers are running. *Why are the passengers nervous and rushing as such?* The reason for such thought is that he grew up hearing, "No hurry in Africa." *Perhaps this might be a hurrying culture.*

In a couple of minutes, the hundred plus passengers that were aboard with Hayet will disappear to go to their homes in Chicago or probably disperse over the other forty-nine states, catching their connecting flights.

In every corner as well as some overhead directories mostly blue, black, and white signs carry numeric and alphabetic scripted information directing passengers which way to go. The thousands of people in the airport exceed his expectations.

What are all these people doing in the airport?

Some run, unintentionally scattering a few of their belongings and are forced to stop to pick up their dropped items. Multitudes walk fast in long strides, while others walk in tiny steps, and a few sleep on the floor and on the chairs. Similar passengers with ample time to relax queue in lines of people that await their turn next to the portable fence to be seated by the restaurant staff.

Hayet, carrying a red and white–striped paper bag, a clearance document that he has been given by the International Organization for Migration, abbreviated IOM, walks along with other passengers. He follows the exit sign and walks through some endless well-lit carpeted passageways. As thousands walk to the exit sign, the same number of people come from the opposite side. Hayet is a skeptic. When the journey looks long, he asks people to confirm that he is going in the right direction.

"Is this the way to go out of the airport?" he asks a young woman carrying four pieces of carry-on luggage.

She glances and smiles at him without saying a word.

"I am coming from Africa and I need help. Which way do I go out?" Hayet stammers a bit explaining accompanied by a reciprocal smile, expecting the woman would have sympathy and help. She still glances and gives him a bright smile. *I did not ask to see your smile; tell me this way or that way if you know the way.*

"No speak English," she declares breaking the smile.

"A thousand-mile journey starts with one step. You are almost there, keep on walking, after about half a mile take a right turn, then immediate left, take an escalator to go upstairs, take the southbound train and get off at concourse B. Then make a sharp right, again walk right through the exit gate, where you will find people waiting for their guest. First, you must get clearance from immigration at one of the booths that you see over there," offers an old bulge faced man.

Hayet froze in confusion because he could not remember all the exit directions.

"I am his wife. We are going that way, you can go with us," she informs him and extending the same kindness to the young woman as well.

"If we do not meet after the immigration clearance, you just ask anybody and you will be shown."

"Thank you for saving me from getting lost." *You are better than your husband is when you give directions.*

American citizens to the right and non-American to the left, a couple of signs direct. *I hope this is the final sign.* He approaches the immigration and custom booths assigned to the noncitizens. The IOM paper bag easily identifies him. Consequently, "Sir, I want you to follow me," states a huge woman. *You should be rich to be as big as you.* Per Hayet's cultural assumption, only rich people are heavy. Nevertheless, because of the officer's service, Hayet gets an expedited clearance and resumes walking, following the crowd to his local connection flight to New York. The boarding gate shuts right after he enters.

At last, Hayet's journey to his home to be in a new city and state comes to an exciting final exit gate. He faces the multitude of welcoming families' friends and perhaps business partners standing in front of the exit gate. He freezes in awe while the other passengers comfortably walk to the front, left and right, leaving him alone. Butterflies fill in his stomach and negative thoughts rush into his mind, as nervous sweat drips from his forehead. He retreats to give himself time to study the welcoming people. Nevertheless, "Once you exit you cannot come back," warns one of the exit-keeping officers.

Mister, during the orientation I learned even old people get kidnapped in America; that is what I am trying to avoid.

In the midst of Hayet's dilemma, two elderly couples come toward him. They hesitantly approach him displaying Hayet's name on a placard and hand him over a bunch of flowers. That is when he meets Mr. and Mrs. GARRISON CALEB, who are his loving adoptive family; in a bigger picture refer to God who adopted Hayet into His family. What a great relieving union; they take him home riding with their nerve-wracking sons, who would be Hayet's scourging tormentors.

Chapter 2

If you do not fall how are you going to know what getting up is like?

— *Stephen Curry*

Hayet's brothers, TOBIAS AND SANBALLAT, who would be the bane of his existence, accompany the adoptive parents.

The sons are so concerned that Hayet might inherit their parents' inheritance. Consequently, they will deploy any psychological, social, and educational attack to ensure that Hayet does not rise above them.

Mr. and Mrs. Caleb feel they have "lost" their children, who deviated from "purposeful living" at their universities. They pray without cease to see the return of the prodigal children and hope not to experience the same with their newly adopted son.

The accompanying brothers are JEZEBEL embodied, shaming, wicked, terrible people, with mindsets of jealousy and manipulation, who'll attempt to persecute and hinder Hayet from getting Mr. and Mrs. Caleb's favor and from reaching his destiny.

Every now and then, everybody has a Jezebel-embodied minion that may appear as a parent or as a child, as a husband or as a wife. As a teacher or as a student, as an employee or as an employer. As a coworker or as a neighbor. As a leader or as a follower for a purpose of persecuting and destroying any intentional person or group.

The name Jezebel is beautiful and courteous. However, because of the connection of a character with a wicked, threatening, intimidating, and murderous woman, it came to be used as a synonym for a wicked person.

A Jezebel-embodied person hates and fights fervently against whatever may be true, noble, right, pure, lovely, admirable, excellent, or praiseworthy in a person. Jezebel belongs to her father, the devil, and she wants to carry out her father's mission on Hayet. Her father is a murderer from the beginning, not holding to the truth, for there is no truth in him.

When a male Jezebel lies, he speaks out of his own character, for he is a liar and the father of lies. A female Jezebel as well has unpredictable, several-faced behaviors, flip flops a million times over one issue, and has no binding obligation to settle on a set agreement. With vicious, merciless attacks, Jezebel denigrates, dehumanizes, and vilifies anyone who opposes her with no regard for age or gender. That is what awaits Hayet from the get-go through his brothers.

A Jezebel frequently brags, "Whoever does not agree with me cannot be voted in or stay in power. I can turn dreams of destiny into a blowing dust."

Hayet believes that there will be a big fight, because his personality does not tolerate and align with Jezebel's.

For sure, whoever holds an office and confronts Jezebel will have a hard time maintaining that office, for she influences collaborators that are driven remotely and who function according to her direction. Her collaborating minions are in the leadership of nations, families, and religious institutions, creating havoc and affliction as well as destroying respected persons' reputations. She has agents even in church leadership who line up to feed her confidential information the moment after a meeting ends. Thus, Jezebel is the first to know every classified information.

A Jezebel always is concerned about her own welfare and the failure of others. Causing others to fail makes her happy. Her intentions are difficult to discern. Sometimes she sheds tears of deception, appearing innocent. When about to be exposed, a Jezebel manages to elude her opponent, using one's own family and coworkers to vigorously defend her, causing dissension.

When a Jezebel takes control, she hides behind her minions, pretends to be peaceful, and says, "I did not do any wrong." She frequently and skillfully manipulates situations, isolating and blaming the blameless and the innocent for no reason. This cunning behavior makes it difficult to catch her. If a Jezebel knows that she is unlikely to win, she comes appearing as the Angel of Light, blinding the sober, giving expensive gifts, until one becomes lame and unable to discern and stand for the truth.

To live with a Jezebel, one needs to be her slave and exalt her. Yet she still destroys her slaves and minions, too, when she is done with her objectives. Only the genuine, who hold on to the truth and never bow to a Jezebel, will win at last.

Tobias and Sanballat terrorize and roast Hayet from the first encounter, giving him a negative impression of the people in his new home and country.

Oh God, I thought America was going to be a restful place for me. How will I live with these boys? Should I go back home? Yet, he is at a place and time where he cannot go back. He is overwhelmed with dread of his brothers.

"Is this all that you have? Did you bring ivories, or alligator's or tiger's skin, or any other precious gemstone?" the boys whisper, belittling Hayet's nameless cheap luggage.

Hayet tries to avoid confrontation. Yet they continue poking him like a thorn in his flesh. Hayet replies, "Yes, this is all that I have for now. However, in due time God will make me prosper far beyond your wildest dreams. I crossed the Atlantic with just one bag, while my ancestors came here empty-handed, with no clothing on their backs and no shoes on their feet. However, the Lord blessed them as well as their descendants and made them into a blessing to others. The same shall happen to me."

"Sonny, are you enjoying the monologue?"

"Yes, Toby. It is making me gag," replies Sanballat, muffling up.

Hayet learns that Sanballat calls his brother Tobias Toby, and Tobias calls his brother Sanballat Sonny.

"If you make it through high school, staying out of trouble and becoming either a musician or sportsman or work in a gas station, that would be great," cracks Tobias.

"One's intent is what matters. Education is one of the ways, not the only means, of making a living. The bottom line is that, if God blesses me with good health, as long as I do not kill, steal, be a male prostitute, or cheat people, I can do whatever it takes to support myself and my dependents."

Sanballat then asks, "So, what would you like to be when you grow up?"

"I would like to be an author, write books. Be a New York times best-selling author."

I like that. Declare your dream, work your dream, walk your dream, achieve your dream, contain and sustain your dream, thought Mr. Caleb

"You would like to be 'an' what?" Sanballat inquires with a contempt as if he did not hear the word "author." Hayet restates his reply.

"Wow, this is unheard of, a shameless babbler. What else?"

"I would like to make family-friendly projects and be an agent of change, a voice to the voiceless, start new projects beneficial to humanity by raising up an army of advocates useful to themselves and to the world."

"What else?" Sanballat asks sarcastically. Nevertheless, Hayet does not pick up on the sarcasm.

"I would like to help parents stay faithful to their children, spouses cleave with bonds of love, the prodigal children return home and decide to again to begin putting God first, prioritizing their lives around serving others."

"I guess; you have neither training nor experience on family matters. How do you intend to fix that?"

"Yes, it is true that I do not have such training or experience. Yet I have one thing that surpasses both. That is guts. I also have a personal conviction, commitment, and dedication to achieving the goal. Additionally, I would help the confused, assisting each of them to identify the great person within them and work to bring that person out."

"What else?" interjects Sanballat angrily.

"I would like to help lessen imports and increase exports, reduce school dropout, and increase graduation rates."

"Is this speech from a trade minister or from a minister of education or minister of trade?" Tobias whispers to Sanballat.

"Neither from trade nor education ministers. You bet, Toby, the next speech is going to be about being a political leader."

Sanballat jokes, "What else would you like to achieve?"

"I would help awaken the minds of presidents, kings, and queens, Prime Ministers encouraging them to abide by the rule of law, fulfill their duty fairly and justly, abandoning lies."

"I told you, man!" yells Sanballat as he laughs a loud manly protracted giggle.

Yet, Hayet continues his speech without interruption, declaring, "Most of the wars that we see are the results of lies. That is the powerful bullying, intimidating, exploiting of the poor and the powerless. I would like to remind each one of us to do what one is supposed to do, eventually avoid misleading wars, contribute to minimizing imprisonments, and help women and children from being victimized by the rich and powerful. By doing all these, I would like to make God and my family proud of me."

Hayet's remarks enraged the brothers. Their nostrils widened and their eyes flashed like blazing fire. "Oh, look at you, Mr. All-High-and-Mighty. I bet you will not be talking so big when you get to high school," remarks Sanballat.

"An outsider fluke with an obscure and unknown background and having an accent, speaking of such great achievement is unheard of and impossible. Refrain from making the prediction of impossible achievement. Failure to achieve could disappoint you," states Tobias with a giggle of scorn.

"I do not know how. That is just how I speak with my internal voice."

"Then, that internal voice is wrong and it must be corrected," rebukes Sanballat.

Hayet adds more enraging his brothers. "Besides, I am not a fluke and God created me not for a *Passa tempo*— for fun, but for a reason. Moreover, be it myself— an African, Albert Einstein, an Australian, an Irish, a German, an Indian, a Russian, an American, or a Chinese genius scientist who speaks with a different accent than yours, it does not mean that any of us think with an accent."

"Again, he is aligning himself with geniuses and scientists," mocks Sanballat.

Mr. and Mrs. Caleb, who are seated in the front seat, appear to be uncomfortable with the duo's grilling of Hayet.

"Can you both stop being rude, please?" requests Mrs. Caleb.

"Father and Mother, we do not want his heart to be terribly crushed the day he fails to materialize his plan. Besides, we have been here for decades and we are stuck. He should not expect such great achievements," replies Tobias.

"Whose fault is it that you have no tangible achievement to show for yourself in a land where anybody can be somebody? You choose not to stay intentional in your education, you choose to commit a crime and go to prison, and you end up having illegitimate children without covenantal agreement and refuse to have parental responsibilities. Whose fault, is it?"

It is our fault.

"When you go to the merchant stores, you purchase food or other items, then complain and vilify an innocent employee or manager over the item's imperfection when there is none. This is not how I brought you up," rebukes Mr. Caleb as he shakes his head left and right repeatedly in quick successions.

"Stealing from a rich thief is smartness," the sons reply in unison, staring at each other.

Hayet notes that the brothers are a compatible duet. They can do good drama or a play without preparation. Nevertheless, such people steal together yet fight when sharing what they stole.

Mr. Caleb is so disturbed. "It is foolishness, not smartness, a different form of shoplifting and a work of Jezebel. Consider that somebody has sincerely labored to make the product ready for consumers, not for shoplifters or grabbers."

"The rich and the powerful to monopolize the market, they confiscate our property and cruelly stiff our hard-earned labor; causing some to settle for less and make others go bankrupt, going out of business. They refuse to give overtime pay to the voiceless. Upon completion of contractual projects, they complain, vilify, and denigrate a reputable and innocent servicer over the project's faultiness, when there is none. They either refuse to pay, claiming dissatisfaction with poor performance or an incomplete job; yet they promise to give you another assignment, on which they eventually will stiff you again.

They obstruct justice using the power of their wealth, unnecessarily prolonging the solvable case for years, causing the poor and the weak to give up their legal right due to a prolonged and delayed justice. Attacking the unjust and unfair is legitimate and smartness," argues Sanballat.

"Let me tell you one story from the Bible to see whether you call it smartness or foolishness. It is written in 1 Kings chapter 21," starts Mr. Caleb.

"Oh, here he goes again Bible," whispers Tobias.

"Be silent and listen. Not far from King Ahab's and Jezebel's palace, there was a vineyard owned by a man named Naboth. One day the king said to Naboth, 'Let me have your vineyard; it is close to my palace, and I want to use the land for a vegetable garden. I will give you a better vineyard for it or, if you prefer, I will pay you a fair price.'"

"'I inherited this vineyard from my ancestors. The Lord forbid that I should let you have it!' Naboth replied. King Ahab went home, depressed and furious over what Naboth had said to him. He lay down on his bed facing the wall, and would not eat."

"His wife Jezebel went to him and asked, 'Why are you so depressed? Why will not you eat?'"

"'Because of what Naboth said to me. I offered to buy his vineyard or, if he preferred, to give him another one for it, but he told me that I could not have it!'"

"'Well, are you the king or aren't you?'" Jezebel replied. 'Get out of bed, cheer up, and eat. I will get you Naboth's vineyard!' Then she wrote a couple of letters, signed Ahab's name to them, sealed them with his seal, and sent them to the officials and leading citizens of Jezreel. The letters said: 'Proclaim a day of fasting, call the people together, and give Naboth the place of honor. Get a couple of scoundrels to accuse him to his face of cursing God and the king. Then take him out of the city and stone him to death.'"

"The officials and leading citizens of Jezreel did what Jezebel had commanded. Then they sent a message to Jezebel: 'Naboth has been put to death.' As soon as Jezebel received the message, she said to Ahab, 'Naboth is dead. Now, go and take possession of the vineyard, which he refused to sell to you.' At once, Ahab went to the vineyard to take possession of it."

"Did Jezebel, the murderer, the land grabber, do what is just and right? Also, how would you feel if somebody else were to do the same to you from your possession?" interrupts Mrs. Caleb.

"Of course, she did neither right nor just. However, take a note that we live in an unjust world whereby the strong take advantage of the weak caring about personal interests. I would feel bad if somebody were to do the same to me," answers Tobias.

"One should treat others as one would like others to treat oneself. Besides, it is better to learn how the rich became rich by emulating and imitating, follow the same footsteps than doing what is not just and right," emphasizes Mr. Caleb.

"God uses whoever is available. He is a rewarder of the hardworking. We have seen multiple times God raises up and uses the unthought of, least likely people contrary to polls prediction; who would win through the electoral vote, failing the popular vote. He uses somebody out of nowhere that nobody has heard about on the news with no training or experience, making it a pleasant surprise. God uses the unknown so that He may bewilder the well-known. Excuse me, how do you pronounce your name?" asks Mrs. Caleb still on the car ride home.

Hayet says his name, but she does not appear to grasp. Finally, Hayet elaborates, "Take the first two letters, *h*, *a,* as in the word *have,* and add them to the word *yet*."

Mrs. Caleb continues to defuse the tension between Hayet and his brothers. "Listen, both of you. Your thinking is unconverted, carnal; you do not understand the doings of God. The person without the Spirit does not accept all that comes from the Spirit of God's doings through people, but considers them foolish, and cannot understand them because they are discerned only through the Spirit." Even as Mrs. Caleb elaborates, Tobias and Sanballat continue to provoke and poke Hayet.

Suddenly, "Honey, stop the car!" Mrs. Caleb commands as if there is an emergency need to flush out the troublesome duo.

Mr. Caleb stops the car immediately. Then, facing Tobias and Sanballat, she begins, "We brought you to be of great help to our guest. However, you have been aggravating and tormenting him in every word you say. If that is all you have to offer, that is not right," she rebukes.

"Sorry," the brothers apologize, insincerely.

The adoptive parents are not aware that Hayet is tough skinned and does not get intimidated or offended by no matter who says what. He does what he said he should and is unfazed. The mocking of the duo does not affect him as badly as it would others that get easily offended, causing crushed self-esteem.

Then, facing Hayet, Mrs. Caleb says, "Son, I and my husband fully trust your gutsy first-blush lecture and pray to see the fulfillment. Whatever God says is yours shall be yours, no matter what and who opposes you. Whether people believe it or not, always declare your dream, work your dream, walk your dream, achieve your dream and sustain your dream. Until then, seek out the hopeless, confused, and torn people like Tobias and Sanballat to show the great person within them. For in God we live, move, and have our being. One time, God causes donkeys to get lost for a purpose. The owner of the donkeys sends his son and a servant to search for them. Their search takes them to a divinely appointed juxtaposition. The son, Saul, who left looking for lost donkeys, returns home as the first anointed king of Israel, filled with the Holy Spirit irrespective of him being from the lowest tribe in his country."

"Honey stop, it is red light," says Mrs. Caleb.

When the traffic light turned to green light, "Now it is green light go," she informs again as if Mr. Caleb is not paying attention.

"Mother, instead of telling father what to do, it is better that you drive," protests Tobias. Yet, Mr. Caleb graciously replies, "Okay honey."

Mrs. Caleb can do multiple tasks at the same time. Then, she resumes, God uses political problems to cause you to leave your country, where you shall meet your divinely appointed place, God's call for your life. You may feel different as if you do not fit in. However, do not get intimidated by what others say about you. Use your difference to reach out to others. We strongly believe that God can use you for His good, for your good, and for others' good in this land. The Lord is able to do immeasurably more than all you ask or imagine, according to His power that is at work within you."

"How confident are you, Mother, that what is being said will come to pass?" inquires Tobias.

"One hundred percent. Often good change comes from God-fearing immigrants or foreigners living among the nationals, though sometimes such people become scapegoats and get blamed for every wrong in the country."

"Mother, give me good examples."

"The young Joseph, a visionary leader saved the country from famine. The young Daniel refused to compromise and worship the king. He was thrown into the lion's den, yet God saved him not from the den, but in the den. By his uncompromising faith, he caused the nation to return and worship the only true God. On the contrary, the people that instigated the accusation were brought in and thrown into the lions' den, along with their wives and children. Before they reached the floor of the den, the lions overpowered them and crushed all their bones."

In another instance, "Nebuchadnezzar set up an image of gold for the nation to worship. However, the uncompromising youngsters Shadrach, Meshach, and Abednego refused to serve the king's gods or worship them. They were thrown into the blazing furnace but God saved them, not from the fire but in the fire. Thus, the king made a decree that the people of any nation or language who say anything against the God of Shadrach, Meshach, and Abednego be cut into pieces and their houses be turned into piles of rubble, for no other god can save in this way. The nationals who prompted false witness were put to shame."

This woman does not know this unknown refugee. How could she say such courteous words so confidently? wonders Hayet, though appreciating her courtesy.

"Mother, those are people the old days. Can you mention a few of the people that we know?" protests Tobias.

"Albert Einstein, Madeleine Albright, Henry Kissinger, Peter Jennings, Dr. Ravi Zacharias, and Arnold Schwarzenegger. Do you want more?"

"Those are enough."

"One important bit of information for you, Hayet," says Mr. Caleb. "I tell you now before it happens so that when it does happen you will not be surprised and stumble. America and Americans in general just as all human beings are generous and open-minded. However, here and there you may encounter the opposite, who would give their own narrow-minded interpretation of American values. In this country, if some people hate you, keep in mind that they hated Jesus first by declaring separation of church and state, getting rid of godly values from our schools and societies. If you belonged to the world, it would tolerate and love you as its own. That is why the world hates and cannot tolerate you. You will be judged for who you are for coming from another country; you will be depicted as lacking intelligence for your accent, denied from getting open positions because people may not trust you. You will be paid less, not get promotions that you deserve, forced to prove yourself more than your American counterparts. They persecuted Jesus and they will persecute you also for who you are and for what you believe."

"Well, Hayet," says Tobias scornfully as they arrive at Mr. and Mrs. Caleb's home, "If you plan to achieve so much, then you will only get there through hard work. No one who wants to become a public figure operates in secret. Since you plan to do great dreams, show yourself to the world and be the best you can be."

"When it is time, it shall happen."

As they enter the bronze-coated elevator located next to the handicap underground parking, Tobias, facing Sanballat, says, "Listen man, let us assume that you achieve all that you intend to achieve. What will be my and my brother's duty in your life?" expecting tit for tat.

"You will still be my brothers," replies Hayet, contrary to what Tobias expected to hear.

Marveling at Hayet's reply, the parents stare at each other.

Mr. and Mrs. Caleb, whom Hayet chooses to call the Gramps, opening the door wide, saying in unison, "Welcome to the United States of America. This is your new home."

They lead him to the first room to the left, a lovely room with a spacious bedroom that has vaulted ceiling, which would be Hayet's dwelling. Their welcome is a great relief after the torment of the duo.

"Please take a hot or cold bath or shower, then you come for dinner at the dinner table. We shall wait for you," instructs Mrs. Caleb.

More than anything else what I need is to get some sleep. I wish you could let me sleep. Nonetheless he says, "Okay, I will come."

After having a quick shower, Hayet comes for dinner. By the rectangular table covered by a long white tablecloth in their respective chairs already sit the Gramps and his brothers. Hayet pulls a brown wooden chair from under the table and takes a seat to the right of his brothers, Sanballat in the middle, facing the Gramps.

Oh God, help me not to be nervous eating with these roasting sons.

The table is set with piles of plates in front of each chair. Multiple forks are set on the left, knives on the right and another set of knives and spoons to the backside of the plates. Still a couple of glasses next to the forks, on the left side.

Hayet is used to eating from one big tray, even in a wedding where eight people eat together from one tray without fork or spoon. He does not know which utensil serves what purpose.

Grandpa offers blessings for the food and dinner begins. Hayet frequently dozes off. He needs to get some sleep more than the choicest unfamiliar foods set on the table.

Be it at the dinner table or elsewhere, he is good at imitating how people do and follow their steps. He survived during the appetizer and soup serving. Then he cut a big portion of steak and put it on his plate. He tried to copy the fork- and knife-holding methods, but he could not do it.

Well, I have to do it my way.

Hayet holds the fork and knife firmly, in a manner one would hold an EpiPen. Then he jabs the steak with the fork and the knife, causing the plate click loud and the table to shake.

"Sonny, is it an earthquake?" inquires Tobias, who is seated next to Sanballat, glancing attentively.

"No! Bro, it is not, but something worse than that," replies Sanballat after pausing for a moment, swallowing the bite that is in his mouth.

"If you come across a person who does not know what to do, shaming and laughing at the person is not a solution; showing is," admonishes Grandma.

Right away, Grandpa stands by Hayet's side and begins to demonstrate.

"Please do as I say. First, pick up and hold your fork in your left hand and knife in your right. Second, hold the food down with the fork tines face downward by applying pressure through the index finger. Third, hold the knife in a cutting position, index finger going to the top, blunt side of the knife. Then cut through with the knife in a tender sawing motion; cut a piece and enjoy."

"Thank you, sir," Hayet says appreciatively and catches the demonstration with some difficulty.

"Before you go to sleep Hayet, I would you like to develop some good habits which could be an investment for your future," informs Mr. Caleb.

"Like what?"

"Arrive early, journal your activities, read books, do not procrastinate, say thank you and apologize when necessary, divide your income between saving, giving and spending, never undermine small beginning, be respectful, and pray consistently."

"Yes, Sir."

Hayet has miraculously made it to the United States through one of the refugee resettlement agencies with a blank slate to show how he has been created for a reason.

Chapter 3

Christianity is not a sprint but an endurance run. Therefore, it is not how we start the race that counts, but how we complete it. How we finish is determined by the choices we make, and those are often formed by patterns we develop along the way.

— *John Bevere, Honor's Reward: The Essential Virtue for Receiving God's Blessings.*

Hayet resides at the heart of the bustling blocks in a high-rise building in New York City where his character and identity will be tested.

In New York, driving is a nightmare; the subways where people would read literature or sleep without daring to socialize with the person on the same seat, the vehicles, the time, the wind, the air, the rain, the train, and the people seem to move fast.

Fitting in with his adoptive community is tough. Within the first few months of his arrival, Hayet asks his brother via phone, "Why is it that everybody appears to run away from me?"

"People know that you are a newcomer. Consequently, when you approach them, they think you will ask help from them. That is why they run away from you. However, when they find out that you can be successful without them, they will come back to you. Until then stick to the ones that love you unconditionally." The Gramps and the United States of America display such true love toward Hayet.

Hayet comes from a communal society where it is easy to go to a neighbor at any time, have coffee, tea, and borrow onions, tomatoes, sugar, flour, as well as other items in time of need. However, in his adoptive country, all appears to be individualistic. He is so scared to talk to or even look at his neighbors.

Hayet faces language and cultural barriers and is indoors most of the time. At school, when his fellow students are talking about the winners of football or Michael Jackson's latest music video, Hayet is still singing folk songs from Eritrea and goes to church whenever the church opens the door for a service. When the students are going to the movies on weekends, Hayet stays at home and watches bible preaching on his old black and white TV.

To escape and protect themselves from their past disappointments of schooling and life in general, the adoptive parents find the best public school for Hayet. He gets along and aligns with the faith of his new family's conservative Christian way of life. Hayet is refreshing to their deferred hearts. Their other children chose to live wild and immoral lives, each act of disobedience driving a wedge deeper and deeper into their hearts. Hayet is the relief for their battered souls, with his unfailing obedience. The parents accept him unconditionally as their own, and likewise, he loves them as he does his biological parents. It is at this time that he consciously and willfully pledges to live chaste until marriage, much to the Gramps' happiness. The practical walking of the pledge would determine his destiny.

Once Hayet gets accustomed to his neighborhood, befriending ungodly people, his attitude on obeying his parents and perspective on the weekly routine requirements of school, study, living, eating, drinking, and the church begins to alter. The routine is not easily adapted to in his new city, and this makes him uncomfortable. He slowly begins to develop a defiant attitude and starts to consider following noble values as useless as chasing the wind.

Consequently, he asks, "Why do we have to go to church whenever the church opens its door for service? It is wasting time and money. I think we, or at least I. should have to go to church only once in a blue moon."

"When you live in this house, going to church is not optional. It is mandatory in all seasons. Besides, God is counting on people who would 'waste' their money, time, and life on Him and His kingdom, which converts into investment. This is what matters most. You truly waste when you do not give full dedication to the Lord, while keeping half to self and giving half to God," Grandma rebukes sternly.

"That is not all," she adds. "Hayet, do not be misled because bad company corrupts good character. Come back to your senses as you ought, and stop spiraling to sinful living. It is obvious, for there are some of your friends who are ignorant of God that cause you to behave like one of them."

"Not really; it is just how things are," Hayet responds.

In his years at high school, Hayet observes his surroundings and friends and begins to behave more like them. He starts to realize that his high moral code has no place in contemporary society.

As the years go by, Hayet has been making poor choices and has become part of a rowdy crowd that misses almost every class. Shortly after the school bus drops him at school, he sneaks out, ditches classes, and spends the whole day in inappropriate places doing nothing. At the dismissal time, he returns to school and goes home with the intentional students. Hayet never perceives that his untimely choices, and prioritizing fun over fulfillment, will jeopardize his future, putting his bright destiny in danger.

The contention over the years with his adoptive parents were so tense. Repeatedly, he comes home late and does not eat, having eaten somewhere else.

"We have to seek a pastoral counseling," suggests Grandma as she muses what to do with Hayet for the hundredth time. She keenly observes the progress of Hayet's unconstructive strange behaviors.

Of late, Hayet has been carrying his black backpack to the kitchen, bedroom, family room, and bathroom too.

The vigilant Grandma, who observed this strange behavior, murmurs, "Why is that Hayet has been carrying his backpack wherever he goes like a baby who carries a favorite toy?"

"I have also observed it. I wonder what is inside of it," replies Grandpa. In the midst of their discussion, Hayet walks to the kitchen while carrying his backpack.

"Son, why are you unnecessarily carrying your backpack?" Grandma inquires.

"Have I been doing so? I have not realized it," he replies, playing it cool. Hayet knows that if he continues to hold on it, the Gramps might forcefully take the backpack from him. Thus, he places it on a zebra-decorated stool between the two brown sofas, the bottom making a clunking sound as it hits the stool.

Immediately, Grandma reaches out and unzips the backpack, effectively destroying Hayet's logical move.

"Grandma, you are invading my privacy without my permission," Hayet says desperately. However, he knows there is no use pulling the privacy card. In this family, there are no secrets. One knows the password of the other. Before Hayet completes his speech, she pulls a silver gun out of the backpack. After realizing what it is, she flings the hateful object away from her and it lands on the stool. Words cannot explain enough how horrified Grandma is.

"I knew it! You will never see those unwise friends of yours again," Grandpa declares as he picks up the gun, holding it at arm's length as if it will explode.

Hayet tries to explain himself. "Please give it to me. I need it to defend the weak and myself from attackers. That is my second amendment right to keep and bear arms."

"For all who draw the sword will die by the sword," Grandpa wisely says, still holding the gun at arm's length.

After locking him in his room, the parents discuss having him transferred to a Christian school so that he might get away from his rowdy pals. The discussion cools off, and Hayet sneaks out of his room to a store downstairs, lit cigar in his mouth as he trots in the cool of the night on the street. It is a late night, except here and there young folks; elderly people are not visible. As Hayet puffs the cigar, suddenly, out of nowhere, Grandpa walks by Hayet toward the convenience store. Hayet freezes like a pillar of snow. *Oh my gosh, this is bad for me. Did he see me?* he whispers as he rushes home.

Standing by the silver refrigerator, pretending to get a snack, Hayet expects another disciplinary lecture from Grandpa.

Grandpa returns home. "Go to sleep," he says and walks away.

*I guess he did not see m*e, Hayet says hesitantly as he heads to tuck in for the night. However, Hayet finds two items tucked in his bed that would torment him for life and freezes in shock and awe.

"This cannot be true," he moans in disbelief as he picks up the items. If Grandma were to be the one that saw him, she would have finished all the necessary lectures with a slap to the face right there and right then. Yet, men and women are different in the way they handle issues. That is why Grandpa used a packet of Rothman's king size blue cigars and a yellow metal lighter for a silent and unforgettable punishment, tucked into the bed.

The Gramps manage to get an expedited transfer for Hayet to a Christian school. Yet they are not aware that Hayet is transferring with the same personality. In fact, at his new school, he will find out the Christian school devil is more destructive than the public school one. What Hayet needs is a change of heart and perspective. Finally, in order to help Hayet achieve the best of himself, regardless of his opposition to an arranged daily life, his adoptive parents who have shown sacrificial love put him in a prison.

"We are taking an action plan which is for your good," declare the Gramps. "Additionally, bear in mind that your father and your ancestors wished to have open educational doors for you that they never had, which you are abusing. When one receives reading, and writing lessons from compassionate slave masters, each one teaches one to read and write. They used such methods to help one another learn. All of them were still living by faith when they died. They did not receive the freedom they were promised. They only saw them and welcomed them from a distance, admitting that they were foreigners and strangers on earth. Your ancestors in their slavery state were longing for a better country. A heavenly country after this temporal one, where there will be no more death or mourning or crying or pain, for the old order will pass away. Now, until you learn how to make use of every prospect to work for a better future, we shall limit your freedom."

Chapter 4

Learn to say 'no' to the good so you can say 'yes' to the best.

—*John C. Maxwell*

Hayet knows that one day he shall be free from the condition that limits his freedom by choosing to walk wisely.

Hayet's mind frequently becomes loaded with numerous assumptions of how life after the prison will be. Imagining survival in prison is the scariest instant of his life. The prison where he is at has no barbed-wired fences, prison towers, or handcuffs. He does not see muscular, assaulting, and extorting inmates. He is all alone, just as in a maximum-security prison. Instead of prison wardens, he has a mentor.

As a thirsty living being thirsts for water, so does Hayet's soul long for freedom. He dreams, talks, and imagines freedom, yet it does not come. It seems to take an eternity to achieve it. Days turn into weeks, weeks turn into months, and months turn into years. The long-awaited freedom comes as expected, in the summer of 1990. It is like a dream. His relatives, friends from near and far, the old and the young come to celebrate his release from the imprisonment of homeschooling. Eventually, he graduates from homeschool high school and receives acceptance into an Ivy League university in New York. It is a double joy with a declaration of his acceptance to the university with a 99 percent scholarship!

It is the happiest moment of Hayet's life, hearing congratulatory greetings accompanied by spicy, salty, minty, sour, sweet, and roasted food. The biggest smiles from the visitors are the first thing he sees on the excited faces. Cameras flash and the colored balloons get released, soaring up high like an eagle to the cloudless sky as all eyes look up through the spacious terrace.

Most of the graduation guests give transitional advice about going from high school at home all alone to an open campus of over thirty thousand students. That is where most students embrace their liberal perspective of spiritual life by the time they graduate from college.

Three distinctive remarks come from little CLAUDIA CLAUDIUS, Uncle JEHU NETANYAHU, and Grandpa.

Claudia is a kindergarten student, but too smart for her age. As she pulls down the braids of her hair, reading Dr. Seuss's *Oh, the Places You Will Go!* she blurts, "Do not follow the crowd, mister."

The congratulatory banner with a black and golden ribbon encircles the living room. The dark and yellow balloons of all shapes float tied with white thread stuck to the wall by a clear tape. Grandpa sits against a charmingly adorned wall and pronounces, "Wherever you go, be it Yale, the capitol, hospital, or jail, we will go, too. Make sure to make gutsy good choices and take us to good places. Now, once you go to college, I want you to have a clean friendship with a good, wise, and attractive senior Christian girl. Take into consideration also that the one who has unreliable friends soon comes to ruin, but there is a friend who sticks closer than a sister or a brother."

"Why should he befriend an older student instead of those of his age? Besides, what does a 'clean friendship' mean?" shouts the stylish EMILY BATTISTELLI, a bothersome friend that Hayet met at the public schools, whom he would love later for the very thing that he hates about her.

Who invited this niggling woman? notes Hayet.

"Mr. Caleb, I totally disagree with your suggestion," she says.

"I understand what you mean, lady. However, it is for his own good," states Grandpa.

"What good comes from befriending an older, wise, friendly girl?"

"Are you interested in having him? Why are you so concerned as such?" he answers Emily's question by a question as he chuckles.

Grandpa sits at the edge of his brown wooden chair and stresses, "There is no point in telling you before you have made such a friend."

Uncle Jehu interrupts as the visitors debate Grandpa's remarks: "I also have a few words to add. Please listen up carefully. We are sending you out like a sheep among wolves, into a destiny, life of purpose, spirituality, and a potential graveyard. Therefore, be as shrewd as a snake and as innocent as a dove. Know how to escape when vicious prowlers or cunning enemies come to distract you from purposeful living. Remember who you are! Make sure to give a good name to the loving, nurturing community, the family that you represent, and the country that welcomed you warmly taking gutsy steps. The only way you will be able to fulfill your goal is by saying no to unedifying habits and ideas."

Uncle Jehu has provided irrefutable advice. If Hayet chooses to adhere to the instruction, he can victoriously make it through college within three or four years. Uncle Jehu continues, "Shortly after I graduated from high school, I left the most comfortable place on earth—my parents' home. My mother packed my yellow leather cases with several blankets that I never used. While holding my wrists, my father gave me lessons that vividly remain in my ears wherever I go. My father's natural advice took me victoriously not only through college; it still sustains me. It is the same instruction that brought me home after my college graduation until I got married, that made me save more than enough money to buy a house with cash and move out of my family's home. Let me tell you what my father instructed me. Listen up carefully, so that you may benefit the way I did and share the secret with others."

Hayet stands to serve other visitors who have just arrived. "This is your day, sit down and listen," commands Grandma.

Uncle Jehu resumes, "She is a lady. She shouts in the road and lifts her voice in the square. She does not hide. Those that seek her find her. When you hear her voice ring in your consciousness, it is unwise to ignore her guidance. She is reliable and can be trusted by all that follow her. Do not abandon her in any season throughout the year, for she will save you from the enemies that enslave your body, soul, and spirit. Wholeheartedly love her, and she will protect you from visible and invisible adversaries. Do all that is possible to have a hold of her. She is the ideal that a person needs for survival in this chaotic world. Though it may cost you all you have, embrace her because she will carry you through a successful life, saving you from calamities."

Uncle, what you are talking about is great qualities of human existence.

"Hayet, give her high regard by cherishing her, and she will honor you in return. Not only that, but she will also keep the highest sustainable achievement in your life, reward you with luxurious awards. She will take you to lofty places that you never thought possible that are far beyond anyone's wildest dreams. Should you embrace her as your companion, you will never stumble. She will make you soar to higher positions. The years of your life will be many. Hayet, would you be willing to love, cherish, and embrace her, to make her be part of your life today? If you do, say 'I do,'" his uncle finishes expectantly.

Hayet gives a rhetorical answer. "For one with such noble qualities that refresh the soul, spirit, and mind and that leads, honors, and sustain success, who dares to say no? My response obviously is, I do. But first, tell me who she is. I hope you are not referring to the person Grandpa is talking about!"

"Although I do not know what Grandpa's statement was about, it could be one way of going about it," Uncle Jehu replies positively. "Follow her steps. She will let you make valuable distinctions. These include answering all the 'who, what, when, where, why, and how' questions of life. Find her. The personified Lady, Wisdom." He ends the conversation, leaving the listeners in bewilderment. And with that, Uncle Jehu introduces Hayet to the next decisive stage of his journey, and that is a college life and education.

Chapter 5

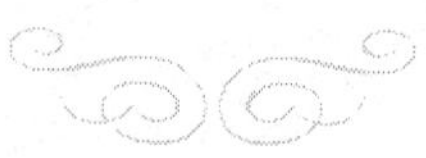

Anyone with sincere religious beliefs cannot say that all religions are true. that is so illogical it is pathetic. all religion cannot be true because some of them are so diametrically opposed to each other.

—*Josh McDowell*

Hayet and Grandpa attend the first international and interreligious experience college orientation, which would determine his life calling.

When the orientation invitation mail comes in, Hayet argues with the Gramps, "I am grown up. I will go alone to the orientation."

On the contrary, the Gramps argue back, "This is an old college tradition, that students should be accompanied by parents." They repeatedly point to the section of the letter that courteously invites all parents or guardians to attend.

Hayet knows why he wants to go unaccompanied, but he does not want to say it openly for fear of offending the Gramps. He just says, "I am a man; I will go by myself."

After weeks of back and forth intense discussion, Grandpa asks, "Are you ashamed of our old age, called to be a son of a white people?"

"No, Grandpa. I am very proud and grateful to be called your son."

"Okay, tell us why? Are you embarrassed of my bald head—which, by the way, you will obviously have in the next couple of years? If those are not the reasons, would you please tell us why you do not want us to accompany you?"

Hayet has kept these feelings inside of him ever since he first went shopping with the Gramps.

"Wherever you go, be it at school, on vacation, at work, in a shopping center, even to strangers on the street, all you talk about is Jesus. That is why I do not want you to accompany me. The reason is that you will be shamelessly preaching Jesus to the students, parents, and to the teachers too, which will offend others of different beliefs. That is not normal."

The Gramps stare at each other in bafflement. Just as Hayet feared, he has poked the Gramps, as one would cause a disturbance to a beehive. Now, the conservative parents will swarm and sting him with their intolerant poisonous stings that would in the end it will turn out for his good. They will keep on talking until he comes to the core and learns the beauty of intolerance.

"It is sad, Hayet, that our mention of Jesus bothers you as such. Knowing, living, and gutsily telling Jesus to others makes one a better person in all that one does. Please tell us whether it is right in the sight of God to listen to you rather than to God. You must judge."

"Of course, it is better to listen to God, but not cool to do so during the orientation."

"Why?"

"It shows how intolerant you are toward other people's way of life, faith, and understanding."

"Wow! What did you say?"

"You heard what I said. I am not going to repeat it."

"Son, what does intolerant mean?"

"One who does not accept the opinions, beliefs, or behaviors that differ from one's own."

"What are we intolerant of?"

"I have already told you the meaning."

"Who should tolerate who?"

"The conservatives should tolerate everybody else, suppressing their true feelings for the sake of being nice and keeping harmony."

"The conservatives tolerating everybody else while suppressing their religious conviction and true feeling is one way. Is it fair?"

"It is not, but that is how it is."

"Okay, what or who are we to tolerate?"

"I have already told you the meaning."

"To tell you the truth, we may be intolerant of ignorance but not genuine wisdom."

"You do not tolerate even the matters that all the literate as well as the illiterate, the president, and the Supreme Court uphold. Do you call all of them ignorant?"

"First, what we may be intolerant of is the liberal ideologies, not the person preaching tolerance. The illiterate is not so ignorant to mess up with an ignorant decision. It is the rich and the powerful who are intolerant. Second, when you accuse us of being intolerant, are not you being one? Third, tell us specific names that are tolerant and we will see whether they themselves are tolerant or not."

"I am not going to tell specific names," says Hayet, because he knows that the Gramps will not stop at it.

"If you do not give us specific names then we are not going to tell you the final 'Yes we are intolerant or No, we are not,' answer. Until then, I will pray until you get to understand the beauty of intolerance."

Hayet got a partial answer and one day he hopes to give specific names of people that preach tolerance.

After listening attentively, referring to the new godless normal Grandma states, "The wrath of God is being revealed from heaven against all the godlessness and wickedness of people, who suppress the truth by their wickedness. Even though such people claimed to be wise, they became fools. Furthermore, just as they did not think it sensible to keep in mind the knowledge of God. God gave them over to a wicked mind, so that they proudly do what ought not to be done. For although they knew God, they neither glorified Him as God nor gave thanks to Him, but their thinking became futile and their foolish hearts were darkened. Though they know God's righteous decree that those who do such things deserve death, they not only continue to do these very despicable deeds but also legalize and approve of those who practice them in the name of protecting minority and human right."

"Grandma, is it right to deny others their constitutional rights?"

"God's law supersedes constitutional rights. Use common sense and judge for yourself, son. Your conscience knows the truth unless it is seared as with a hot iron. The leaders that approve the despicable deeds neither they nor their children practice them. Using your authority, authorizing others to practice what you would not do for yourself is a hypocrisy. For a sensible brain, those should be good reasons to analyze right versus wrong."

"Son, I pray that the God of our Lord Jesus Christ, the Father of glory, may give you the Spirit of Wisdom and of revelation in the knowledge of Him. Having the eyes of your heart enlightened, that you may know what is the hope to which He has called you, what are the riches of His glorious inheritance in the saints, and what is the immeasurable greatness of His love toward you. As for us, for we cannot stop speaking about what we have seen and heard about the name of Jesus," declares Grandpa.

To finally end the lengthy discussion, Hayet agrees to have Grandpa accompany him.

The first day they step out of the car at the parking lot what Hayet feared would happen happens.

They are almost immediately greeted with an incoming student and his family.

"Hello, my name is Garrison Caleb, from New York, and congratulations for making it to the university."

"Thank you! My name is ENOCH ELIAS, from Sweden."

"That is great, what lovely names of two people taken to heaven without experiencing physical death," Grandpa begins.

"Do you believe that?" Enoch replies.

"Yes, I surely do. In fact, some day, I expect the same to be fulfilled in my life."

"Good for you, but I do not believe."

"Bad for you for not believing. Why don't you believe?"

"It is not scientifically proven and violates many laws of science. Besides, I have to see it to believe it."

"You do not believe because you have not seen? Blessed are those who have not seen and yet believe in the biblical truth."

"Good for them, but I do not believe."

"Pity for you."

"I am fine with my unbelief because, honestly, there is no God."

"The fool believes in his heart and confesses with his mouth: there is no God."

"Are you telling me that I am a fool and what you believe is better than what I believe?"

"Yes, what I believe is better than what others believe. If it is not, I would not tell others about it."

"How intolerant of you."

Hayet flinches when he hears the word "intolerant" and says, "Grandpa, we have got to go now." *I knew it. That is why I did not want you to accompany me.*

"Okay, son."

"Enoch, may I invite you and your parents for dinner tonight?"

"That would be great instead of going somewhere else as long as you promise to pay and not to mention church stuff."

"I promise. Can I mention Jesus?"

"Do not mention either."

"How about if you ask a question about them, then can I answer?"

Enoch is not so sure what to answer. Anyhow, he thoughtlessly replies, "Yeah."

"Thank you, sir, for telling our son what he often needed to hear at a time he does not want to hear. This is a fulfillment of God's promise. Before we meet for dinner, God will convict Enoch," Enoch's parents say in unison.

Hayet is not happy about Grandpa's intolerant remarks. As they keep on walking on the pedestrian walkway, "Grandpa, keep what you believe to yourself. Do not force your intolerant belief on others, especially if they are not interested."

"By saying what you are saying right now, aren't you being intolerant?"

"What I mean is, please do not initiate any Jesus and church discussion."

"Thank you for your coward remarks. Nevertheless, whether they like it or not, I will tell others about Jesus. Am I now trying to win the approval of human beings, or of God that I should keep Jesus and church just to myself? Or am I trying to please people by eclipsing the Lord? If I were still trying to please people, I would not be a man of God."

Grandpa continues to attend the orientation with Hayet. Except for the mention of Jesus and the church stuff every now and then, his mere presence is reassuring as Hayet becomes acquainted with the school, students, and faculty. Hayet is overwhelmed as he visits various facilities and the department faculty amphitheater they visit shows a glimpse of what is to come. They frequently bump into Enoch and his parents.

At the end of the orientation day, the students, guardians, parents, and professors meet in an outdoor auditorium. Professor Brat Hildebrandt, the university chancellor, makes the first welcoming remarks. Then, professors and deans give presentations and talk about life at college. One of them is a resident advisor (RA), Dr. Zack Thompson. Dr. Thompson makes the students' college life smoother and easier. The RA is like an engine of the campus, for the success of the students serving as a role model abiding by all university policies, federal, state, and city laws. He is always reliable and available for residents to come to him with the diverse issues they may be facing. The RA is able and keen to identify potential crises and addresses them before they become overwhelming threats. For the issues at hand, the RA provides an appropriate resource and makes right referrals to health, counseling, and financial dealing as necessary. He also develops a sense of unity and solidarity that will allow residents to have fun together, to learn from each other through the academic, social, recreational, and community-related services to make the learning process holistic.

Professor Bell Brannon is the most graceful, fair, and just of all the lecturers. He is a person who listens intently, nods patiently, and has a million-dollar smile. He throws up his arms in the air as he makes his speech.

"Dear students, on behalf of faculty and staff, it is my pleasure to welcome you to our summer 1990 orientation. This university is the only institution where you shall find such a distinguished faculty and staff. The admissions department selected your application from a pool of outstandingly talented candidates from around the world. Our university is where you belong. Congratulations."

Loud applause echoes through the university. Startled birds resting by the London plane trees scatter at the thunderous noises.

Professor Rebecca Soyinka, the academic dean, adds, "The four years that are ahead of you will possibly be trying, challenging, and exhilarating, and they will fly by quickly. Before you know it, you shall be prepared for commencement and perhaps for employment openings or graduate studies."

Professor Jonathan Connor articulates, "We have all kinds of people on campus. I would like to warn you to be prepared to be stared at, have words or items howled at you, and receive racist, bigoted, xenophobic, and homophobic comments for those of you with differing value positions. It may seem that there is no one to turn to, and some can become engulfed in such a situation. However, I would like to tell you that our staff, and, hopefully, many fellow students, are available to help at any time. Gear up to make it through the academic and social challenges by learning and by teaching us from your experience. Take advantage of every good person's help. Your hard work and dedication will eventually lead you to harvest a worthwhile future."

Dr. TRACY TRAVIS, the tallest professors is rumored to be one who grades a person instead of their work. She is the most unprofessional and dishonest of all professors, would be Hayet's terrorizing professor.

"If you hand in your project one minute late, you have already lost three points for the day. Make sure to hand in your homework on time. At all costs, avoid plagiarism; it will automatically give you an F for an assignment. Be honest with your work."

Losing points for not turning in (NTI), assignments on time is going to be Hayet's red flag, for he is used to turning in assignments whenever he wishes. Grandpa's remarks, *Arrive early, journal your activities, read books, do not procrastinate, say thank you and apologize when necessary, divide your income between save, give and spend, never undermine small beginning, be respectful, and pray consistently will be an investment for you,* rings in his ear hears.

On final exams Hayet most of the time gets 95% or higher; which is less than 40% of the final grade. He has to discipline and organize himself because he cannot make it, because everything in college depends on wise time management.

"Next, I am going to lead an interfaith silence prayer for people worship the same God but express it in different forms," she announces.

"May I ask a question before you do the interfaith thing?" asks Grandpa.

Oh, here he goes again, knowing that Grandpa will not tolerate such a thing.

"I cannot hear you clearly. Would you please come over here?" asks Dr. Travis, motioning with her hands.

Grandpa is a gutsy man. He makes his way to the front of the crowd. "Doctor, when it comes to prayer, there is nothing like interfaith. Scripture clearly says, do not be yoked together with unbelievers. For what do righteousness and wickedness have in common? Or what fellowship can darkness have with light? What congruence is there between Christ and Belial? Or what does a believer have in common with an unbeliever? What agreement is there between the temple of God and idols?"

"Sir, we have to account for all faiths. This is no longer a Christian institution and no longer a Christian nation."

"We may have fallen, but we shall diverge, comeback and put America at the rightful place when God brings up a revival and courageous leaders who would restore whatever has been taken away by the liberals. When it comes to social issues, at work, in the market, I have no problem and can work together without any issue. However, when it comes to prayer, we cannot have an interfaith prayer."

"Sir, even during the days of prophet Jonah, each of the people aboard prayed to his or her own God."

"Yes, doctor, but which God saved and answered Jonah's prayers?"

"Only one God answered and saved Jonah in the belly of the huge fish." However, Dr. Travis would not admit the truth. Instead, she adds another approach to support her interfaith belief. "During the days of prophet Elijah also people prayed to their own God."

"Yes, doctor, but which God answered the prayers? Baal or God?"

"Only one God answered. The Lord's fire fell and burned up the sacrifice, the wood, the stones and the soil, and licked up the water in the trench. Yet we want people of all faiths to feel welcome."

"Not in spiritual matters. When you go to Islamic countries, you would be required to adhere to their way of life? When you go to Hindu, Buddhist, or communist countries as well you are required to follow to their belief. When people with different beliefs come here also, we get required to tolerate to their way of life. That is not acceptable. Instead of going to them, God has brought them to us for a reason and we need to use the open door to reach out to them. Let these people turn to us, but we must not turn to them."

"So, what do you want to do now?"

"One has to offer a Christian prayer."

"You know what, go ahead, do what you want," she authorizes, expecting that he would not do so.

Then Grandpa prays. As soon as he pronounces "Amen," a rather loud applause echoes through the university.

As Hayet and Grandpa get in the car to go home, they are approached by Enoch. Enoch says, "Mr. Caleb, thank you for sharing your thoughts. I guess I would say now I believe in God. I want you to pray for me right now at this historic place where we met first and I want to go to church with you." Grandpa prays with Enoch, who accepted God into his life.

"Mr. Caleb, since God has done His job in Enoch's life, please allow us to have a family discussion and you can meet with him some other time and take him to church."

"That is fine," replies Grandpa.

As they drive home back he says, "So, son, is intolerance bad?"

Hayet has seen how Grandpa's intolerance convicted Enoch. "Sometimes it is good," he replies.

Hayet loves to help Grandma when she needs him, but he also wants to enjoy the freedom of college life. Grandpa is so concerned as Hayet prepares to move to live on campus. The reason is that many good students drop out than graduate and get spoiled at the universities, as the Gramps have experienced firsthand with their own children.

Consequently, he once more suggests, "Hayet, would you like to live off campus?"

"No, Grandpa," Hayet refuses for fear of more homeschool-style imprisonment.

"From what I have observed of the life in college, I tell you that unless your exemplary way of living and righteousness surpasses that of the unbelievers, you will certainly not enter the kingdom of heaven," emphasizes Grandpa.

The reason why he says so is that there are multiple changes in college life between their time and the current generation.

Anyway, the orientation ends and regular class begins.

The college randomly pairs Hayet up to a room with someone who is tall and skinny as a bamboo cane: MAKERERE NYERERE, an African student. The other students know him for a skinny person with a funny name. The two have diverse cultural upbringings, but now they share a small room. The food, the money, the culture, and the weather are new to Makerere. It is his first time out of Africa. Makerere is brilliant, a fast learner, and a man of few words. A virgin like Hayet, he makes education his priority, not fun. Finding a place in the city where he can eat his traditional food, which is a boiled, cooked, and mashed banana, to make him happy is another priority.

During the first-class sessions, the professors give the students a schedule with a summary of the semester's workload. The professors have one consistent theme: use time wisely.

Using his time wisely will be a challenge to Hayet. Although the Gramps taught him how 'even one second matters,' he did not embrace the value of time wholeheartedly. Thus, at times, he suffers from procrastination. He is faithful, honest, and confident of his work, and he never plagiarizes. Nonetheless, procrastination drags him to the chasm of breaking his academic integrity. On the eve of the due date, he does not sleep until he finishes with his assignments. Working behind schedule gives him less time to study, worsened by the time needed to play sports and do other extracurricular activities such as volunteering and tutoring kids.

Just as other professors hinted, the most dedicated professor, Dr. Albert Huckabee, who desires to produce high-quality researchers, slams the students with a large writing project. Hayet hates writing related works as much as he hates the torment of his brothers. The twenty-five-hundred-word assignment is five times longer than anything Hayet has ever written. He seeks advice on how to make an outline from Ms. MARTH LINUS, a teacher's assistant (TA). She helps organize his thoughts according to priority. The TA is a stunning woman.

She prefers her initial interactions to take place in a safe, well-lit area where thousands come and go to, the library. She is loyal to her academic integrity.

Ms. Linus is calm and has a pleasant voice. "Have an idea what you would like to write about? Come up with a thesis statement, develop an outline, and start the initial word, and before you know it you will have more than twenty-five hundred words on your first draft," she states confidently. "On your second and third drafts, you will modify, trim, and add some relevant ideas to make it an A plus project."

Hayet goes to see her a second and third time, for the same project. *You are a man; dare to stand alone.* The fourth time he meets her still on that first project, he says, "Sorry for bothering you."

"You should not apologize; that is what I am here for. Besides, I wasted many years of my life, and I still made it, thanks to tireless and loving classmates, professors, and parents. You too will make it through. Believe that you can, and be afraid of nothing."

"You do not look like someone who has had to struggle."

"Do not judge a book by its cover."

Eventually, Hayet earns an excellent grade on the first project. Then he declares impulsively, *This means I can write a book,* not knowing his declaration would materialize in due time.

At college, he surrounds himself with like-minded students who maintain the same spiritual, academic, and social values. He actively participates in the Campus Union fellowship (CU). The CU mentors eagerly help students in their spiritual, social, and academic life. Hayet's musical talent will take him to the top. However, it takes a character to keep him there. His musical ability, depending on how he uses it, could have a significant effect on his life journey.

As a university student, Hayet has a fair shot for achievement and the ability to choose his life course with a fresh start. It will all depend on the choices he makes and his skill in identifying the right direction in the road of life with a particular GPS, which is God's Positional System, God's Plan of Salvation, and put God first, Prioritize your life, Serve others. This GPS never fails and it is far more valuable and accurate than the average satellite-based navigation system. This GPS has countless benefits. It elevates him from being nobody to being somebody and guides his lifelong journey in the land that God gives to him. This GPS is incomparable to silver and gold for whoever utilizes it wisely, fairly, and justly anywhere on the globe.

As the days go by, Hayet becomes friends with many students. In fact, he has more friends than any of the other freshmen. Some of his friends have a GPS, but most do not. He makes other groups of friends by joining the Frisbee and soccer teams.

At the soccer field, he meets two new friends. These friends are the muscular EMMANUEL HOPE and the skinny FELIX CAIN. They are unpopular and appear to be great soccer fans. The duo would cause him to throw in the chastity pledge he made. Hayet also befriends intellectual and dedicated students named PAULA PAULO, LEE DYLAN, and GUPTA GANDHI. He also befriends the brilliant but party-crazy BERNARD TIM, SANDY SHAKUR, and SHIAN CARSON. He spends most of his weekends giving rides to his partying cronies.

In about the same season, Hayet encounters two dazzling college girls. He has never encountered anyone like them before he meets these stunning campus queens. They are the girls that have toned bodies and flat abs. They are "ANGEL and DEMON," the girls that every male would love to date.

Hayet feels uncomfortable walking all alone through the campus between classes. Although he has more friends than any other freshmen, he desires a *close* friend like everybody else. The yearning to have a real friend bothers him deeply. He searches among the thirty thousand plus students to find one.

At college, Hayet meets and deals with hundreds of students from all backgrounds, including modern, ethical, and philosophy-oriented peers with fascinating ideas. He is in a new generation and in an educational institution where all kinds of temptations exist. For the shortsighted and untested students who appear to live just for themselves having fun, wandering from purposeful living is not a big deal.

Hayet has choices to make with significant consequences. These choices are life and death, blessings and curses. He should be aware of the blessed, ingenious, and innovative person within him whose discoveries could possibly turn the world upside down. Hayet has all he needs to start something far bigger than what he could ever imagine. The people around him realize his potential, and they are ready to follow, if he is ready to lead.

The entirely distinct religious, social, and educational environments prove to be a challenge. Moreover, he feels inferior academically and alone.

In classes, Hayet sits in a lecture hall. Most of the halls have a sloped floor and a semicircular auditorium. The students in the back sit higher than the students at the front.

The back seated can see the professor behind the stand.

Hayet takes the second row from the front, on the left side of the center aisle. As it is his habit, he most likely will sit in the same seat for the remaining years of college life. The students on Hayet's left and right write fast every word the professor says with intelligence and thoughtfulness, while Hayet appears to miss almost the entire lecture. Puckering his face and scrunching up his nose, he pensively sways his Afro-haired head. "Excuse me, what did the professor say? I did not get it," Hayet says to the students that are on his right and left side nervously.

"Sir, we are taking notes and you are distracting the lecture," rebukes a deep-voiced student to the left.

As Hayet grudgingly contemplates on the harsh admonition, "Let me take notes now and I will show you after the lecture," whispers Emily, a young woman that he knew at the high school glancing at him. She is blessed with large beautiful long-lash-adorned eyes with an inexpressible genuine gifted heavenly glimpse. Her eyes glow with the depth of sensational loving and caring service.

"Thank you," Hayet says, offering a smile of apprehension. *If you help me to survive this season of my life, it would be an honor to be part of your future life.*

Grandpa habitually says, "Watch out what you say. The very words that you say could chase you until you see the fulfillment." Hayet's thoughts could chase him until he sees himself being part of Emily's life.

While Hayet contemplates why he thought so, she says, "I will help you not only to survive but also to thrive." Emily shocks Hayet as if she heard his thoughts.

"Thank you."

During the lecture, the students seem to know everything the professor is talking about and Hayet feels left behind.

Even after the assurance of Emily, due to his inability to catch the lecture, every now and then, Hayet mumbles, *I am wasting my time here.* His hopelessness to excel is so intimidating; he begins to feel sorry for himself, blaming his homeschooling and his unwillingness to do more studies than what is needed. Nevertheless, he remembers what Grandpa habitually cries: "Do not be intimidated by the mighty strength of the people that you see around you. Strategize, if necessary, reposition yourself, do not procrastinate, and do plan your time ahead. Have less fun and study more, and then you will make it through the rainy days. What does not kill you makes you stronger."

Hayet's survival and competency with his competitive colleagues is at stake. Not only that, but he also has a couple of other challenges.

Socially and spiritually, he is a misfit, which is also another indication of the challenges he faces. The majority of the students drift from intentional academic integrity, spirituality, and religiousness.

Although he meets a few students that are not ashamed of publicly saying who they are and what they believe at the first encounter, for most of the students, spirituality is fading, becoming out of date.

Hayet also has social challenges to overcome. He feels isolated when he hears bigoted and filthy words, which is not how he grew up. In a few instances, Hayet hears intolerant remarks and people stare at him. He receives death threats for no reason. Nevertheless, a few students such as Emily who recognize the values he has have helped him develop.

At times he thinks, *Being in college is hell on earth. It is extremely hard to come across accepting students.* A couple of students have already transferred, and a few more are transferring to another college this semester. Hayet does not blame them; he would do the same if he could. However, he is stuck with the scholarship he receives. Besides, any decision should involve his adoptive parents because they have sacrificed a lot for him.

A few of Hayet's colleagues, just as others, begin to shower themselves with alcohol, drugs, and in sensual pleasures instead of focusing on their studies. It is no surprise to walk into a room on campus and see the scrambling of the students trying to hide their drinks.

Hayet also begins to notice the interactions between men and women on campus. Instead of treating chastity like a serious subject, they treat their activities as something fun and carefree, with "no strings attached." Hayet begins to wonder if he took his vow of virginity way too seriously.

The lack of academic priority and school-related discussion replacing it with fun contagiously spreads through the men and women. It is hard to predict how many students will make it to graduation. Hayet, depending on the choices he makes, determines his destiny. Good choices will help him graduate, while bad choices will cause him to drop out.

Time flies fast. Years ago, Hayet pledged to stay a virgin until marriage. However, the situation at the time he promised and the setting at the university vary. The pressure to be like most of the students pushes him to compromise with his pledge to stay chaste until marriage, and he searches to have a cute student for a companion in campus, because he is fed up walking on campus all alone.

Chapter 6

The only really happy people are those who have learned how to serve.

— *Rick Warren, The Purpose Driven Life*

Hayet often walks across the campus in the cool of the day alone with an untimely urge that could jeopardize his education and threaten his fate.

The urge to have a friend is so strong that he cannot take it anymore. *Befriending a good, wise, older, and friendly Christian girl as Grandpa suggested, would not be harmful.* Eventually, he befriends LEANN LEHMAN, a graduate school student. She is wise, straightforward, and older than Hayet, a friendly, gorgeous, and a phenomenal woman. She has an adequate height for her weight, a flat stomach, tanned skin, green eyes, and a sweet smell as fresh as heavenly flowers. Moreover, she is kindhearted.

From the beginning, LeAnn showers Hayet with the respect a man ought to have. In reciprocity, Hayet gives LeAnn the love and respect a woman deserves. LeAnn proves her love and respect shamelessly by a public display of affection (PDA). She gives hugs, plays, speaks affirming and loving words, and holds Hayet's hand as well as puts her arm around his shoulder. Hayet feels discomfort over LeAnn's touchy PDA. He appears nervous the moment he stands by

LeAnn. He often removes her pleasant yet tempting hand from his shoulder. He feels guilty for being with such a loving and head-turning woman. LeAnn knows Hayet's discomfort over the PDA, but she annoys him by doing it more often.

"It is normal," she assures him. However, she fails to draw a boundary line regarding how much is normal and how much is not.

Huh! Normal gets underrated. If this is normal, then what is abnormal? If she goes one more step beyond what she has been doing, I will openly tell her to stop it. He reinforces his pledge before it is too late.

In the subsequent weeks, their outings become habitual. They meet everywhere on campus, grab lunch, talk, and hang out for hours at the library doing schoolwork and eating food together.

LeAnn takes him to memorable historic sites in the city, and she introduces him to her family and friends, which Hayet cannot resist. Slowly, Hayet comes to love the PDA and responds likewise. Nevertheless, he cautiously observes the new border he has drawn. "Getting to know LeAnn is the best thing I ever did," he often says.

One of the most memorable moments is when they go on a trip to the World Trade Center (WTC) towers observation deck. In the elevator, they meet a man who is in his mid-twenties wearing an elegant white suit, striped black shirt, and a black tie. The man stumbles backward into LeAnn's chocolate ice cream, which leaves a mark. It looks like a perfectly designed stamp in the middle of his suit. Nevertheless, the man appears to be calm.

"Never mind; it is my fault," he comforts LeAnn.

That is how they happen to meet Mr. SAMUEL SPRINGER, whom she would eventually marry. He takes them to where he works, WTC 1, around the hundredth floor. Moments after he takes them into his office, he comes back with a clean new suit.

"I love that," LeAnn comments with a smile on her face.

A short time after exchanging addresses, Hayet and LeAnn resume to the tower's indoor and outdoor observation decks, taking two speedy elevator rides. On the outdoor viewing platform, the weather is moderate. Hayet looks in all directions, as far as his eyes can see.

"This is an endless city," he calls out, his voice carried on the wind.

As time goes by, Hayet adjusts to college life. In early winter, a couple of friends tell him, "The hottest girl in the school is looking for you, man. How did she notice *you*, of all the students? Perhaps she wants to exploit your uniqueness. You know, she is a strikingly lovely girl with smooth, creamy-white skin, a toned body, level abs, pearly white teeth. She is the whole package, dude."

During those days, Hayet has been staying home to help Grandma, who has shortness of breath and a rapid heartbeat.

Many times people are not satisfied with what they have. They want to get something new and better if they can. That is why they do not take action to seal their friendship by getting married. His friends, such as Bernard, say, "Dude, please, let me be with you when you happen to meet this girl."

"You already have a bunch of girls. Why would you speak of the only girl that has been looking for me?"

"You may have all the girls I have got if you are willing to trade me with the one who has been searching for you. She is a woman who has a noble character, not easy to find, worth far more than rubies."

"First, she is not a property that I would trade with you. Second, my parents instructed me to be loyal; when you befriend one, stay with that person until the end."

"You are old-fashioned; have fun with as many women as you can. There is no accountability checklist."

"You are wrong. What I have learned is that each of us will give an account of ourselves to God."

"You are wrong, Hayet. The world is the way it has been for centuries. I have never seen any sort of accountability giving."

Right then, LeAnn arrives and interrupts the conversation and pulls Hayet aside. "Listen, Hayet. The majority of the boys and girls on this campus are close minded, rich, ill-informed kids who have grown up in luxury. Shortly after they come to college, they develop character flaws. Then they end up being unable to live without sensuality, drugs, partying, and alcohol. They become drunk every night and have hangovers in the morning. A few others also drink during the weekend. Anybody who does not behave like them has a hard time fitting in socially and academically. They hang out together most of the time. It is a mystery to see how they handle the intensive academic workload.

All they do is loiter leisurely, play wildly, drink uncontrollably, and flirt promiscuously. They are identical in the way they dress and walk, they often use slang, and they are intolerant, not friendly with people that are smart and separate from them. Always be vigilant of the students that you happen to meet, and stay connected with the helpful ones. At the same time, separate from the spoiled ones. Do not think you will change them to your way—they will change you!"

Hayet knows that LeAnn's advice is to his advantage. He applies LeAnn's recommendation and sifts through useful information to achieve immediate and long-term goals. Hayet is curious. His curiosity is not to see her enchanting charm of the student that has been looking for him, but to find out why she has been looking for him while she could find other cool students.

It has been a couple of months since the school opened its doors for the semester. The initial months of classes and other extracurricular activities could potentially predict who is who academically, socially, and spiritually. The first semester foretells how a student is most likely to adapt to the four years of campus life, unless one shifts from fruitfulness to unfruitfulness or vice versa.

Meanwhile, the Gramps' 1990 silver Toyota 4Runner, a stylish SUV with large rims, that Hayet drives makes him well known as a celebrity all over the campus, even by people who have never seen him. Thus, he befriends more people than any other student, including the partying, transportation-lacking trio of Bernard Tim, Sandy Shakur, and Shian Carson. Academically, they are talented students. They are aggressive and have no hesitation asking for a ride to and from clubs on the weekends and sometimes weekdays. Hayet's SUV ownership is what connects them, which could have a lifetime effect on him.

Chapter 7

Direction, not intention, determines your destination.

— Andy Stanley

Over time, Hayet has developed a misguided notion of how to help his partying friends every weekend without weighing the possible negative consequences.

Every year, several potentially endowed college and high school students die or get in car crashes because of over-the-limit alcoholic intake. They consider that passing out, throwing up, being totally drunk can be relieved by sleeping it off with only a passable hangover the next morning. Regrettably, taking drunk behavior as easy as they do could threaten the drunk person's and others' lives.

When Hayet's friends get drunk they cannot take care of themselves and are prone to harm themselves and others, including Hayet. Consequently, he needlessly takes the responsibility of providing them with transportation, cleaning their vomit, and ensuring their safety from the clubs to their dorm.

Sunday morning late winter in 1990. Cottony, feathery, white, shimmering particles cover and transform the landscape, making it a dreamlike terrestrial fairyland suggesting an unexplored landscape.

The balcony outside his bedroom clearly displays snow pummeling the city. The crisp flakes rest on the roofs, walkways, streets, parks, and trees. All visible areas have turned snow-white, as the cold morning breeze of gusting wind hits New York City, affecting the homeless on the streets and the early-morning workers.

At home, the heater constantly blows hot air. The dining table is full of sizzling blackened shrimp, broccoli, green peppers, snap peas, chestnuts, mushrooms, and carrots, with a brown curvy clay jar of water set in the middle of the revolving table. Three empty cups are on the left side of each plate. The food is drizzled with a spicy sauce and topped with parsley. Three overripe blackened bananas are in the old brown fruit basket. The savory, spicy, cheesy, and garlicky aroma of the fresh homemade food overwhelms the dining room. Grandpa often implores, *Because you do not know what the day holds for you, before you go out of the house, make sure to fill your empty stomach.*

The table is ready to serve their watering mouths with satisfying food. However, nobody is eating or even talking. The silence makes Hayet nervous. *There could be a problem going on between them.*

To break the silence, Hayet says, "Good morning, Gramps," while pulling out a brown wooden chair from the dining table. However, none of them replies or even dares to look at him.

Perhaps I could be a problem, he reasons as he gazes at them.

"The food smells fabulous. Thanks for preparing it. Sorry I did not help you cook."

Breathing with a shallow huff from her nostrils, Grandma gives him an unkind gaze without a word.

"What is going on?" Hayet asks Gramps to initiate a discussion.

Grandma grumbles, "How did you expect to wake up early and assist in the kitchen after coming home only a couple of hours ago? I cannot take it anymore. I do not like the way you are going about at night. If your friends stay up that late, we do not want them to bother us every weekend at odd hours. Inform them to hire a cab! If that is what they want to do, tell them clearly that our car is not a transportation resource for their crazy antics. I trust your openness. However, you should realize that he who associates with the wise grows wise; a companion of fools suffers harm."

"Grandma, my friends live their life and I live my own life. How dare you call my friends fools, and how dare you say for being a companion of my friends I will suffer harm?"

"It is the Bible's proven record of many years of experience that says so. Trust me, eventually, a companion of fools suffers harm. If you do not see it today, you will see it tomorrow."

Grandma speaks openly, portraying him as a fool. However, Hayet does not want to admit it. In fact, it is his first driving experience in such windy, snowy, and unpredictable conditions of limited visibility. It was only with difficulty that he made it to the club, to the campus, and home. While making a turn, his SUV skidded at two intersections, barely missing pedestrians both times. Bumping other cars and the curb was the worst part. He had two accidents and received two at fault tickets. It is a miracle that he made it home with a drivable car and no injuries.

Hayet knows that acknowledging the truth will require him to stop helping his friends.

"Grandma, you are looking at only one side. I have a concern for their safety, especially keeping the girls from attackers should they become drunk. That is why I give them rides from the clubs whenever they give me a call."

"You are neither their watchman nor their chauffeur. If they want to be safe, let them walk and stay in the Light, with a capital 'L.'"

"I always find them walking or standing under the light."

"You think so?"

"Yes, Grandma."

"Had they been students that walk in the Light, they would not be loitering like an owl at night. By the way, I am talking about the quality of Light, which is brighter than the sunshine that glows during the night and the day; it fills one's mind with overflowing joy. I do not mean the light that goes on and off daily."

Meanwhile, Grandpa is resting his right elbow on the dining table while rubbing his wrinkled chin with the tip of his fingers. He silently listens throughout the heated conversation. When he is still, it is not good, and Hayet does not like it. Usually, the quietness comes before the expression of an indisputable conclusion that uproots, tears down, destroys, and overthrows in order to nurture, soothe, and reconcile.

"Honey, I cannot take it anymore. I have repeatedly told you about it. However, you do not take any action. You should stop him now before it is too late," grumbles Grandma.

Hayet knows what has been going on. He feels awkward and cannot look them in the eye, so he bows his head as a sign of defeat because he knows if he argues, the Gramps will try to limit him from helping his friends in their times of need.

Chapter 8

We have a right to believe whatever we want,
but not everything we believe is right.

— *Dr. Ravi Zacharias*

Hayet envies the imprudent life journey of others and desires to walk like everybody else, forgetting his identity, the call to influence others' lives for their good, for his good, and for God's good.

For a few moments, all is quiet at home except for the wintry, frosty, hissing wind. Grandpa clears his throat, a sign of willingness to talk. He walks slowly, unstraps his white apron, and places it on the old brass hanger. He is an untraditional man who helps Grandma with every home chore.

"My son, keeping quiet does not mean that I do not know what has been going on with you. I have several reports of the places you have been and what you have been doing."

Hayet confidently asks, "Such as where and what?"

"If you insist, let me tell and show you the most recent incidents." He pulls out a drawer and puts it on the corner of the dining table.

"You went to notorious places where illegal transactions take place. That is where the nasty stuff happens. The worst part is that you parked in a handicap spot and got a ticket that we still have to pay, a wasteful five hundred dollars." Hayet could not deny the fact.

"Yes, it is true; there was no parking in that area. I went inside to call my friends out, and suddenly I found the ticket under the windshield wiper. *In fact, you should be thankful that nobody drove off the SUV, because I left the key inside while the engine running.*"

"Which friends did you go to call?" Grandma interjects. Hayet pauses, eying Grandma.

"You know who. Bernard, Sandy, and Shian."

"I knew it. Those are the same people that are troubling us every weekend," she mutters as she intentionally looks to Grandpa.

"Not only that, on the following day also, you parked by a fire extinguisher and we have to pay a hundred-dollar fine. I expected you to tell me about it, but you did not."

"I planned to tell you, but we did not happen to sit and talk."

"That is not an excuse. If there is a will, there is always a way."

"By the way, this morning I also had two accidents and two tickets," reveals Hayet, knowing the violation mail will come to the home address.

Furthermore, he adds, "By offering help, I was trying to explain to my lost friends the greatest love of all. That a person will lay down his life for his friends. I desire to lead them to the Right Way," Hayet elaborates. He is trying to help his friends. However, his approach varies from the Gramps' method of helping others.

"My son, you are using the right key for the wrong purpose. Not only that, but you are also spending your time in useless pursuits. So far, I would say all your fuses are intact. That is why we are trying to protect you."

"Protect me from what?"

"From failures in life, by teaching you from our experience so you can avoid repeating the kind of mistakes that we made. Son, you are not in darkness so that a bad day should surprise you like a thief. You are a child of the light and child of the day. You do not belong to the night or to the darkness. So, you should not be disobedient like others, who are asleep, but be awake and sober, discerning bad from good. For those who get drunk at night and call you to give them a ride, staying with or around such friends could one day put you in a troublesome condition. Just pray for your friends."

"Grandpa, first, I am careful nothing bad will happen to me; second, prayer without action is dead."

"You know the truth. However, be aware that sin is hunkering at your door, and it desires to enslave you. You must rule over it before it is too late. The enemy has sown tares in your heart that have been germinating their shoots. Once they grow bigger, the one that you crave to be a slave of will sit in the throne of your heart."

"I am a free man. I have never been a slave to anyone, and neither do I intend to be one," Hayet insists. He has a different understanding of freedom from that of the Gramps.

"Let me finish," exclaims Grandpa as he repositions his chair. "Yes, you are certainly free, but only to do what is right. Above all, God requires of you to act justly, to love mercy, and to walk humbly before Him. Remember also that freedom has boundaries. Besides, though it may sound unbelievable, you were a slave through your ancestors for more than a century on different continents. They suffered in order that you may have a good life because of the price they paid. I can see now you are craving for the worst form of slavery. By the time you realize it, your hands and feet shall be banded. You will not be able to reverse the entrenched wrongs of your life. If you choose and decide to walk that path, afterward all your fuses will blow out. If you abuse your freedom when you have the time, then given what it takes to rectify it; the time will come that you will want to correct it but no redemption will be available. Then you shall come to understand the true meaning of freedom is doing what is right." Gramps clearly want to protect Hayet as a precious jewel.

"Once you blow out one fuse, you will crave more, to the point of the blowing all of your remaining fuses. What I want to say is that, up to now, you have been a decent person, not contaminated with the world. However, if you continue associating yourself with the people to whom you have been giving rides, then slowly you will end up being like one of them. Mark my words, should it occur, it will be more difficult to detach yourself from such habits than it is for the people to whom you give rides," says Grandpa. Grandpa's statement does not convince Hayet. "Grandpa, you have the wrong perception of the kind of person that I am. Being a man, I am aware of what I do and the places I go. Do not worry, and do not be overprotective of me. Leave me alone."

"We are mortal just like you," says Grandpa. "However, you cannot live without Him in who you live, move, and have your being. Remain in Him, as He also remains in you. Because no branch can bear fruit by itself, it must remain on the vine. Neither can you bear fruit nor handle by yourself unless you remain in Him. Jesus is the vine; we are the branches. If we remain in Jesus and Jesus in us, we will bear much fruit. Apart from Him, we can do nothing. Also, if you think you are standing strong, be careful not to fall. You are overconfident. Who do you think you are? You should learn a lesson from the 'unsinkable' *Titanic*, which sank. Do not make the mistake of thinking that you are out of reach of the devil and out of reach of God. Tell me, what is the description of a man?"

"A man does not necessarily mean male gender. A man is one who is willing to provide, protect, and serve himself and the community," replies Hayet. He has heard this statement numerous times.

"Thank you for the correct answer. Note that one earns the title of manhood by avoiding problems and making wise choices, not by looking for trouble. I have lived on this earth better and longer than you have and witnessed several aspiring individuals unconsciously deviate from purposeful living. They squeezed themselves into being someone they are not and ended up in places where they did not want to be." Grandpa starts to walk away in dismay.

"You do not have to do that. I am listening," shouts Hayet. He knows where Grandpa is going and worries about it. It is better to receive physical punishments than hearing the nerve-racking song. Hearing the song is as painful as adding salt to a wound.

"You do not want to hear the truth!" Grandpa declares as he sits on a three-legged, zebra-striped stool. "You will know the truth, and the truth will set you free. Besides, what you do not want to hear is frequently what you need to hear. In the future for the very speech that you hate us now, for correcting you, you will love us. Above and beyond, that is how my father dealt with me, and this is how I treat my son."

Hayet waits for his foster father's message. Taking his guitar from its stand, Grandpa sings a lesson about how King David gave himself away to slow, fading vulnerabilities before he crumbled into Bathsheba's bosom. One sin leads to another, and finally, David murders her husband to cover up his wrongdoing.

Then Grandpa sings the Casting Crowns song "Slow Fade": "It is a slow fade when you give yourself away."

"Hayet, that is the message for you," he says, placing the guitar on its stand and sitting on the floor with legs crossed.

Hayet numbly contemplates the song while rubbing his chin. Regardless of Grandpa's depictions, Hayet is confident and believes that he is cautious of temptations and vulnerabilities. Silence overtakes them with no further song and no discussion; each of them sits awkwardly.

A brief lull takes over inside the house while outside wild wind hunkers down in New York City. Then Grandma utters, "The car is the one putting him in trouble. Before all sorts of disaster strike him, the best thing would be to take the car away from him." At the same time, she places freshly brewed ginger scented black tea in a blue kettle on the table. As she watches the vapor exit the pot, Grandma expects to hear Hayet's remorse.

"If that is what you think would be the solution, then so be it. I can use the subway, which is hassle-free, or I will borrow or purchase a car."

"Listen, son, if you do not have enough money to pay for the car, you should not buy it on credit, which would make you a slave to the creditor," warns Grandma. The Gramps drive no-frills cars, though they can buy classic cars.

"To save yourself from debt, during the good times divide the money you get between saving, spending, and giving. Then in the days of need, it will be a treasure for you. Furthermore, remember that the Scripture says that the Lord your God will bless you as He has promised, and you will lend to many nations but will borrow from none. You will rule over many nations, yet none will rule over you."

"Taking the car from him right now might be premature. However, if that is the only solution, we shall do so," affirms Grandpa.

"You can take whatever action you want. However, I want both of you to know that whatever I do, it is with good intention, to serve people," insists Hayet.

"Son, I do not have to repeat myself. Instead, the food is getting cold. Let us eat."

The conversation is embarrassing, and Hayet feels misunderstood. He has no desire for the delightful food. Nevertheless, to fill up his rumbling stomach, he pours the hot ginger tea into his cup. After adding four teaspoons of sugar, he stirs the tea gently with a silver spoon. He then sits motionless, his finger drumming on the table while staring at the tea.

Deep within his heart, Hayet believes that he should obey his parents even if he disagrees with them. Instead, he uses his own reasoning to do what he wants to do.

Well, now that they have caught me red-handed, at least I can avoid parking tickets. I would better use another method to be of good service to my friends. The best thing is to avoid coming home on weekends. Then take my friends to their destinations early, stay in the parking lot, and do schoolwork while I stay in the car until they finish their fun.

Gradually, the mood changes and they resume typical family discussions. However, Hayet still has one issue that has been bothering him.

Chapter 9

Weakness of attitude becomes weakness of character.

— ALBERT EINSTEIN

Hayet's promise pledge, "True Love Waits," engraved on his ring, bothers him more than anything does in college, and he wants to disavow it.

As Hayet takes the first sip of the third cup tea, he decides to share his concern.

"Grandpa," he calls out.

"What is that you want to say?" Grandma, who has a Type-A personality, replies instead.

"Nothing," answers Hayet. He is too shy to speak of his concern.

Grandpa walks around, pulls up his favorite zebra-colored stool, and sits next to Hayet.

"I believe one that we do not know is troubling you. Let us discuss it man to man, and I will help you with all that I can."

Grandma sits as well. She never seems to leave the room to give space for a man-to-man discussion.

After a moment of fidgeting, Hayet says, "Well, it is about growing up, which has been troubling me since the first day of college."

"What is it?" Grandma interrupts.

Hayet pauses, being wary of talking about it, after staying faithful to his chastity pledge for years.

"Tell us! What is troubling you?" Grandma reiterates, waiting to hear the information.

Hayet does not know how to break the news, and Grandpa listens, finger drumming on the table. Grandma casts a darting glance at him.

Hayet gazes at the Gramps and then opens his mouth to say what has been tormenting him.

"Wherever I go, people ask me, 'Are you married?' I feel so ashamed to explain to people who do not seem to appreciate my values. Eventually, people make fun of me. I feel like I am a loner, a fish out of a water, in a distinct world where I do not belong. I hate having this ring on campus, and it feels right to take it off while there."

Grandma becomes nervous. She sits on the brink of her chair and says, "Baby, I am glad that you brought up the sad attack on humanity's chastity heritage. From what you are saying, I can tell that this could be the beginning of the end for you. Chaste living should not bother you. You ought to feel proud of yourself for having the pledge. To tell you the truth, the people who ought to feel ashamed are the ones that do not have what you have. They tampered with their purity and had no regard to their prospective spouse. If any student or teacher asks you about it, tell them that you pledged to God to remain chaste until marriage, out of respect for your future spouse."

"This is a speech that I do not want to make. It is not popular and is tormenting me. Sometimes I put on gloves to cover my ring, and other times I put my hand in my pocket to evade questioning."

"Hayet, it is sad that you feel that way about it. Tell me which one is better. To be chaste or unchaste?"

"It is best to be chaste. However, it is okay for people that live in the jungles. For the contemporary generation, especially for men in college, high school, and middle school, it is uncool. A man ought to try out the water first before immersing to swim. The reason is that when a real situation that needs swimming comes, you know how to do it, so there will not be teasing when you get married. That is what my colleagues say."

"Would you rather listen to God or to your immature and untested colleagues who cannot tell their right hand from their left?" *To God.*

The old-fashioned intolerant conservative Gramps and the young man desiring to try all before the appointed time have numerous differences. Many times, the Gramps wake up as early as 2:00 a.m. to faithfully commune and speak face-to-face with the Lord, and everybody in the neighborhood can hear. Frequently, Hayet prays, *Lord, please answer their prayer right now so that people in the neighborhood and I may get some sleep.*

"Honey, what is going on with the current generation?" asks Grandma artfully.

"Same as what went on during our generation."

"What I am trying to say is that they dress the wound of my people as though it were not serious. They say 'cool' to unholy choices."

"Son, you do not need to try any of that. You will know how when you get married, without taking trial lessons. Trust me, a one-time trial for which you yearn could be the start of an endless failed and promiscuous life journey. Besides, the marriage bed is to be kept undefiled by all people in the city or in the jungles, male as well as female, including your friends that lure you to deviate from your chastity pledge. Hayet, for the sinful friends that entice you for wrongdoing, never allow your life to compromise into their ways. Do not go along with them; do not set foot on their paths."

Grandma adds, "You know son, when Grandpa and I got married, he was inexperienced in what you are talking about."

"So were you!" Grandpa pronounces slyly.

"Of course, both of us were naive; that was new, the first time for both of us. However, we were and still are compatible with each other. Therefore, will you be, too, when you get married. I kept myself pure for honey, and he did the same for me. Besides, it is you who chose to wear the ring; you pledged willingly, and nobody enticed or forced you to embrace chastity!"

"Yes, Grandma, but that was then and this is now. Times have changed. My friends say you do not have to wait to have it until you get married or have a marital obligation or covenantal agreement. One can have it without being married or even having a commitment."

"So, do you believe that?"

"Yes!"

"The simple believe anything, but the prudent carefully consider their steps," she rebukes Hayet.

"Are you saying that I am a simple?"

"I would say yes. Additionally, you shall know the truth and it will set you free."

The Gramps is worried about how to make Hayet grasp what they are saying. They can no longer homeschool him. He has grown beyond what they can handle.

Finally, Grandma says, "Son, thanks for your honesty. We can see your dilemma. It will help us understand you better. So—um—," Grandma hums and pauses as if she has lost the right word. "What do you propose for a solution?" she lastly asks bluntly.

"Well, right now I believe taking the ring off my finger is the best solution."

"That is the beginning to the end!" she shrieks, throwing her hands up.

"Grandma, please understand. I will keep myself chaste, but this ring will not be on my finger. I will feel more accepted without it than with it. The ring is just a piece of metal."

"My son, I do not see the ring. What I see is the message it conveys!"

"What message does it convey?"

"It declares to the world that, 'I am not free to open my precious gift to anybody until the appropriate time, which is while waiting for marriage. I belong to a spouse who is yet to come.'"

"What if she does not come?"

"Though it seems slow in coming, wait patiently, because she will surely come. He who did not spare his Son, but gave Him up for us all, will also along with Him, graciously give us all that we need. Until then, seek first His kingdom and His righteousness, and all that you need will be added to you as well," Grandma asserts. She appears to be more concerned than Grandpa is.

"Honey, don't you think that the current generation has a deficiency of some DNA?" she asks ingeniously.

Grandpa chuckles over her remarks. "You bet! Nevertheless, what DNA are they missing?"

"They are missing the DNA of holiness. They are unable to discern between the noble and the common, the wise from the foolish decision. It is the same deficiency that drives a mature man to behave like a boy and a fully-grown woman to behave like a girl."

"You know, honey, you are being sarcastic. Don't you remember when we were in high school?" Grandpa begins.

"Stop that! I do not want to talk about my past. I have buried it behind me."

"Okay," replies Grandpa out of respect. Although Grandpa wants to tell of his experience so that Hayet may learn from it, Grandma hates to talk about the past hurt.

After a minute of silence, Grandma says, "Baby, it is easy to tell that you are trying to be someone else. Be gutsy and be yourself. Whoever accepts you will respect you for who you are, with or without your chaste ring. Those who have screwed up, enticing you to be as one of them, have lost their GPS. I beseech you, son, by the mercies of God, not to give up your noble values; instead present your body a living sacrifice, holy and acceptable to God. This is what you need more than fun. The rumor that will spread without your ring will be worse than if you were to keep it. Do you know that?"

"I do not know. However, getting rid of my ring is what I am thinking now. I wish I could be a free man," Hayet mutters as he occasionally runs a hand through his Afro.

"Indeed, you are free. Yet, you are yearning to be a slave of your fellow students, whom worms are consuming. You dare to stand up for who you are, not for what others say about you. It is what you believe about yourself that matters most, not what others say about you. Take responsibility for your life and action. Plunge the guidance of the Holy Spirit into your life, not to the pressure of your colleagues. Every choice you make has a consequence."

"Grandma, what worm eats a person while one is alive?" asks Hayet with a giggle.

"I am talking about the worms of compromise, tolerance and worldliness that erode one's reverence of God."

Returning his chair to the table, Hayet picks up the used utensils and places them in the sink. He usually does not enjoy cooking, but he likes washing and putting the kitchen in order. He puts on an old yellow apron, then pours scented detergent on the sponge and opens the faucet for the water to run. The fragrance of the detergent and the hot water give the sink a pleasing lemony aroma. While washing, he often turns his face and gazes at Gramps, who is in deep silence, mulling over the troubling news.

The clattering of pans echoes through the kitchen as Hayet washes the plates and porcelains.

Suddenly, the doorbell rings. Hayet wonders, *Who could be coming so early without prior notice?* It should be a close relative or friend. Grandma straightens her clothes and hair braids as she walks to open the door. The door opens. Grandma stretches out her arms, smiles, and shouts, "Hallelujah! Hallelujah! Come on in." The guests are her religious ultraconservative friends, the Grannies: Mrs. ANNABELLE LIONEL, Mrs. CELINE KLEIN, Mrs. JENNIFER JACKSON, and Mrs. GWEN BALDWIN. They live in the same condominium building as the Gramps. These women are the backbone of the church and the country. Usually, it is when they have a local or national concern or a personal problem that they come together to pray. Whoever the target is, woe unto him, her, or it; they never let go until they receive at least an assurance of what they prayed for.

Chapter 10

Crying is all right in its own way while it lasts. But you have to stop sooner or later, and then you still have to decide what to do.

— C. S. Lewis

Grandma's friends are prayer warriors; they will offer a supplication that would have a seed of return planted in Hayet's soul long before he deviates.

When they pray for one, they feel one because they mean it. They carry the overwhelming crushing concern on themselves as they unleash each meaningful supplication before the Lord.

The coming of the Grannies at an unusual time alarms Hayet. *Who could be the target?* Hayet, who is on the verge of giving up hope of developing a tolerant attitude, dries his wet hands on a towel, takes off his apron and places it on a wooden hanger, then approaches to greet them.

"It is a pleasure to see you, adorable women!"

"Thanks for the kind words. How is school going?" Mrs. Baldwin asks while standing and holding the door handle.

"At the beginning, I was a little nervous about the amount of work. However, I am getting used to it and doing well."

"How is the campus social and spiritual life?" Mrs. Jackson adds.

"Well, as long as I become progressive, tolerant, follow the crowd and the stars, believing what they believe and doing what they do to blend and fit in, I will be okay."

"What do you mean by progressive?" Mrs. Jackson inquires.

"One who is not stagnant conservative that embraces old tradition, one who advocates and implements social reforms that are liberal thoughts."

"Out of the billions population of the world, God has only one you to be who you are meant to live. Why would you vacate the only Hayet to conform, settle, fit in and blend in instead of standing tall for the purpose you have been created for?" questions Mrs. Jackson.

If I am like no other, then abandoning myself to fit in and blend in is not worth it. "Furthermore, when we started college, the faith and the creation theory were giving me a hard time to comprehend. Most of the school body does not believe what you people believe. Of course, you will not be comfortable with it, but when you hear the contemporary college discussion, you will come to appreciate the scientific theories and social life. Now that I have a clear understanding, and am learning how to tolerate, the adjustment is coming easier."

Hayet hints at the new, unbelieving perspective on life that he has adopted in college. The faithless inclination did not appear overnight—it took hold when he was back in Africa. The reason he felt this way was that God did not intervene when the powerful authorities mistreated his father. He comes to believe there is no just God who intervenes in unjust proceedings.

He tells the women, "All that you need to live in this world is power, money, and a connection with appeasers that I call a lie-synthesis."

At the college and in high schools as several students do, not only has Hayet grown lukewarm toward faith, but he is also likely to abandon it all together. The Grannies have several questions to ask.

"Why would you follow stars while you could follow the *Son*, which is the best of all?" says the baffled Mrs. Klein, spelling the word, "*S-o-n*."

The Grannies do not seem to understand Hayet's message.

"Stars are the celebrities and VIPs of the world that I follow."

Mrs. Klein inquires, "Oh, and what will the stars give you for following them? Do your stars know you, and how do you communicate with them?"

"They give me nothing, they do not know me, and we have no personal relationship or communication."

"Why would you follow people who do not know you, who you are not related to or have two-way communication with, which would give you nothing?"

"I don't know."

"Son, you may not know how to give a gutsy answer as to who the stars you follow are and why. But, I know the one that I follow and whom I have believed in. Let me tell you. I have a star. My star knows my name and where I live. He is merciful and compassionate, feels all my pain and walks with me and talks with me day and night. In my days of trouble, I call upon my star and He avails Himself instantaneously. My star is my refuge, my provider, my defender. If I were you, I would abandon all others and commit to following the star I am talking about, the one who is the same yesterday, today, and forever, the one that gives me abundant life."

"I would love to add to the list of my stars and follow that one, too."

"No, no, and no! You should not make a mistake of combining my star with other stars. My star is all-sufficient and can stand without any support. One time, the Philistines captured the Ark of the Covenant, which was the earthly representation of God to a place called Ashdod. Then they carried the Ark into Dagon's temple and set it alongside Dagon. When the people of Ashdod rose early the next day, there was Dagon, fallen on his face on the ground before the Ark of the Lord. They took Dagon and put him back in his place. The following morning as well, when they rose, there was Dagon, fallen on his face on the ground before the Ark of the Lord. His head and hands had been broken off and were lying on the threshold; only his body remained. So, take note that my star exceedingly transcends all other stars," explains Mrs. Klein.

Furthermore, she confidently clarifies, "Everyone who follows your stars, perhaps for the majority of them that did not complete high school or who did not go to college, that are not able to handle their achievement could be disappointed and will look for more; nevertheless, whoever follows my star certainly will not go hungry or thirsty, will receive satisfaction, and search for no more."

Mrs. Klein's lips dry up as she speaks. She grabs a small tube and an oval mirror from her huge handbag. As she looks her skinny lips over the mirror, she applies the lip balm.

Then she resumes. "It is the same star that Polycarp of Smyrna followed and spoke of when he was pressed to recant: 'Eighty-six years I have served Him, and He never once wronged me. How can I blaspheme my King, who saved me?' It is this confession that led him to burn at the stake."

Hayet scratches his Afro with his pinky fingernail. He can tell that Mrs. Klein still has more questions, and he does not want to answer them.

"Besides, what does a lie-synthesis mean? I know photosynthesis, but not that term. Does that term convert unacceptable wrong lying into an acceptable truth?"

"It does, sort of. You cannot find it anywhere else. A lie-synthesis is a method that does not punish an ally or a friend over punishable offenses and crimes, yet it allows a punishment of an enemy over an unpunishable offense. It also rewards an ally for unsatisfactory accomplishments while withholding and opposing legitimate reward from an enemy. It is a way of legalizing the illegal, using, manipulating and perverting of the law," explains Hayet.

"What else does it do?" Mrs. Klein asks.

"A lie-synthesis covers up the wrongs of an ally to evade punishment by adjourning an ally defendant's lawless crimes. If you hate a person or a nation because of their refusal to be enslaved, you manipulate your friends to hate what you hate and to love what you love. To get support from the poor, one bribes or threatens the poor with severe consequences, purchases votes for a benefit, paralyzes and forces one to muzzle up from speaking what is just and fair. Should one speak against it, one is considered an antagonist or unpatriotic or is labeled other names."

"We are old school and we need an explanation in simple words. Can you give us an example of a lie-synthesis?" inquires Mrs. Lionel.

"A lie-synthesis is self-explanatory," Hayet explains. "It is a perverted legal process that does not allow punishment of an ally, even for atrocious offenses. If your ally does wrong, you cover up the wrongs using excuses, so that your ally may evade punishment. On the other side, if an enemy commits the same, a lesser crime, or an unpunishable offense, lie-synthesis mobilizes others, even fabricating reasons to punish the enemy. It extravagantly rewards an ally for unsatisfactory endeavors while plundering, squashing and opposing legitimate remuneration from an enemy. It is a way of legalizing the illegal using and distorting the law. A lie-synthesis postpones an ally's unruly penalty deserving act."

"Hayet, please explain using real examples so that we may understand your message," Mrs. Lionel implores.

"Okay, here is the first one. In 1964 President Lyndon Baines Johnson created a fabricated lie-synthesis. He wanted to commit more troops in Southeast Asia. He and his advisors made up a lie-synthesis of an unprovoked attack on US ships by Vietnamese torpedo boats. The president used Senator Fulbright to create a lie-synthesis for a resolution in Congress to retaliate, and Fulbright received eighty-eight out of ninety senate votes. The two senators, Wayne Morse and Ernest Gruening, who voted no, in objection to sending American sons into a war in which we had no business, were not reelected because their constituents were mesmerized by the lie-synthesis of the people in power. In reality, there was no attack."

"Here is the second one. The law says anyone who communicates, furnishes, transmits, or otherwise makes available to an unauthorized person, or publishes, or uses in any manner prejudicial to the safety or interest of the United States or for the benefit of any foreign government to the detriment of the US any classified information is guilty. Lie-synthesis holds guilty, imprisons, and fines thousands of dollars for people with one or two crimes. Yet it intentionally covers up for mishandling thousands of pieces of classified information without imprisonment or fine to the offender with the same standard that holds others accountable, sealing it with Medes and Persians no decree or edict that the authority's issues can be changed. Lie-synthesis makes the rule of law apply not to all to certain people."

"Wow, that is a great revelation. I got it. Who is going to fix the prevailing lie-synthesis?" replies Mrs. Lionel.

"Somebody with a unique perspective of just and true service," replies Hayet.

"Perhaps you could be the one fixing such failings. In addition, why is Hayet making a distinction between himself and us?" Mrs. Jackson whispers, turning her face to Mrs. Baldwin.

"That is what I was about to ask!" Mrs. Lionel booms. She does not have a whispering voice.

Grandma, who had gone into the kitchen, replies, "We have had such a discussion for some time."

"Do not tell me it is true," calls out Mrs. Jackson.

"Yes, it is true," exclaims Hayet.

"We hoped that you would be the gatekeeper and represent all the values that we uphold. Who has persuaded you to turn away from your faith? Before you started college, Jesus Christ was on the throne of your heart. Who has bewitched you to fall spiritually downward, spiraling to your current state?" rebukes Mrs. Jackson.

"Mrs. Jackson, I want you to know that I did not fall. Scrutinizing of religious myths and being tolerant is a sign of the maturing of a person whose eyes opened to a new perspective of intellectuality," Hayet argues.

Grandma is furious, *Mamma mia!* declares and rebukes Hayet. "We did not follow cleverly invented myths when we told you about our faith in the Lord Jesus Christ. Our faith is not a hollow experience, fairy tale, or worldview. It is about having real and personal experience with God. God has adopted you into his family. What this means is that your identity changes and God expects of you to live out His love for everyone to see, be it at school, at home, or in the street. You are accountable for living out your faith, speaking out to anyone you meet about the hope of salvation since you never know if your words and actions will be the seed of the word of God planted in a lost person's heart."

"Do you have anything else that is part of opened eyes to a new perspective of intellectuality?" inquires Mrs. Lionel.

"Yes! When it is Valentine's Day, you can say Happy Valentine's Day. When it is Saint Patrick's Day, you say Happy Saint Patrick's Day. When it is Easter, you say Happy Holiday. When it is Christmas, you say Happy Holiday. In this generation, all non-Christian experiences, including in the reformation landmark places of Christianity are welcome. However, anything that has to do with Jesus Christ, who is divisive, people should refrain from speaking of in public. I have come to learn that it is okay one can believe in nature, animals, or other beings. However, upholding conservative Christian values is intolerant and it is often interpreted as a sign of simplemindedness."

"In China and other non-Christian nations people can wish Merry Christmas, yet we cannot. It is too sad. The first shall be the last and the last shall be the first is being fulfilled. Also, did you say the liberal perspectives that are a conducive breeding ground of terrorists which are making Europe a spiritually choked continent are the signs of maturity of a person whose eyes opened to a new perspective of intellectuality?" asks Mrs. Lionel.

"I guess so! You should not speak words that offend others. Be tolerant," replies Hayet.

"Do you know what happens when a nation abandons God's laws in order not to offend others in the name of tolerance, for whatever reason?"

"Nothing!"

"The ground gets cursed because of you; through painful toil, we will eat food from it all the days of our life. It produces thorns and thistles for us. If we disobey God's law, He brings up people among us who would become barbs in our eyes and thorns in our sides. The same would give us trouble in the land where we have lived in peace for generations."

"Banning such people or building a sky-high wall might be a solution."

"Showing God to such people in colleges and in our neighborhoods and in work places is the only solution; banning or building walls increases the enmity. The reason is that Christ himself has brought peace to us. He united Jews and Gentiles into one people when, in His own body on the cross, He broke down the wall of hostility that separated us."

Mrs. Lionel is not yet done arguing with Hayet. "Son, I refute your elaborations and claims of simplemindedness. These should be the signs of the opposite of your claim. Dr./Mrs. Klein is a retired scientist, investor, and a billionaire; Mrs. Jackson has a Ph.D. in math; Dr./Mrs. Baldwin is a cancer specialist; the Gramps have a Ph.D. in pharmacology; and my husband, Dr. Lionel, and I have Ph.D. in law. The truth is that the message of the cross of Jesus is foolishness to those who are perishing, but to us who are being saved it is the power of God."

"So, are you saying that I am among the perishing?"

"The perishing believes and displays contrary to the message of the cross of Jesus. Judge for yourself whether you are of the perishing or not."

"What else?" inquires Mrs. Klein.

"When you see expectant women do not refer them as pregnant women or mothers to be."

"Why?"

"Because there are some women who identify and consider themselves as men, they get offended."

"What should we refer the pregnant women as?"

"A pregnant person."

"Is it a man or a woman that get pregnant?"

"Of course, it is a woman."

"Thank you for answering the question accurately. Daydreaming, identifying and considering yourself what you are not does not abrogate reality and make you to be what you daydream."

Right then Grandpa walks away. Hayet immediately knows where he is going. He grabs his banjo and sings MercyMe's song "Greater."

The song deals with what happens when the accusing voices of others may say intimidating, demeaning, or crushing words by making fun of you for who you are and for what you believe. The song challenges the accusing voices, asserting that what matters most is what God, the Greater living inside of you says is who you are, not what the one who is living in the world says about you.

The Grannies are not happy about the way Hayet is speaking words that are not compatible with the biblical truth. After a moment of stillness, Mrs. Klein cries, "We are in the end times. Our children face hostility to their faith on one side and indifference to anything of importance on the other side. The secularism influence infuses them, and they graduate as liberal scholars. Sadly, the casualties are high by the end of the college years."

Grandma says, "I do not understand what has gone wrong despite having a secure biblical grounding and a clear understanding of the faith. We thought Hayet would repay us for what we did not achieve from the older children."

"Perhaps it is his choice. Besides, sometimes we do fail to teach the college bound students real-life applications of justice, fairness, and service from a truth perspective. Frequently, we do not live by what we profess. We claim to be believers, yet our actions display otherwise. The anti-biblical liberal professors deflate the clean conscience and smear their infectious toxins to the knowledge yearning, uncorrupted mind. We need to safeguard our college students from venomous indoctrination. Our instructions at home should revolve around all that the anti-faith liberals use, and we should equip them with appropriate discipleship from internal as well as external attacks," explains Mrs. Lionel.

Furthermore, "Maybe that is why we are here. As for us, we are Christians, believe in one nation under God to protect us from unseen calamities. In a hard work, a family where married male and female live, a powerful army to defend us from foreign aggression, keep our guns from home intrusion. Abortion, secularism, communism and liberalism thoughts who do not accept a defeat graciously are dangerous threats to humanity. Jesus Christ is our savior, and we pray God to bring a leader who would bring jobs back to America and return the Ten Commandment statues and Godly values back to our societies and court houses" she says.

Physically, she is the feeblest woman, yet she is gifted with a thunderous, powerful voice.

"We should not blame the university instructors for every wrong choice our children make. The verdict is, the Light has come into the world, but people loved darkness instead of light because their deeds were evil," comments Mrs. Klein.

In the midst of the discussion, "That is not all. He also yearns to do some *practice*," Grandma says, intending to expose him more.

"Practice makes perfect! What is that he wants to practice? Is it operating mechanical, electrical equipment or doing some surgical procedures?" asks Mrs. Jackson.

"I wish it were so, but is not. He craves to sleep with a woman so that he may not be teased by his wife after marriage," explains Grandma with a whimper.

Grandma, who appears to have more to say questions, asks, "By doing adult activity prematurely do you think it will make you seem more mature?"

"No. However, I feel like I will not be cool if I do not."

"Putting all your self-worth in someone else's judgment to be cool is not healthy."

I am aware of it, yet I will try it out.

"Bring the oil," orders Mrs. Lionel while pulling out Grandpa's favorite stool.

Grandma walks to the kitchen hurriedly.

"We want you to kneel down here. We are going to say a prayer for you," orders Mrs. Klein.

Hayet opens up his mouth to say, "No, thanks."

The ladies are too quick for him. Instead, he impulsively says, "Sure. However, before you pray I have one more point to say. I want to have a tattoo of Jesus or the cross. How would you feel about it?" Hayet presumes that the Grannies always have something to say from the Bible.

"Why would you want to have a bumper sticker on your body? Don't you know that you are fearfully and wonderfully made? Will inscription, drawing Jesus, or the cross symbols on your body make the procedure holy?"

"I guess so?"

"Do you know that you would pay more to undo it than to have it done?"

"I don't know."

"Well, son, if you do not see that from a financial point of view, scripture clearly says do not mark your skin with tattoos. Take a note that you have been fearfully and wonderfully made. Besides, God has engraved you on the palms of His hands. You show that you are a letter from Christ, written not with ink but with the Spirit of the living God, not on tablets of stone, on your skin, but on tablets of your heart," argues Mrs. Lionel.

I knew that.

Immediately, they encircle him with no way out, in the manner that ferocious predators surrounding a gigantic prey to poke it from all directions. While Hayet kneels on the cherry hardwood floor of the living room, Grandma brings oil in a little black clay jar brought from the historic city, Jerusalem.

"Shut your eyes and open your heart," orders Mrs. Lionel.

How can I shut my eyes and open my heart while being in a spiritual surgical procedure, unless you induce me with anesthesia?

Hayet is the target. The best thing he can do is to cooperate with them so they finish quickly.

"Would you lead us with a worship song?" Mrs. Lionel asks Grandpa.

Grandpa gets out of his chair. He is a great jazz artist who can play the saxophone, all types of guitar, accordion, and the piano. He picks up his banjo and plucks an introductory interlude.

"Hmm," he hums. Then he utters the first sentence of the song with lifted arms. "We need you, Lord. Yes, Lord, we need you." The women echo the song of praise and prayers would go to the throne of God as fragrant incense.

As the song progresses, the women jump, shout, wail, and howl while yelling, "Come out devil!" Mrs. Lionel blasts her divinely empowered voice right in Hayet's ears.

Should the devil be within me, unless muted with deafness, he has to hear and come out, making the tension end quickly.

The neighbors' discomfort over the abrupt, noisy commotion is Hayet's main concern. Some of the neighbors might be sleeping; others are studying or working from home. The women are in high spirits with lifted arms and eyes closed.

"The neighbors might be—"

Before he finishes the sentence, Mrs. Lionel says, "Never mind about the neighbors; they all know that the old Grannies are up to serious business."

It is taking longer than expected. Perhaps I should have said no thanks faster. However, for the Gramps and the Grannies, I am aware that even if I were to say 'no' thanks, on issues pertaining to Jesus and the Bible, no thanks is not an appropriate answer.

The only option he has is to enjoy the spiritual ride. The women intensify the prayer. They shake him in all directions. Not only that but they also squeeze and press him down on the floor, as one would do to drain wetness out of a wet substance.

At the climax of the song, the shaky Mrs. Lionel pours oil on top of his head. The oil rolls down to his forehead, eyebrows, face, and cheeks, a few drops falling to the chair and on the floor. The oil that does not drop from his face makes it over and under his clean Sunday clothing. The oil spill makes the room slippery and hazardous.

"I have to bring a mop and wipe this mess," Hayet mutters. He motions to fetch a mop, but they force him down to his knees.

Physically, they seem to be shaky. Nevertheless, Hayet wonders where the Grannies acquire such strength when they pray. In spite of their jumping, walking, and shouting, they never become tired or weak. Their strength renews as they go as if they are self-recharging. Then, one by one, they dip their fingers. They smear his lips, ears, feet, tongue, and hands, making every part of his body heavy and oily.

After a fierce fight with the devil for control of the soul, either they give up or by faith, they accept answers to their prayers. They end the prayer ordeal and say, "Amen."

"Thank you." Hayet breathes a sigh of relief. A couple of them go to the kitchen sink, and the rest head to the bathroom to wash their oily hands.

While they are returning to their respective chairs, Grandma asks with a grin, "May I prepare coffee or tea?"

"Do not worry; this will do for me," pronounces the outspoken Mrs. Klein, pointing to a water bottle near the stainless silver fridge. Eventually, all of them choose the same.

Grandma hands a bottle to each one of them as she walks around the table.

"It is so tight that I cannot open it," whispers Mrs. Klein as she labors to open her bottle.

"I will have mine room temperature, please. This one is too cold," requests Mrs. Baldwin. Grandma brings the requested water and gives it to her.

Mrs. Baldwin opens her mouth wide and opens the bottle with her teeth.

Meanwhile, Mrs. Klein struggles to open the water bottle by herself.

"Mrs. Klein, why do you have to struggle to open the bottle? Give it to the young man, and he will do it for you," says Mrs. Jackson.

"I used to be able to open them easily, but these days my arthritis makes it hard," mumbles Mrs. Klein as she attempts yet again.

"You know that you are growing old," replies Mrs. Jackson, disapproving of Mrs. Klein's endeavor.

"Thanks for your remarks; however, remember that I am a German woman." Mrs. Jackson giggles hearing the reply.

The two personalities of the women bewilder Hayet. When they pray, sing and worship, they act as energetic as toddlers. But when they sit down for discussion, they return to being Grannies. There is no sign of the prayer attack that just happened. No sign except for the oil spill on the floor.

"How come when you pray, you appear to be so strong, and yet other times you do not?" asks the baffled Hayet.

"Have you not heard that those who hope in the Lord will renew their strength? They will soar on wings like eagles; they will run and not grow weary; they will walk and not be faint," replies Mrs. Baldwin.

As Hayet hands the open bottles to Mrs. Jackson and Mrs. Lionel, Mrs. Klein shouts, "Yes, I did it. I do not want to depend on others for all that I need."

Shortly after the fierce spiritual fight with the devil, Mrs. Jackson asks, "How do you feel now?"

Hayet wipes oil from his eyelashes. "Well, frankly, I feel the same as before the prayer, just a little oilier. Moreover, I do not understand why you claim to be keeping me from captivity and wrong ways as if I have been taken away by somebody."

"The Lord knows why," replies Mrs. Baldwin.

"It does not make sense that you do not know why you say a prayer and make the Lord responsible for what you did."

"Son, we do not know what we ought to pray for, but the Spirit Himself intercedes for us through wordless groans," stresses Mrs. Jackson. Furthermore, she says, "You do not understand the effects of the prayers right now. However, when you see yourself snatched out of a bad crowd and delivered from near death, you shall know the outcome of today's prayers. Besides, ignoring our prayer if you decide to go away from a purposeful living, I want you to take note that you are not the only one that will pay the price for your untimely choices. It will affect your family, including us, as well as your descendants. Additionally, somebody has paid a price for you to be here. Choose to pay the price for someone the way the Gramps paid for you. Be a man and say no, courageously, to untimely choices. If not, one day you will regret not holding to your pledge."

Meanwhile, Grandma mops the floor, clearly hoping that the Grannies will not do *that* again. Hayet says, "Excuse me, ladies and Grandpa. I have to take a bath and change my clothes."

"I don't think we will stay until you return because we have to go to the first service," Mrs. Klein replies.

"We are also going to the same service. If I see you, fine; if not, that is also acceptable."

Hayet takes a bath with extremely hot water and soap to get rid of the oil, and then he changes his clothes. By the time he returns from the bath, the Grannies have already left to do the Sunday routine and church commitments. Hayet and the Gramps as well leave for church and return home at noon.

In the late afternoon, Hayet says, "I am going to campus. Have a nice week."

As usual, Grandma replies, "Behave yourself and drive safely."

"Grandma, I have heard that sentence a million times, as if I cannot think for myself. You are limiting my life. Please stop hovering over all that I do."

"My son, we have visited and buried multiple youngsters that walked your walk and talked your talk, ignoring their parents' warning to behave themselves and drive safe," interrupts Grandpa.

Hayet leaves without further discussion. In a few minutes, he reaches the campus parking area, where he meets a gorgeous student, who every man wishes to date.

Chapter 11

We are born bad. Children did not need to be taught to behave badly — they are born knowing how to do that. We teach them how to be good. We become good by being reborn — born again.

— *J. C. Watts, In New York Times*

On a snowy, cold early evening, Hayet receives an ultimatum that will influence his life journey from one woman and a brief warning from another woman whom he would love in the future for the very thing he hates and ignores.

Feathery and thin hazes of ice-crystal cirrus clouds blanket the horizon. It is breezy this late Sunday afternoon. By the time Hayet arrives on campus, the high-rise buildings and skyscrapers block the sunbeams. The time change and bad weather make it worse.

Before it turns five o'clock, it is pitch dark. Hayet parks the large-rimmed silver Toyota 4Runner near the dead-end sign. Out of nowhere, an elegant, a retrofit and flare silhouette comes toward him in stylish red, silver-studded high-heeled shoes. Hayet's heartbeat grows ragged; his blood teems, as he looks at her sideways. *Who is this woman?*

The silhouette approaches, leaving tiny footprint marks through the un-trudged fresh bright white snow. Hayet glances at her and realizes it is ANGEL.

Although it is obvious she is approaching, he pretends not to see her while brushing off his black leather jacket.

After all, she has no business with me.

Angel is as white as a Cherokee rose in the midst of the choicest flowers. Her speech, walk, smile, appearance, and touch are all angelic. She is dressed in an unseasonable miniskirt with a bright smile not affected by the frosty weather. Her tamed hair spreads out over her large breasts and down to a naturally endowed hourglass-figure tiny waist. Every time she walks on campus, she is as happy as a bird in flight. Every day she dresses in fashionable clothing from Christian Louboutin, Chloe, and other stylish designers. Whether it is day or night, she looks as if she is going to a coronation ceremony.

As beautiful as Angel is in her adorable gorgeousness, she is sick, with a disease that nobody notices. Angel's sickness is not a bone-eating disease or one that contaminates her blood with abnormal cells. Her sickness is not something that slows or increases the heartbeat. Physical medicine cannot treat or cure Angel's sickness. Her sickness is not one that afflicts her with painful sores from the soles of her feet to the crown of her head. If she were to have a feeling like irritants in her eyes and thorns in her sides, she would have sought medical help. However, her sickness is not anything like that. Her sickness is a spiritual problem, the habit of lying. When she lies, she creates wild fabrications off the top of her head, and it is not easy for her to tell anything with full honesty. A spiritual problem needs a spiritual solution. Thus, only God can heal and deliver her from her lying habit. She has to return to where she left to reclaim what she left.

Angel keeps on walking toward him. Although Hayet has no previous kissing experience, her glittering lips are enchanting. *Will I survive this enticing woman?*

"Hi, I am Angel," she pronounces, flashing her flamboyant smile.

"Hi, Angel. Your name and face are familiar. How are you doing?" Hayet replies, extending his hand for a handshake. He wants to see for himself her soft angelic handshake. A rumor has spread that she never shakes hands to the point of touching her hand web, using the tip of her fingers, the way Her Majesty Queen Elizabeth and His Majesty Emperor Haile Selassie do. It proves to be true.

"I am fine," Angel replies, as simple as that.

Hayet tries to curtsy as he greets her and appears confused. He does not know what he is doing. He stands by Angel's side and wishes he could take a picture as a souvenir. However, he has no camera.

Angel twirls her hair with her manicured index finger. She also frequently licks her glittery and attention-grabbing lips with the longest tongue Hayet has ever seen. Straightaway, she gives him an ultimatum.

"Hayet, I want you either to sleep with me or else I will tell everybody on campus that you are a gay."

While Hayet contemplates on what he heard, she adds the day, time and the place where they should meet.

The ultimatum to sleep with her is unlike anything he has ever heard in his life. Then she leaves the vicinity calmly as if she has not stunned the young man, carefully trudging on the same footprints that she stepped on coming to meet him. The ultimatum drains his strength, and his body turns sweaty in the middle of the wintry parking lot.

While Hayet reprocesses the ultimatum, Emily Battistelli arrives. She is a peer who wishes to help Hayet but has had multiple unproductive encounters with him, wishing to win Hayet's heart.

The moment she nears him, she says, "Listen, Hayet," displaying a V sign with two fingers. "I heard the girls in the dorm plotting to entice you to swap your V card using Angel. So, watch out when she comes to meet you."

"Emily, please listen. I usually never deposit myself and swap my card at any location. To tell the truth, I do not see how you are different than the girl you are talking about."

"Believe it or not, I am not such girl. I am a woman of noble character, worth far more than rubies. Only the blessed one will legally take me to be a wedded wife at the right time. Whatever I say right now is with a clear conscience. In fact, I am one of the two girls on this campus who have any concern for you."

"Oh, you are concerned about me," mocks Hayet sarcastically.

"The thing is that you cannot show up at every turn and dictate how I should live my life. I kindly ask you to leave me alone."

"Fine, I shall leave you alone for now. However, remember how to deal with Angel. She will approach you for the wrong reason."

She already came by and gave me an ultimatum. "Do not worry about me. I am a man and can handle myself."

"Okay . . . but . . . Remember that in the future the very thing that you hate and ignore me for now, you will love me for."

"Not to you, Emily."

At the same time, *What does she mean?* The thought engulfs his imagination as a staggering light that Emily did not observe in flashes around him. Emily's "*Remember that in the future the very thing that you hate and ignore me for now, you will love me for,*" hit Hayet's heart like a sledgehammer that breaks unbreakable rocks into pieces. Of course, Hayet assumes that it is broken pieces of rocks that can fit in multiple areas in life than a huge solid rock. Something needs to be broken in Hayet's life to be convenient for himself and for others. *When, where, and how is what Emily is saying going to take place?*

Hayet numbly rethinks Emily's words. Then she adds, "Also, think of the unsinkable *Titanic,* which sank with all the people who could have been saved; so can you too perish for your ignorance," she says as she walks away, waving goodbye.

"Don't worry I will not perish for my ignorance; I am not an ignorant."

As soon as Emily leaves, Hayet thinks, *She shows up and troubles me one time for a prayer meeting, another time for Bible study, and today she talks of Angel. I am right, and she is wrong.* Nevertheless, Emily's nagging speech awakens the importance and rewards of Hayet's godly walking. Deep within his heart, he thinks, *Perhaps she could be a messenger sent to warn me.* However, he is always confident of his skill in handling challenges and temptations on his own.

He proceeds to the cafeteria. *Maybe Emily is an angel sent to protect me from the wrong person; she could be the answer to the Grannies' prayers. However, she does not know how strong I am. I am not easily swayed.*

Hayet walks to his group's usual dining table. The cafeteria is noisy, and students occupy all the seats.

"Good evening," he greets the usual trio.

"Where's your dinner?" Bernard questions.

"I did not get it yet and I am okay. Besides, I have no appetite."

"Are you in love?" Sandy interjects.

"Is that what love does?" Hayet answers her question with a question.

"If not to everybody, at least it did to me," she says with a wink.

"I have also had the same experience," confirms Shian while sprinkling cheese on her hamburger.

"What is up? Did you get some sleep?" Shian adds.

"Yes. I did get some sleep. However, the Gramps barked at me for the early phone call you made, but that is not my main concern right now."

"Sorry for bothering you and your family. However, you are the most reliable person that we know. That is why we depend on you and we will keep depending on you as you stay dependable. So, what is going on?" asks Sandy.

"I met Angel, and she gave me an ultimatum that is so confusing."

"She did? You are in big trouble," Shian laughs. "We know what you are talking about. It has been an ongoing rumor around campus. People say that she knocks down old-fashioned men like you. What amazes us most is how vigorously Emily and LeAnn are defending."

The discussion goes contrary to Hayet's expectations, leaving him confused.

"My friend," shouts Bernard with a manly giggle. "You have dodged the enjoyment of manhood for years. Now the opportunity has come through an extraordinary girl. Go and have fun. I wish I were you."

"Listen, Bernard, the enjoyment of manhood that I know is using my gift to help others. Additionally, my father once told me, you who are young, be happy while you are young, and let your heart give you joy in the days of your youth. Follow the ways of your heart and whatever your eyes see, but know that for all that you do, God will bring you into judgment. Therefore, the only way I see to stay on the path of purity is by living according to God's word and serving others."

Shian says, "I trust you so much, Hayet, that no matter what, you are not going to do what Angel requires of you. Nevertheless, should you decide to go for such pleasure before you legally get married somewhere, let me be the beneficiary of your first-time love so that I may brag about it."

"No, let me be the first one!" objects Sandy as she winks, facing Shian.

"Since you are our best friend, instead of swapping your V card for a girl that you do not know, let one of us be the recipient of your first experience. It is a good deal," reasons Shian. His friends' advice annoys and leaves him more confused than before he met them. They are not as concerned as he is, or as much as Emily. Hayet does not want to tamper with his pledge before it is the right time with the right woman.

Abruptly, he hears, "Hi, how are you doing?" A soft touch accompanies the charming voice at Hayet's shoulder. It is LeAnn.

"Hi, how are you doing, LeAnn?" replies Hayet.

"When you finish with whatever you are doing, please see me in the lounge," she drawls with a fuzzy look and a fretful grin.

"I suppose I am finished. Thanks for your ideas," says Hayet to his friends, following LeAnn.

"Hayet, remember," Shian yells, wagging her manicured index finger to indicate herself and Sandy.

"If that is what friendship is about, then I do not want it. Besides, I treat you as my sisters and I do not expect such words from you."

"We also treat you as one closer than a brother and that is why we do not want to see you go for anybody else other than us."

"See you later," declares Hayet as he walks away.

"Whichever way it goes, we wish you good luck," bids Bernard.

"Whichever way it goes; I do not believe in luck. I trust in the destiny making God." Just as LeAnn is exiting the cafeteria, Hayet catches up with her.

"Did you hear the rumor going around campus? I have already hinted about it the other day," speaks LeAnn.

"What rumor?"

"Well, on this campus, whatever good or bad goes on, word of it spreads faster than wildfire."

"What rumor are you talking about?"

"It is about you."

"What about me?"

LeAnn looks around and observes no one is nearby except for the black and white handmade portrait of the university founders before the American independence. It is hanging at the corner of the high-ceilinged artifact-decorated wall. Right then, the old brown wooden side door opens wide for a handicap student. Gusty wind whooshes through, blowing LeAnn's hair and dress wildly right up over her head. She does not attempt to hold her hair in place while struggling to hold her dress down from the merciless raging wind. The automatic door shuts right after the student enters.

LeAnn then says, "Hayet, after several futile attempts, the students got together and have planned to lure you into bed, using Angel. She will approach you soon, if not today, then before the weekend. If you are not careful, she may knock you out, as she has done to many others, to throw in the towel of chastity."

"She already talked to me and gave me an ultimatum."

"Oh, my God. You are in big trouble. I knew it!" LeAnn whispers, standing motionless. Hayet is one step ahead and looks back at her.

"So, what're you going to do?"

"Well, I do not know. That is what I am about to ask you."

"I suggest that you do whatever your heart tells you. Yet, beware, because a lot of times the heart is deceitful. Follow God's word. Moreover, think and pray about it. I have survived middle school, high school, and four years of college, and I am still doing well in graduate school. I do not want to give myself to a man who is not my wedded husband, not before the appropriate time."

"At this age and time do we really have people that treat chastity as noble and keep themselves until marriage?"

"Not going far, I am one, and you are two."

"Besides, how do you know the appropriate time and the right man? You are growing old and you should get a man before it becomes too late."

"I trust in God with all my heart and will lean not on my own understanding. In all my ways, I submit to Him, and He will make my paths straight. I collaborate with God, who is the perfect planner, do what He requires of me, and He will make the remaining connections by Himself. God is more concerned about me than I am about myself. I just cast my cares on Him, and He shall carry my burdens, fight for me, and give me the victory."

"So, you let God do your thinking for you?"

"Absolutely. His thoughts to me are so precious. How great is the sum of them! If I should count them, they would be more in number than the sand of the sea. Senseless people do not know; fools do not understand God's idea for me. Additionally, by putting God first in my life, I want to see and enjoy the good He has for me. By doing all that is right in the sight of God, I want my father to walk me down the aisle and present me on my wedding day. I would feel proud to present myself a virgin woman to my husband. If you are cautious how you handle Angel's issue, you can choose to make a wise decision."

"Who are the fools and the senseless people?"

"The ones that act independent of God ignoring their conscious warning and their parents' advice."

"Okay, I want you to tell me how satisfied are you of being dependent of God?"

"I am so thrilled. The decree of God is flawless, uplifting the soul. The laws of God are dependable, making wise the simple. The principles of God are right, giving joy to the heart. The guidelines of God are glowing, giving light to the eyes. The reverence of God is pure, durable forever. The rulings of God are secure, and all of them are virtuous. They are more precious than gold, than much pure gold; they are sweeter than honey, than honey from the honeycomb. By them one gets warned; in keeping them there is a great reward to one's self and to others."

LeAnn adds, "You know, when I started high school, I heard one of my mother's buddies, Mrs. GILLIAM LEON, talk to my mother. 'Are you going to put LeAnn on birth control?'"

My mother acknowledged, "I have full confidence in my daughter. She loves putting the most important priority first. Now her priority is education, and she will never consider what you are talking about as an alternative."

"My mother's reply always makes me proud of myself. My parents raised me like an eagle that stirs up its nest and hovers over its young, that spreads its wings to catch them when they are about to be crushed and carries them aloft. I shared their food, drank from their cup, and even slept in their arms. For my parents, who paid more than I could ever imagine, I can make choices that would make them happy and proud of me. My mother and father failed in matters of chastity, yet they instructed me how to survive, learning from their mistakes."

Furthermore, LeAnn says, "Mrs. Leon, as well, failed on her walk of chastity, for instead of teaching her daughter, Layla, how to avoid the mistakes she made, she taught her how to avoid pregnancy. After dodging pregnancy for some time, my friend has ended up where her mother would not want her to be, starting from middle school when she lost her chastity, got pregnant and dropped out of school."

"LeAnn, I do not think you understand how old I am."

"What do not I understand? Did I skip being your age to get where I am now, or am I an elderly woman with such dead emotions that I do not feel what every young person feels? I choose to be intentional. Before I graduated from high school, my flirtatious friends, who had multiple ex's by the age of sixteen, brought me a young rich athletic man who would not stay with one person even for a week. They said, 'You cannot graduate before having a boyfriend.' I refused their coercing, knowing my destiny and focusing on my educational priority. Internally, my friends wear off, are dissatisfied over the carefree and unreliable relationship that depletes their heart. Here and there they come and tell me about their dissatisfaction for what they call fun, yet externally they appear to be happy. I have gone and I am still going through the temptations you are facing. Choose to live with the godly convictions that satisfy the heart, please your parents and God."

"Thanks for sharing your story. I feel like saying no, but I am terrified and do not have the guts to say so. Angel is the pinnacle of beauty."

"Stop kidding yourself! Watch your words. There is power in your words. Whatever you say, it will catch you. I am serious. One more thing is that the girls say that Angel never forces any man. However, by her glamorous appearance and charming words, she succeeds in seducing, attracting chaste and decent men to go after her."

They discuss several options for Hayet and settle on two: not to show up for the appointment or to report the harassment to the police. However, Hayet considers both cowardly.

"Thanks for your concern. I will go home to share this with the Gramps."

"Hayet, it does not matter whom you talk to about it. What matters is what you decide to do with it. Remember that the final decision is yours," LeAnn says solemnly.

Angel has threatened Hayet, that either he goes to bed with her or she tells every one of the backward life he has led and has tried so hard to hide.

Chapter 12

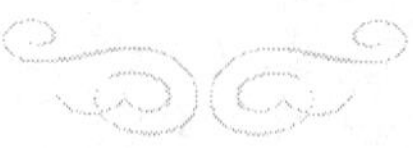

It is not the situation, but the way we respond
to the situation that is important.

— *Zig Ziglar*

Hayet is under a microscope—everybody seems to know of the ultimatum that could have a great effect on his life.

I am in a catch-22, he frequently laments. He comes to campus to start his assignment early. However, it proves difficult to concentrate in the face of Angel's demand, to sleep with her. The ultimatum's crescendo rings in his ears as loud as a shuttle rocket as it creates the thrust necessary to lift it from the ground.

He zips up his black jacket and puts on his gloves before heading home. The sliding door opens and a windy gust slams his face.

Hayet has stayed just one hour, and so his windshield is not very icy. The defroster takes care of the little ice buildup. He pulls away from the dead-end sign and drives cautiously. Except for a few pedestrians and little traffic here and there, the streets are empty. Excluding restaurants and bars, most of the businesses have shut down for the day. By the time he merges onto the highway, the blizzard swirls, making the sky hazy. The sparse traffic makes his driving easy. In a few minutes, he is home.

The door hinges screech, and his adoptive parents stand there in awe. "What happened? Are you okay? You look depressed," Grandma shouts. She pats Hayet's arms while encircling him impatiently.

Hayet places his jacket to the right of the door, between two black coats. "I have no broken bones. It is another challenge!" Grandma's eyes narrow and she frowns.

"We have been through it just this afternoon," Hayet hints.

"What did we talk about?" Grandpa asks, amused.

"I met Angel," Hayet replies with an elation.

Grandma's eyes widen. "What about an angel appearing to you?" she shrieks hysterically. "I have never heard such testimony before, that an angel appears even to the current generation. Did the angel tell you good news?" She grabs Grandpa's shoulders.

"Honey, please let him tell us what the angel said! Was it Michael or Gabriel?"

"Grandma, relax. You are asking and answering the questions all by yourself. It is neither Michael nor Gabriel. It is a student named Angel."

"What a lovely name. I wish I had such a name," Grandma sighs languidly. "What did she do?"

"She made me see hell today. I am so confused and do not know what to do," Hayet utters, pacing impulsively. He sits down with legs and arms crossed while the Gramps stand in front of him.

"Tell us what she did."

"Angel, a student with a glittering smile, gave me an ultimatum."

"Tell us what the ultimatum is," Grandma insists.

"For next Friday, she gave me an ultimatum to sleep with her in one of the five-star hotels in our city. She declared, 'If you refuse, I am going to tell everybody on the campus that you have a different lifestyle, no interest in women.'"

"My first question to you is why do you call her Angel when she is such an insidious person? She ought to be called a demon," says Grandma.

"Well, Grandma, the first thing I will ask when I meet her on Friday is that question. Besides, we also do have another student named Demon. Creepy, huh?"

"The name is not my main concern. Let me make sure that I understand the ultimatum correctly. If you do not sleep with her, she will tell everybody that you have a different lifestyle with no interest in women?" Grandma reiterates, seeking clarification.

"Precisely, but it goes a little more than that."

"That should not bother you," Grandma cries. "Tell her openly that you already have a different lifestyle than she does, that you vowed an allegiance to follow Jesus and pledged to stay chaste until marriage. In fact, she is the one who has a romping lifestyle that is wayward to how God intended her to live."

Hayet takes a long sigh. "Grandma, I do not think you understand what I am trying to say. If I refuse, she will tell everybody that I am a gay."

Grandpa is silent, standing with arms crossed while he leans against the wall. Then he pronounces, "I would like to thank you for your honesty. I am glad to know you are an honest person. Whether she is an angel or a demon is not significant for you right now. What matters is who you believe you are. In the days of creation, God created male and female. Accepting any other belief that makes you less than who you were meant to be is a perversion."

"Hayet is our son," interrupts Grandma.

"Honey, please let me finish. Nobody will take him away from who he is unless he fully wants to drift from that intentional living."

Grandma walks away spontaneously, grabbing dinner utensils from the dining table while vigilantly monitoring every word from the kitchen.

"Remember son, what does not kill you makes you stronger. That is what makes one a fighter. Besides, countless wrongdoings exist in life. To mention a few: stealing, cheating, child abandonment, discrimination, exploitation, racism—you name it. If is not clear, I want you to read 1 Corinthians 6:9–11; that is what my father once read to me.

'Do you not know that wrongdoers will not inherit the kingdom of God? Do not be deceived: neither the sensual immoral nor idolaters nor adulterers, nor men who sleep with men, in parallel– women who sleep with women, nor thieves, nor the greedy nor drunkards nor slanderers nor swindlers will inherit the kingdom of God. That is what many people were. Nevertheless, once they chose to diverge, they were washed, sanctified, justified in the name of the Lord

Jesus Christ and by the Spirit of our God.' Now, son, what makes Angel's ultimatum different? Take note that whosoever violates one law is guilty of breaking all."

"Grandpa, what you are telling me is subjective relativism."

"What does subjective relativism mean?"

"You know what it means." *It is the understanding that weakens the belief of morality to a personal level rather than to the set standard. The value that you consider true for you may not be so for another*

"Where did you get that ungodly understanding from?"

"I learned it. Besides, when you are faced with two evils choose the lesser evil."

"What do you mean, son?"

Hayet certainly knows that the Gramps are so serious and do not compromise on matters that are not compatible with their biblical belief and he has to explain what he meant.

"The current generation parents allow and do not rebuke their children saying 'You shall not commit adultery or fornication,' when they see and hear them practice."

"Is this the lesser evil?"

"I guess so."

"Why would the parents not rebuke their children being aware of them doing adult premarital activities?"

"Because they presume if they do not show interest on the opposite gender even if they have a religious conviction, they are afraid that their children could turn or get libeled the other way."

"Is this the greater evil?"

"I guess so."

Grandpa stood and said in a loud voice, "Hear the young generation that are being cheated by their governments and their parents that are falling into ungodly practices that would not satisfy the thirst. Let anyone who is thirsty come to Jesus and drink. Choosing lesser evil would not make one good."

"Now son, first, who determines the level of lesser or greater evil?"

If I say God, Grandpa will question me why I put God's word into question. If I say the contemporary society, the government or other institutions he still will ask who would I rather obey? Consequently, "I do not know," answers Hayet.

"Second, will choosing the lesser evil make it right in the sight of God?"

"No! But, by choosing the lesser evil you become nice and cool."

"You do not become nice and cool by disobeying God's word. Well, what do you think is the solution to the ungodly predicament which is hovering over you? Think of the solution being based on 'Where there are no oxen, a stable stay clean, but from the strength of an ox come abundant harvests,'" Grandpa observes calmly.

"To begin with, Grandpa, we have been through it a lot of times. You do not want me to enjoy life like any other student."

"Wait, wait, wait," shouts Grandpa, facing Hayet.

"We live in a free country where one can be whatever one wants to be. Winner or loser, educated or uneducated, powerful or powerless, chaste or unchaste, gay or straight—the list is endless. As Grandma mentioned earlier, you chose the chastity walk. About enjoying life like any student, if you think tampering with your purity for fear of libel about who you are not is worth it, then go for it. The only way a young person stay on the path of purity is by living according to the word of God. Additionally, the life enjoyment of a person that I know should be standing on a solid rock, serving others while sacrificially holding the flag of allegiance to the Truth, who is also the Prince of Peace."

"Tell us what your decision is," interjects Grandma.

"Get it over with," Hayet replies concisely.

Immediately, Grandma yells, "That is the end! He blew it!" The reply hits Grandpa like a bolt of lightning, and he stands stunned like a pillar of salt. Hayet gives a hug to both.

Grandpa gains his composure. "Can an apple be an orange for fear of libel? Alternatively, can an angel be a devil for fear of libel? I call Angel's ultimatum a perversion. If the ultimatum drives you to be who you were not meant to be, God's investment in you would be in vain. However, I have confidence that the Lord will not make it happen."

As forecasted, a northern winter storm is hitting the city. The snow visibly builds up outside the window. Grandpa's spirit and will, too, hit the ground.

"What will you gain by 'getting it over with'?" he questions, breaking the silence.

"I never had relationship experience and want to try out for myself what the big deal is. I am tired of hearing how great it is from my colleagues. Besides, people think a man not active in a premarital relationship is uncool."

"Out of all your peers, you are the only one who is chaste?" Grandpa asks.

Hayet pauses for a moment. "Well, not really. There are others, too. However, I am the most popular."

"Thanks for your honesty. Millions and millions of chaste youngsters are thriving. If you do what is right, God will accept you. Nevertheless, if you do not do what is right, wickedness is entering your heart; it wants to make you devious, but you must subdue it. Additionally, do not make me repeat myself. If you have an interest in women and want to keep yourself chaste until the right time, say, 'Yes, I have.' You should not bother yourself about what people who may not even know you will say about you. Think and live by what God says who you are, not by what people think and say about you."

Hayet's unreasonable rationale puzzles Grandpa.

"What amazes me most is that you spend more time proving who you are not than who you are. If I were you, I would spend time on who I am, not on who I am not," he states.

"My dear, if abandoning your chastity is your decision, then go ahead. You willfully and consciously are stepping into enemy territory, squeezing yourself into being someone who you are not. An ungodly temptation is assaulting your mind; it desires to derail you, but you must overcome it. If not, then later you will suffer heavy consequences and will find yourself in an irreversible situation of regret."

"Grandpa, I understand what you mean. However, I want you to remember that I am a man and can do whatever I want. In fact, I am tired of both of you dictating what my life should look like. That is your view, and this is mine. Please do not force your beliefs on me. Allow me to live for myself."

"First, I want you to know that you are a steward, and cannot just do whatever you want to do, rough and tumble, and get away with it. Second, one day the dust will return to the ground it came from, and the spirit return to God who gave it, which you cannot resist. You will give an account to God of how you utilized the life He gave you. On that day, you will be either happy or dismayed with what you decide to do today. Last, you have grown so fast, especially since you went to college. None of us will force our belief on you. The only thing we can do is give you our suggestion and inform you, to help prioritize your life. However, remember that if you do not listen to the advice of your parents now, the time will come when it is too late. You shall look for help, and you will not receive any."

Grandma interrupts. "Honey, please sit here. You cannot stand all night long." She pulls out his favorite stool.

"Thanks, sweetie," Grandpa utters appreciatively. He grabs a cupful of water and sits.

He raised the cup for a drink. Yet, placing the cup on the table, "Well, it seems you are at a crucial time, in the same way, as a young person who once utilized his GPS. In fact, he was a couple of years younger than you are, at seventeen years old."

"What about the young man? What did he do? Tell me."

"He was a physically well-built, handsome, intelligent, insightful boy, a born leader. Traders forcefully take him out of his home to a country where the people speak another language. It is a place he probably never thought of going, where people easily sway under its influence and moved there for all sorts of ungodly pleasures. The moment he lands in the new country, an influential rich government official picks him up. His shrewdness helps him rise through the ranks from a regular person to an overseer of the official's household and estate. As a result, he comes into command and care of the house that the entire the family owns. His physical handsomeness becomes carnally attractive to the official's wife, and she wants to sleep with him when the man of the house is not home."

"So what is the big deal if she loves him? Is he also in love with her?"

"I do not know about that. What I do know is that she casts her lustful eyes on him. She repeatedly pleads with him and attempts to seduce and take him to her bed. One day, while he does his daily chores, she approaches him near the bedroom. She wants him to sleep on their colored linen coverings on the myrrh-, aloe-, and cinnamon-perfumed bed with her, take a break and have an afternoon nap with some sensual pleasures." Hayet listens attentively.

"The absence of witnesses, her suggestive lingerie, and her fashionable and alluring black-salved lashes make the offer appealing. She supplements it with seductive eye glare and affectionate words. The young man has reasons to justify accepting his mistress's invitation; she has the power to hire or fire him. He is in a tempting situation: either offend his mistress by rejecting the invitation or betray his master by going with his wife behind his back. The young man refuses to give in to his mistress's demand. Does his refusal to accept Mrs. Potiphar's coercing deserve to have him referred to as one who has no interest on women?"

"Maybe not. I guess he is living up to his moral, religious, or ethical convictions."

"He refers to her plea as a wicked thing before God. On the final attempt, which ends the ordeal, she grabs him by his cloak and pleads, 'Come to bed with me.' However, he leaves his cloak in her hands and runs out of the house. An African proverb says; 'A thief, when seen, smiles; when not seen, steals.' Had he agreed to quench her lustful drive, she would have kept it secret. Instead, for his refusal to accommodate her demand and upon learning that he is not likely to do so, she accuses him of rape and has him unfairly incarcerated."

"He could have dodged prison by agreeing to her demand," Hayet comments.

"You think so?"

"You bet."

"I do not think so. Had he agreed to her demand, at that moment, all would probably have been fine. Nevertheless, when a day exposes him, his wrong deed would turn for the worse. Let me tell you of another person who did the thing you advocate," Grandpa says while sipping his water before he continues.

"His birth was supernatural because an angel brought the good news to his old, barren parents. It is difficult to believe his birth, yet it happens. He grows up blessed with tremendous and paranormal physical strength. He is matchless when fighting one on one or even a group against him. The Maasai warriors of Kenya and Tanzania, equipped with a spear and a knife, must kill a lion as a rite of passage to be married. Unlike them, this man could tear apart a lion with his bare hands. His mere existence was a threat to his enemies. However, he was blinded by untested love affairs, and after several near misses, he finally gives up the secret of his strength. Not to his mighty male enemies but to a seductive woman. The man had walked as a powerful hero but turns into a powerless fellow when he disobeyed the God's plan of salvation for his and others' lives. His enemies gouge his eyes out and put him to work grinding grains."

"Sorry to hear that, Grandpa."

"That is what he chose, and that is what he received. Out of these two men, which one would you rather be?"

"To tell you the truth, I would rather be neither of them. However, compromising a little and giving the mistress what she wanted would probably have saved the first one from prison."

"Stolen water is sweet; food eaten in secret is delicious! However, little do you know that the compromising guests of such a person are within the realm of the dead. What if the husband caught him fooling around with his wife?"

"Too bad—shoot him with an arrow."

"What if it were you with Angel?" Grandpa asks, expecting fair judgment.

"Well, I would expect him to set me free," replies Hayet as he laughs.

"You need to have fair and just judgment for everybody," Grandpa sternly rebukes. "I want you to listen carefully, son. You do not know if the girl called Angel might be someone's wife. How would you feel if someone were to do the same with your wife? If you love her, first marry her, then date her for life as you go along."

"This is a distinct case, Grandpa. The current generation first dates as many people as are available for months or perhaps for years and when one finds the right person, then marries. I understand that you do not like that, but that is what the contemporaries do."

"Would you rather obey God or the contemporary life style?"

"I would rather obey God but that is not cool."

"Beloved, I am afraid to tell you that once you put ungodly relationships before your educational priorities, switching between women like they are used tissues, your reproductive years shall pass wastefully. By the time you are ready for marriage, you may not be able to beget children after you or understand the mystery of true love and marriage."

"That applies to women, not to men. A man can impregnate at any age."

"In the eyes of God, whatever applies to a woman should also apply to a man."

"Further," adds Hayet, "It is fun to have premarital relationships, and with no long-term accountability to anyone. Above and beyond, she is the one asking."

"A man who commits adultery has no sense; whoever does so destroy himself. Kicks in the teeth and disgrace are his lot in life, and his shame lives forever. Whether she asked or you asked, that does not matter. What matters most is doing what is godly. Accepting what you call her ultimatum will lead you to foolishness that is difficult to return from. Let me tell you how each man's story ended," He states as he takes another sip.

"After years of incarceration, the first man receives vindication. The king has him released from prison, not to the previous position, he held before the imprisonment, but to the second-highest position in the country, instantly, without a matching résumé and previous experience. The other man dies in vain without becoming a husband or a father. Whichever woman he goes after; others take her away. The faithfulness of the young man rewards him with the promotion. The pride of the older man rewards him with a demotion, eventually ending his life without being a husband or a father, not minding to diverge to where he ought to be. These men are Joseph and Samson of the Bible."

It has been a long day.

Finally, Grandpa concludes, "We have discussed all that you need to hear. As a matter of fact, you know the right answer. Life and death, blessings and curses, obedience and disobedience, chaste and unchaste are set before you. I suggest that you choose life, blessings, obedience, and chastity so that you and your descendants may endure to tell about it."

Finally, the Gramps walk away, leaving Hayet behind. Hayet sits on a rocking chair, processing Grandpa's words. *The Gramps are right and I have to obey them.* He gazes downstairs from the balcony. Except for a sporadic automobile moving here and there, the neighborhood is silent. Finally, he reaches a decision. *I will go to the appointment to meet Angel, no matter what the outcome may be. After all, just standing a couple of minutes with her would be a considerable achievement.* He anxiously envisions for the D-Day.

Chapter 13

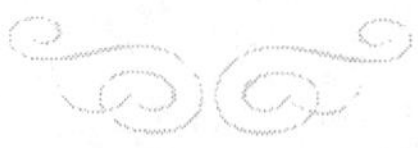

A person does not have to change who he is to become better.

— *Sidney Poitier, The Measure of a Man*

Friday, D-Day, late afternoon, Hayet arrives for the crucial and decisive appointment a few minutes before six o'clock, carrying his guitar in one hand and a cup of coffee in the other.

A black Cadillac Brougham limousine appears by the curvy pickup and drop-off awning, crushing the snow that blankets the driveway. The limo blows Hayet away. He can imagine a commercial for it playing through his head. *This limo is a dream car to ride in between high rises on the golden streets and bridges while viewing the memorable sights of New York and being stylishly dropped off at one of the five-star hotels for dinner.*

Whomever the limo picks up or drops off today must be an important figure of the university, a son or daughter of a president, or the CEO of a notable company. Slowly but surely, the chauffeur parks right in front of where Hayet stands.

While rotating the steaming coffee cup in his hands, Hayet moves to the right behind a concrete pole to avoid the limo. The chauffeur follows, trailing him. Hayet's heart bangs hard, his eyes widen, as he wonders what is going on.

The well-dressed chauffeur emerges from the limo, turns around, and opens the passenger door.

"Come on in, mister."

Hayet glances behind; there is no one there but him. "Surely not me, sir," Hayet speaks, distancing himself from the courteous invitation.

"I am not mistaken. Come and have a ride. You are the VIP," affirms a soft voice as sweet as molasses from inside.

The affirmation leaves Hayet frozen on the windy pickup area. A fascinating woman with golden auburn hair spilling over her shoulders and down her back invites him.

"Get in," she calls while gesturing.

She wears retro fit-and-flare black sassy, short, trendy stretch draped-sleeve mini dress and black knee-high boots. The smile on her flawless face lightens Hayet's mood after his weeklong troubled emotions. It is Angel.

"Angel, you look so beautiful," utters Hayet.

Angel's emotions and spirit seem high, and she is singing Diana Ross and Lionel Richie's "Endless Love" along with the music.

"Thanks!" she replies, pausing temporarily.

"It is so cozy in here," says Hayet upon entering the limo. "However, why do you have to come with such a luxurious ride?"

"Do not worry; all has been paid for."

"You sound like the Gramps when you say 'all has been paid for.'" Angel glares at Hayet in disorientation.

"We may have similar backgrounds," she affirms.

"Are you a Christian?"

Angel is silent. For she knows what she intends to do is contrary to Christian and holiness belief. A moment later, she replies, "Yes, I am—we both are." She pauses awkwardly, appearing to hide what is unexplained to Hayet.

"Sometimes the person chooses a ride on a horse-drawn carriage. However, today I chose a limo, knowing that you do not enjoy cold weather," she speaks, baffling Hayet.

How does she know that I do not like cold weather? That is not all. She knew where on campus to find me.

"I would love to have a horse ride over the summer. Would you?" Hayet asks.

"Yes, I would. It is breathtaking. I have had few sleigh rides over snowy, scenic forests in Wisconsin. The ride usually is on a palomino Belgian draft horse."

"Wow, I have never had such a ride. I have seen some people have horse drawn carriage rides, though."

Displaying some giddy feelings, she occasionally sings to "Endless Love," leaving Hayet's eye to wander around the limo.

"You are talented. How did you acquire such an angelic voice? Could that be the reason why they call you Angel?"

"I am talented, huh?" she says, accompanied by a shallow, long whine while nodding her head, displaying contempt.

The angelic voice compliment has stuck like a bone in her throat. She flashes back to the squeaky-clean years where she poured out spirit-filled angelic melodies that blessed the Lord and His people with high-lifted holy hands over the awakening meetings.

"The talent is the brightest part of my life. However, now I am living in a boy-crazy purposeless and perverted life journey without a GPS. The GPS-less life is the dark side of an unpredictable lifestyle that I chose, and I am unable to extricate myself from it," Angel says more to herself than to Hayet.

Angel seems to be in deep remorse. In a short while, the giddy feelings vanish from her face like a smoke blown by a wind.

What is going on? She seems saddened, hushes, and does not sing again.

Minutes have passed since Angel uttered her last words. *What does she mean when she speaks about the bright and dark parts of her life?*

Angel is a girl one would see on the front cover of a college catalog or a bulletin that tells about becoming a fitter, to-be-seen girl on campus. Not only that, but she has what it takes to appear in Victoria's Secret, best-selling magazines for clothing and shoes, and the finest promotions. She is the most likely to escort an athlete, golfer, CEO, spoiled governor, or disgraced preacher to ballrooms. She is also the most likely to pick to dress in a new bikini style. She has an astounding smile for the cameras and, in person, is appealing to sit by, take a walk along, or have fun with. She glows every second of her life. She is academically intelligent. *Still, she does not seem to be satisfied*, what is she lacking? notes Hayet.

The synchronized traffic lights make their drive to Angel's choice of destination, not far from the banks of the Hudson River, the Gansevoort five-star hotel, faster. They go through the courtesy entry. Door attendants dressed in black double-breasted overcoats buttoned to the neck greet them.

"Good to see you and welcome," pronounce the door attendants, one after another with big smiles. The attendants put on their police-like hats and are busy opening car doors and accompanying visitors inside.

Angel, with your mini dress, exiting the Limo, without flashing your knickers is going to be a challenge. Right then, pressing her knees together, she swings her feet on the ground outside. Holding her right hand, "Lady and gentleman, you are most welcome here tonight. My name is STEPHAN MARTINO," greets the maître' d at the entrance to the dining room.

While gently smoothing her dress, "Thank you, Stephan," Angel replies as Hayet follows her.

"Would you like to have this enjoyable night over the rooftop or over the first-floor restaurants?" asks Stephan as he glances at both of the guests with an anticipation.

"What is the difference and where would you choose?" inquires Hayet facing the maître' d as he takes a brief look over the map and direction arrows placed between the two green live queen palm trees that are loaded up with bunches of ripe yellowish date fruits.

"It depends upon your personality. However, for your information, most of our guests over the rooftop are younger because it has live music; while the first-floor restaurants are family friendly and ideal places for businesslike or memorable discussion."

"We would rather be over the first-floor restaurants," Angel replies as she leads the way, showing off her head-turning and eye-catching peahen silhouette catwalk beauty on the red carpet. She confidently sashays, with her mini dress comfortably fitting her curves. Her flaming curls bounce with every tiny step she takes.

"I wish you a memorable evening," says Stephan after he leads them to their seats in the dining room.

"That is what we are here for," replies Angel with a dazzling smile.

At this point, Hayet appears frightened. He anxiously waits to see what will happen next.

Chapter 14

If you board the wrong train, it is no use running along the corridor in the other direction.

— Dietrich Bonhoeffer

Angel leads and Hayet follows through the decisive night that would determine her destiny backfiring on her.

Dim, silver wall-hung lanterns and sporadic scented candlelight of the Gansevoort full-service resort makes Hayet's visit memorable. For it is his first time ever to step in such exotic and soul-refreshing place. Angel deserves a big thank you and a kiss to the lips from across the table. However, he is unlikely to vocalize the thank you or give the kiss because it could portray that Hayet is crushing on her.

The restaurant's attractive layout offers a variety of seating options based on the type of service one needs. Stationary and classy adjustable-height swivel barstools with cushions in black and pink colors with as well as without backrests encircle the bar in the middle of the restaurant. Two additional rows of bar-stand tables and matching chairs arranged according to their height are spaciously set enclosing the encircled bar. Standard comfortable chairs and sofas that have backrests high enough for viewing only over the heads of people sitting in front or back of other diners spread throughout the dining area.

Hayet is anxious as to how the night might end and how failing to fulfil his walk of chastity may affect his future. His apprehension is displayed on his face as he bites his nails restlessly, and he hopes Angel does not notice.

Hayet is not too hungry because he had a late lunch. However, in order not to disappoint Angel, he decides to order a small dish. "Which way do I go to wash my hands?"

"You do not have to go; you will be served by the acclaimed lady coming from behind you," informs Angel, winking her left eye.

"Hi, my name is LINDA ROSSETTI. I will serve you tonight," says the old blonde, petite server as she hands them the menus and certain steaming contents that look like ducks facing each other on a big woven basket plate.

I guess Angel knows that I am an uncivilized African. It would not hurt to ask. Is this food? He does not want to spoil the dinner by making a laughable wrong move. In a case such as this, he usually either asks what to do or waits patiently to learn from what others do.

Angel, the trendy girl, methodically wipes her hands using only the tail part, while the other parts remain intact. The steaming contents are nothing but towel origami. "How did they make such marvelous work out of a towel?" asks Hayet as he wipes his hands, disintegrating the duck-shaped towel into a lump of bumpy folds and uneven creases.

"I do not know how they do that, but I have been served in the same way multiple times. Actually, it is for the high-quality service and artistic presentation that this hotel charges more."

Angel, you have been served in the same way multiple times? With who?

"Sorry for interrupting you. If you are ready, I am available to serve you with your orders. I guess that you know, alcoholic drinks are not served in the dining area," informs the server as she pulls an order pad out of her mini black round apron and a blue pen out of her apron's pen pocket.

"Ladies first, please," declares Hayet smiling and gesturing go ahead. Letting Angel order first will help Hayet to buy time to go through the colored menu, which is as big as a booklet.

“Thank you,” replies Angel accompanied by a charming grin. In the same breath, she orders without any glitch, which can be half of a page when written. Hayet did not catch any of the order. The menu words are not familiar to him. Orders from McDonald’s, Chick-Fil-A, or other fast food restaurants are not as complicated and twisted as such.

“I have got you, ma’am,” affirms the server pointing her blue pen toward Angel.

Right away she asks, “What about you, sir?” pointing the same pen toward Hayet.

Hayet is not gifted memorizing strange types of food. Therefore, the easiest way for him to order is either by order number or by pointing his fingers. Thus he says, “I would like to have these two. Are these good?” he speaks pointing out his orders.

“Trust me, they are good, and you will love them. However, if you order these two, you will skip the first course.”

Hayet is not aware which one is the first course, second course and so forth.

“So, what would you suggest I order?” he asks, trying to play it cool.

The freshly scented server, who appears to understand Hayet’s barrier, comes near him. Placing her pen on top of the order pad on the table near the black clay flower jar flips a couple of pages. Pointing her manicured finger, she says, “This would make a perfect order, but it is a little more salty, spicy and lemony than the other orders we have.”

“That is great. I love those kinds of food.”

Hayet, this is not the kind of food you need when you accompany me. These are so spicy and you will tear up and start sweating like a pig in the most unattractive way, thought Angel.

“And I love customers that are as gentle and understanding as you two,” the server tells them. “One little thing, we are short staffed in our kitchen. Please understand that your order will take a little more than an hour. However, I will bring your drinks in a couple of minutes.”

“No problem. Thank you for letting us know, though,” replies Angel.

What are we going to do until the food comes? thought Hayet.

"So, as we wait for our food, please tell me about yourself," asks Angel. Hayet's eyes widen. Taking his hands off the table and leaning back to the chair, he wonders, *Why and what does she want to know about me?* as he openly stares at the oncoming server carrying multiple drinks at lightning speed. It is his first time to get such a question.

"Look at the server, Angel. In spite of having a heavy load of a tray full of drinks and wearing high-heeled shoes, she comfortably walks balancing with the tips of her left-hand fingers and thumbs high up from her body, while her right hand-grabs the little black stand," marvels Hayet.

"I know! She is the star of all the servers. Even if twenty patrons order, she gives the orders to the right person without making a mistake. That is why she still works despite her old age. Shhh! She is coming this way."

"Here is your lemon water with ice, Angel, and here is your plain water without ice, Hayet," the server says as she picks one after the other from the little black stand. The liquids inside are a little higher than half of the cups.

"Thank you," reply Angel and Hayet simultaneously.

In Hayet's country, people greatly appreciate giving and receiving an overflowing drink to receive, "May God give you full blessings." The culture values blessings by others. In this case, Ms. Linda would be yelled at to fill the cups either until they overflow or at least are full.

"Should you need more lemon, here it is," whispers the server as she picks up freshly cut from underneath the silver lemon wedge slicer and putting them on a flowery porcelain saucer.

As Angel takes her first sip through a straw lid minding her lipsticks and lip liner,

"Please tell me about yourself," she repeats.

Hayet is puzzled and does not feel comfortable answering this strange question.

Consequently, he says, seriously and somehow loudly, "If you want me to tell you about myself, first you tell me about yourself."

"Sorry, my friend. Let me make it clear," apologizes Angel. She clears her throat, takes a second sip while sitting at the edge of her seat, nearing Hayet.

"In the American way of life, when you get asked to tell about yourself, it is just for getting to know you better; there is no hidden agenda. Besides, you know my story; it is no secret, as open as the universe."

Angel is not as tormenting and intimidating as his brothers Jezebel embodied, Tobias and Sanballat. Instead, she is as gracious as the Gramps. She graciously and courteously explains to Hayet what she meant.

"Oh, thank you for your explanation," he says while taking his first and long sip, drinking every drop. Hayet narrows his eyes staring at his empty cup while still holding it.

Is not he the thirsty one?

As young as he is, he has had a rough life and does not know where to start and where to end.

"So far, my years have been few and difficult to tell about. It could take multiple volumes of books to tell it. Do you want some or all?"

How few and difficult? Not going to the Hawaiian beach in the summer and eat ice cream? Not having Tibetan Mastiff dogs and a couple of Allerca cats? Not buying the latest fashion clothing? Not viewing new movies?

"In order to get to know you better, I would rather hear all, starting with where you come from and how" she counters.

Chapter 15

God can take your most monstrous failures and turn them into triumphs such as you never could imagine.

— Dr. Tony Evans

Hayet narrates his past, present, and what he anticipates in the future. A gracefully slender man without adequate width holding a booster seat walking toward them distracts Hayet and he asks, "Angel, who is the tall man holding the child booster seat walking this side?"

"It is the manager of the hotel. He usually comes out as much as four times per table, ensuring customer satisfaction, serving as much as or even more than the regular servers do. I guess he is bringing the booster to serve the guests behind you," answers Angel, stretching her back straight across to look. "Please do not worry about that, just keep on telling me all about yourself."

Hayet is the fifth born of nine children. His birth country, Eritrea, one of the few African nations that live with less or no foreign aid is the historical home to some of the oldest known human developments. It is an ancient name, from the time preceding the Exodus, which took place around 1500 BC. The name Eritrea appears in older translations of Bible, history books of Moses. God delivers the Israelites through the leadership of Moses. They cross the Eritrean Sea, currently known as the Red Sea. At the time of Hayet's birth, the country has about a million people, with nine tribes and nine languages.

The injustice of the imperious superpowers that God has elevated to administer justice causes the instability in Eritrea. Nevertheless, the political and social injustice shapes Hayet's life perspective for good.

"I want you to tell me all," restates Angel.

"Settle down and listen then."

Eritrea has glamorous beauty and abundant natural and agricultural resources that include silver, gold, copper, oil, zinc, salt, and coffee. Rocky mountain chains, black stones, white stones also known as flint stones, and the greenstone belt that formed of volcanic rocks, mainly in the Red Sea coastal plains, which is one of the hottest places on earth.

The spiraling mountain roads feature numerous switchbacks, zigzags, and hilly hairpin twists with guardrails that cannot be relied on to provide protection from falling off the cliffs. The most populous area is a road about six hours from the capital that leads to the Red Sea. The road descends from nearly eight thousand feet above sea level to sea level in less than sixty-five miles.

Thick mist hovers through cliffs of dense natural forest that surround the mountains. Through the intertwined mountain chains, a loaded locomotive trains chug, cutting through tunnels and blasting a horn that echoes through the sparsely, if at all, populated valleys. These are areas with a higher concentration of monkeys and apes than anywhere else is in the country. Every day, farmers wake early to protect their dew-covered groves of oranges, bananas, grapes, guavas, and vegetables from the invading and consuming untamed animals.

Unfortunately, the abundant fortune of the region's natural blessings has also become its curse, causing several powerful nations to become involved in the area through agreed-upon, as well as forced, relationships. These relationships have been with the Arabians, Greeks, Egyptians, Turks, Portuguese, Italians, British, Americans, Russians, Cubans and Ethiopians.

In 1941, the army of Great Britain liberated the nation, chasing out the Italians after seventy-two years of occupation. The Italians had set foot in the country in 1869 and declared it a colony on January 1, 1890. Neighboring

Sudan was under British rule, Djibouti was under French occupation, and Somalia was, like Eritrea, an Italian colony. The Ethiopians experienced five years of Italian colonization before fighting and chasing them up to the Mereb River, which eventually became the dividing border between Ethiopia and Eritrea. The Ethiopians were capable of liberating Eritrea from the Italian colony. However, they never attempted even once to go beyond the Mereb river be it during the leadership of Emperor Menelik II or Emperor Haile Selassie.

Downsides to the country's loveliness, wealth, and strategic location are her tiny size and that her children suffer preventable deaths. Such deaths are a direct result of unfair and unjust relations, a condition known as lie-synthesis. A lie-synthesis states that the country is too small and unable to become an independent state. A lie-synthesis federates the country with Ethiopia, as per United Nations Resolution 390 A (V) of December 1950, which is a violation of basic human rights. The reported reasons include protecting the country from Islamic invasion of the region and defending Israel in the time of need from across the sea.

The invasion and disturbance of the Falkland Islands by Argentina is not acceptable because of its link and interest with the superpower. Invasion of Kuwait by Iraq is not acceptable either. However, the same rule would not apply for the right of Eritreans, which would eventually consume about two million people from both sides. Due to the lack of implementation of the Algiers peace Agreement of December 12, 2000, that the two parties reaffirmed the on Cessation of Hostilities, they live on no war no peace situation causing thousands to become refugees in search of peace. Worse annihilating fate is expected and could ignite anytime for the people of these two nations unless a just savior comes to the rescue.

Angel raises her cup to drink water. Before she does so, "Excuse me, Hayet, what do you mean by lie-synthesis?" and she places the cup back on the table.

"It is the process of doing the illegal using the law as a tool to fulfill the powerful ones' wrongful desires."

The ice in Angel's lemon water is about to dissolve as she motions for Hayet to continue his entrancing story.

The well-built Italian architectural infrastructure and many large murals make the city of Asmara popular and lovely, prompting the nickname *Piccola Roma*, meaning Little Rome. Asmara means the act of creating a reconciliation, unity, and oneness by feminine genders. The root word for *Asmara* is *Simret*, which means coming to unity and oneness, as of that between two or more warring parties. In the old days, the men were fighting among themselves. Four women initiated the unity, peace, and reconciliation. That is how the name Asmara came into being.

Asmara is a city where about century-old Peugeots, Fords, Opels, Volkswagens, Fiat 600s, Corvette, and Balillas still rumble, in one of which Hayet's search for his father's tormentor gets revealed during one ride. The city is a kilometer or so away from the open field and the streaming brooks in the jungles of *Frusta Le* (the forest), where Hayet spends most of his time studying, hunting, and resting on his homemade rocking hammock. Asmara has moderate weather all year long, and sometimes it can get as cold as about —6°C with rain that produces icy pellets of hail as big as pieces of bubble gum.

Through the formation of the colony, the Italians control governance, employment, and education. The colonizers offer employment to Eritreans only in menial positions, which include conscription into the Italian army, which paternal and maternal grandfathers were part of.

The segregated schools teach mainly in Italian language courses for learning, allowing limited education for the locals. Electric lights are sporadic for the natives. The citizens study under the nearest streetlight or use smoke-bellowing lamps that burn paraffin drawn through a wick made of woven cotton. The students who study by the streetlights endure severe weather and mosquito bites, yet they earn top marks. The Italian language is not one the common people use in life; consequently, the language does not survive except for a few words and names of places that are still commonly used.

"Please tell me how your childhood upbringing was. What is the difference between growing up in Africa and in America?"

"In Africa, everybody is somehow religious, there is some sort of reverence to a Creator; while here, it is not the same. While life in America appears to be individualistic, in Africa it is communal society; it takes the whole community to bring up a child. Customarily, the younger obeys the older. If an older community member catches young folks doing something wrong, he/she could discipline, punish and admonish them; they obey and accept the chastisement graciously. The high regard giving reverence of a Creator, obedience to the parents, the older people, and the community makes growing up in Africa different and better for families."

Hayet tells Angel of how his father's struggles that he witnessed during childhood, accompanied by his concern for social and political injustice, shaped who he is as the family moved from place to place in search of a green pastures.

Chapter 16

Let us help people get on board with what God wants to give them, but what we do not want is the process. Everyone wants the product.

— *Chip Ingram*

Hayet's family moves into the capital, Asmara, a place that shaped his life for good.

They reside first in Arbate (four), Asmara, and then in Casa Kenisha, meaning house/neighborhood of Protestants, at the Dembe-atal (pen of goats) compound.

Casa Kenisha is one of the last neighborhoods by the exit to the port of Massawa, on the Red Sea. In December, the winter's freezing wind hits and then rolls through the palm tree–adorned Asmara through Casa Kenisha and Hayet enjoys the aroma of the foggy clouds that fill the whole city. The Massawa road is the route through which Russian armored military vehicles and hundreds of thousands of troops roll into Eritrea. These vehicles kill scores of civilians due to reckless driving, but the reckless drivers get away without justice.

For Hayet's family, the toll is high. Hayet's first-born brother, whom God blessed his parents with after years of childlessness, is one of those lost in action in a place called Hashenit. Additionally, an artillery shell strike on their home also killed one of his twin sisters. The other twin survived with minor injuries.

One Saturday midafternoon, incoming artillery mortar shells whistle and sound blast echoes throughout Asmara. Panic-stricken birds fly and the citizens run for their lives, not knowing which way is safe.

"How did you escape and where were you at that time?"

On Saturdays, he usually does not go out. However, that day for no reason he decides to take a long walk, far away from home. Neither his older brother nor older sister nor his parents were home at the time of the incident.

"Then what happened?" inquires Angel sympathetically.

"The artillery shell strikes Dembe-atal compound, landing between two outsized flint stones and an enormous log, smashing both into bellowing dusty particles that reach high into the sky. Hayet's mother, Wa-euro, often used to say, *This huge wood will produce enough fire to boil, roast, cook, and bake for my daughter's wedding*. But after the accident, nothing of the log and stone survives."

The direct impact area leaves a deep crater and pockmarks through the entire compound. The artillery shell badly damages Hayet's house on the Dembe side. It eventually becomes a door.

The relocation to Casa Kenisha is like any other relocation for a family in search of a better living. Up to this point during his life, though still young, Hayet has no vision to pursue and no hero or role model to imitate, since his father is often away. He has several challenges to face and must figure them out by himself to survive.

Hayet has an identity crisis, does not know who he is or where he belongs, because of his parents' constant moving from one place to another.

His peers debut him as 'the new kid in the neighborhood,' and Hayet does not like it. Thus, "Would you please let me go back to our previous neighborhood?" fighting tooth and nail. He beseeches his mother every time they move which he is not comfortable with.

His parents always speak the truth with love whether their children like it or not.

Thus, his mother says, "Son, I am sorry to say, but we are not going back. This is the best place for our family."

"It might be for you but not for me. I have no friends; I hate this neighborhood and the school nearby," cries Hayet, refusing to cooperate with his parent's choice.

"The schools that we need are available in this neighborhood. It is the best path for your future. You should do all that you can to adjust. We adjusted to all other places we have been; you can choose to do the same," his mother insists and will not make the slightest move to accommodate Hayet's pleading.

As a result, *I will not make any friends or adjust into this neighborhood,* vows Hayet silently, refusing to change his bad attitude.

Hayet struggles to gain acceptance among his new neighborhood peers, who have diverse upbringings, interests, and clothing styles. His peers wear leather shoes and Adidas sneakers, whereas Hayet puts on a homemade shoe known as *Harambe*, made of worn-out tires. Four nails hold the shoes together, two at the front and two to the back. Sometimes he puts on a Congo, a factory-made rubber shoe, a point of national pride in the country.

"Why did you have to wear homemade shoes?"

"Because my father was not financially wealthy. However, socially, my family is conducive for love and the best family to be part of."

Hayet uniquely wears short sleeves and no-name pants while his peers put on popular brands such as Wrangler Jeans. Furthermore, he fetches firewood from bushes, surviving wild animals and landmines going up and down through the hilly mountainous terrains, whereas his pals buy from the shops. These differences are nearly insignificant for an adult. However, for Hayet, they are heartbreaking and crucial for his survival. These lethal challenges could either break or make him stronger which depends on the survival venue he chooses.

In the midst of the storytelling, "Sorry for the interruption. Would you like to have some more water?" asks the manager.

"Yes, please," answers Hayet as he hands over his cup to the manager for a refill.

Hayet remembers his need to put in an effort to overcome the depressing pressure of peers. These efforts are within the bounds of wisdom. A dozen bullies that do not understand justice, fairness, respect, and love marginalize and physically intimidate him.

They taunt him because of his strange style of dressing and a funny accent.

At the time of relocation, academically, he is a year behind his peers, a first grader. In the villages, schools are rare. That is a reason to taunt and dehumanize him, considering his first-grade stage for his age as lacking intelligence.

To prove the lacking intelligence claim, the wildest tormenting big boy challenges, "Which one is more, negative ten or positive ten?"

The question is above Hayet's grade level. His inability to give the correct answer reveals him as one lacking intelligence, which is not true. The peer's wrong perception of Hayet infuriates him. Like in the animal kingdom, where the powerful survive, every day Hayet has to face uncertain challenges that may go for or against him and he has a choice to make as to which way to go.

He is the only southerner among northern and central province kids. The central province friends live surrounded by uncles, aunties, grandparents, and relatives who boast of their heritage. They undermine people from other regions. Nevertheless, depending on how he chooses to handle life's unfair dealings, the very peer pressure that set him apart can take him precisely where God wants him to be. Thus, he comes to believe that in God's eyes favoritism has no room, no matter where one comes from. "The earth is the Lord's and all in it, the world, and all who live in it."

Casa Kenisha has more advanced living standards, such as running water and availability of lavatory, whereas the other places his family has been do not; one has to go to the rivers and mountains on the open fields to do so. Hayet does not like the environment, though, as he feels like a stranger. However, the move turns out to give birth to a new person, along with a resurgence of an innovative perspective that will purge, shape, and equip him with a purpose for the rest of his life.

The outcome depends on his overcoming the choppy hurdles of self-acceptance or self-rejection. He can endure and grow up with good values, knowing God, prioritizing his life, serving and protecting his community and the world at large. Otherwise, he may remain in defeat, swallowed by adversities, in self-pity, paranoia, and depression worsened by his father's absences.

Chapter 17

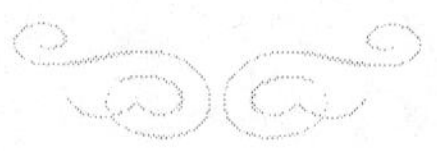

I am not a product of my circumstances. I am a product of my decisions.

— Stephen Covey

Hayet does not see his father much while growing up, mainly on Sundays and holidays; he goes where he is needed most, for work.

The holidays more than any other days without a father feel so heavy. Sheden usually comes home only after weekends and holidays, perhaps once per month, then he goes back.

Angel, as well, has never enjoyed a father-daughter relationship and always envied the girls that had such closeness with their father. She identifies with Hayet and feels his agonizing pain.

"I know how hard it is growing up without a father, I have seen it."

"I was a shy child and lacked confidence because of it. The best way to communicate with others was writing my message," tells Hayet.

"Communication through writing could make you a good writer and author in the future."

"I did that because I was unable to talk face to face to people due to shyness."

On Sundays, Hayet goes to church. His friends earn hugs, kisses, and visits from their relatives. However, for Hayet, nobody knows who he is, and nobody visits, be it the church community or his own relatives, who have excommunicated the family due to their contact with American missionaries. The absence of Sheden aggravates the isolation. No one knows the day or the hour when he will come home from work. Nevertheless, when he does come, it always becomes a happy day of laughter and socialization. The moment Sheden takes a seat, the entire family bows willfully to kiss his hand or kneecap and wash his dusty feet with water in a tray in return for a highly-regarded blessing, *Brook Kun*, meaning, "be blessed," (for male) *Brktee Kunee*, (for female) with outstretched hands. A foot washing is an acceptable tradition to one who comes from long distance.

During his days of isolation, Hayet pledges, *When I grow up, I shall always be present for my family.* He does not understand his father's endeavors, desires, and the sacrifice he makes to be with his family. Nevertheless, the few evenings that Sheden comes home are tormenting for Hayet. Nobody comprehends his sufferings.

On one Tuesday in the early evening, the sun sets behind the cloudless horizon. A neighbor's bougainvillea flowery house blocks the view. The moment Hayet steps into the square cement kitchen floor, his young sister announces, "'*Aboy*,' meaning 'my father' has come."

Hayet makes his way through the shadowy corridor with a large bookshelf on the left and opens the yellowish living room door. Sheden sits all alone on a yellow sofa chair in a dark room, huddled in a white *gabby,* which is a cotton shawl, by the window and the road stands between the house and the black stone fenced public clinic and Isaac T. High School.

Here is Aboy again, moans Hayet, seeing his father, not for the first time in a condition that suggests unresolved issues. *I do not like this! It overwhelms my soul with sorrow to the point of death*. Yet there seems to be nothing he can do to ease the situation.

"God, if you exist, please intervene in my father's unexplained anguish," Hayet repeatedly cries, bitterly. For Hayet, the intervention determines whether to believe or not in a God who hears.

It is minutes after six o'clock. On the street, all is as calm as a school at night. In the stillness, one hears sporadic gunshots aimed at whoever violates the curfew. It is easy to smell the gunpowder polluting the air. There will be no rescue to the shot citizens until sunrise, after the curfew. The curfew declared by the Ethiopian government requires people and livestock to remain indoors between 6:00 p.m. and 6:00 a.m.

Once the curfew hour is up, all citizens and animals enter their homes for the night. It is so tiresome to be indoors every day for twelve hours. In Dembe, out of twelve families, only one has a television. That is where the neighbors watch World Cup soccer on the occasion that the inconsistent electric power comes up. Endless unpredictable power cuts trouble the residents. In one World Cup soccer season, several citizens who violated the curfew were shot and killed. At times, having a TV could be an inconvenience to the owners. It causes people to risk their lives to go to other homes during the curfew to look for TV and stay until the end of the program.

The busy road behind their house has been desolate for nearly an hour. Hayet is standing on the step of the living room, holding the brass door handle.

Something is wrong with Aboy. Is it only I who goes through this undeclared anguish? I wish I could listen to the inner suffering from his heart to lighten all that makes him sit in darkness. I am willing to pay what it takes, even to the point of giving my life!

Hayet understands his father might be tired. However, he wants to hear the burdens that keep him sitting in darkness. His father's chronic gastritis, common to people with unresolved issues, only increases Hayet's desire to have his questions answered and to find a solution.

Hayet contemplates for a while by the doorstep. Then, without turning on the living room or the corridor's light, he greets his father, "*Salaam, Abo,*"— Greetings, Father!

"*Salaam, z-we-day*"— Greetings, oh my son—replies his father, unwrapping the *gabby* from his gray-speckled bald head and, rising from his chair, offering signs of respect, usually done the other way around. Sheden gives Hayet a sincere kiss to the cheek and places an arm around his shoulder, which is the second thing that Hayet needs.

"How have you been doing, and how is school?" school is the priority that Sheden emphasizes in life and ensures that his children to take advantage of it. By his sacrificial provision, Sheden wants to ensure that his children have better educational doors than he did.

"School is okay. I have been doing well."

"Listen, my son; I do not own an inheritance to leave to you. However, if you hold on to education, it could be the greatest wealth for you. Always put God first, prioritize your life, which is an education in your case, and serve others fairly and justly and your dedication will reward you in return. In order to be successful in life, always live and work to please someone through your living; be it your parents or God."

"Why live to please someone else not myself?"

"By living to please someone you would have a purpose to live. If you live to please just yourself, you would live only to eat, drink, sleep, and have fun, caring about yourself; making you less responsible."

"Okay father, I will obey you."

"What would you like to be when you grow up?"

"I would like to be one who serves the people and God fairly as well as justly."

"If serving is what you want to do, that is great. However, if you happen to work, especially in the church, I suggest that you be financially self-supporting."

"Why?"

"The reason is that, if you are not financially stable, you could be tempted to tolerate the intolerable and compromise the uncompromising truth to please people, rather than God. Wherever you go, you will find Jezebel-like people who are there to threaten and intimidate. There will be people who come to discourage you. If you do not please such people, they will fire you, leaving you to a condition where you have no job. Besides, I have learned that we are in a time when people do not put up with sound doctrine. Instead, to suit their own desires, they gather around them a great number of teachers to say what their itching ears want to hear. If you serve to please God, you will have a hard time fitting in; those with unregenerate hearts will persecute you. Having stable finances could help you stand in the face of adversity."

"Why don't you do the same if that is the best way to live?"

"This was the only option I had, perhaps which God has set for me."

Hayet expects his father to explain why he sits in darkness, which is what Hayet needs to hear more than anything else. Yet to Hayet's disappointment, Sheden will not open up. *Perhaps he does not love me.*

In order to give Sheden time, Hayet exits and stands by the square cement corridor. He leans against the wall, facing the shelved books. *Abo,* (Father) *what is it that is tormenting you? I wish you would tell me*, he contemplates, until someone interrupts, coming through the corridor. Hayet eventually sits up in the darkness on the late night and early morning, making it his daily routine.

"Did you do anything to alleviate your father's struggle?" Hayet sighs and clasps his hands tightly. His eyes moisten. *Sorry Hayet, I feel your pain.*

"I never knew what the problem was. So, I could not bring a solution. I wanted him to tell me but he never did."

As the fluctuating curfew time allows, when all the neighborhood children go home, Hayet proceeds home, too. After a short while, he returns and sits by the dilapidated sundeck or roams the dark locality. He asks, *How can I alleviate my father's untold cries?*

In the absence of Sheden, at the time of curfew, Hayet goes home and sits in darkness on the yellowish sofa, internalizing his father's anguish.

"I hope one of the orders that Ms. Linda has is ours," states Hayet in anticipation.

Nevertheless, she serves others, not Angel and Hayet's table. As Ms. Linda returns, "When are you going to bring our order?" Hayet inquires.

"Your order will come after five orders ahead of you, each having between four and ten people. Sorry for the delay," she informs him with an apology.

The main thing Angel wants to hear is Hayet's entire life journey.

In the mornings, Hayet wakes up early and sits in darkness, where he meditates on questions that are beyond his age.

My father never seems to explain his unarticulated moans. My mother and older siblings never appear to know what is going on, or maybe they do not want to tell me about it, he worries. Nevertheless, who will answer and give him information? As a result, Hayet gives it an all-out effort, doing detective work, developing a spy mentality, and finding crafty ways to work. He begins to figure out answers by connecting the dots that seem to relate to his father's sufferings.

At last, *My father's work might be the problem,* he determines. Meanwhile, he embarks on personal training. He wants to fight potential enemies. He pledges, *People will take advantage of you, so make sure not to trust anybody—especially the rich and the powerful.* Consequently, he trains himself to fight, having a distrusting mentality toward whoever approaches him. Concurrently, he desires to bring up an unconquerable army of world changers who would be useful to themselves and to others, fighting for the right of the weak and serving others fairly and justly.

It is at this time that he offers his sincere prayer, *O God, please give me strength to defend and help the weak.*

God grants his request. As a kid, Hayet needs physical strength. However, when he grows up he needs a brain to fight and win legal fights. The people that Hayet helps say, "*Brook Kun.*" As per the blessings received, Hayet eagerly waits to see God's blessings in his life.

To spy on enemies, he climbs the black pepper trees, the neighborhood clinic, and Isaac T. High School. These are perfect places to attack the disobedient and get away with it. In addition, these are the spots where he hides his hand-propelled missile, bow and arrow, and a slingshot apparatus after daily practice in *Frusta Le.* He also scavenges suspects' trash cans in hopes of finding useful information.

Hayet knows that his father organizes and documents what he does. *Searching through his written documents for information might not be a bad idea*, he reasons in distress. *I cannot stand my father's agony anymore.*

In the evening, after everybody else in the family goes to bed, Hayet begins flipping through pages of documents. He finds more than he anticipated finding. One of the letters shakes his inner core. Such a letter would keep a loving and caring father sitting in the darkness accompanied by tormenting gastritis. Although consisting of few words, Hayet cannot take his eyes off it, as he reads it multiple times for accuracy. However, each time he reads, it gives him the same message.

It requires a divine intervention that the ostracized Sheden cannot handle singlehandedly, before the deadline of June 30, to vacate the house. Hayet freezes in awe. His heartbeat increases tremendously as he wipes his uncontrollable, salty sweat with a dirty arm. He lifts his eyes to the bluish ceiling.

"Hello, God, are you there? Are you seeing what is going on? My father needs your intervention. Just seven days remaining and somebody needs to do something to stop this notice before our family gets disrupted," cries Hayet in noticeable moistened eyes. However, there is no visual intervention the young lad could observe, be it from God or a whooshing and dawdling superhero who comes forth to help save the day. *What're we going to do?* Hayet cries within and deeply sighs. *What will Aboy do?* he ponders, moaning in distress.

Chapter 18

Every happening, great and small, is a parable whereby God speaks to us, and the art of life is to get the message.

— Malcolm Muggeridge

Hayet makes a pledge, which would eventually guide and direct his life journey for a good cause.

The written document leads Hayet to conclude that the administration personnel where Sheden works is the problem. The finding will shape his life forever.

At this moment he pledges, *When I grow up, I will never treat a human being the way these people have been treating my father. I shall live to serve and treat humanity fairly and justly, living a life worth remembering before people and pleasing to God. It shall be so until I see the fulfillment of my mother's wishes. Fight the unfair and the unjust, never give up, and let no one intimidate me.*

Hayet disciplines himself for a tough life: fighting evil and protecting the weak, the poor, the elderly, and animals. Advocating for animals is unique in his culture, yet Hayet does it. He commits to being crafty in living, and he pledges,

I will not let anyone outsmart or take advantage of me. Seldom does he have a conflict with his mother, though others take advantage of her.

One evening he declares, "Mother, you should not allow anybody to take advantage of you."

His mother smiles and continually rebuke him, "Do not fight with an evil person. Listen, my son," she stresses, "if anyone slaps you on the right cheek, turn the other cheek. Likewise, if anyone wants to rob you, and take your shirt, you should hand over your coat as well." However, Hayet has trained himself to do the opposite: smack down anyone likely to attack him. One thing he and his mother both agree upon is not to turn away from those who want to borrow from them and to give to the needy.

"What did the finding of the letter mean to you?"

"The letter revealed and brought closure to the quest for information about the unfair and unjust treatment of my father."

Hayet is still not sure how to deal with the problem. That is, is it the whole group, or a few individuals who are oppressing Sheden? He is convinced of the target and vigorously connects the dots to zoom in on his mark. He applies the same measure when dealing with his friends, connecting dots and reading their faces; he knows their intentions before they utter a word.

One more challenge is the timing, taking revenge now versus later. Culturally, people say, *A person who does not take revenge is a donkey's son.* Only mediation and reconciliation by the elders avoids revenge and bloodshed. Joining and learning from the Eritrean liberation factions is the best way to be part of a precise mission accomplishment. However, Hayet is too young to join. Therefore, revenge military style is unlikely to happen soon. Hayet has to find an alternative way, that is, befriending multiple, undisciplined gangs that will help him achieve his secret plan. Hayet decides to have revenge on the overall group at one of their meetings.

One Saturday in the late afternoon, the granite-walled exclusive apartments of Aba Ha-bash casts shadows over the park of Bah-tea Mess-Kreme Square. Extraordinary aromas of freshly brewed coffee with hot pastries across the street at Ugo Café, as well as spicy beef stew at Langano Restaurant, entice passersby to enter inside to eat or to play billiards or pool games.

Hayet and his friends are picking date fruits from the left side of the Bah-tea Mess-Kreme Square entrance. Hayet is on top of the prickly palm tree, reaching out for bunches. A smiling man, named Mr. CHEKAN YEHUDA, stops by the highway. "Do you want a ride home?" he yells out. The neighborhood kids do not have cars. Car rides are cool and something that they fantasize about, even if it is only to ride for a few meters. Hayet comes down at once; his friends are already crammed in the car.

Right then, Saint Mary's and Cathedral's somber bells ring. Mr. Chekan Yehuda starts a conversation. For all of Hayet's friends, it is just a car ride that they are not likely to remember as special. However, for Hayet, it is an impeccable day that he has wished to see for years.

"Tell your dad that I gave you a ride," Mr. Chekan Yehuda says.

Right away, Hayet connects the dots. *Hey, wait a minute. All of my friends have fathers. Why did he single out my father and inform me to tell him of the favor?* Mr. Chekan Yehuda's statement is puzzling. *This is nothing but the confession of my primary target.*

"Did you get to share your burdens with your parents?"

"No, because they will not approve of my tit-for-tat retaliation."

From that day onward, Hayet is absolutely convinced of the primary target and focuses on studying his route to attack the man alone. Hayet believes in punishing one for one's sins; there should be no collective punishment. For maximum secrecy, Hayet will act as a lone wolf. He plans his mission exceedingly well; no matter how long it takes; he is determined to get away with it.

In the meantime, the imprisonment and unjust killing of Eritrean citizens under the Mengistu regime as well as the use of intimidation and rape grow ever more rampant.

The death and imprisonment of nationals are widespread.

In one such incident, a relative of Mr. Chekan Yehuda orders the ruthless militias that he manipulates, "Kill WE-HA-THEE," that is, Hayet's brother. We-hathee is a masculine-gender name meaning something that flows ceaselessly.

Usually, the militias as well as the soldiers, could kill any person and then say, "They are rebels," and get away with it without justice. Nevertheless, "This man is courteous, and we shall not kill him," protest the militias this time.

"Our God is a God who saves; from Him comes escape from death," declares Angel.

After surviving one imprisonment, to avoid death, Hayet leaves the country, leaving his life behind.

On the eve of Hayet's departure, Sheden manages to take him out to Capri Restaurant, which is in the same block as Cinema Roma and Cinema Dante for the first and only time. Hayet orders the coldest, tastiest banana juice he is ever had, and then they start their conversation.

"Behold, my son," announces Sheden. "I would love to bring you to places like this all the time; however, I have no money."

The statement mercilessly cuts Hayet's inner core. Hayet hears directly about his father's financial struggles for the first time, which he never perceived before. *I wish you told me before. I never would have done some of the things that I did.* Anyway, after drinking the best juice he is ever had, they return home.

The following early morning, Hayet leaves home, receiving his parents' blessings and prayers. "May the Lord answer you when you are in distress; may the name of the God of Jacob protect you. May He send you help from the sanctuary and grant you support from Zion. May He remember all your sacrifices and accept your burnt offerings. May He give you the desire of your heart and make all your plans succeed. May the Lord bless you and keep you; the Lord make His face shine on you and be gracious to you; the Lord turn His face toward you and give you peace wherever you go."

"Thank you, father."

"My son, the Lord is with you. Be the best you can be. When you come to the Promise Land bring the cloak that I left incomplete and my scrolls, especially the parchments. A Jezebel-embodied leader did me a great deal of harm. The Lord will repay him for what he has done, I do not have to have revenge. My son, you too, should be on your guard against such, because they strongly will oppose your destined walk. The only way to win and make your enemies angry is by doing what they don't want you to do and being what they don't want you to be."

"What do you mean?"

"Your enemies want you to fail in life and be useless. If you fail and become useless they become happy."

"If becoming successful and doing right makes my enemies angry, that is easy and worth living for."

"My son, at my first local defense, no one came to my support, but everyone deserted me. May it not be held against them. However, the Lord stood at my side and gave me strength, so that through me the gospel message might be fully proclaimed that the unbelievers might hear the Truth. God delivered me from death when I was caught up between two war fronts. The Lord will keep on rescuing me from every evil attack and when I die, will bring me safely to His heavenly kingdom."

Hayet is hesitating to ask his father whether the one that did him a great deal of harm is Mr. Chekan Yehuda or not.

Father, I know you are also going to talk about gratitude.

Sheden is a priest and knows how to invoke priestly blessings. "My son, although I do not know how and when; the Lord will bless you and take you to the Promise Land as He said He would. However, when you have eaten and are fulfilled, praise God for the good land He has given you. Be careful that you do not forget the Lord your God, failing to observe His guidelines, laws, and rulings that I am informing you this day. Otherwise, when you eat and are satisfied, when you build fine houses and settle down, and when your wealth grows large and your silver and gold increase and all you have is amplified, then your heart will become proud and you will forget God, who brought you out of this land. Always remember God, for it is He who gives you the capability to produce prosperity, and so confirms His covenant, which He swore to me, as it is today. If you ever forget God and follow other gods that appear in different forms including wealth and worship and bow down to them, I testify against you today that you will surely be ruined."

Sheden prays all night for Hayet's safe journey. However, for Hayet prayer is meaningless; he has come to believe that God neither exists nor hears prayers, because He does not seem to intervene in his father's case.

After receiving his parents' blessings, Hayet has taken a dangerous journey en route to safety, not knowing what would await him. He is walked long distances through the jungles as hungry lions roared and famished hyenas laughed, giggled, barked, and walked alongside him, searching for the best opening to devour him.

"Were you frightened the moment you saw the wild animals?"

Hayet was so frightened and panic-stricken. "Obviously."

Moreover, his feet are swollen. He cannot walk any more comfortably. He walks, dragging his swollen and blistered feet. He is not used to walking long distances.

Were his companions to leave Hayet only a few meters behind, it could isolate and expose him to the wild animals that create a diversion and attack the weak.

"We are almost there; we have to cross the border before sunrise. It is better to walk a little more with pain than becoming dinner for the ravaging beasts you see and hear or get caught by the government patrols," encourage his companion, Asher, and the guide. As they continued walking through the bushes under the night cover, "Stop!" two men order at a gunpoint, brandishing Russian-made Simonov refiles. The runaways and the guide panic.

"This is the end," Hayet cries in despair.

"Go straight ahead," order the captors trailing the runaways.

The runaways and the guide walked to an undisclosed location. It is in such places that perhaps more than half of the political refugees perish. Some die because of hunger, thirst, buried by the Saharan sand dunes, eaten by wild animals, or end at the hands of merciless captors and smuggling rings. Others who escape from the perils in the land drown in the sea. Very few make it to safety and live to tell about it.

The only reason the few that flee from the hand of the persecutors give for their actions is this: *If we stay here we shall die. If we attempt to go to another safe country, we could die. If people that find us on the way spare us, we live; if they kill us, then we die, and they try the journey of faith.*

It is a terrifying moment for the runaways and their guide.

"My feet are in pain; I cannot walk anymore," Hayet says, who always has the favor of God before the people that meet him, as he pleads.

"Well, if you cannot walk, bring money; we will set you free. If not, we deliver you to the government patrols," the captors say. The government patrols could be torturers, gropers, and rapists of women, far much worse than the local patrolling militias.

"Listen," whispers Asher in a language that the captors do not understand, "if they hand us over to the government, Colonel Mengistu will kill me because I am a national service escapee. We have got to fight, give money, or manage to snatch and turn their guns towards them."

They engage in a brief negotiation. Then, "Bring your watch and money," orders the shortest captor. He is dressed in khaki shorts and a camo T-shirt with dark sunglasses over his eyes, even at night. The captors have the power to do whatever they want to do. Hayet's heart-throbs in dread. What else can he do? He cannot defend himself against the threat of the armed captors. He reluctantly hands over his Citizen, which is sparkling in the moonlight, plus some money. The captors release them without searching their pockets. Hayet and his companion make it to safety, crossing a little creek to Kenya.

Becoming a refugee, Hayet lives in camps in Kenya, where he is able to influence people for good. The financial restriction of having no money coming in causes him to develop a chronic worry, *What will happen to me when I run out of money?* The thought makes him sleepless. Before he left his home country, though a teenager, he was financially stable, involved in a wholesale and retail business. Hayet is in the transition from having plenty of money to no money, from self-dependent to a dependent and unpredictable condition.

To relieve him from the chronic worry he opens a Bible that his brother gave him, reads a transforming word: "I tell you, do not worry about your life, what you will eat or drink; or about your body, what you will wear. Is not life more than food, and the body more than clothes? Look at the birds of the air; they do not sow, harvest, or store away in storehouses, and yet your heavenly Father feeds them. You are much more valuable than they are. By worrying, can you add a single hour to your life? Why do you worry about clothes? See how the flowers of the field grow. They do not labor or spin. Yet I tell you that King Solomon in his entire splendor did not dress like one of these. If that is how God clothes the grass of the field, which is here today and tomorrow is thrown into the fire, will He not much more clothe you, you of little faith? So do not worry, saying, 'What shall I eat, drink, or wear?' The godless people run after all these, and your heavenly Father knows that you need them. Nevertheless, seek first the kingdom of God and His righteousness; He will give you all that you need as well. Therefore, do not worry about tomorrow, for tomorrow will worry about itself. Each day has enough trouble of its own."

Upon getting such a turning point message from the Bible, *It makes sense. Maybe I can try not to worry.* The financial scarcity could teach him a lesson to trust in God for his needs. Being in unpredictable conditions, Hayet inspires a number of people to move from where they were to where they ought to be. By doing so, Hayet helped others to find themselves. Will he be able to discover himself?

Chapter 19

I am only one, but still I am one. I cannot do everything, but still I can do something, and because I cannot do everything, I will not refuse to do something that I can do.

— *Helen Keller*

Hayet's story entrances Angel and touches her heart in a way that no one has for a very long time which could be the best encounter in her life.

As innocent-looking as you are, you have been through a lot. If it were not for the prearranged betting, I would have let you keep on walking your chastity walk or at least marry you. Men such as you are useful and strong. Sorry, after this first day, you will end up being promiscuous like me.

At last, "Sorry for the delay. Here is your order," Ms. Linda informs them while mentioning each order.

As Ms. Linda lifts the orders to put them on the table for the patrons to eat, Hayet thinks, *Thank you Grandpa. You humbly showed me how to hold a fork, knife and spoon, what I needed to learn at a time when I did not want to learn. However, now because of you, I can comfortably eat with this popular girl.* An overwhelming appreciation fills Hayet's heart. He then silently offers blessings to the food without letting Angel know. Angel as well does the same, both of them hiding their true Christian identity, neither wanting to offend the other.

Angel cuts the food, places the silver knife on the top of the plate sideways. That is when she positions the food for a bite as she takes a pause to talk. Then, she switches the fork from the left hand to the right hand and eats.

Hayet starts with a salad. It has juicy grilled shrimp, black olives, hardboiled eggs, tomatoes, all on Bibb lettuce and tossed with a creamy avocado dressing.

In the midst of the meal, Hayet fiddles with the yellowish flower napkin and gives Angel a shallow, tentative smile.

"If you need anything else I am here to serve you," Ms. Linda says politely whenever she takes a walk through the patrons' tables. As he scoops the last of his dessert, a classic cheesecake with graham cracker crumbs, strawberry sauce, and whipped cream, Angel tells him, "Relax. You look astonished."

"I am relaxed," he replies, smiling at her with a gleam in his eyes while hiding the nervous feeling on the inside.

After they ate all that they could and discussed all they had to talk about, Angel announces, "Let us go to our room," she holds his hand for the first time. What a fantastic night. Hayet feels mystified by her; it is embarrassing to tell her to let go of his hand. He carefully slides free of her grip and places his hands in his pockets.

The main dining room exit is next to the silver-paneled elevators. A concierge staffer stands by the elevators. Uncle Jehu's advice during graduation ceremony flashes in Hayet's mind like a frightening thunder.

Remember, we are sending you out like sheep among wolves. Be as shrewd as a snake and as innocent as a dove. Know how to dodge when vicious prowlers or wise, sneaky enemies come to divert you from your destiny of purposeful living. Remember who you are! Make sure to give a good name to the loving community and family that you represent. The only way you will be able to achieve your goal is by saying no to worthless ideas. Say yes to what is true, noble, right, pure, lovely, admirable, and praiseworthy.

At one escapable point Hayet thinks, *This is my only moment to say goodbye and escape before I enter the elevator.*

He casually looks for an accessible escape route.

"Why do you lag behind? Come on," Angel says as she hooks her angelic hand to Hayet's for the second time.

"No one will ever know that you were with me. You will enjoy this night. Do not worry about the consequences because there will not be any. What happens in Vegas stays in Vegas! I have taken care of all. There is nothing to worry about, and there is no reason you should not have a pleasure this day!"

I have learned what happens in Vegas does not stay in Vegas. He is afraid to resist and cause an argument in front of the diners and other visitors. The guests are already glaring at her stunning beauty from the high and low bar chairs as well as the reception area.

Angel wears exclusive Saks Fifth Avenue clothing, accompanied by fashionable makeup from Champs Elysees, Paris; Bond Street, London; Via Montenapoleone, Milan; Bahnhofstrasse, Zurich and so forth. Not only that, but Angel also has a fruity, entrancing, and alluring scent.

In addition, her touch is angelic, her mouth is softer than silk, and her talk is sweeter than honey. She has charm in her voice, and her words pull him to herself like a magnet. She is captivating, wise, and talented. She has glittering, expensive jewelry on her fingers, wrists, and neck.

The minute they enter the elevator, Hayet feels like a sheep being led to the shearer, silently walking toward a foolish decision.

They step out of the elevator. "Wow, the hallway is so silent," Hayet declares.

Angel scans her card, and the door to the room opens. Immediately, she coerces him with a sloppy, wet kiss on his cheek to test the water. Although as a result of the sensual kiss sends a ripple effect of shock waves to the novice's innermost being, the kiss on the cheek being his first; at the same time, he wipes the kissed cheek repeatedly by his sleeves as if she muddied him with a red dirt.

"Thanks for accepting my invitation," Angel articulates seductively.

Hayet displays a delightful expression that causes the corners of his mouth to turn up, while his lips shut, having seen the extravagant layout of the room. *Beautiful place*, he exclaims.

"Look at the towel origami on the bed," Angel tells Hayet, walking ahead of him.

"How did they make this peacock and peahen?"

"Well, these people are set for business. Customer satisfaction is their priority. They know what makes the customer happy. That is what they do every day."

Meanwhile, Hayet slides open the patio door, and Angel follows him to the stylish Juliet balcony. He stares out the foggy balcony.

"Wow, the view is magnificent. The city sparkles," Angel raves.

"Yes, it is because of the Christmas lights," he affirms. As attractive as the vibrant city scene is to enjoy the invaluable nightly panoramic vicinity, the cold chill forces them to retreat.

The room has quality contents. The walls, the bed, the pillows, the long draperies, are light blue with white. The loveseat and the mahogany oval study table and brown recliner and revolving chairs are on the left side of the patio door behind the brownish mod-style sofas. It is seductive to be there, even for a night. Nonetheless, it is not affordable for him unless somebody else pays for it.

"Isn't it amazing?" Angel asks rhetorically as she opens draperies and drawers. Then, she gleefully jumps into the side of the tufted king size white bed without touching the origami and unzips her boots, dropping them off from the bed. The boots fall sideways. After she soaks up, she picks up her Hermes alligator exotic skin black handbag.

"Excuse me for a minute or so," she declares and walks into the restroom.

Just as would be expected of a trendy girl, Angel has perfect feet with a proper pedicure. Meanwhile, Hayet's heart pounds quickly. *What next?*

For the time being, he positions himself on the study desk next to the exit door, ready to run away if anything unpleasant happens. *I should have chosen to stop playing with fire of immorality from the first time we met. I already missed openings to escape before I entered the elevator. Perhaps this is my last chance. It is also hard not to cooperate with her demand.* Hayet blames his indecisiveness. He hears water running and some shuffling. *What is she doing? It has been ages since she went inside.*

Finally, the restroom door opens wide. A moment later, Angel emerges. The instant she appears Hayet thinks, *What I see cannot be true.* He glimpses her spectacular silhouette and twinkling, soulful, piercing eyes. It is Hayet's first time not only to be near but also to see an angelic woman's body. She looks like an enhanced angel as drawn by Leonardo da Vinci or Michelangelo. She has a toned body, flat abs, and stimulating curves made by the best artisan that designed Eve from the ribs of Adam. Right then, Hayet turns his face the other way so that he will not sin by looking at her lustfully.

Angel is shameless; she trots in a transparent and a revealing lingerie as if she is going to sleep with her husband on the day of her wedding. Her golden auburn hair spreads over her shoulders gracefully. She walks in front of a young man who is not her husband without any intention to hide under the blankets or use a towel to cover up her nakedness. Instead, she approaches nearer. She finally sits by the table, placing her right leg on a chair with her left on the ground. She smells as desirable as heavenly captivating myrrh. Again, Hayet turns his face the other way, yet she drags his chin by her angelic scented hand and makes him look at her. Yet he still looks sideways.

In the meantime, Hayet's pulse surges. Shortly, what LeAnn said comes to mind. *Angel never forces any man. However, by her glamorous appearance and alluring voice, she seduces the chaste as well as the decent men to go after her.* Hayet could fall for Angel because he has fully immersed himself in an irresistible situation.

Chapter 20

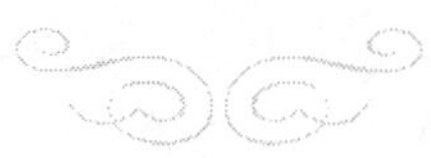

If you do not stand for something you will fall for anything.

— *Malcolm X*

It is possible to save others from a wasted, addictive, promiscuous lifestyle to *diverge* to purposeful living and yet be unable to help yourself.

Hayet sits on a chair, facing a phenomenal myrrh-scented curvy silhouette. He is at a pass or fail stage. Because of his nervousness, he has no courage to look straight at her engaging face. He attempts to dart for the door, shooing away her grip. She gawks at him with fluttering sky-blue eyes. Stretching her disarming arms, with her manicured nails, she blocks his move and pins him back to the chair.

I should have refused from the very beginning before I submerged myself in this alluring situation.

Angel warns, "I know what you want to do. Should you ever touch the door without my permission, I will scream and accuse you of rape."

In that instant, Hayet knows that his life is in considerable danger. *Exiting would cost me more, probably taking me to prison.* Not knowing what to do, he sits in distress.

Moments later Angel purrs, "Relax, you are halfway through and almost done. Today will be a memorable moment in your life."

She grabs his well-built shoulders and massages them, providing his body with a sensational and irresistibly pleasurable feeling, but he has butterflies fluffing in his stomach.

"Memorable day—huh, it could be your memorable moment, too," Hayet echoes thoughtlessly. He has no idea how to flee from her grip, though.

In the midst of apprehension, "Angel," he asks hesitantly, "You admitted you are a Christian. How can you display this behavior, so contradictory to biblical teaching on how unmarried people are expected to live, if you profess to be one?"

Angel for sure knows that God does not allow any premarital ungodly relationship, be it fornication or adultery for whatsoever reason, even if it is consensual. Nevertheless, she seems more focused on getting what she wants than on answering Hayet's question. As he anticipates her answer, her spritzed and freshened hair sways in his face, tickling him. Then sharply, "I am not going to answer that question," she sneers. At the same time, she pins him to the chair as she blows the loose strands of hair from about her eyes.

The visual stimulation makes Hayet somehow respond physically. Nevertheless, he has mixed feelings of fear and fretfulness. He does not know how to make the first move or what the result will be. It comes to mind that LeAnn and Emily were right when they warned him: *It is impossible to escape from Angel's bait. Avoid her at all cost.* Now that he is her bait, the only thing he wishes is to get loose from her grip even for a moment, which is unlikely to happen unless she has a swift change of mind. In spite of the fact that the situation at hand foretells the inevitability of Hayet's fall, deep down in his personhood echoes, *Every cloud has a silver lining.* Yet he is not aware where and how to find the relief that will help him to fulfill the walk of chastity.

In the meantime, grudgingly, he wonders, *How can I go against my pledge so easily?* With what feels like his last breath, he says tentatively, "Angel, I have one question to ask you, please."

"Whatever question you may have, save it for later, after we finish with what we are about to do."

"This is serious. Listen, Angel, for the whole day I have been cooperating with your demands. Please answer my one question so that we may have an enjoyable night," he insists.

Man, life is so short enjoy it. Do not be so serious, mumbles Angel. "Well, make it quick. What question is it? Ask me," she pronounces, pulling her hands off his shoulder and placing them on her hairless smooth knees.

"How did you come to have the best name I have ever heard, Angel? I told my family about you. I promised them to ask why we call you Angel."

Angel stares at Hayet blankly. "You discussed such matters with your family? That is great. Keep it up! The openness, living to please your parents and transparency shall keep you safe."

"From what?"

"Do you want me to tell you all or some?"

"Please tell me all," he responds to buy time.

Angel extensively knows how to maintain a healthy lifestyle, by living to please her parents and God.

The best teammate in the world, her mother, based on the word of God, guides her along the best pathway for her life and counsels her with a parental and godly loving eye on her. Thus, she can truly teach about life principles about finance saving and spending. In fact, on her sixteenth birthday, she managed to buy a $16,000, 1989 Acura Legend Coupe with her own money. She is aware of how to protect her identity, monitor her credit score, determine her needs versus wants, the importance of having all types of insurance, prioritize her life, and you name it.

When Angel first came to college, she lived a transparent and honest life, giving willful consent for her parents to access her academic, attendance, and of course financial records at any time even without her presence. Those years were the safest and best moments in her life, the days that she reported every happening to her parents as her teammate. Later, ungodly students began to taunt her for being a dependent university student and Mommy's girl. Without regard to her accountability and integrity, she first hides a tiny and insignificant information from her loving parents. Then, minute hiding gives birth to more of the same as well as hiding where she had been in the evenings and doing the same for all her grades.

At one time, she disallows the communication between her parents and the school. Giving full access of reports to her parents would have kept her safe, but she became foolish that she made the change. As the days go by, she does not have the loving communication with her parents, relatives, or church community. Angel did not want to hear what she often needed to hear, parental guidance, which could keep her from terribly falling.

The reason as to why she cut the caring communication is that she gave up her position in Christ; she effectively isolated herself and created her own "acceptable ghetto" instead of living by God's standard. She failed to realize that cursed is the one that preaches and creates his or her own standard even if herself, any pastor, Governor, President, Prime Minister, King, Congress, Parliament, Court, or an angel from heaven should preach a gospel other than the one declared in the Bible to her!

The biblical abnormal became her normal. The only thing that people know about Angel is that she did not drop out of college and she is not dead, but nothing else. One sin giving birth to another sin, she broke her accountability and integrity to her parents and to God. Finally, she lost her God's Positioning System, which leads to God's Plan of Salvation. She abandons prioritizing her life for fun instead of fulfillment.

As she continues explaining how the name Angel came into being, she says, "It is good that you do not know the origin of Angel," and pauses for a while.

"It is a long story. The name has a negative implication that students labeled me three years ago on a hot and tropical summer Friday. You know that on this campus, unless one intentionally says no to all that is disadvantageous, so many temptations and peer pressures occur.

Beloved, you too should have said no to my invitation. To be part of an exclusive group, one could be tempted to do unaccustomed practices and go to wild places. Should one do any wrong, it spreads throughout the campus with the details exaggerated. I do not want to talk about that. The more I talk and think about it, the more it brings an additional hurt I inflict on my damaged emotions caused by one day's mistake, which could only be healed by God's redeeming power." She falls into silence.

Hayet is keenly waiting for Angel to carry on her story. "Please tell me why we call you Angel," he insists.

Instantly, her face, ears, and cheeks turn red. She takes her feet off the chair and gathers her enticing, fragrant, ticklish hair into a sideways ponytail.

"No, I am not who the students and the teachers nicknamed me. I am who I was meant to be, not a *fallen angel*," she cries.

"Is the word *fallen* a prefix to *an angel*?"

Suddenly, her eyes widen and she gapes at Hayet almost angrily. After a moment or so, she nods her head.

"Yes!" she howls helplessly. "You do not understand how disgraced I felt when the students called me a *fallen angel* in the beginning. However, later, I got used to it. I set my mind on earthly things. My destiny turned to destruction, pleasure and fame became my god, and my shame became my glory." Her eyes moisten and she finishes in a low, anguished voice.

"I did not mean to hurt your feelings. It is just that the Gramps and I were really curious to know why you are called Angel," comforts Hayet.

"You should not feel sorry. A sinner deserves punishment for her sins."

"Everybody sins. If God punishes all sinners for their sins, no human being will stand on the earth. There is a God who forgives and accepts you as you are by His unmerited favor."

Angel covers her body with the peahen towel, leans against the window, looks down the lawn past the tall, hardy palm trees, and weeps. She wipes her welling eyes and runny sniffling nose with the peacock towel.

It is heartbreaking for Hayet to see an outstandingly beautiful young woman in such despair. He gives her a hug and says, "I am sorry for what you have been through. Whatever you have been through, you are through it."

He wraps his arms around her neck tightly, and she hugs him in return, still weeping.

"I wish I were through, but I am not," she shouts furiously.

"What am I going to do?" she asks, her voice choked with grief.

"If you want to find your real name and identity, return to the place and time where you lost and abandoned real you. Find the real you, by diverging and returning to the God of all creation. Come out of your wasted life and be separate, for the Lord. Do not touch the unclean thing, and He will receive you. He will be a Father to you, and you will be a daughter to Him," affirms Hayet.

She looks into his face while wiping her tears of mirth. *If you really knew who this wretched woman was, you would have stayed away. Besides, even if I return to the place and time where I lost my real name and my identity, where I went partying with Valerie, there is nothing to find and no broken pieces to mend. All is gone, it is irreversible shame.*

Although she knows that there is a redeeming grace somewhere in the universe, she does not perceive that grace could pluck her out of the mess she has willfully immersed herself in.

Because of her intentional foolishness, she is not certain to receive forgiveness. As a result, she says, "Even if I return, I cannot have a grace that abounds with mercy. I am wretched and shameful to my family and to the community that I represent. I ruined not only my life but also the lives of other aspiring young students and professionals. I lost my dignity from the highly-regarded woman of God to the point of earning a *fallen angel* nickname. The worst part is that I accepted the nickname with pride, forgetting my real name and identity."

"What real name and identity?"

"A daughter of God, justified, a citizen of heaven, blessed, blameless, redeemed, a saint, a dwelling of the Holy Spirit, an overcomer, protected, and one whose life is hidden in Christ by God. I took my disgrace as my splendor."

"Sorry to hear all that you have been through. I assumed Angel was your name. What is your real name, then?"

"Corey Kerry! That is my real name," she whispers. "Slowly all good eclipsed from my life. As we speak, there is nothing valuable left in me. Look at my eyes. I am a walking dead."

Hayet is troubled that the tsunami of regret could cause her to collapse. Consequently, he says, "Angel, this is—"

"Please stop calling me by that nickname. I have had enough of it!" she shouts.

"I am sorry. I will never say it again, Corey."

"Thank you for calling me by my name."

While wrapping her in his arms, Hayet says, "You are welcome. You have a life and you are still alive. That is most important. Today could be your memorable day where your healing begins. Do not let go of this moment in time. Then you shall receive healing from your spiritual, emotional, and social brokenness by diverging to where you belong, to God. Please give me a moment to sing a song of healing." Hayet sings Tenth Avenue North's "Healing Begins."

The song focuses on how one like Corey can receive healing from her tormenting sins once she departs from them.

While singing the song, Hayet frequently glances at her. Tears gush from her blacklined eyes, creating tracks down her cheeks. Corey sits down on the floor, looking as withered as a dry flower cut off from the sources of life. She is not the outgoing, cool, popular girl that everybody knows.

From such brokenness, the only way out is her return to where she fell from, reasons Hayet. "Corey, yesterday is gone. Forget the former failures and do not dwell on the past. New and wondrous inheritances shall come, and you shall be acceptable as you are."

"I wish I could be accepted as I am; I would give all. I intentionally tampered with all the dreams and aspirations I had, ignoring the warnings and good values that my parents imparted to me based on the word of God. I have been part of and am in a basket of deplorable, done despicable, disgusting deeds, and I have been to filthy places. There is no mercy and hope for me. I am dead inside," she howls timidly.

"Please be assured, my sister. God is the most compassionate and merciful to accept as well as to forgive you. As long as there are breath and life in you, there is still hope and a good future for you. I tell you, the optimal time to receive your healing is here and now. You do not have to pour very expensive perfume from an alabaster jar to gain acceptance. All that you need is to accept the call. Do not let go of this divinely appointed instant in time. The only place you can begin your healing process is where you are at, and the impeccable time you can choose to do the same is right now. This day will open a new and clean chapter in your life. Promise to diverge and return. Once you return you shall sing exciting songs of the redeemed like a bird that escaped from the fowler's snare; the snare shall be broken and you shall escape," pleads Hayet.

"Brother, I have already told you. I would give all to gain acceptance. Nevertheless, even if mercy avails for everybody else, I do not deserve compassion because of the terrible deeds that I have done." No matter what comforting words Hayet uses, Corey's eyes continue spewing tears.

Hayet considers stopping his exhortations, yet he does not know how. He gives her a few more assuring words.

After a short while she speaks, "Thanks for the song. I told you that godless living has become part of my life. I have done terrible deeds, more than anybody else has. There is no hope for me. I am at a point from which I can never return."

What terrible thing did she do that she cannot forgive herself? Could it be the shedding of innocent blood? She seems to refuse every forgiveness, grace, mercy, hope, and healing, promising words.

"What a terrible thing you did, that you condemn yourself so. It is not about what you did. It is what Jesus Christ did on your behalf. It is not about where you have been; it is where you are going, having a new life through Jesus."

"How could that be? I fell from that grace. I have tasted the goodness of the word of God and the powers of His redeeming grace and have fallen away. It is impossible for me to come back to reconciliation. To my loss, I have crucified the Son of God all over again, subjecting him to public disgrace."

"Corey," implores Hayet, "Come near to God and He will come near to you. Wash your hands from sinful ways and purify your heart. You are within the reach of God. You cannot fall forever this fast, thus far causing you to be unable to return when you get lost.

I remember a man who terribly fell from God's call for his life. From a highly respected a godly Nazarene to a godless entertainer. If there were a person that you would not expect God to hear, that would be him. Yet, at a time when nobody expected him to resurge, he manages to pray, 'Sovereign Lord, remember me. Please, God, strengthen me just once more.' The God who is nearer to him than his breathing instantaneously restores his strength, enabling him to achieve what he asked for on the only request from God in his entire life. Therefore, so shall it be with you, too. Your future life will be far much better than the past. Just diverge."

Corey is no longer concerned about having the enjoyment that she originally planned when she set up the appointment with Hayet. She fights for her existence, to clear up the guilty conscience that has tormented her for years. Accepting Hayet's speech makes sense. Yet the guilty feeling repels her from self-acceptance though the word of God that breaks a rock in pieces will consume and crush her hardened heart once she gives Him willful access.

Chapter 21

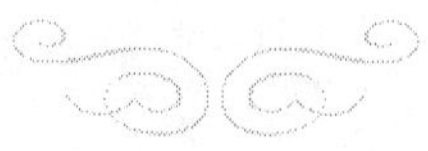

I am who I am today because of the choices I made yesterday.

— *Eleanor Roosevelt*

Hayet and Corey continue to discuss how to set her free from the guilt trip that torments her and how diverging to a spiritual freedom would usher her into a brighter future.

Corey gazes at Hayet with blurry eyes while blowing her watery sniffles. *As long as she hides in her ungodly life, she cannot receive healing emotionally, spiritually, and psychologically.*

After fidgeting for a couple more moments in her squatting position, she stretches out. A terrific rattling noise arises as if dry bones were coming to life. It is a sign of the opening of new beginnings. Then she abruptly unfolds her story.

Hayet learns that Corey grew up in Vermont, during the Christmas season enjoying Wassail parades, where they sing along accompanied by jingling horse bells. During the summer, she goes hiking in the woods. While growing up, aside from school, the church was the most important part of her life. She has an uncontested godly and spiritual foundation. She receives and develops a melodious singing voice.

She has loving parents that practice daily devotion and prayers after the lovely time of fellowship at the dinner table. When he is not on business trips, which could be as few as five days per month, her father, Mr. WILLIAM KERRY would be home by seven o'clock at the latest. During the absence of her father, her mother, CHLOE KERRY assumes leadership in the social, spiritual, and academic aspects of life. As much as Corey loved her father's presence in her life, his job makes it impossible to spend time with her when she needed him most. She survives the choppy waters of her early teenage years without her father's company. The good thing is that the father provides more than enough for all that her family needs and wants. Also, the family uses homeschooling to prepare her for college.

At college, Corey continues the family tradition of having personal devotions without parental supervision. She enjoys participating in Campus Union fellowship, surrounding herself with supportive people focusing on serving humanity, academic, and spiritual area of life.

Until she nearly completes the first year of college, she has never dated, kissed, or touched a man illicitly. Her parents sternly instructed her to avoid the untimely dating games until she finds the right man to marry, then date for life. That includes dodging prom and having a party at home instead. She is working to keep herself pure and chaste for marriage. She wants to have her first kiss on her glorious day at the altar.

To strengthen her commitment, whenever asked to go for a date, she would reply, "If you are serious enough to go up to marriage, allow my mother to go with us." However, the men that have hidden agendas, who love dating games, hopping like a kangaroo from one untested relationship to another beseech her. "Come on, girl, you are a grown-up college student. You do not have to adhere to the old-fashioned parental instructions, enjoy life," repeatedly says the grouchiest young man who has a crush on her. Yet, with no apology to anybody Angel boldly replies, "Until I get married I belong to my parents. After marriage, I belong to my husband. How glorious and beautiful it will be to keep my virginity intact until marriage for my spouse. I have come to realize that what our generation refers carefree wallowing, indulgence in the heat of the moment as coolness is a foolishness. True love waits. Waiting and 'holding out' to have a matured, a super-solid and a lasting relationship in the face of adverse temptations and peer pressure is not easy, but possible. A man should take a woman only when given by woman's family; a woman should not give herself to a man of her own free will. The reason is that, most of the relationships that do not involve family end up in despair, breakup, and one hurting the other. It is better to be safe than sorry."

When asked, "How about if your spouse would not do the same?" she customarily replies, "It is his problem. My main responsibility is doing what I am supposed to do."

As her first year of college is ending, she eases a little, envying the cool and popular college girls who accept any man's invitation, who are not as good-looking as she is, but who are going out almost every night. At one point she wonders, *Why is it that my friends enjoy life while I do not?* She yearns for that kind of reckless and ungodly enjoyment. Little did she know that what she yearns for would turn out to be detrimental to her life journey.

Corey willfully creates a void in her life through misguided nostalgia. Consequently, she associates with fallen people that have no regard for putting God first, prioritizing their lives and serving others fairly and justly. These people loiter leisurely, play wildly, drink uncontrollably, and flirt promiscuously.

Her yearning has a possibility of crossing her through endless tunnels.

It has been months since she started moving away in slow motion from purposeful living, the anchors of her faith, the conscious alarm, the warning calls of a loving family and friends.

Corey's ungodly raving prompts her to befriend a senior graduating student, VALERIE CONSTANTINE.

"I want to invite you for the school's end-of-the-year party," says Valerie. At the same time, the Campus Union fellowship announces another party. The choice of going with Valerie or to the CU fellowship overwhelms Corey.

In the decisive encounter, Valerie insists, "You have had campus fellowship the whole year. You still have three more years to go. Come and have fun with us, *just for today*."

Corey's soul sounds an audible distress call for her not to go, because her parents trained her, if something is not worth repeating, do not do just *for today* or *just for tonight*. At the same time, her body wants to have fun.

"I will come to fetch you by 7:00 p.m.," Valerie maintains, leaving Corey in a catch22.

The day of the party, Corey takes a bath, dresses up in a pink tank top and a skirt that matches and waits for Valerie.

I will never give Valerie a coin phone call, promises Corey. She creates spiritual excuses and prays, *Oh Lord, if you do not want me to go with Valerie, please do not let her come.* Corey casually prays instead of giving Valerie a firm *yes* or *no* answer obeying her inner convictions.

Concurrently she vows, *Should Valerie come; I will go with her and would never do what God would not want me to do prematurely, and will witness about God to the people that I meet.* Oh, foolish Corey.

As agreed upon, Valerie comes on time. Valerie has the determination to derail Corey. They walk through the covered passageway and across the campus, passing a busker singing an old childhood song. The busker eyes Corey aggressively.

O be careful little feet where you go
O be careful little feet where you go
There is a Father up above
And He is looking down in love
So, be careful little feet where you go

Corey stands motionless, listening to the challenging song that brought her up as a child. *It is better to return my feet to the campus.* Nevertheless, "We are late; we have to go," says Valerie as she drags Corey.

Corey keeps looking backward, glancing at the busker until she can no more see and hear him. "Where are you taking me? I have never been here," probes Corey.

Valerie twitters while flashing a phony smile. "You will be fine, and I will tell you when you reach there."

Finally, they enter a high-rise building. The elegant building is familiar, but Corey has never been inside; she does not know what transactions go on there. It is bright, and a concierge stands by the elevators. Corey still has fresh memories of that day.

She remembers every detail and feels it as if it happened just yesterday.

Corey, Valerie, Lupita Lopez, other three women and accompanying men arrive at about the same time. Each girl hooks up with one welcoming young man. In total, six men, six women, and six bottles; the number is familiar: 666. The other mates, including Valerie, are not ashamed to do wild, sensual, caressing acts right from the start.

Corey hooks up with one man. However, she pledges to herself, *I am not going to let him touch me. I am not his wife.* She certainly knows that she should not touch or be touched by someone who is not her officially wedded husband.

Straightaway and without any warm-up or dialog, the man coerces, pats, and pesters her inappropriately, as if she were his wife.

"Stop it! I am getting out of here," she sternly prompts. He is very pushy and is deaf to what Corey speaks. It is AMNON MASON. Amnon who is a groper, tries to make a move to kiss her, just pushing himself on her and in return, she pushes his face away, "Stop it," she retorts.

"Why?"

"No," she restates, trying to play it cool. She is not quite sure if she really wants him to stop because she feels she needs a kiss, no more beyond that, though. The moment he gets near her, she internally senses butterflies hovering in her being because nobody has ever been so close as to kiss her. That is not all; he sits with her, puts his arm around her, touches her body, but she moves his arm away.

After several futile attempts, Corey feels like giving up, telling Amnon to take his hands from her body. The worst thing is that she still stays in the room instead of running out. Although she does not like what he is doing and wants to remain a virgin until marriage, at the same time she wants to prove to Valerie and other girls that she is a desirable, hot woman.

Some girls consistently taunt her for not being outgoing despite her phenomenal looks.

Upon seeing Corey's resistance, *Valerie, what kind of wild girl you brought today?* Amnon leaves but comes back right away. "Here we go," he says, offering her a bottle of wine.

"Thanks, Amnon. However, I have never had an alcoholic drink. I am not going to have it," Corey insists.

"I have never had a drink, either. Are you a spiritually committed person?"

The answer is obviously *yes*. It could let her go home peacefully. However, she does not feel comfortable saying it, in order not to offend Amnon. Instead, she pronounces, "I am allergic to wine."

"How could you be allergic to wine, when you just said that you have never tried it?"

"I mean I do not like it," she says, correcting herself.

"Let us have a little *just for today*," he insists. She boldly turns down the drink offer. It is good for her.

Meanwhile, Amnon continues pestering her body. She resists yet does not vocalize it seriously. She resists hesitantly to the point of letting him take off her pink underwear. "I promise I am not going to hurt you," he buzzes, and she trusts the mugger to keep her safe. As the situation progresses, he lays her down on the squeaky couch, spreading himself on top of her.

"Amnon, you promised you were not going to hurt me. What're you doing?" she asks.

"Of course, I swear I am not going to hurt you," he insists for the second time.

Meanwhile, he continues to press more. Once more, she resists, but she does not do so seriously. Afterward, Corey endures irritable, demanding, and painful minutes. Then he rests on top of her, motionless.

"Yes! He did it," Valerie shouts.

With the same ease, Amnon caresses Corey's virgin bosom and pours out his lust on her. It feels like it did not happen. However, the stains witness, it certainly did happen. It is too late to undo it.

Corey is confused and does not know what to do. Valerie and the others are making fun of her. She weeps hysterically for tampering with her one-time irreversible, delicate membrane, her God-given gift. It happens in a place, at a time, and with a person that it should not have. She walks to the bathroom to wash, and nobody comes to her rescue.

The moment she comes out of the bathroom, all others except for Amnon have left.

Amnon appears to be guilty about what has happened, and he is beating himself up.

"I did it again," he has frequently stated with an identifiable fake smile. He bows his head and gives Corey a consoling hug. "I am sorry. I did not mean to do that. *It just happened*. The situation was irresistible, and I had to surrender. However, no matter what, I will be there for you," he fumbles sweet-talk assurance. "It is going to be all right. Soon you will forget the guilt and will rush for more of the same behavior."

In the midst of her grief, Corey declares, "This is a one-time mistake. I will repent and never do such a thing again. I am not that kind of person."

Little does she know that the momentary foolishness could prompt her to sniff for more unless she *diverges* and renews her pledge.

Corey's remarks enrage Amnon. Then he belittles her. "That is what the failed people say when they casually cross the boundary they set or one set for them. Now, I have another appointment at this place. I want you to stand up and get out of here right now!" he commands.

Corey wants more time to nurse her wounds; however, he will not let her. Pushing her away is worse than what he has already done to her. She walks back to campus disappointed.

In such a simple way, she crosses a boundary that she promised herself she would not approach until marriage. The main concern she has as she walks back to the campus is *Am I pregnant or will I have an STD?* They were not ready for it, or rather she was not ready for it. They did it without birth control protection. She betrays herself, her faith community, her future spouse, and God. As Corey pours out her painful story, Hayet says, "I understand what you mean. However, remember that it is not the end of the world. You may fall seven times, but remember to rise seven times, rectify your wrong, and resume your stalled life journey."

Corey frequently shrugs her shoulders and sobs, wiping her wet eyes and runny nose by the edge of the blue towel. She takes sharp breaths and lets them out with a lengthy huff.

The first outing with Valerie has devastated Corey. There is sufficient time to make it to the Campus Union fellowship and throw herself at the feet of Jesus in the presence of the brethren. However, she feels dirty, unholy, unfaithful, and unworthy to join the group that has a clear stand about premarital relationships that for a year she taught, the untimely biblical violation that she has just committed.

Listening to Corey's story, Hayet understands that Corey has been through a lot. To encourage her to diverge, he urges, "Corey, you have got to bury your past behind you, or else it will bury you."

"How could I forget? It happened to me. I will always remember until I find someone who will turn my mourning into gladness, giving me comfort and joy, taking away the sorrow that I have embraced."

"Only Jesus can do that, not the men that you have been seeking temporal satisfaction from. Besides, yesterday's sin should not haunt and control your today and your tomorrow. What you must do is to diverge, confess, shake it off, and continue your life, beauty for the ashes. God will bring forth great achievement out of the hurtful condition that you have been in. God loves you so much and does not want you to settle for less important achievements. Besides, I have one more song for you. It is Laura Story, 'Blessings.'" The song reflects the idea that sometimes God uses trials, pains, tears, and brokenness to speak to us to accept his wisdom, receive His blessings, and take us to where we belong.

"Thank you for the song," Corey says appreciatively. She wishes to forget, but she cannot. Her wrongdoing seems as if it will haunt her for all the days of her life. That is not the only thing. Days after the experience with Amnon, the guilty feeling distances her from the affirming fellowship. Eventually, she throws in the towel and continues doing the same thing more often; it finally becomes an insatiable habit.

Gradually, Corey embraces teachings that come through hypocritical liars, whose consciences seared as with a hot iron. These liars are not ashamed to hold other people to some higher standards than they hold themselves. They teach the purity of relationship ideals but fail to live up to them and engage in the same behaviors they condemn others for. The more Corey spends time with these hypocrites, the more she compromises with the godly influences that she loved while growing up. Eventually, she learns to love a promiscuous behavior that will never satisfy her and considers it enjoyable. She mercilessly consumes multiple men's lives, then wipes her mouth and takes her perverted action for smartness, adamantly saying, *"What is wrong with that?"*

Corey refuses to diverge to her reverent upbringing. Even after serious counseling and the relentless pleadings of another aspiring cool girl previously known as DEMON.

Chapter 22

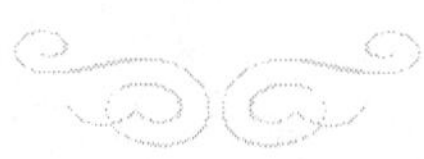

You can never fall too hard, so fast, so far that
you cannot get back when you are lost.

— *Unspoken, Who You Are*

It turns out that Corey has delivered Demon from an addictive, promiscuous lifestyle to purposeful living, yet she refuses to embrace Demon's help to *diverge* when the tables are turned.

Hayet hears from Corey that Demon had a difficult childhood, her unwed mother informing the father, "I am pregnant."

"I do not want an illegitimate child," he says and disappears from Demon's mother's, KELLY ROBB'S, presence for good. The irresponsible mother carries the pregnancy without any support from the man who shunned fatherhood responsibility.

On the day Demon's mother, Kelly, gives birth to her, her grandmother cuts the cord, washes her with water and wraps her in a swaddling cloth. She is despised and unwanted before birth as well as right from conception. No one cares or has compassion for her but God.

Kelly does all that is possible and expected of a responsible parent to protect her daughter. Kelly protects her daughter from the unfortunate events that befall on her. Kelly provides the best education a parent can give to a child. The little girl proves to be brilliant, having an analytical brain.

By the time she goes into middle school, she grows as quick as sunflowers as she enters puberty. Her breasts form a little, though not fully mature, and her hair has grown tremendously. During those days, Kelly becomes so busy working sixteen hours per day, seven days a week, that she barely sees her daughter.

"I do not want you to have a mother like mine and eat welfare food the way I did," Kelly cries. By saying so, Kelly ensures that her daughter has bread to eat and a home in which to lay her head.

Kelly comes home from work totally worn out, and she immediately goes to sleep before the routine of waking up early in a few hours for the next day. In the moments Kelly sees her daughter, she says, "Be careful and do not do what I did. I did not take advantage of the educational open door; I prioritized fun over fulfillment; that is why I have to work while standing for sixteen hours every day. My friends the ones that made a good choice, stayed faithful to their education work a few hours a day, which earns them more than enough money for their needs and wants. Operate by the fear of God, prioritize your life, and serve others in fairly and justly."

"You do not trust me, Mother?" Demon habitually replies as she dazzles with jewelry, arm bracelets, necklaces, rings, and earrings that Kelly, her only provider, did not buy. The unearned gifts are an early warning that she is receiving gifts for which she did not work.

Demon's academic excellence and beauty make her popular in the school and the neighborhood. She attracts multiple visitors, of whom her mother would not approve, and who arrive at her house as early as a minute after her mother leaves for work. Demon stays home, spending time with uninvited visitors instead of attending classes.

Consequently, she lags in her schoolwork.

Her guests are a new breed of generation slackers that does not understand the value of education. Their ancestors were heroes and heroines, who fought for their rights and those of others. However, they give birth to sons and daughters that are not as industrious as their ancestors were. The new-generation fathers do not understand the use of belts. The fathers sag their trousers and the mothers whale tail; their children do the same as their parents. They wear pants that sag so that the top is below the waist, revealing much of their underwear. Demon learns from her suitors how to dress up out of age, indecently. She whale tails: her pants reveal her underwear. When she stoops and bends, she exposes above the trousers for people behind to see her whale tail.

Demon becomes pregnant before she is a teenager. It is a shock for her hardworking mother, who has done her best to keep her daughter from such calamities. Her friends and family give various "legal" suggestions and options for ending the pregnancy so that she may be able to complete her schooling.

"The legality of terminating the pregnancy does not make it right. I refuse to victimize the baby, be it now or even after birth. Every year, we murder about one million unborn children. I am not going to be one of such and make the second evil," Demon declares, carries the baby, and gives birth to a son on a weekend.

The following Monday, "My dear, you have made untimely choices, and you have to reap what you sow; go to school," orders Kelly.

Demon has only one choice. That is to obey and go to school. She is tired and sore from giving birth. As she grudgingly exits the house, "I hate you," she yells wildly, to the point the students at the school bus stop could hear, causing them to take a glance toward her house in contempt.

Kelly has a right to give an appropriate response. Instead, the heartbroken mother, "Father, forgive her, for she does not know what she is saying," cries, devastated by her daughter's inappropriate cussing.

"In the future, for the very thing that you hate me now, you will love me," declares Kelly.

That is not all; as she enters the school bus, "Good morning," greets the school bus driver with a sincere smile.

"I hate you. Get out of my face," she screams, pouring out her displaced aggression as she sits out of her assigned seat.

The driver has a right to write her up. Instead, he says, "Thank you, God bless you, and I love you! I want you to remember in the end, after wasting years of your life, eventually, you will do what is right."

She is very scruffy. Her disorganized, wiry hair spread all over her face and shoulders just like that of a newborn's hair. Leaning her head on the window, *God, why would you let this thing happen to me?* she cries, amassing tears.

"A person's own folly leads to their ruin, yet their heart rages against the Lord," replies one of the hypocritical students who had an encounter with her, while the gossiping girls spread their venomous whisper.

As the students exit, "My dear, remain behind," orders the driver. "I want you to wipe your tears, have a smile, and fix your hair before you exit. Know that God loves you and this is not the end of the world. Be strong. Please do not show even a single outburst of anger toward anybody lest you be put into trouble."

As she fixes her hair in a ponytail style, she wipes her tears and sniffles. "I am sorry for what I have just said," she apologizes, as she receives the first loving hug since she got pregnant.

"You are welcome. You can take more napkins."

"No, I do not need anymore. You have dried up my tears and returned my smile by your encouragement."

Demon walks in the schoolyard as a mother. Frankly speaking, it is a hellish experience. Yet the driver's encouragement helped her to overcome the gossip and the discouragement of the day, regardless of her sitting and walking isolated.

Deep in her soul, she regrets the mistakes she has made. However, it is impossible to undo them. The worst part is that she refuses to admit and apologize to her mother for her wrongdoings.

Shortly after the birth of her son, she invites multiple boys, one at a time, to take a paternity test, though it is in vain. After eleven tests, she is unable to identify the father of her baby.

Subsequently, her mother announces, "My beloved, for your arrogance you deserve punishment. However, Jesus paid the price to make me who I am and forgave me; I want to do the same and give you a second chance."

Kelly employs a wet nurse for the grandchild. Additionally, she cuts her work hours to take care of Demon's baby. The pregnancy and the birth of her child have slowed Demon's behavior for a little while, but not all together. Before the baby is weaned, Demon continues spreading her legs with increasing promiscuity to anyone who comes to her. Nevertheless, due to her mother's unwavering support, she completes school and enters college, where she meets Corey.

At college, the moment Corey sees Demon, she feels pity for her. Demon is weary and lives like an unleashed dog left to run out of control.

Although Demon has a different lifestyle than Corey, mysteriously, she loves Corey. Corey frequently eats lunch with Demon. Whenever they meet, they happen to read Ezekiel 16 and John 4.

"Last night's outing was terrible. I hate my meaningless existence."

"What happened?"

"I almost died," desperately says Demon before she takes a bite.

While Demon is chewing, "Listen, Demon," Corey says, "You may be having what you call fun right now, but in the end, you should do what is right. You need to diverge toward God. Let your past stop with you."

"What do you mean, having fun? Didn't I just say it was terrible?" Corey cryptically ignores that question and plows on.

"You have lived such a life for years. Let that kind of living end with you, and do not let your descendants inherit any of that. Resolve to prepare your life for a better future."

"How?"

"I am going to tell you. What you need is a sincere lover who'd lay down His life for you. The men that you go with will drain your heart and tear you apart. However, the lover that I would like to introduce you to will soothe your wounds inflicted by other men. The physical aspect and enjoyment of sleeping with men is temporal; while the spiritual aspect of it goes far beyond that, you cannot forget and break up from those men. Your body does not belong to any man until he legally marries you."

"I own my body and can do whatever I want to do with it."

"Not really. God owns you and one day, you will give an account of how you lived your life. I know a woman from a place called Samaria who lived as she wished. She had five men in her life. The sixth she had also is just like the previous five. If she were to live that kind of life, she would have reached probably one hundred or so, and at the end, she would have gained nothing. However, one day she meets the genuine lover and she instantly breaks up from the depleting kind of relationships she had once and for all. The genuine lover accepts her with all of her imperfections; she becomes His, and He becomes hers, sealing their love with an unending covenant."

"I wish I could get such a lover," Demon replies. "That would be enough for me. I do not think I deserve such lover because I have gone much further than that woman has. Besides, he may not be interested in my kind of dirty person."

"He is, if you are willing to be His alone."

"It looks like you want to set me in an arranged relationship. As the woman from Samaria remains settled in such a kind of relationship, I would be willing to be his, and his alone if he would be willing to be mine alone, too."

"Yes, He will be yours and accept you with all your inadequacies. The woman of Samaria was satisfied by the genuine love and she hysterically goes on telling everyone of her new relationship to all the people of her country to start the same relationship."

Corey's instruction about the genuine lover cuts Demon to the heart, and she longs to find such a relationship.

Demon says, "Corey, what shall I do? I am fed up with this kind of madness. It has got to be stopped."

"Repent, return, diverge, and abandon your old ways and you will be accepted as a new creation by the sincere and genuine lover. His name is Jesus."

"That kind of relationship I would like to have. Let us make a deal, though. I will stop drinking, smoking, putting myself first, taking advantage of the weak, and any other bad habits. Can you allow me to keep only one, which is going out and sleeping with men, which will be the hardest of all to quit? That would be a great thing."

"To begin with, I do not make the rules; God does. I am as weak person as you are. If you keep your best to yourself, you will not get any benefit from God. God gave us His best, and in return, He expects you to lay what you love most at the feet of the cross and sacrifice it. Then He blesses your sacrifice and gives you back many more folds to be a blessing to others. Moreover, if you pile up preconditions you will never be able to get answers to your questions. You just come to God with all your imperfections as you are, and He will accept as well as wash you clean."

"Wash me with what?"

"It is good to know that He gave himself up for you to make you holy, cleansing with water through the Word that became flesh, and to present you to Himself as a radiant bride, without stain or wrinkle or any other blemish, but holy and blameless. Once you get washed by accepting Him, you will never seek temporal satisfaction from men, for He will satisfy your hunger the way He did to the Samaritan woman, who found her wholeness in the same lover."

"I do not deserve the kind of lover that you are talking about. Let me make it clear to you who I am and what I did before I make the first move."

"You do not have to tell me. God knows your every whim. The day you encounter Him, you will shout, 'Come, see a man who told me all I ever did in bewilderment.'"

"Okay, what about if He refuses to accept me for being extremely unworthy?"

"I guarantee you, to seek and save that which was filthy is the main reason why He came to the earth. You are the best candidate to receive His grace, mercy, love, and forgiveness. With your return, angels will rejoice in heaven and you will find overflowing peace and rest."

"That is what I am lacking. I cannot sleep during the night or even the day. Besides, if I come with the habits that I cannot abandon, what will happen to the habits?"

"You just come to Him as you are, cast all of your cares upon Him, and He will carry them for you. If you return to Jesus, He will remake you. If you remove wickedness from your life and dispense your chunks to the dust, your high-quality gold to the rocks in the ravines, then the Lord will be your gold, the best inheritance for you. Then you certainly will find happiness in Him. You will pray to Him and He will hear you. By doing so, you shall be blessed and be a blessing to others," explains Corey.

The moment Demon hears Corey's explanation, one side of her feels guilty and another side of her feels hopeful to be receiving peace. Then, "Well, I am in," Demon promises, signaling her intention to diverge.

"My family history has endless sad chapters," resolves Demon.

"The endless sad chapters of life do not have to be your future. God can stop the generational garbage here and now. You do not have to pass the sad chapters that you inherited from your ancestors to your offspring. You can begin a new chapter."

"I like your idea. I will *diverge*, accept, and walk that route," she says, and proves it true by her walk.

As a result of Corey's friendship as a good Christian witness, she delivers and transforms Demon from her despicable, addictive, and promiscuous lifestyle a couple of months before Demon's graduation. That is when she earns the nickname Demon, which they intend to mean Delivered Demon. Her real name is RAHAB ROBB.

Rahab *diverges* and shows a radical change, becomes a fruitful citizen. Right after graduation, the college hires her and she becomes a resident advisor, replacing Dr. Zack Thompson, who has left to start his own business.

Rahab does not wait for the students who need help to come to her; she goes, searches, finds, and rescues others, even by going out of state, if necessary. She snatches the lost, depressed, and confused from the flames of aborted destiny. She shows mercy to still others, but does so with great caution, hating the sins that contaminate their lives. Rahab is perfectly made for the RA position. Because of her role, the dropout rate falls nearly to zero. There is nothing more beautiful than when an employer becomes free from prejudice and lie-synthesis. Consequently, if everyone fits in the right place, doing the right thing in the course of life, there would be peace and no more war in the world.

Too late is better than never, and Rahab embraces God's Positioning System for her life.

Afterward, Rahab is indoors—no more going out without a purpose. At the end of the school year, SCOTT PIERS, one of the prodigals that Rahab delivered to diverge from a wasted life, proposes to be her soul mate. As a result of her return, Rahab envisions a bright future. The proposed marriage would make her the only person legally married in the family. In her family, her uncles, aunts, their children, grandchildren, their parents, grandparents never married and gave birth to children who would also do the same. The inclusion and acceptance of God's plan in her life could make her a historic person among her kin.

"There is one condition," declares Rahab to Scott. "I have lived a wasted life and do not want to live such again. I will not touch or allow any man to touch me until the day I get married. Would you agree to affirm my pledge?"

"That is what is expected of delivered people. I was about to tell you of the same intention. We are in the same boat," affirms Scott.

That is not all. The initial day she turns herself from her old ways, her father appears on the campus and for the first time she meets him. Rahab never had a father-daughter relationship. She has until now hated anything that had to do with fatherhood because she never had one. However, the day she turns her heart toward God, she finds not only her biological father but also a Father who is more concerned about her than her natural father is.

As Rahab enjoys God's Father-daughter relationship, her father appears and declares, "I am your father."

Immediately, she jumps into his arms joyfully for a genuine and loving hug such as she has never had. She wraps her arms around his shoulder like a toddler for a good number of minutes, weeping uncontrollably.

As the rejoicing cools down, her father speaks in tears of laughter.

"I never fathomed that you would accept and embrace me as such. What made you accept mi in such loving way? I am deeply sorry for abandoning you."

"I found a loving Father who forgave all my wrongdoings and accepted me as I am, with all my filthy behaviors. I should do the same. Besides, I have been without a father for over two decades. I do not want to be fatherless again."

Meanwhile, the Campus Union chaplain, Dr. MICHAEL OLSEN, friends, and resident advisor Rahab advise Corey to turn away from her newly adopted direction. However, she distances herself from the loving community. The best move is to admit her wrongdoing and *diverge* from her wayward ways. Instead, she believes the new lifestyle is cool and goes on a promiscuity fling, involved in despicable deeds worse than any that Rahab ever partook of.

On one of those days, a Friday early evening, Corey dresses in a golden mini skirt that reveals her hourglass curvy figure. Her waist up and hips are proportionate to each other. Her upper body as well is balanced with the length of her lavish thighs and hairless legs on which she wears high-heeled golden shoes. As a stylish lean woman with seamless body composition, she knows how to choose the type of outfit for the season that enhances and puts emphasis on her natural waistline. *Do I look fit to be seen?* As she combs her golden auburn hair while applying facial makeup to match, she glances at her entire body in the oval dorm mirror as she figures out a smile that amplifies her beauty. She is ready to go out for a couple of parties.

Previously, Corey used to tell others, "Dress modestly; the way you dress on the outside expresses your inside. Be careful that the exercise of your rights does not become an obstacle to the weak. For if someone with a weak conscience sees you, with all your knowledge, practicing or eating in an idol's temple, will not that person be encouraged to eat what is sacrificed to idols? Therefore, your failure of practical application of your knowledge destroys this weak brother or sister, for whom Christ died. When you sin against them in this way and wound their weak conscience, you sin against Christ. Therefore, if what I eat or how I dress up causes my brother or sister to fall into sin, I will never eat meat or dress up indecently again, so that I will not cause them to fall." Now, all she does is the opposite of how she used to teach just living for herself, not minding others or God.

Due to Corey's influence, Rahab currently dresses up as beautifully and decently as any woman should. As their difference grows wider Rahab says tersely, "Corey, I want to talk to you not as a resident advisor, but as a sister. It is not a secret what you have been doing. I want you to be aware that your family will fall into dysfunction and disintegrate because of you."

"Ha-ha," Corey laughs out loud. "My parents established their marriage on a solid rock. It will never happen," scorns Corey.

Contrary to Corey's word, however, her family *is* on the verge of disintegration due to Corey's abrupt insane behavior. The joy of the family is gone; her parents were not on speaking terms. One parent blames the other for not doing enough to protect her. In reality, it is Corey, who is to blame for her untimely choices.

"First, believe it or not, if dysfunction and disintegration did not happen so far, but because of you, it will. Second, I want you to tell me the exact words that you used to rescue me from my wasted life. Possibly, the words might ignite the dwindling gospel light in you."

Corey for sure knows the exact words that she used to deliver Rahab, yet she struggles to hide.

"By living an immoral life the way I used to, you have shown utter contempt for the Lord's name and Christianity. There are good numbers of guiltless citizens and foreigners that are searching for good examples to imitate, looking for righteousness, an intentional person to show them the Way. Due to your failures to show the Truth and virtue, some innocent people get lost at home; while others leave our shores to become Jihadists and Jihadi brides; by killing innocent people think they are offering a service to God. You failed to show your inheritance the right Way, the Truth, and the Life. You are responsible for the lost lives and the ones that stumble because of you. God wrote in the Bible, I do not know where exactly though, the unbelievers shall turn to you, but you shall not turn to them. If we do not show them the Way, they will show us their way, which will be hard to overcome. Instead, you are embracing an unbeliever's lifestyle."

Because of her deviation, the favor of God in Corey's life vanishes in the manner it did with Samson of the Bible.

Corey habitually testifies about God to any people she meets, no matter the place. To one group of students she says, "You have to become a Christian to find true life."

While the others stare one another, a courageous student answers her with a question.

"What do you mean when you say so? Does it mean people that are not Christians cannot find true life?"

"What I mean is that there is true life and happiness that never ends, which makes one seek happiness in no one else but in God."

"Do you have that true life, happiness and if so how has that benefited you?"

Everything departed since the day I went out with Valerie. "It is a promise given by God. Whether I have it or not and whether it has benefited me or not it all depends on me."

"Honestly, there is no absolute truth and life, only the truth and life that one happens to believe. What you believe does not make it superior to what I believe. It all depends on what and how you define true life."

Corey previously used to answer obviously for such questions. However, now because of living mixed-up life, she is not sure to do so.

"Besides, I have known you for some time. You do all that we do."

"What do you mean?" asks Corey assuming that he does not know all about her.

"You do ice, I mean drugs, and we do. You fornicate and we also do. You drink alcoholic drinks and we as well do. What is the difference between you a

Christian and others? If becoming a Christian makes me be a hypocrite like you, I do not want it. I live better than you do."

"You have to look to Jesus, not on me."

"How can I look to Jesus that I do not know while the one who claims to know Him does not live showing His principles?"

Rahab lovingly rebukes Corey. Although she does not admit it, Corey is confused.

Rahab is worried for Corey's well-being.

"There is a problem in your thinking. You should be mentally drained. A normal person would not do what you have been teaching others not to do."

"A normal girl who wants to be cool, well known, and popular as you were, grows up and frequently does what she taught others not to do."

"That is hypocrisy, risking your health and your future for misguided perception. What you have to strive for is to be knowledgeable, not to be known, because being well known does not make you knowledgeable. The main reason people, mainly celebrities, terribly fail in life is because they are well known but not knowledgeable. Moreover, strive to make God known, and in return, He will make you everlastingly known. Over and above that, if the kind of life where you delivered me from is the way to be popular and a cool girl, why did you deliver me from that kind of life? By the way, do you know who the most popular people on campus are?"

"Girls like you are popular," Corey replied. "The reason I feel this way is that when I see girls flirting with boys, my way of life makes me feel like I am not even worth it to boys so I do not want my spirit to be crushed. My friends dropped me. I became the only college student without a friend. I frequently have to agree to go out with whoever picks me up to find favor and make someone happy."

"First, this is a bad reason because giving or losing a part of yourself just to make someone you do not have a covenant with happy is not a noble reason. A noble woman makes noble plans and by noble deeds she stands."

"What is second?"

"Second, favor is freely given, not earned. Moreover, you do have the favor of God that gives you an everlasting love and the sincerely caring family of brethren in the Campus Union fellowship, which you cannot find anywhere else. Therefore, since such a great cloud of witnesses surrounds you, throw off the misguided perception that hinders and the sin that so easily entangles you. Run with perseverance the race marked out for you, fixing your eyes on Jesus, the author and finisher of faith. For the joy set before Him, He endured the cross, scorning its shame, and sat down at the right hand of the throne of God. Consider Him who endured such opposition from sinners more than you do, so that you will not grow weary, lose heart, and have a crushed will and spirit."

"I hear what you say, but I want to enjoy life. Being popular makes me feel like I am pretty, noticeable, and cool—not just a well-dressed girl."

"Not really. First, men who reduce your value do not determine your worth. God determines your worth; He demonstrates His own love for you in this: While you were still a sinner, Christ died for you. Second, the most popular shining-star students on campus that others honestly would envy are not the yes-girls that go out with everybody or the same boys. It is the chaste girls like you and boys like Hayet who live intentionally, focusing on academic, social, and spiritual life, while offering help to others. Previously, everybody wanted to befriend you. Now, because of your deviation, you have lost your value and your new nickname is surfacing."

"What nickname?" asks Corey in surprise.

"Fallen Angel."

"You need to return to where, what and who you left to get what you left. A prostitute is paid by her suitors, but you give presents to all your lovers and bribe them to come from everywhere to sleep with you, and none of them satisfies you. What a shameful girl! You saved others, but you could not save yourself. Perhaps you need to see a specialist or a physician."

"I do not need to see anybody. I am fine the way I am. This is the way to be cool. And what are you talking about, a specialist? What specialist can work on me?" Corey laughs.

"You for sure know the specialist, for you have seen Him operate. He caters to every part of your life and does not charge you a penny. He paid all your debt in advance. He uses a remote access word, which is sharper than any double-edged sword that penetrates even to dividing soul and spirit, joints and marrow, that judges the thoughts and attitudes of the heart and heals the inner being. The same specialist healed the woman who was bleeding for twelve years. The specialist is the one who gave the Samaritan woman living waters. He is the same one who set the woman caught in adultery free from the accusers that came to stone her, to whom a forgiven woman poured an alabaster jar of very expensive perfume. He changed my life from the ungodly practices that eclipsed my name for years, Delivered Demon, to Rahab. This specialist is the Doctor of Doctors, the Judge of Judges, the King of Kings, and the Lord of Lords. His name is Jesus," shouts Rahab.

How fast did Rahab learn about all these divine revelations? wonders Corey. On her new failed avenue of life, Corey is dissatisfied with herself for her irrational actions. Nevertheless, she will not admit defeat and return with her tail between her legs.

Rahab dearly wants to see Corey's transformation. If Corey could wait patiently, God would fulfill her heart's desires with gratification.

"Wait on the Lord, for He has good plans for and in you. Then you will experience fullness in your life. Patience gives God the consent to do His will in your life. Do not go ahead of Him. Follow His guidance. He loves you so much to give you minor satisfactions," says Rahab.

Corey knows the appropriate answer; she has heard it come out of the mouths of many sinners before: yes, Lord, I have done wrong and come as I am. Accept me and forgive me for my wrongdoing. However, she is silent.

Corey plainly knows all that Rahab is saying, yet she chooses to be silent.

At that instant, Rahab cries piteously for she knows what Corey is yearning for, the wasted kind of life from which God had delivered her.

Rahab, please don't cry, you are making me guilty and jealous. "I have a deep, deep wound that nobody can heal."

"Trust me, there is no wound that Jesus cannot heal, because He is the healer. He will take your wounds and make scars. He, himself has a lot of memorable scars. Jesus' wound is much deeper than yours. He was despised and rejected by mankind, He was oppressed and afflicted, nails and a spear pierced through His arms, feet and His side. The wounds were verified by Thomas the doubter, who put his finger on the wounds and saw the hands, he reaches out his hand and put it into His side. Jesus' as well as your wounds and scars are testimonies of the past to redeem others for a better future."

Corey twiddles numbly.

"Please say the words that rescued me," Rahab persists.

"I am not going to say any of those words. If you want, go and read Ezekiel chapter 16 and John chapter 4," fumbles Corey.

Corey shrugs her shoulders. "Your body is the temple of God, not a toy for men. The men pursuers will say sweet talk and do all that will make you happy until they get what they want from you. The moment they get what they want from you or perhaps impregnate you, you will never see them again, giving you shame that you will have to carry for the rest of your life. That is what I am doing. Take a note, in the end, after wasting years of your life, eventually, you will do what is right."

"What do you mean?"

"If you do not do what you are supposed to do willfully when you are able, eventually you will be forced to do it and you are not going to like it."

You are right, Rahab.

"I am telling you the truth since I have been there. If you want to do what you have been doing, get married legally, and then you date for life. I cannot tell you how filthy and hurtful the deeds you have been doing are to see them when God opens your eyes."

"That is fun."

"Corey, hurting yourself is not fun. Even if you forget about the spiritual aspect of life, if you look at it from a medical point of view, many things can hurt you. During the years of my foolishness, whenever I went to see a doctor I was always concerned what she would find in me. Now that I have settled the matter with God, my sins were like scarlet, they have been washed by the blood of the lamb of God, and they are white as snow. My sins were as red as crimson; they are now as white as wool. To tell you the truth, I am reaping the consequences of my foolishness and I do not like it."

"Such as what?"

"For my thoughtless choices, the doctors say, unless there is a miracle, I will never be able to give birth," pours out Rahab. Nevertheless, at this point in her tale, Corey is at a point of no return that could cost her dearly.

Chapter 23

In the end you should always do the right thing even if it is hard.

— Nicholas Sparks, *The Last Song*

Corey tells Hayet how she fell from the grace of God that had sustained her. As time goes by, her grief over swapping her V card subsides. She not only embraces the fact but also searches for the same thing that she reluctantly did with Amnon.

Meanwhile, in the early days of the deviation, Corey attends a Sunday service. A man called ELTON MIDDLETON, their youth coordinator, who walks in godly ways, whom people call a mouthpiece of God, says, "Corey, the spirit of fornication is attacking you. It is better for you to return to where you belong to find yourself where you got lost before it is too late. God has greater plans for you and hates to see you settle for less."

Corey becomes embarrassed. The embarrassment is not for disobeying one of the Ten Commandments, "You shall not commit adultery," or why she forsook her decent upbringing, no kiss before marriage. It is amplified as every congregant stares at her questioningly. It appears as if she is the only person doing such immoral premarital activities. Elton is the first to cast a stone at her. Immediately, her normally serene and pleasant appearance changes and her expression is distorted in an all-overwhelming anger. Her nostrils widen, her eyes flash like lightning, as Elton's remarks enrage her. Outrage controls her emotions.

The moment the congregation is dismissed, Corey walks all alone, humiliated, as if she has a communicable disease. In fact, what she is involved in is communicable. She got it from Valerie when she strayed from who she truly was. Valerie also got the same disease from JENNIFER PRESTON, and the list goes on. Abandonment of promiscuity is contagious, too.

Just as a hungry predator ambushes its prey, Corey waits for Elton by the concrete parking lot next to the broken stop sign.

"Preacher, thanks for embarrassing me in front of people that have a high regard for me. You will pay the price and regret the shame that you caused me when you missed the elegant villa that you have prepared for marriage and other bill payments. Certainly, you will not be here next week, and I will make sure there is no safe haven for you." Elton knows that he is in a big trouble.

"Corey, I know because of the influential lie-synthesis you have that you can have me fired from this position. However, I am convinced that what has been said is from God. It is for your good, and I am not scared of what you can and will do. The genuineness of my innocence shall justify me in admiration, exaltation, and diligence when the truth reveals itself. Then the harm that you threaten to cause me shall embarrass you. Remember that I have the greatest attorney of all, who beats all attorneys and never charges me a penny for representing my case."

"We shall see who wins!" threatens Corey.

"My attorney: haven't you heard that the eternal God is my refuge, and underneath are His everlasting arms. He will drive out my enemies before me, saying, 'Destroy them!' You are fighting with my God, and you cannot stand against Him. You will surely come to ruin!" Elton asserts confidently.

"Also remember," he adds. "In the future, the very thing that you hate and persecute me for now, you will love me for."

Internally, Cory knows that Elton is the best kind of man that every woman dreams to have, *I wish I could have you but that is not going to be possible*. However, since she declared a war on him, and knowing the impossibility, "Not to you, Elton," replies.

Elton is wise and organized, lives an upright life, according to the Word of God. It is difficult to find fault in him. The only way to trap him is by making up false accusations.

In her foolishness, Corey rehearses all her lies, and she knows how to attack her prey even from among the church brethren. She approaches her prey in sheep's clothing, yet inwardly she is a ferocious wolf.

Corey is a hypocrite, who is like a whitewashed tomb, which on the outside appears to be beautiful and blameless. However, within her heart, she is full of dead men's bones and all uncleanness that God detests.

Corey is not yet done humiliating Elton. She wants to damage his emotions and reputation beyond repair. Right after the service, while the tears cascade, she approaches each of the church leaders separately and reports, "Elton molested me for several years. When I confronted him, saying that I will no longer be silenced, he spoke against me, lest I expose him."

Corey's report shocks and awes the elders and the whole congregation.

"Elton lied to us," says each of them in shock.

It is not Elton; it is I who lied to you! Corey's guilty conscience screams out.

The influential elders are jealous, spiritually blind, and have no personal relationship with Jesus and lack the spirit of discernment. They are more concerned with getting money and keeping the old traditions of the church that do not bring one sinner into a conviction or to a personal relationship through the message of repentance. In fact, they were looking for a reason to attack Elton. Now that they found one, they are happy. Elton challenged the double-standard elders to live according to the Word of God. They hate such statements.

The business administrator convenes an emergency meeting and catches up with Elton before he exits the parking lot.

"Excuse me, sir! We are having an emergency meeting and you are required to attend," the administrator informs him hurriedly as he catches his breath.

"Mr. JAMES STRONGMAN, in case you have forgotten, my name is Elton Middleton," shouts Elton angrily.

"My main concern is to convey the message to you, not the calling of your name, which has a bad reputation."

"I was there with you; why didn't you tell me earlier? I am coming. You just go ahead," Elton tells him as he follows.

Mr. Strongman sternly gawks at Elton, appearing ready to catch an escapee. "I want to ensure that you come to the meeting."

"I am not a thief; you do not have to wait for me," objects Elton. As he walks, following Mr. Strongman, "Hi, Mr. HILL'S family," calls out Elton, and he gestures to give a hug to the college student's daughters.

"No, you do not have to do that," protests Mrs. Hill, distancing her daughters from Elton, displaying an unrealistic smile.

"Mom, this is Elton," protests the junior Hill, who is the outspoken one of the family.

"Honey, I know what I am doing, didn't you hear what is going on?" reassures Mrs. Hill.

"We have to live per the Truth, not by lies invented by twisted defiant liars," speaks Hill junior, dissing Corey.

Lord, the war begins here, cries Elton, having seen Mrs. Hill, who used to connect her daughters to mentor them, instantly distancing them from him.

The yellow color painted conference room is located on ground floor, within the east side of the main sanctuary, where the somber bell stands. The room is secure and safe from all kinds of natural disasters and an unwanted intrusion. It is a building within a building. That is where employees are encouraged to run for safety during an emergency.

By the time Elton enters, dragging his feet, six out of seven elders, Corey, and Reverend RUSS HOLMS are seated around the boat-shaped brown conference table.

Everybody else is silent. However, Corey sobs, scattering her sinewy hair over her face. She most likely knows that if she were to look at the elders face to face, some of the discerning ones could read her face and declare her guilt. Elton pulls up a chair and takes a seat in front of Corey.

"I do not want to see the face of this monster," she protests in a coarse voice and walks barefoot and moves to the opposite end from Elton and sits on the floor.

Mr. Strongman walks holding a folder that Elton signed when he was hired. “The time is exactly one o’clock in the afternoon. As you all know, we called this emergency meeting because Elton displayed unchristian behavior to one of the people that we entrusted him to lead. There may be other victims too. Corey, please tell us what happened to you,” he invites in the same sentence.

“She already told you her version privately. Why would you want to hear it again? Please allow me to give my account,” protests Elton.

“We have heard you speak for many years. All that we need to hear is the truth from Corey. Elton, are you afraid? You should not have done what you are accused off,” mocks her uncle, Mr. ADAM STEINBECK, who is an influential chairman of the elder board.

“I am not afraid of what you will and could do. I speak the truth, and the truth shall set me free.”

“Well, we are going to hear the truth from Corey. Please tell us,” says her uncle.

Corey always has a double standard. At the church service, she put on a red backless dress that does not cover her back and shoulders. Right after the service and before she met the elders, she changed her backless apparel and put on a long golden embroidered one that covers up to her ankles. She has forgotten that long clothing covers her body, not her sins.

Dr. GERRY NGUYEN, who is the shortest of all the elders, appears to be uncomfortable and disturbed the way Corey acts. *The accusation does not make sense to me,* he whispers. He is a prayerful man, who has personally known Elton and Jesus for many years. He speaks boldly and is not afraid of anybody.

“To begin with, Corey, I want you to gather up your hair sit on the chair facing each one of us.”

“Doctor Nguyen, how do you expect a woman to behave whose heart is deeply disturbed to pour out her great anguish and grief to the elders? She is not vacationing to do what you expect her to do. She is a little girl. Do not take her for a wicked woman,” defends her uncle.

Thank you, Uncle, for defending me.

In the midst of the conversation, everybody keeps silent, giving time for Corey to speak.

"The man seated on the other end of the table," declares Corey in a trembling voice, pointing with her right hand in a sideways curve, and pauses. She never looks to the face of any of the people that she is speaking to.

"Corey, in case you have forgotten, my name is Elton Middleton," Elton says, protesting Corey's refusal to call out his name.

I do not want to call out your name.

She restlessly sobs, slathering her saliva and sniffles. The pause takes longer than it should, as she cries aloud.

As Dr. Nguyen challenges, "Okay, tell us what the man on the other end of the table did to you."

Suddenly, an extremely powerful reflective light, brighter than a sunshine slant at Corey through the door.

The relentless reflection put her in the spotlight and appears to press her to *speak the truth*. Corey's hands fumble over her head and face while wiping watery discharges off her forehead with the edge of her apparel.

"Okay, tell us what happened?" presses Dr. Nguyen, who still has more questions to ask.

"I am telling you that he molested me for several years."

"If he has been doing what you accuse him of for years, why did he choose to discontinue this time?"

"Ask him! Here he is," yells Corey.

"It is you who brought up the issue, and it is you who should answer."

Doctor, stop roasting me. I do not want to be exposed, drawls Corey. The more Corey is pressed, the bigger the lie becomes.

"I am having a hard time believing and connecting to what Corey is telling us," Dr. Nguyen says, showing his doubt by glancing to each of the attendants. "We all have known Elton for a long time. Has he ever done something like this? He has always proven himself to be a man of God, so this accusation seems made up to me." Dr. Nguyen looks at Corey with piercing eyes. Some of the elders appear to believe to what Corey is saying, while others do not. A vote that the elders usually take would determine the consensus of Elton's fate.

"Well, the decision does not rest on only your shoulders, Dr. Nguyen. Besides, as we all can see, Corey is being tormented over what has happened to her, whereas Elton displays no remorse whatsoever. Let us put this case to rest, voting either to fire or keep Elton. The business administrator will take over the voting session," announces the chairman.

"Well, as per the chairman's recommendation we shall take two brief votes. If your vote is 'Yea,' fire him, vote first. One, two, and three," the administrator counts. Then he resumes. "If your vote is 'Nay,' do not fire him, vote now," he opens the floor. Then, "One, two, and three," he counts.

"The vote is even, Mr. Chairman. Three yea and three nay."

Dr. Nguyen breathes a sigh of relief, hoping that Elton would keep his position and the revival to spread out far beyond the four corners of this church, as well as to the nations. However, the chairman is determined to fire Elton.

"Elton, do you admit to what you are accused of?" asks the chairman.

Elton knows that whether he admits or not, it will not make a difference. The reason is that, no matter what Elton replies, the chairperson will do what he intends to do with or without a vote, applying lie-synthesis. Thus, Elton chooses to give no answer.

"Elton, do you refuse to speak to us?" the chairperson asks. "Don't you know that we have power either to keep you or fire you?"

"You would have no power over my case if it were not given to you from above. However, no matter the outcome, the one who accused me to be judged by you is guilty of this innocent man's blood," Elton calmly replies without naming Corey.

Corey's uncle is greatly disturbed, unable to reason calmly. The vote did not go through as he had anticipated. He could circumvent the vote or create other ways to achieve his goal if he wants.

"Let us leave it here and pray about if before we take any action," Dr. Nguyen says to buy a time that could possibly save Elton from being fired.

"That is not going to happen. We have to help the offended, not protect the offender," her uncle insists wildly.

"Who is the offender and who is the offended?" Dr. Nguyen pours out his dilemma.

"I am the offended and that man is the offender," Corey says, pointing toward Elton.

"What proof do you have?"

"You have to trust what I am telling you. Because I am a woman."

"There are as many women liars as there are men."

"Doctor, why are you defending the accused offender?" the chairman questions.

"In my entire life and profession, I have never defended an offender. I am just speaking the truth that sets free. Perhaps the people that undercut the success and revival brought in our church wanting to discredit accomplishments and desiring to sidetrack God-loving employees should examine themselves as to whether they are defending the liar or not," Dr. Nguyen says.

The chairman knows that once Dr. Nguyen starts talking on what he believes is true, he will not budge. Therefore, Mr. Steinbeck takes another abrupt turn to cover up his misjudgment.

"Since this is an emergency meeting, we do not want to waste more time going back and forth. Let me make a phone call to elder Mr. THOMAS, who is on a business trip and see if he is willing to vote. If we cannot get hold of him, then we will make a final decision today somehow or wait until he returns tomorrow," he proposes.

Elton is aware that no good comes out of elder Mr. Thomas. For he knows that Thomas lacks a stability of character, and he is easily swayed by any wind of coercion.

"No, you cannot wait until tomorrow. My conscience has been ripped apart by this man," cries Corey.

"Mr. Strongman, please make the phone call," instructs the chairman.

Mr. Strongman clears his throat as he slides his revolving chair and grabs the new phone that is equipped with a speaker from the center of the table. He has a good memory of phone numbers. He dials the ten-digit number. The phone rings and rings.

Elton is relaxed; no anxiety is displayed on his face. Dr. Nguyen prays, *Lord if it is your will please do not let him pick up the phone.*

"Hello, this is Thomas. How may I help you," Mr. Thomas replies.

"How have you been doing, Thomas?" Mr. Strongman inquires.

"I am fine. My wife just called and informed me what the imposter did. How are you coping with it?"

The chairperson hijacks the phone call. "Mr. Thomas, we are at a crossroad in the history of our church. We are in a meeting to decide how to handle the issue. Six of the elders, the reverend, Corey, and Elton are here too. We want to take a vote to fire or keep Elton. We have three yea and three nay. Your vote is crucial to me," the chairperson says, coercing the coercible Thomas. Without courteous thinking, "Let him be crucified. Let him be fired," replies Mr. Thomas.

Mr. Thomas's reply does not surprise me, Elton laughs aloud.

"Thank you, sir. That is all we need to get from you. Be safe," concludes the chairman.

"Mr. Thomas's vote brings to a conclusion the votes, four yea and three nay. Thus the motion passed; we will fire Elton. Mr. Strongman will take over the rest of the action to be taken," announces the chairman.

"The truth is that, per the church bylaws, we cannot condemn people without investigating the allegation, before hearing them and finding out what they have done," protests Dr. Nguyen.

"I asked him and he chose not to answer."

"You did not give Elton as much time as you did to Corey."

"Before we end this meeting, Elton, do you have anything to say? Perhaps a confession to make?"

"Sir, you need to address such a question to your niece, not to me. History repeats itself. Esau got betrayed by his own brother and his own mother. Joseph got betrayed by his own brothers. Samson got betrayed by his so-called lover. The righteous Jesus as well was handed over to his people by God's deliberate plan and foreknowledge for good purpose. His own people with the help of wicked men betrayed and put him to death by nailing Him to the cross."

"Elton, who is wicked and who is not? Who is betraying who? Who is righteous and who is not? This is a serious matter," says the chairman, rapidly turning red face with little specks of spit flying from his mouth.

"Are you sure that you do not know the answer?"

The chairperson pauses going into deep thoughts. *If I say Corey is wicked in betraying him, with my help, he will ask me why I question his God-given authority. If I say Elton, you are righteous, the one who is being betrayed, he will challenge me as to why I defend the offender.* Thus, the chairperson chooses to answer, "I do not know; tell me the answer."

"If you do not tell me, neither will I tell you. However, one thing I do know. You shall know the Truth, who is a person. Then the Truth shall set you free from being a servant of the father of all lies," answers Elton.

Elton challenges the chairperson. To escape from further questioning, "Reverend, please close the session by the word of prayer," he invites.

"Reverend, before you pray I want to say a few things to you, Elton." Dr. Nguyen responds.

"There are going to be people and moments along your life journey who'll try to challenge your indisputable achievements. Never give up. Keep your eyes on God. Do not let the perverted twists of life detour you. Someday, when you get to where and what God has in store for you, you will look around and you will know that it was the Lord and your perseverance who put you there through paths that you would not choose, yet it was God's choice for your life. That will be the greatest joy to you and to the Lord."

The reverend stands to speak. "I understand that I have no voice over your vote. However, I would like to speak few words. I feel like we are in the days of Prophet Jonah. My prayer is just like that of the sailors that threw Jonah overboard: 'Lord, please do not let us die for taking this man's life. Do not hold us accountable for killing an innocent man, for you, Lord, have done as you pleased.' Our action might bring irreversible remorse on the offender like that of Judas Iscariot after he realized betraying an innocent man departed and went and hanged himself," he cries loudly.

The reverend's prayer is a big blow to Corey and the sneaky chairperson. Thus, "Reverend, you are making us guilty," the chairperson protests.

"Clever words will not cover up awful measures. Two wrongs do not make a right. It is your action that justifies or condemns you, not the words of my prayer," replies the reverend.

The business administrator furnishes a red sheet of paper, writes Elton's name, checks a couple of boxes and informs him, "Elton, we have terminated your employment because of the serious allegations made against you and because we cannot have a hypocrite lead the members of this church."

"Thank you and God bless you for firing me."

The administrator hands Elton a separation notice, thus applying a lie-synthesis. Dr. Nguyen previously witnessed practical application of the church bylaws serving every member justly. However, that law does not seem to apply to Elton's case. The firing from his job disqualifies him from receiving unemployment benefits. Corey has won, getting more than what she planned, though only for a time. She walks out of the meeting victorious on the outside but crushed with a haunting guilt and regret on the inside for intentionally hurting an undeserving young man.

Chapter 24

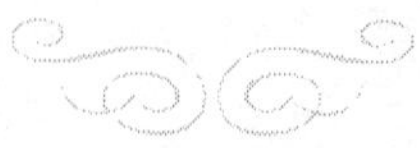

Be bad, but at least do not be a liar, a deceiver.

— *Leo Tolstoy*

What are my parents going to say for the made-up accusation and the action taken on Elton? I know, they do not trust me, because I am the worst liar. I hate my lying habits; I know that it will lead me to a bad ending, Corey thought.

The car that was creating the powerful reflective light happens to be that of Corey's parents. Corey's main concern now as she approaches them in a tiny step is what they would say to the firing.

"Corey, tell us what happened," says Mrs. Kerry.

"Sorry to tell you, but they fired him."

"How dare you blackmail an innocent and a trustworthy man."

"*It just happened*. I did not expect it to get so out of hand."

"Would you like to say sorry and ask Elton for forgiveness?"

"No, I am not going to ask for forgiveness; he should."

"Why?"

"For offending and being intolerant of me, telling the congregation that I am a fornicator and touching me where it hurts."

"Which part of the body does a physician treat?" questions Mrs. Kerry.

"The area that hurts."

"Why?"

"That is where healing is needed."

"Corey, Elton gave you the right dose and you should have accepted it gracefully. When you hear the truth, do not harden your heart. It will cause you to have a haunting guilt for accusing an honest man of God. If you do not diverge and make a U-turn in your life right now, you will be a vagabond and die in vain, which we cannot afford. It is the same kind of guilt that tormented Joseph's brothers for about twenty-two years for betraying an innocent brother and selling him to be a slave. Judas also betrayed an innocent Jesus; the guilt tormented him to the point of ending his life in vain. Reconsider your actions," pleads her father in a voice of despair.

Dad, you sound as if you heard the conversation we had in the meeting.

Mrs. Kerry continues challenging, "If you want to get healed from your sickness, you ought to get an honest touch where it hurts from the one who loves you, not excuses from one who covers up your wrongs."

"Mother, I am not sick. That young man hates me. That is why he exposed my wrongs to the world. My uncle is the one who loves me. He defended me and got that man fired."

"To tell you the truth, Elton loves you; your uncle hates you. I would rather have one who rebukes me when I am wrong than one who keeps silent or one who covers up my wrongs."

"What do you mean?"

"It is only the people that care for you who rebuke and instruct you to rewrite your wrongs."

"In this generation, if you see someone doing what is wrong according to your understanding, you just keep your view to yourself, do not rebuke anybody."

"That is wrong, my daughter. I wish I and your dad had a person like Elton in our lives; we never would have done the irreversible wrongs in our lives. When it comes to your uncle, he is one of the people that I love after my husband and you, our only child. However, in spiritual matters, we do not agree with him. He is the devil's advocate who keeps on bedeviling. He got positioned in that leadership to destroy the church. Tell me, how many lives did your uncle bring to God's kingdom? How many lives did Elton do the same?"

My uncle disperses; Elton gathers up whatever my uncle dispersed. My uncle brought zero souls and Elton thousands.

"My daughter, do not make light of the Lord's discipline and do not lose heart when He rebukes you through your parents and leaders. The Lord disciplines the one He loves, and He corrects everyone He accepts as His child. This rebuke has come either to cause you to turn your life to *diverge* from the wrong avenue of life or becoming a worse person. The choice is yours. At last, he who rebukes a wrongdoer will find more favor than he who flatters with his words. I want you to be aware also, in the end, after wasting resources and years of your life, you will ultimately do what is right."

After frequent glances, "Here he comes," announces Mrs. Kerry. Their eyes catch Elton. The family is perfectly positioned to meet Elton, giving him no other way out. Elton is so worried and nervous. How in the world would he start life over again and gain trust after he has been destroyed, betrayed, and fired from work?

Am I called to serve you, Lord? Maybe I am not. How could you let such a thing happen to me?

Elton casts a dilemma about his call to serve.

Lord, what am I going to do? How will I face the family that trusted me so much? I wish the earth would open its mouth, swallow me up, and I would die. I am worthless, he cries as he walks.

Son, you do not have to die. Because I died once for all. Do not be afraid, for I am with you.

At once, Corey's parents rush toward Elton as fast as a powerful tsunami that gobbles, sweeps up, and destroys everything in its way. On the contrary, Corey walks away in the opposite direction just like a repelling magnet and takes a seat under a leafy shade, to see how the unscripted drama would unfold.

Elton decides to stay put to avoid a head-on collision with the parents. *Lord, please give me your grace to bear their displaced aggression.*

The moment they come within reach of Elton, they throw their arms around him and cry bitterly. "Please forgive Corey, for she does not know what she is doing," pleads Mrs. Kerry in a choked voice.

Is this hug for real, Lord? Elton mumbles. At no time did he ever think or hint that they would treat him so. This is a tough moment for Elton. He has been hurt badly by a woman that he did not expect would do so. He is left all alone in shambles, at his lowest point in life. He looks around in disbelief, wondering what happened and how he would handle the humiliation.

Giving forgiveness is not as easy as it sounds. With time, as Elton moves forward and as the hurt subsides, yes, but for a fresh hurt caused by one closer to one's self, it is so devastating. Just as Corey's parents do, Elton of course expects people who are not walking in his shoes to lecture him to forgive. He even tells God, *Lord, Corey falsely accused me and I lost my job,* as if God is not aware of what is going on.

The worried Elton prays, "Lord, there is no one like you to help the powerless against the powerful family. Help me, Lord my God, for I depend on you, and in your name I have delivered your message. Lord, you are my God; do not let the plans of the mere mortal Angel and her uncle prevail against you. Please help me."

"Just a couple hours ago I taught, 'Blessed are the merciful, for they will be shown mercy. Blessed are those who are persecuted because of righteousness, for theirs is the kingdom of God. Blessed are you when people insult, persecute, and falsely say all kinds of evil against you because of me. Rejoice and be glad, because great is your reward in heaven, for in the same way they persecuted men of God who were before you.'"

The practical application of what he taught is going to be a real test to Elton. Giving and receiving forgiveness is a choice. Forgiving the undeserving Corey will prove that he lives by what he teaches. Refusal to forgive will show how hypocritical he is, he tells others to do so and not being able to do himself.

After going through excruciating emotional thoughts, "Please, allow me to go home and get some sleep. I am so exhausted; I have no strength. All that I need is to go home and rest," replies Elton.

Mr. Kerry pleads, "Elton, please forgive her for heaven's sake. She does not know what she is doing. She is a foolish girl."

"Mr. and Mrs. Kerry, please be assured things will be alright with Corey," persuades Elton.

Mrs. Kerry cries, taking her arms off Elton. "What proof would you give us that things will be alright?"

"Soon, Corey will come asking for forgiveness from me. You will see it in your own eyes," reassures Elton.

"We cannot force you to forgive her today. Nevertheless, Elton, I am reminded of Joseph—who was sold as a slave. They hurt his feet with fetters. He was laid in irons. Until the time that His word came to pass, the word of the Lord tested him. The king sent and released him; the ruler of the people let him go free. He made him lord of his house and ruler of all his possessions, to teach his elders wisdom. The same shall happen to you after this difficult season. May the God whom you serve faithfully keep you safe in the in the lion's den and the blazing fire of life journey," says Mr. Kerry and he lets Elton go.

The day Elton got fired, he prayed, "Lord, what would you like me to do? I said what you wanted me to say and lost my job."

Shortly after the prayer, a good woman named ABIGAIL MITCHELL, who has confidence in Elton rather than the bureaucracy of the church, finds him a better-paying job. The new job would be a place to hide until the disturbance caused by Corey gets cleared by the truth of the gospel that convicts the sinner. In the end, Elton knows that he is called to preach the gospel.

Time flies fast. It has been a couple of years since Elton lost his job. The look on his face in the subsequent days and years turns radiant and happier than before, and it drives Corey crazy. She mercilessly wants to devastate Elton beyond recovery, cast out from the presence of the brethren forever. Yet the opposite happens. Elton got hired for another job, appears happy; his dedication to never quit the church drives Corey insane.

The day Elton confronted Corey to *diverge*, instead of admitting and returning from her wrongdoings, she decides to cover it up. She creates an accusing story, which is a worse mistake. Hayet is stunned upon hearing Corey's entire heartbreaking account.

"Your story is so captivating. Wow, I have never heard such compelling information. However, the only exit I see from your brokenness is to ask for forgiveness. Go meet Elton and ask for forgiveness."

"Huh, after doing intentional harm to Elton? I will be crucified if I ask for forgiveness."

"If Elton is the person that you say he is, obviously, he will forgive you. He has received forgiveness, too. The sooner you ask forgiveness, the faster you will receive healing from the deadliest poison that imprisons and binds you. By asking forgiveness, even if he does not accept it, you will help the most valuable person in the world, which is yourself. Be aware also, in the end, after hiding the truth for years, you will in due course do what is right, admit and ask for forgiveness."

"If you believe that Elton will forgive me, please allow me to start with you. I planned purposely to knock you down from your walk of chastity. Will you forgive me?"

"Sure, I have already forgiven you!" Hayet assures her.

Corey is happy for receiving forgiveness. "Thanks for your forgiveness and for ending my day well. I hope not to follow such a lifestyle again. Please do not do all that I did. The only thing that you will ever get is torment and hurt."

After giving him a kindly hug, she walks toward the bathroom, carrying her black handbag. Hayet expects another hour's delay; however, she returns within less than one minute and puts her shoes on. "Hayet, thanks. You ended my day perfectly. Now I feel like I am born again! However, I still have no courage to confront Elton. Besides, I must ask forgiveness from the leaders whom I manipulated, as well as from my parents and Reverend Russ."

"Well, Corey, as a friend, my duty is to suggest to you what to do. Nevertheless, the decision of whether to do it is up to you."

"Then I will try to talk to him on Sunday," she promises.

They immediately exit the room and the hotel together, hiring a taxi ride up to college. The moment they step out of the taxi, wherever they walk the students ask them, “How was it?” Finally, Hayet comes to realize that all that Corey did was prearranged. The good thing is that it turns out for her best. She *diverges* from a purposeless life to embracing her abandoned GPS, that is, God’s Positioning System and God’s Plan of Salvation. She goes from a fallen angel to a daughter of God and she stingily anticipates meeting Elton.

Chapter 25

Real integrity is doing the right thing, knowing that nobody's going to know whether you did it or not.

— *Oprah Winfrey*

Corey decides to meet with Elton Middleton to ask for a crucial forgiveness.

The first Monday after Corey's failed attempt to break Hayet's chastity vow, she comes to meet him. The sun is behind thick clouds, making the weather somewhat cold.

Bernard tells Hayet, "Angel wants to see you downstairs by the swirly railings. Maybe she wants to give you an astounding reward for Friday's outing. By the way, how was it?"

"It was a miraculous transformation from the fallen Angel to Corey," replies Hayet.

"I know and trust that you are not an easy person and are capable of escaping temptations. You won and escaped this time. However, it does not mean that you won once and for all. Be prepared that the same enemy will return with many sneakier tactics to exploit your vulnerabilities. The reason is that most people pass the impassable and fail in the infallible. The survival in the deep and impassable condition does not guarantee you survival in the shallow, easily passable conditions. By the way, did you manage to talk to Sandy and Shian? I bet they know that the outing did not go as expected." As Bernard is still speaking, Hayet heads downstairs.

This time, Corey appears much elated than during the days before.

Hayet asks, "What is up Corey? What makes you smile with such elated look on your face as bright as the morning star?"

"Because I encountered one who elates and received new life through Jesus," she replies, unable to suppress her broad grin. "Let me tell you the good news."

Shortly after Sunday service is over, Corey takes her parents and Reverend Russ with her to accompany to meet Elton. Her parents have been arguing and on bad terms for the past three years, because of Corey's deviation. They know that divorce would devastate Corey and manage to persevere, stay together for the sake of their daughter, which estranged parents should imitate. This is the first time in many years they have gone to church at Corey's request which also brought reconciliation to the whole family.

Elton in a gray polo shirt tucked into belted white jeans with a cell-phone holster at the hip walks alone, though he seems happy and relaxed. He is leisurely walking on the cement pedestrian walkway, in front of the ponytail-haired little triplets that happily play hopscotch on a white chalk-etched sidewalk.

As the girls stop playing to hear the adults converse, "Elton, I want to talk to you for a minute," Corey speaks boldly.

"You have already threatened to do all those bad things to me. Why would you want to talk to me today?" Elton replies warily.

"I am here to tell you that whatever I said about you that made the elders fire you from your job is not true. I did that intentionally to attack you for rebuking me in front of everybody. Although I do not deserve it, I am asking you to kindly forgive me."

The words that Corey articulates shock her parents and the reverend. This is her first time admitting her sin and speaking up openly. Although Elton knew that Corey's accusations were false, he still stands perplexed, motionless, and stunned, gawking at her blankly.

Elton sighs, twiddling his thumbs, and runs a hand through his shaggy hair, without saying a word. Corey avoids his deep penetrating innocent eyes. She stares at the ground while combing her golden auburn hair with her manicured fingernails.

While waiting for his reply, she repeats, "I am sorry for the damage that I have caused you." She meets his gaze briefly, attending for one sentence: *I have forgiven you.* It never seems to come.

Another lull takes over. Corey's father wants to see the practical application assurance that Elton made years ago. That is, "*Soon, Corey will come asking for forgiveness from me. You will see it in your own eyes.*"

Mr. Kerry says to Elton, "Did you hear what she is requesting?"

"Yes, sir."

"So, answer her!" presses Corey's dad.

"The only person that I have an issue with is Corey. Please allow me to talk to her," whispers Elton, facing Corey's companions politely. Then he turns to Corey and speaks to her directly.

"If what you stated and did are true, I want you to say yes."

He begins to list the accused wrongs as if reading them off a piece of paper.

Corey does not expect the grocery list of the damages she inflicted on Elton, for she already knows them all in detail. However, he continues to list them.

"Corey, did you say, 'You will never be here next week.' the week of the accusation?"

"Yes."

"Did you intentionally manipulate the church elders to fire me from my job? Did you?"

"Yes, yes, I did," Corey stammers on the verge of tears.

"Did you threaten that I would pay the price and regret the embarrassment that I caused you, hinting I would miss my mortgage and other bill payments?"

"Yes!"

Elton is not yet done with his list.

"Corey, because of your selfish actions, parents distanced their children from me, reported me as a child molester, and I experienced social isolation."

"I know what I did. Although I do not deserve forgiveness, I am asking it for the sake of relieving myself," she cries, admittedly dismayed with grief.

The pronouncement of forgiveness is taking a long time. Will Elton ever forgive Corey for all the wrongful deeds itemized in the list?

After several excruciating moments, Elton speaks. "Corey, I was prepared and have been waiting for a moment such as this. For all that you stated and did to me, not only have I forgiven you, but also I am willing to accept you as a wife. I love you with all my heart. I cannot live without you. Will you marry me?" he kneels right in front of Corey.

The glow of his eye cuts through her guilty conscience. It is shock and awe for Corey, her parents, and the reverend, leaving them speechless.

Corey's tears amass on Elton's forehead and face. Her dad stands in bewilderment, his arms crossed, and her mom cries, "How could this be possible?"

The moment Elton pronounces, "I forgive you," it feels like a ton of bricks lifted away from her guilty conscience. That is not all. His proposal also rejuvenates the vision of marriage and family that she abandoned years back. Now she foresees dressing up in a wedding gown and walking down the aisle. She anticipates her father presenting her formally to be a wedded wife in front of family and friends, and eventually becoming a wife and a mother.

Her family has been through sleepless nights and days anticipating a phone call about her death because of her wild living. The proposal is like a dream. Corey feels undeserving to say yes to one who walks upright, to the same person that she inflicted harm on with false accusations, which caused him the loss of a job and the confidence of the community. Her body is saying no; nevertheless, her spirit says yes. She is stranded between saying yes, accepting forgiveness, or no, harboring guilt.

Corey knows that she has tossed herself from man to man frequently. Each encounter with men has drained her life passion. Inwardly, she is wasting herself, abandoning her dreams and aspirations with so-called lovers. She has been to wild partying ballrooms. The more she parties, the more her heart depletes. None of the men that she has spent time with has spoken kind, uplifting, and loving words the way Elton has. "How can you propose to love and live with a wretched woman?" she stammers, wiping away tears of shock. The bright midday sun rays blind Elton's eyes as he explains, still while kneeling.

"I do not see you for the wretched woman and for the fallen angel that people see and know you are wearing filthy clothes. I see you for a woman whose filthy clothes and sins have been taken away, forgiven, and who has been dressed in new clothes, one raised up with Christ and seated in the heavenly realms in Jesus," he assures.

Elton has lost his mind; he can not only propose to but also speak such kind words to a wretched woman.

"My love for you never dies. Please say yes today. You are the choicest woman that lightens my life. Will you marry me, Corey? Do not let go of this impeccable moment," beseeches Elton.

"I have class. Please tell me what happens," Hayet says, interrupting her story.

"Wait, I have class too," states Corey. "Just let me finish."

Then she asks Elton, "Why would you want to have a long, lasting relationship with a woman who intentionally inflicted harm on you, and much worse, who lives a promiscuous lifestyle?"

"Corey, I know all that, and I do not see you for what you did and where you have been. I see you for who you are and for what you could be. It is never too late to begin again. Please say yes," begs Elton.

Corey is anxious that Elton could be pretending to love her yet planning to take revenge later, after marriage. She cannot say yes. Besides, they have more differences than similarities. He is chaste; she is unchaste, to begin with. After hasty consideration of the torment Elton went through, she convinces herself to turn down the proposal.

Nevertheless, based on her knowledge of Elton's behavioral predictability, her heart cries, *What if Elton's proposal is for real?* However, trying to calm and turn the offer down methodically, Corey cries, "Elton, you know several girls who are as good as you. What makes you come after a girl who has messed up, behaved immorally, and made shameful accusations about you?"

"Corey, I do not see and measure you by the past. I see and measure you by the redeemed future person in you. You should say yes if you believe that is the right decision for you. As for me, I say what I mean and mean what I say. Please say what you mean to say, and rest assured that I have forgiven you and will accept you as a virgin, or rather as a new creation in Christ," assures Elton.

Most of the congregants have left at that time. The remaining few observe the unfolding drama. At that moment, the cathedral's harmonious bells ring for the next service.

Corey strongly believes she has to *diverge* from her wasted life and make a fresh start. *However, I do not think that I am ready for a committed relationship right now,* she thinks. What is more, can she say yes to Elton? Whether yes or no, she should give him an answer. The words that he speaks are from deep within his heart and show on his smiling face, which is as pure as the waters in Sandy Springs. Corey pauses, gazing at him with tear-blurred eyes.

Lastly, she comes to a point where she must give him an answer, whether he likes it or not. She kneels right beside him on the wet floor. Compared to the forgiveness she received, kneeling on a concrete floor is painless for the girl with flawless skin. She whispers her answer into his ear. Elton jumps to his feet. He picks her up, hugs her, and turns her around, the way a jubilant skater would a partner, though with no kiss. For he knows that she is not his wife yet; he cannot give her a kiss. What a wonderful day! It feels like a new birth to Corey.

"Yes, I will marry you—on one condition. My parents have to agree with your proposal."

The girl who lived as she wished embraces the forgotten virtue and seeks parental affirmation. What a miracle-working God!

The woman who never experienced true love receives a sincere soul mate. Elton promises to fulfill her deepest longings of true love and her sense of purpose with a fresh start. The moment is as light as two paired balloons soaring up in the same direction.

"Hayet, thank you, not only for saving me from premature death but also for opening a new chapter in my life. Because of your saying gutsily what I did not want to hear at a time when I needed to hear it, I have received the most cherished gift every woman dreams to have, only a couple of months before my graduation. I was dead and am alive again; I was lost, but now have found a hopeful future. Although I intended to harm you when I met you, the Lord meant it for good. Thank you for being the catalyst of change in my life. Do not undermine the healing gift that is within you, and please be sure not to walk a mixed-up life the way I did. You saw all that comes from the pain and suffering caused by one day's mistake."

"Congratulations, Corey! Remember also that it is the same couple of months before graduation that you gave Rahab a future and a hope. Keep your life aligned to God's Positioning System. It is a pleasure for me to have some time with you. I am so glad that all has turned out for your good. See you later. I have got to go," says Hayet, and he takes off for class.

Eventually, Corey graduates. After graduation, the university promotes Rahab to another position.

"The best person to take over the RA role is Corey," recommends Rahab. Corey graciously accepts the RA position, and she performs the duty beautifully.

Hayet has been useful to many students in succeeding spiritually, academically, and socially by putting God first, prioritizing their lives, and serving others fairly and justly. Will he be able to continue intentional living up to the end? It is not the beginning but the end that matters. Let us read further on Hayet's life journey.

Chapter 26

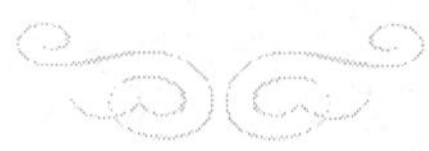

Sin is crouching at your door; it desires to have you, but you must rule over it.

— *Rev. Kidane Adhanom*

The days of college fly as fast as Dr. Rebecca Soyinka predicted during freshman orientation; Hayet the fourth-year student now goes to a club which changed his life forever.

The students reveal visual and physical changes. The men have grown full-blown mustaches. Some of them have grown muscular, and others are not so fortunate. The women have become curvier and prettier than when they started college. They are anxious to graduate and go to the field of service that is a practical application of what they learned.

Some students choose to be professional athletes, representing their college near and far. Intellectually, the hardworking students increase their knowledge. A few others do not make it through the first quarter due to deviating from purposeful living, forgetting the reasons for coming to college. One example is Mr. TYLER TAYLOR, the first student to drop out of the batch.

Tyler is always critical of everybody. He spends more money than he earns and blames others for taking better jobs instead of working. The batch enters their fourth year, energized for the final sprint.

For his academic excellence, Hayet earns a free scholarship for graduate studies, and he hopes to apply for significant job openings at home and overseas. Nevertheless, he must graduate before thinking about jobs and graduate studies. In the meantime, Hayet cannot find someone to replace LeAnn's companionship. Thus, he walks alone on campus. LeAnn has been a role model for Hayet and others to follow in all aspects of life. He searches for a person like her on and off the campus.

Meanwhile, he looks for a good job to enable him to make credit card payments until he graduates. Perhaps he should have listened to his adoptive parents when they advised him to avoid unnecessarily incurring debt at all cost, as well as their willingness to pay the whole amount for the car. However, due to his pride, he has turned down the offer. He now should pay for his reckless and an unprecedented financial obligation, with no idea of what it will cost.

The trio, Bernard, Sandy, and Shian, decide to stay on campus for the long Labor Day weekend of 1993. Hayet goes to campus to pick them up. The entire ride, from the moment they climb into the silver SUV until they enter the Piccolo nightclub, each one tells how horrible the summer was, and it was not due to a lack of food to eat, books to read, places to go, or other fun activities. The reason is that their parents (all Ph.D. holders) were simultaneously on vacation to invest time with their children. The parents were always there with their children, giving the college students no opportunity for unseemly practices.

At one point, Hayet asks his friends, "Why would you live for your parents? Learn to live for yourselves. You should be responsible and consistent, be it in the presence as well as in the absence of your parents."

"Hayet, you do not know the fun life that we are talking about. You better not comment," scorns Bernard.

"Well, I am glad that I never knew it, and I do not wish to know it."

"Man, that is what I used to say before I tried it. Just you stay the way you are—you do not need to be out partying with us. Who would give us rides if you did? If you screw up, we shall replace you with a credible person," replies Bernard.

"Today may be your day," interrupts Sandy as she exits the car.

"I heard what you said. You go and check out the situation before I leave," declares Hayet.

A couple of minutes later, Bernard returns with a lanky man who has a brownish handlebar mustache. He wears a light blue sleeveless safari shirt folded up to his enormous muscles. He has no traces of tattoos.

"Hayet, this is Morris Norton, the owner of Piccolo," Bernard introduces the man.

"Hi, Morris, it is nice to meet you."

"Nice to meet you, too," answers Morris. "I have seen you do extraordinary favors for Bernard and his friends. Their safety means a lot to me. I always wanted to come and thank you. However, I have not managed to do so."

Morris readjusts his cowboy hat before he resumes. "Anyhow, today I have come looking for another favor. Tonight, a couple of my musicians are out, and others called in sick. Phone calls to locate the reserves never seem to work. Bernard told me that you knew how to play musical instruments. I am kindly requesting you to play in the club, whichever instrument you may feel comfortable with, to save my day. I will pay you fifty bucks per hour. The main reason customers flood in from near and far is to enjoy our live music. Please do me a favor, *just for tonight*."

Hayet says, "Bernard, you should have told Morris the answer yourself. You know that I do not play such games. Why would you refer a club owner to me?"

Hayet is questioning Bernard's integrity in their friendship with a furrowed brow. He then addresses Morris.

"Thanks for the offer. However, these hands of mine are holy, and they play holy songs to holy people in a holy place. Sorry, but I am not going to play here. Moreover, I counsel, teach, and mentor Christian ethics. Accepting your offer would portray me as a hypocrite and a bad example."

"I told you, he is still a mama's baby boy," interrupts Bernard.

Morris does not give up. "I respect your integrity to your family and the faith community that you mentor. I am not forcing you, just asking if you are willing to do so. Not only that, but I would be willing to offer you a job for a couple of hours on weekends, with the same pay rate and without jeopardizing your school priority. By the way, although we have never had it before, you are free to play holy songs by your holy hands to the unholy people in this unholy place. Perhaps, who knows, the unholy people may turn out to be holy, hearing your holy presentation."

Hayet answers, "No!"

Shortly after he replies, he climbs back in the SUV, ready to drive away. However, an unfamiliar sound buzzes in his ears like a twisting tornado: *Do not miss this opening. How else am I going to pay my debt?* The thoughts dash in and out of his mind. He attempts to crank the SUV multiple times. However, his fingers are unable to twist the ignition key as he thinks about Morris's offer.

The surrounding area is dark. Hayet shuts his eyes and reclines in the car, stretching out in the driver's seat. He aimlessly scratches his Afro with his long pinky fingernail. Some of the payments he pointlessly incurred are due to start soon. Hayet feels like a ship that has lost control, floundering in the ocean and pushed all directions. He has no time to discuss the matter with Gramps, LeAnn, or other trusted friends. Furthermore, he realizes that they obviously would say 'no' and do not approve for Hayet to play music or dance that does not glorify God. He must decide and do what is right by himself. Whichever way he chooses there is a reward or consequence that would impact his life.

This might be my only means of making good money as a student.

In the past, he has seen divine intervention whenever he needed it, provision coming right on time. However, now, while there is a money-earning way, waiting for divine endowment or asking for a contribution from other people is unreasonable.

Years ago, he believed and experienced that God supplies seed to the sower and bread for food would supply his need. However, while an opening is at hand, he is not so convinced that he will see such an endowment. He does not want to miss this opportune moment. He contemplates going ahead and preparing himself to pay his debt. At least one payment is due next month, and he has no money to pay.

This could be divine Providence, an interventional exit, a saving grace for me. Besides, of what value is a car without a driver, an airplane without a pilot, and a horse without a rider? The same is true about my talent if I do not capitalize on it. Morris offers better pay compared to what I earn in my part-time job.

Furthermore, *The church does not pay me money. Capitalizing on my musical talent here does not appear to be a terrible idea.* Hayet uses that kind of reasoning to do what he wants to do. *Besides, Morris has allowed me to play holy songs for the unholy people, believing the unholy people could turn out to be holy.*

As the sliding whiny door shuts slowly, Hayet shouts, "Morris," while motioning with both arms. Hayet unenthusiastically stands right in front of Morris, who waits expectantly a couple of steps away from the open door.

Sensing the cold air from the club, Morris moves away from the sensor of the sliding door. "What is up?" Morris asks, looking at Hayet casually.

"I want to assure you that I will do it, *just for tonight*," promises Hayet. Bernard's eyes widen in bafflement; he clearly never expected Hayet to agree.

"Thanks! Your service is a million-dollar gift for me. I do not want to disappoint my clients. It is live music entertainment that the customers enjoy here," Morris says, clapping his hand on Hayet's back.

"You are welcome," replies Hayet.

The time is already late, and customers have been asking Morris why there is no music in the club. He immediately leads the way with a bright smile, tucking his hands into his pockets; Hayet trails him. The club is somewhat dim. Flashy strobes glowing and whirling give it the illusion of slow-motion lights. Morris walks quickly toward the stage, creating a significant gap.

Hayet walks cautiously, minding his steps. Suddenly, a woman bumps into him. She blurts defensively, "I am not drunk."

Her speech speaks for itself that she is drunk.

"Whoa, this is your first taste of the club life," notes Bernard. He is couple steps ahead.

"You will be amazed to hear that the same woman will drive her car and go home."

"Woe unto the innocent citizens of our city that shall be victims of this drunkard's onslaught," pronounces Hayet sympathetically, not knowing that he could do the same soon.

"Huh? Walking on staggering feet and driving home is simple compared to the battered black eyes and split lips that regular club attendees often receive," Bernard utters with a chuckle.

Hayet cannot comprehend what Bernard is saying. As a result, he asks, "How can people be customers where battering is prevalent?"

"That is what I used to say before I stepped in the club. When people become intoxicated, they become judgment impaired. The alcohol controls them. That is why they think, behave, reason, walk, and talk abnormally."

"I am glad I am here *just for tonight*. I will never be a regular attendee of such a place."

"Again, that is what I used to say before I became a regular. You are so far, so good. However, since it is the end that matters, we shall wait and see how your life shall end up," says Bernard.

Morris holds a cordless black microphone. "Attention, attention please," he calls out and receives a response from the intoxicated customers.

The light on the stage is bright. The flashy strobe lights twirl in the general area. The bright stage light makes the veins of Morris's hand very visible.

"Ladies and gentlemen, sorry for today's inconvenience. However, I am pleased to announce to you that today we have a special guest who is knowledgeable in all kinds of music to entertain us." Chants, whistles, and cheers interrupt the announcement. "Okay," repeats Morris several times until the applause dies down. "Allow me to give the stage to Hayet! Finally, yet importantly, please allow me to make one final remark. Hayet plays holy songs with his holy hands. Please allow him to play the holy music that he is used to."

Morris stretches out his right arm toward the stage and then gives Hayet a second clap on the back.

Gramps usually say in all that you do, make sure to do that which glorifies God. If not, stop what you are doing even if it pays good money. It is better to trust in God, who can convert the wilderness into fertile land and vice versa.

Despite the experience of observing God's faithfulness, Hayet decides to lean on his own understanding and chooses to go on his own way without regard to God's guidance.

Consequently, failure looms in Hayet's life.

Chapter 27

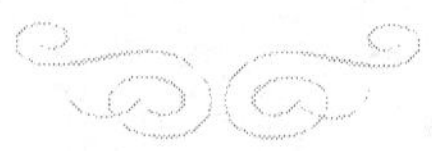

Ability can take you to the top, but it takes character to keep you there.

— Zig Ziglar

God has imparted Hayet with the gift of playing music for His glory, yet with unwise wistfulness, he uses the gift for an ungodly benefit.

Hayet has had a conservative upbringing and has never been to a club, let alone on a club stage, be it in Africa or in America. Morris invites him to play music for money. With misguided longing, Hayet ventures toward unfamiliar territory. The moment Hayet steps onto the stage, Morris welcomes and gives him a platform.

The strobe lights' flashing makes it difficult for Hayet to identify who is who while gazing past the instruments. The chanting, the shouting, and the jubilation show that customers are lively.

Hayet faces Morris and says, "I thank you all for welcoming me warmly and giving me this opening. I hope that we all shall have a blessed night, I mean, uh, a happy night," he corrects the slip of the tongue of the spiritual terminology.

Morris then walks Hayet to the instruments. Before Hayet seizes an instrument to play, servers with a tray full of drinks come to the stage, announcing, "Here is a paid-for drink for you." Here comes 'the paid for' again.

"Thanks for the offer. I do not drink. Besides, I am the designated driver."

Most the servers accept Hayet's refusal and go away. However, one remains behind, Delilah Samson. She is a server with a gratifying tongue whose lips drip sweet words.

She points to a person that Hayet cannot identify. "The one in a yellow jacket seated on the black revolving bistro chair and table bought you this drink so that you may become bold," she indicates.

Delilah's remark is nerve-racking and touches on Hayet's real problem: shyness. *How did she know that I am shy?*

Delilah continues, "Everybody knows about you." In addition, she says, "I cannot take the drink back to the customer. Please, take it from the tray and save my day. It is a martini, a little glass, and it is just one sip." Hayet resists; Delilah persists.

Finally, Hayet sees the enhanced red color of the drink. It is pleasurable to the eye, and it is also desirable for gaining confidence and boldness. *Just for tonight*, he declares and gulps the drink.

The drink causes a light burn and indescribable irritation in his throat. He coughs and chokes, clearing his throat. His eyes moisten with slight tears. He grins with hazy eyes as Delilah freezes, staring at him in the emptiness. "Why do you stare at me in such a way?" Hayet asks as he wipes tears.

"I was about to give up begging you. We never assumed that you would accept even a sip."

The other bartenders return and yell, "Why did you accept Delilah's and refuse our drinks?" They turn out more aggressive than Delilah did, surrounding him with no way out.

Hayet always talks about fairness and treating everybody equally. The principle of treating all equally makes it difficult for him to say yes to Delilah but not to the others. That is the moment a thousand alarming panicky thoughts dash through his mind. *This is not about fairness. It is about doing right versus wrong*. Nevertheless, after a little more nagging, he opens himself up for more drinks.

A couple more sips will have no effect on me. Hayet fails to perceive that wine is a mocker and beer makes one brawl; causing one to fight, and whoever is led astray by them is not wise. He accepts all the drinks he is offered, and then wipes his teary eyes.

Bernard, Sandy, and Shian come from nowhere to block the way across the stage, hindering further drink offers. By then, Hayet has emptied the remaining glasses and is seeking more. Immediately, he develops a visible boldness and warmness on his forehead with an increasing intensity and a blurry sight. He has fuzzy vision. Other than that, he shows no other sign of immediate alcoholic effects.

Finally, Hayet, having had enough to drink, gains boldness and announces, "Since this is the Piccolo club, let me start my first music with a piccolo clarinet," he tells the audience. He picks up a piccolo to fulfill his *one-day* pledge. He closes his eyes, cradling the piccolo in his arms like a lover longer than he should. At the same time, he tries to prevent something that wants to come out of his mouth. Suddenly, he feels dizzy, and his stomach is upset. He walks toward the restroom and staggers a bit, bumping into a server he met before. Without warning, he is out cold.

Chapter 28

The Christian shoemaker does his duty not by putting little crosses on the shoes, but by making good shoes, because God is interested in good craftsmanship.

— *Martin Luther*

It takes one little wrong to derail one's aspiring life journey from good to bad, from fruitful to fruitless, from constructive to destructive, and from heaven to hell. That is where Hayet finds himself, just where he would not want to be.

The first day Hayet has made a choice to drink, he hears Sandy, Shian, and Bernard talking with the Grannies, despite of the fact that he is asleep. *It should be a dream. The trio never met the Grannies in person.* Hayet denies the reality of the fact that rings in his ears.

Bernard says, "Although you have appealing ideas, no one ever told me all that you are sharing. I grew up with my parents, who do not care about religious stuff. However, after seeing the sacrifice Hayet made on our behalf, I am willing to diverge and change from my old way of life."

"Me, too," affirm Sandy and Shian simultaneously.

Right away, the Grannies funnel endless truths, forgive them, encourage them, and strengthen them with prayers accompanied with a thanksgiving.

The moment that they all pronounce, "Amen," Hayet opens his eyes and looks around. He finds himself in an unfamiliar situation. He attempts to wake up from the bed but cannot. He looks down. Bandages wrap his arm and there is an IV needle stuck in the back of his right hand.

Head bandaged, and his chest plastered with several devices, he wonders, "Is this real? How did I come here?" fumbling spontaneously.

"It is real. Settle down, my son. Behold, you are in a hospital," says Grandma while she opens the curtains to show him.

"I cannot believe it. How did this happen to me? Am I okay?"

"A man's irresponsible, reckless, careless, and foolish behavior and his wrong perception brought him here," an irritating voice says.

Hayet does not want to look at the one speaking. "I know such judgmental, intolerant, annoying and even worse words come from Emily," Hayet whispers without looking at her. He understands that replying to her remarks costs him more annoyance; keeping the peace is the best thing to do.

Emily is not the only visitor who is Hayet's bane of existence. Tobias and Sanballat are there as well. The moment they step in, "Toby, somebody in his country—", announces Sanballat.

"That is too broad; minimize it, brother," cuts in Tobias.

"Okay, somebody in this hospital—,"

"That is too broad again."

"Okay, here is the final one. Somebody in this room knows how to talk the Christian talk."

"However not walk the Christian walk. Where was God at that time?" Tobias finishes the other half.

Hayet feels ashamed and foolish for harming his dignity and self-respect in the face of the people that love to see his good as well as those that wish to see his failure. Then, dissing Tobias and Sanballat, he says, "Listen my enemies; do not rejoice over me. When I fall, I will arise; When I sit in darkness, the Lord will be a light to me. I will bear the outrage of God, because I have made mistakes against Him. One day, He will bring me forth to the light and restore me back to Him and I shall see His loving kindness. Then they who are my enemies who said, 'Where was your God?' will see, and shame will cover them. My eyes will see them and will regret what they said against me."

At the same time, an enchanting woman stands in front of Hayet. She leans upon the arm of a physically well-built, shaggy-haired man. It is Corey with her husband, Elton; they got married right after she graduated.

"Sorry, you have to see me in this condition. *It just happened*."

"Huh? It just happened. It cannot *just happen* unless you wanted it and willingly participated," scoffs Emily with a girly laugh, showing a cold shoulder.

"I went to work, and the drinking part *just happened*, okay?"

"Effect can by no means happen in your life unless you willfully and intentionally permit it. Do you remember the principle of cause and effect?" she taunts as she moves toward Corey and Elton and stands right in front of Hayet, displaying a smirk.

Hayet does not want to look at Emily. He turns his face toward Grandma, who is still holding open the curtains.

"Nobody has ever ridiculed me the way you always do, Emily. I have had enough of you. You cannot show up wherever I go and dictate how I should live. I am a man."

"Oh, would you please tell me what the measure or description of a man is?" Emily jeers.

Corey cuts in, "The measure of a man is his willingness to provide, serve, and protect his family, as well as the community, enduring hardship."

"Thanks, Corey," says Emily. "Hayet, tell me where you see your manhood per Corey's description."

Hayet knows the precise answer, yet he does not want to speak. Arguing with Emily will expose him to more confrontation. He decides to keep silent.

"Tell me," she persists.

"Nowhere," yells Hayet. "Yet remember that I am a student with few opportunities, struggling to find wider doors to make it to the top," he says instead of admitting the truth.

"Thanks for mentioning the word *few*. If you are faithful in small dots right now and right here, God will appoint you to handle greater responsibilities in the future. Bear in mind there are no shortcuts to purposes worth pursuing."

Emily's rationale is true, however, sickening to a young man who wants to avoid her factual yet nagging words. *Finally, I cannot take her simmering and searing words anymore. I have to sit up and defend myself from her intimidating remarks.* He attempts to sit. His body turns dizzy and weak, leaving him with no strength to sit up on his own. Tears surge down his cheeks, dropping onto the blue gown and white pillow.

"I know what you want to do. Let me give you a hand, buddy," pronounces Bernard, and moves to help.

Grabbing Hayet's right arm, he pulls him up gently. At the same time, Emily zooms in and positions the pillow behind Hayet's back. The others also help make him comfortable. The moment Hayet sits, the dizziness worsens, Emily's criticism having galvanized the situation.

As Hayet struggles with the dizziness, Shian tells him, "Do not be angry. Lean back and take deep breaths; relax, and you will be fine."

"Why should I not be angry? Do you see that she is driving me mad?" He gains his composure after a minute or so.

"Emily, you are making my blood boil going under my skin. Why do you follow me wherever I go and lecture me?"

"Wherever you go, be it Yale, jail, the capitol, or a hospital, we will go, A*migo, porque Dios te ama*, (friend, because God loves you,") she retorts.

"Who are you to dictate to me? I am not your baby."

"First, I wish you were my baby. I would have made you listen with a rod of love. Second, I am a woman who knows her identity and who walks as well as lives intentionally, fully utilizing her GPS. I am concerned to see you with some new perspective. Do you understand? You lost your GPS and identity, and you are moving away from who you are meant to be in slow motion."

The pillow slides as Hayet attempts to rise to a seated position.

"If I do not know my identity and who I am, I suppose you do," he screams, placing his right hand on his chest.

"Of course, I sure do! You are the son of a man who dreamed the American dream decades ago. Your father endured unfairness and injustice and still lives serving, providing, and protecting his family and his community. You ought to carry on his legacy. Besides, if you do not know who you truly are on the inside, then you do not know what you are entitled to. Follow Jesus to find your identity."

"Can you tell me who I am and what I am entitled to?"

"You are a child of God, entitled to receive grace, peace, and safety amid a storm, and abundant blessings because you are made for more."

Hayet does not want to heed Emily's reasoning. "You know, Emily, East Africans say, 'One who knows more than the owner is a witch.'"

"I do not care how the African saying labels me. My main goal is to see you *diverge* and have a new perspective on life."

"Where do you want me to *diverge* from? I am neither lost nor confused without perspective. I know where I am and where I am heading. Whatever I do, I do it with full understanding."

"Ha-ha," Emily horselaughs scornfully. "I wish you knew what you were talking about. You are a fish out of a water. Do not cover it up. You should admit that you are lost so that somebody can lead you to the exit where you could receive healing, if not today, then someday, if not here, then somewhere. That is why we found you, and you found yourself today at the hospital. I am afraid to say that you will find yourself in hell at the end of your life. Bear in mind that the day you know the Truth, the Truth shall set you free."

Emily's horselaugh enrages Hayet. In the meantime, the word "*diverge*," that Emily pronounced echoes in his ears repeatedly as a recurrent pain. It is getting out of control.

"Emily, do you remember what I told you during our last conversation?"

"Yes, I surely do! On that icy Sunday afternoon in the parking lot, you asked me to leave you alone."

"Thanks for remembering. Please do not make me repeat it. I still stand by it."

"Do you also remember what I replied?"

"Yes, I surely do. 'I will leave you alone for a time.'"

"Thanks for remembering. I still stand by it." Furthermore, she says, "I want to assure you that for the very speech that you hate me for now, you will love me in the future."

"Not really for a bane of my existence."

Suddenly, silence prevails. Hayet's heartbeat returns to normal. During the silence, Corey speaks.

"It is sad to see a man who transformed my filthy past fall into the hole from which he rescued me. You have heard the discussions. Now I want you to listen carefully, Hayet. Yesterday is gone. Will you please promise today that you shall never do such a thing again?" she rubs her pregnant belly as she speaks.

Corey has braced for intentional and purposeful life. A look at her face portrays how joyful and thrilled she is about her new avenue of life. She lives in full pursuit of her passion, embracing the forgotten virtues, and nothing can slow her down. However, her nickname, Angel, still lingers in campus, even after she is gone.

Hayet understands Corey's words are indisputable, and her intentions are for his good. However, he does not want to promise and fail.

"Please just promise. It is the right thing to do."

"I cannot promise. It is a job offer."

"Pretending a problem does not exist will not take it away. So, are you saying it is your job to become drunk?" Grandma asks.

Hayet keeps silent and bows his Afro head.

"I am talking about the drinking part. If you have to drink, know your limits," explains Corey.

Hayet replies, "I understand what you mean. As I stated earlier, I cannot promise. I did not intentionally go to drink, but to work. The drinking part *just happened*."

"If the job entangles you the way it did, then you better not take that job. Elton can hire you for a better-paying job until you graduate. We want to save your life."

"Save my life from what?"

"From the spiraling, futile life for which you yearn, where I wasted my womanhood, dignity, and precious years of my life."

"Do not worry *and do not cry*. I am careful and will not fall."

"How can you be careful while shifting in slow motion like a frog in slowly boiling water? The evidence is that if one puts a frog in boiling water, it will jump out. However, if it is set in cold water that is gradually heated, it will not realize the danger until death. Your failure or unwillingness to *diverge* from slow-moving danger will kill you before you know it. By the way, *I am careful* is what I used to say. I have told you before that my downfall started before the day I went with Valerie. One yearning led to another. The wrong yearnings wrecked my life beyond repair, until the time when you found and rescued me. No word can describe God's love for me that flows through you," Corey screams in a remarkable voice, for the special gift of the redeemed life she got from God.

Corey continues, "You do not understand what you are talking about when you say you are careful. If you were to be careful, you would not be where you are at today. When you hear the voices of truth, do not harden your heart. That is what you did before the rebellion progressed and got you where you are now."

Grandpa adds, "Remember who were those that ended up in jail, with an aborted destiny and dreams? They were aspiring individuals with a good future, and they started well. Whose body is it that falls in the city streets? Was it not of those who rebelled against their destinies? To receive a rest for your body, soul, and spirit you need to *diverge* from your perverted perception. Accepting Corey's job offer could prepare you for a better future. Previously, you were using friends as an excuse to go out and to be like a night owl. Now upon hearing from your friends that they will not go back to their old ways, you are using a job as an excuse. Do not reject Corey's job offer."

The discussion touches Hayet's friends like never before. Bernard has earlier stated, "For the hours that I have been with you, I already feel an unceasing peace and rest that surpass my mere understanding. I wish I knew it earlier. Using this opening on behalf of myself, Shian, and Sandy, I would like to ask forgiveness of Gramps for putting our friend Hayet in such jeopardy."

Hayet says, "Good for you, Bernard. I never knew that you could preach. I know what you are going to say, years before you say it," adds Hayet, demeaning Bernard.

"Knowledge by itself is nothing. Just as Tobias and Sanballat have mentioned, it is doing what you know and living by what you know that counts," adds Shian.

Hayet sarcastically replies, "Whew—. I never knew that we had two preachers here."

“I am afraid the last shall be the first, and the first shall be the last fulfilled, in your life,” affirms Sandy.

“Thanks, third preacher! Why is it that all of you turn against me? I do not need your criticism,” cries Hayet.

At that moment, nobody dares to say anything. After moments of stillness, Corey then says softly, “None of us has turned against you. Perhaps you should examine yourself. It is you who turned against yourself, and you need to *diverge*.”

How could I turn against myself? Nevertheless, by refusing to listen to the cries of his friends and loved ones, Hayet continues an unprecedented life journey that will determine his fate at a cost that may be hard to pay.

Chapter 29

The biggest devil is me. I am either my best friend or my worst enemy.

— *Whitney Houston, in an interview with Diane Sawyer*

It is possible that a person's number one enemy one wrecks one's destiny, which one cannot defeat, can be oneself.

That is what Hayet is fighting against. As he examines how he could turn against himself, there comes a knock at the door.

"Come on in," utters Grandma.

The door opens. "It is Dr. Hadas Selassie," says Chenguang Chao, the acclaimed nurse of the year who is on duty.

"Hello, everyone," the doctor says in greeting.

The moment the doctor enters, "What is going on?" shouts Tobias with an outburst aggression.

Sanballat and the Gramps know the reason for the displaced aggression. Even before Dr. Selassie, when Dr. Mohammed and Dr. Patel came in, Tobias expressed the same feeling. However, both were so gracious and ignored his ignorant remarks, completed their duties, then left.

"Do we have actual physicians, medical personnel's or nurses?" protests Tobias.

"No, we do not. The supposed actual physicians got lost, prioritized fun over fulfillment and you will not find them in places such as this. You will find them at Central Tavern since April 1st 1985."

April 1st 1985 is the day Tobias and Sanballat dropped out of college and they have been regular visitors at the Tavern. Dr. Selassie knows Tobias and Sanballat personally.

"Sir, take a note, if you do what we did, you will get what we got. If you want to get what you lost— the real physician that you lost, go back to where you lost."

It is a clear call for Tobias and Sanballat to return; for Hayet not to follow footsteps of his brothers.

"Okay, let us not get destructed. Hayet, you must be dearly loved to have all these visitors at one time. Other patients have one or no visitors at all," the doctor says as she pulls gloves from a drawer near the metal sink by the corner.

"This is his first hospital admission. That is why everybody is shocked," explains Grandpa. "Morris has pledged not to eat or drink until Hayet gets discharged out of the hospital," he adds.

A golden bangle bracelet and necklace adorn Dr. Selassie. Placing a blue stethoscope on her shoulder, "Okay then. I guess we will just have to get you out of here in a hurry, Hayet. Let us see what we have today. Do you want your visitors to stay here or leave the room?" the doctor asks as she read the X-ray results.

I would never let them hear the discussion. If I allow them to stay, they will use the same discussion to ridicule me. By letting them stay out of the discussion, I will be able to guard my privacy against the remarks they can use to mock me.

Hayet seriously stares at the visitors one by one. He begins to rethink what to say. He should look at it from a few perspectives. First, he has nothing to hide; second, he has nothing to confess and renounce; third, he believes that he did not do anything wrong. Last, if his job requires him to drink, then it should be understandable.

"So, what is your decision?" probes the doctor expectantly while reading the reports.

"Let them stay," he mumbles.

"I can also stay?" asks Emily.

"You use what you know to attack me. For what you do not know, you research it for the same purpose. I know you are going to use the information against me. My decision about you in this regard is that you may also stay."

"Whatever I say is for your own good. Do not push me to give you a loveless irrational promise. For the very reasons that you hate me now, you will love me in the future. I have said it to you time and time again," she replies.

"And I have said 'not really' to you time and time again."

Now that Hayet has approved of everyone's staying, the doctor asks, "So tell me why you are here."

"The four of us can tell you the entire story," cuts in Morris, swiftly, pointing to himself, Bernard, Shian, and Sandy.

"No, I want to hear from him and see whether he is sober or not."

"Please listen to the people who know the entire story and brought me here."

"No, I want to hear from you," insists the doctor.

"All that I know is that Morris offered me a job, and I accepted the offer. Multiple servers came with free drinks. At first, I declined the drinks. However, one insisted that I drink so that I may become bold. I took the first, second, and third cups. It became unstoppable to the point that I do not know what happened. Then I found myself here."

"Do you know the names of the drinks?"

"No, I do not. Most of them had no label, served in tiny little cups. Moreover, I was so nervous and did not ask the names of the drinks. One thing I know for sure is that all the drinks burned and irritated my throat."

Bernard declares, "It was Bacardi, Everclear, vodka, whiskey, and other high-alcohol drinks."

The doctor says, "No wonder they served it in a little cup. These drinks are repeatedly abused by underage college students. It is a good thing that he is alive. What else do you remember?"

"That is all I know," replies Hayet.

"As witnesses, maybe we can fill in the rest," pronounces Bernard.

The doctor nods. "Hayet cannot tell what happened, so please go ahead."

Bernard resumes. "A college dropout server who enjoys inflicting pain on aspiring students offers Hayet a thirty-four-ounce beer. However, Hayet refuses to take it, knowing that it is too much for a novice drinker. When the servers insist, Hayet accepts the drinks in small containers, having refused the large drink. The young man who offered the beer becomes angry that Hayet accepted the drinks selectively. The man harbors rage in his heart and takes Hayet's action for discrimination. While Hayet walks to the restroom on staggering feet, the man ambushes and punches him. The relentless punches, after the high-alcohol-content drinks, cause Hayet to pass out, and his blood pools in the hallway. If it were not for the club security's intervention, Hayet would have been in heaven by now."

"In hell, you mean," shouts Emily.

"I told you to be quiet."

"The uppity self-important people do not like to be corrected; they never ask for advice from those who are wiser."

"May I know who are wiser? No doubt that you are going to be one of the wise people."

"A wise man is he who built his house on the rock. The rain came down, the streams rose, and the winds blew and beat against that house, yet it did not fall, because it had its foundation on the rock. A foolish man is he who built his house on sand. The rain came down, the streams rose, and the winds blew and beat against that house, and it fell with a great crash near the bathroom in the Piccolo night club and is misfiring at the New York University Hospital of Columbia and Cornell. In that case, you are the foolish one; everybody else is wise. I hope I have answered your question."

Hayet sternly gawks at Emily without blinking his eyes. Nevertheless, she is as bold as brass. After a short while, Hayet asks, "Where's the man now? Who is he and how can I find him?"

"He is under control. It is a young man named Mr. Tyler Taylor," replies Morris.

"I know him. With the same measure that he inflicted pain on me, it shall be measured to him."

"The words of the godly are a life-giving fountain; but the mouth of the wicked conceals violence."

"Am I the wicked?"

"You know yourself. What I intend to say is that, I do not want to hear about revenge. Violence brings only violence. Hate does not get even with another hate. Darkness does not drive out darkness; only light does. Do you know the light I am referring to?" protests Grandma.

"Jesus is the light," yells Emily.

What am I going to do with you, Emily?

By then, the nurse has unwrapped Hayet's head bandage. The bruises, swollen forehead, puffy and bloody nose, and battered and cracked lips are ugly. Hayet can hardly see. His eyelids and cheeks are puffed up severely, as from a bee sting.

In the meantime, Emily takes a mirror from her black handbag and tosses it onto Hayet's lap. "Look at yourself!"

"Do not worry, honey, I have one," replies the nurse, holding a mirror in front of the battered patient.

It is unbelievable what the mirror displays. Hayet utters, "Is this me?" At the same time, he sneezes, and tears gush down his face from the pain. He wipes the tears with his salty hand, and the salt burns his wounds.

Emily zips in swiftly, giving comforting, tender touches to his shoulder as she sits by the bed. She not only wipes all the tracks of his tears but also clears the sniffles from his nose. Because of Emily's loving service, Hayet feels no more burning. *I do not understand why she treats me the way she does despite my looking at her with a suspicious eye.*

Hayet manages to utter "Thank you" with a smile on his swollen face as he continues to heal under her loving care.

Upon seeing Emily's kindness wiping his tears and sniffles, Mrs. Lionel, whose voice is like the lion's roar, says, "She could make a good and a caring wife for the acting up Hayet."

"In the natural sense, it does not look like it; because they appear to be antagonists; however, in the spiritual sense, with God all that was impossible is possible," replies Grandma.

A moment later, "It is okay; you just let go of it," whispers Grandma feebly from across the bed, entreating Hayet not to seek revenge on his attacker.

"How can I let go of it after seeing the unpleasant condition of my face? What would you do if it were you?"

"I would do what Jesus would do, and that is to forgive."

"Be assured there is no forgiveness!"

Here the nurse speaks, addressing Grandma. "About the legal proceedings, do not worry. Hayet will have to give a statement to the police, who will talk to him within twenty-four hours."

After reading the X-ray report, the doctor says, "The cuts, scrapes, and bumps on the head and face that you see are only external. The good news is that he has no concussion, fractured bones, and no internal bleeding. Dizziness and headaches, which are common symptoms in these situations, will subside. I will discharge you today. Finally, I would like to tell you to try not to drink again. If you do drink, make sure to know your limit."

Upon hearing Dr. Selassie's instruction, Grandma yells, "That is enough, doctor! It feels as if you are encouraging him to drink. We have spent a sleepless night, and we do not want to see him drink ever again."

"I understand what you mean, Mrs. Caleb," says the doctor.

"I wish it were enough. However, it is not. I am afraid to warn you that this is the beginning. Be prepared for the worst."

"Doctor, there is nothing worse than this—bringing shame to himself and to the family's reputation. None of us has behaved the way he did."

Dr. Selassie smiles and says, "I can tell the kind of life perception you have of what you are saying. By the way, you sound like my mother. Drinking and deviation from purposeful living have become an epidemic in college. Students leave the home environment to go to college, and they become excited by knowing that they are free. They do not have to explain to their parents or guardians every day where they are or where they are going, who they are or were with, or what time they return to the dorm. The freedom of being in charge of their lives gives them the freedom to explore all that they did not try at home, and eventually, they become lost. A lot of them fail to comprehend that they are responsible for the choices they make." Dr. Selassie's explanation does not impress the visitors.

“Doctor, your explanation sounds good for a freshman student. However, Hayet is in his fourth year,” exclaims Grandpa, who looks saddened by Hayet’s wrong choice.

“Oh, I perceived that he was a freshman. Still, some students start exploring late. That is not all. He may end up behind bars for some DUI (Driving Under the Influence.) He might also be accused of stealing, larceny, and other crimes when he lacks the money to quench his cravings.”

“Will I ever live to see what you are talking about?” Grandma cries.

“You are seeing the beginning of what I am telling you. My prayer and wish for Hayet and other lost students is to embrace purposeful living, reacquire their GPS. I also pray to God to open their blind eyes so that they may see and give priority to their academic integrity, never hungering again for a wasted life. I have friends who started well yet ended up destroying their lives. A few started terribly and ended well. A number who chose the wrong avenue of life are dead. Some of them are wasting brilliant minds in prison, doing prisoner jobs. Others are living paycheck to paycheck. If they go to where they left they could get what they left.”

After listening attentively, Hayet declares, “I do not like the words *lost and blind*, doctor. Why are you referring to me as one? I am not lost or blind. I am in command of my life.”

“Doctor, you should not be offended by what Hayet is saying. We agree with your remarks. He is confused and lost. That is why we found him at the hospital,” exclaims Grandma.

Furthermore, Grandpa tells Hayet, “Although you have free will to do whatever you want, you are entrusted with the life that you have. One day you shall explain how you make use of the days of your life. If people could do whatever they want and get away with it, it would be unfair to the decent. A reward or a punishment wait for all that we do.”

Hayet laughs and replies, “Do not give me the old-fashioned, unrealistic sermon and threaten me about living my life. The world is the way it was millions of years ago. It shall be the same in the future, too. As long as I do well for the sake of heaven, then I will be passable. All roads lead to heaven.”

"You are wrong! That is not a message of the true gospel of salvation that diverts from the only Way, the Truth, and the Life. Don't you comprehend that in a race all the runners run, but only one gets the best trophy? Run in such a way as to get the prize. Therefore, Hayet, since we are surrounded by such a great cloud of witnesses, let us get rid of everything that hinders and the sin that so easily entraps us. Let us run with determination the race marked out for us," challenges Mrs. Klein.

"I am good. Don't worry about me."

"Son, you cannot be good enough to please God on your own. It is only when God's grace covers you that you become passable and acceptable. What agreement is there between the temple of God and the idols? We are the temple of the living God who lives within us. God has said, 'I will live with them and walk among them, and I will be their God, and they will be my people. Therefore, come out of your perverted thinking, have a godly perception and be separate, says the Lord. Touch no unclean and ungodly contaminants and I will receive you. I will be a father to you, and you will be my son,'" rebukes the outspoken Mrs. Klein.

Right then, Elias, Gupta, Paula, Lee, and Makerere arrive at the hospital room and stand in the corner, opposite the sink. Hayet rolls his eyes in shock the moment he sees them.

Before Dr. Selassie exits, she says, "Should you have any questions, you may ask any one of us. Otherwise, I wish you a quick recovery. Get well soon."

"How did you hear that I got admitted into the hospital?" Hayet asks the new visitors.

Elias replies, "You are like a light that shines during the day and night in our college. Not only that, but you are also like a city upon a hill that cannot be hidden. Should any cloud hover over you, anyone can tell what is going on. Nothing that you do and say remains a secret. Everybody, the current students and graduates that are out in the world, know whatever you do."

"Corey is a witness of the former graduates," states Emily.

"Keep quiet; nobody asked you," howls Hayet.

"Oh? I did not know that," pronounces Elias.

"Regardless of what happened, you are alive," emphasizes the bashful Paula.

As the patient and the visitors chat, two more visitors whom Hayet does not want to see at his hospital bed show up. It is LeAnn and the man they met on the WTC tour, Spring Springer. She married him, and she appears to be expecting.

The moment Hayet sees LeAnn and Mr. Springer, he cries, “Oh, no, why would you also come?”

“Tell us one reason why we should not come?” replies LeAnn simply.

To divert everybody from the heated discussion, Hayet inquires, “Are you still working at the WTC?”

“Yes. We just renewed our contract. It ends at midnight on September 11, 2001,” responds LeAnn.

The nurse interrupts the discussion. “In a short while, you shall be set to go after the IV removal.”

“We still did not make the payment. You want to let us go for free?” probes Grandpa.

“Nothing is for free unless it is paid for,” replies the nurse.

Here is the paid-for statement again.

“The bill is paid. Morris paid it all,” informs Bernard.

“Sorry, I did not tell you about that. I feel responsible for the entire incident, and so I paid it all,” discloses Morris meekly.

“Thanks for your kindness. However, you should not have done that,” declares Grandpa.

“It is my pleasure.” In the meantime, the nurse continues removing the IV from Hayet’s wrist as well as the tape from his chest.

“Ouch, it pinches,” growls Hayet, squeezing the spongy pillow.

“Sorry, that is the downside of IV and removing a tape from a hairy chest and arm.”

After a little more pinching the nurse informs him, “You are set to go now. I hope to see you soon.”

“It hurts,” Hayet slurs, wiggling his puffy and hairy wrist.

Grandma probes attentively, “Excuse me. What did you wish?”

“I hope to see you soon,” repeats the nurse strictly.

“You wish people to become sick?”

"That is the daily prayer of every medical practitioner and the people that work in health care. If people do not become sick, then we cannot work to pay our bills. My remarks should not be new to you. The mechanic wishes for vehicles to break down. Lawyers wish people to be in trouble. Teachers wish people to go to school. Graveyard and funeral home workers wish for people to die. The list goes on. We are interconnected. I cannot live without you, and you cannot live without me. Sorry, my words might be offensive, yet it is a reality," explains the nurse.

"Do you wish to become sick, be in trouble, or have your car break down?"

"No!"

"Be fair! Treat and wish others as you would like them to treat and wish for you."

The nurse's unkind yet realistic reply stuns Grandma. Yet she manages to say a thank you. At the same time, Grandma opens the wardrobe.

"His clothes are wet and blood-soaked," she says as she checks out the clothing items one by one. "You cannot put on these clothes until they are washed."

Grandpa suggests, "It is faster to buy more than to go home to bring more or to wash them. Bernard, you know his size. Please go with me to the store." Bernard nods. "We, too, will go with you," whispers Shian as she glares at Sandy, and they trail the men out of the room.

By the time Hayet finishes bathing, Grandpa slips in and hands him the new clothes. After an expedited discharge from the hospital, they arrive home quickly and in a few hours, Hayet plans to go again to the same club, against his loved ones' protests.

Chapter 30

Be nice to nerds. Chances are that you will end up working for one.

— Bill Gates

Family and friends are happy to bring Hayet home without any broken bones and wish him to stay, never to make such a mistake again, which he is most likely to repeat.

Hayet pulls out his watch from his pocket repeatedly. He often seems as if he has to go somewhere important.

At home, almost all is in the same place as when he left. However, the light appears to be a little brighter. It feels as if he spent an eternity at the hospital.

"I am glad to be home," Hayet remarks in a shallow gasp.

"We are glad, too. We hope that you will never get into such mischief again, for the sake of yourself, your family, and your community," declares Grandma sharply. At the same time, she sets a brown popcorn bowl on the slab table and then pours the corn in a hot oily cooker on the stove. Sizzling popcorn rattles with small explosions. The buttery aroma fills the room, and the popcorn fans salivate in anticipation.

Bernard places his flat cap on his skinny kneecap and slouches on the floor, eagerly waiting for the popcorn. Suddenly, the red-hot popper's lid accidentally falls to the white vinyl tile floor.

"The popcorn is safe," assures Grandpa as he pours it into the grass-woven old brown bowl. Immediately, each of them scoops up a handful, crunching large volumes of hot, buttery, sugary, sensational popcorn. They quench their thirst with water and juice.

Early in the evening, the moderate wind blows gently throughout the city. The sun sets in a hurry. The universe turns dark and cloudier than ever.

It has been hours since birds and human beings began nesting in their respective residences. The highways have few people walking and others driving.

Bernard, Sandy, and Shian have been listening to endless lessons from the Gramps.

While accommodating the visitors, Hayet frequently glances at his watch. *I am late*, he thinks repeatedly, wishing several times that they would stop for the day. However, the discussion never seems to end. Finally, he prays, *O Lord, please let them stop for the day.* However, they seem to be far from wrapping up. Hayet's wishes and prayers never seem to work. He dresses up and interrupts the flow of lively conversation.

"I have to go to work. Morris is expecting me."

The announcement overturns the friendly and peaceful atmosphere. It is a significant blow to all of them, and it makes Grandma stagger. She grabs her rib cage on the left side and falls to her recliner.

"Are you okay, Grandma?" cries Hayet as everyone rushes to her. She gains her self-possession in a moment or so.

"I am okay," she assures them.

"Honey, I want you to relax. Please do not leave me so early," pleads Grandpa.

"How can I relax while my house is on fire and I am seeing my dear son whooshing to an endless tunnel that leads to eternal death? I have to say or do what it takes, even if it hurts," retorts Grandma shakily.

"I am going to work, Grandma, nothing else."

"It is foolish to disregard what your parents taught you; it is wise to accept their correction. Therefore, obey your father and mother, or else the result will be irremediable hurt," Sandy rebukes him.

"I knew that long before you."

Shian says, "We did not say whether you know it. First, you never informed us. Second, if you were to have genuine knowledge, at least you would stick with what you know."

The lectures exasperate Hayet. "I want all of you intolerants to hear me clearly. I am a man and can do whatever I want. I do not want to hear any of your criticism. You should not stand between my hopeful job and me. Besides, three of you have no audacity to rebuke me."

"Constructive criticism is good, not intolerance. Besides, telling a rebellious fish out of water that he is wrong requires only courage," declares Bernard.

Grandma cries softly, "We are opposing the walk of life that has crept up on you unnoticed, not a job offer. We prayed and worked diligently to ensure that your humble beginning will lead you to a prosperous future and that your influence spreads to the four corners of the earth like a tree planted by the water. It is in such a place that the birds come and perch on its branches; humans and animals rest under the shade. We are troubled to see that you are drifting from intentional living. Your wrong choice may sift you slowly. Like an eagle teaching its young to fly, catching them safely on its spreading wings, the Lord shall take you on life adventures. Therefore, God will help you. He will lead you into the wilderness and speak tenderly to you. In the wilderness, the troubles and intimidation will hammer you mightily. You shall groan because of the hardship you shall face. There, you shall respond as in the days of your childhood. Regrettably, you shall transfer to another university, abbreviated UOW, until the devil cooks you."

In slow motion, Hayet is heading to a way that appears to be right, but in the end, it can only lead to death.

Chapter 31

In the end, it is not the years in your life that count. It is the life in your years.

— *Abraham Lincoln*

"Hayet, sad to say that you are transferring to another university," declares Grandma.

Occasionally, she uses an expression relating to what determines Hayet's fate. He needs more explanation as to what UOW is.

"What kind of university are you talking about?" inquires Hayet.

Grandma explains, "In the world, we have outstanding universities such as the University of Cambridge, Harvard University, the Massachusetts Institute of Technology, Yale University, the University of Oxford, and so on."

Grandma appreciates the value of the productive force that these educational establishments pour into the field of service. However, UOW produces students that are much more qualified than those the Ivy League universities train.

Hayet asks, "What makes the university that you are talking about different than other institutions?"

"UOW is an institution where eminent graduation can take effect immediately once the enlistee declares an allegiance. At UOW, the past, the first earned credit or demerit, does not count. The enlistee for the program is required to start fresh, with a clean chapter. Unlike the Ivy League universities, which are limited to a few places, UOW has many branches in all countries around the world and has a minimum requirement to enlist. As long as one meets the minimum requirement, that is, not quitting, one is safe to stay on the course.

UOW is the institution where Moses Amram, William Carey, Abraham Lincoln, Susan B. Anthony, Harriet Tubman, Mahatma Gandhi, Watchman Nee, John F. Kennedy, Martin Luther King, Woldeab Woldemariam, Mother Teresa, Benazir Bhutto, and Nelson Mandela graduated with honors. They dedicated their lives to their calling. All these graduates share a few commonalities: serving humanity justly, fairly, and honestly."

"What makes the graduate of UOW different than graduates from other universities?" inquires Hayet.

"The thing that makes the UOW graduate different is that it teaches practical lifelong lessons, unlike the learning institutions' training that ends in about four years or so. Some of the trainees received the baton from like-minded team members just like in a relay race. Some of them may have initiated, dreamed, and created their own batons, working to fulfill their own destinies. No matter how they got a baton, each one of them stretches an arm to hand over the baton so that someone else, such as you, may take it in turn until the team wins. Each human being is responsible and ought to be willing to take part in the race to make the sacrifices paid by the servants of justice workable for future generations."

At one point, out of concern, Grandpa cries, "If you walk away from the truth, you shall never prosper in whatever you do until you rectify your perspective. *Diverge* to where you belong, first to God and then to a purposeful living."

"Also remember that it is easier to enter into something than to get out of it," says Emily.

Internally, Hayet cries, *Stand at the crossroads and look, ask for the right street and the old way which you deviated from, walk in it, and you will find rest for your soul.* However, externally he still utters, "I am going to work, nothing else."

Hayet perceives that all of them are wrong and are intolerant of him, and he is right. *All that they are saying is because I am different. Furthermore, they do not want me to enjoy life, earning good money to achieve the American dream.*

Hayet seems to have missed the fact that a person achieves the American dream through hard work and purposeful living, not by deviating from intentional living.

Corey cries piteously. She sobs -as if Hayet has transferred to a place where there will be weeping and gnashing of teeth, demeaning lifelong learning, and hellish torture. "You do not have to cry, Corey. By the way, I promise to all of you that I will never transfer to any university. Should it happen, rest assured it shall be to a better one," he states.

Hayet does not seem to grasp what Grandma is saying. He does not realize that he has already been in the process of transferring. "Grandma is talking about the University of Wilderness," Grandpa states openly.

"Huh! The University of Wilderness?" echoes Hayet.

"By the way, no one could ever be compared to the earlier mentioned faithful servants, the harbingers of justice, fairness, and service," Hayet says as he walks toward the door.

"You know, son, when you say no to one, you are saying yes to another. That is how the faithful leaders that I mentioned started their journey of service," declares Grandpa.

"If I say no to all, refusing to conform to everybody else's pattern of life, that would be intolerance, a heresy making me a heretic."

"Yes, you are an intolerant heretic for good on the inside and you need to bring it out to the public. If not, you would be less effective, a follower rather than a great leader, settling for less."

"We have previously discussed intolerance. Do you know what heresy is, who heretics are, and what they do?" asks Grandpa.

"Yes, I do know. Heresy is any provocative belief that opposes generally accepted norms and is different from the established and acceptable beliefs. A heretic is a supporter of such statements or beliefs. Heretics are rebellious charismatic people who do not conform to the status quo."

"Good. How do heretics appear?"

"Heretics come in black, white, and all colors and from religious as well as nonreligious backgrounds. Heretics may be male or female; they may have accents or not. Physically, heretics may be petite; however, internally they are very rooted and strong."

"How do heretics survive?"

"They have an unshakable faith. When they pass through the mighty waters, they survive. When they walk through the consuming fire, they stay alive. The flames will not set the heretic ablaze because their eyes are set on destiny."

"How do they identify what is beneficial?"

"Heretics are visionaries; they start doing and saying unheard-of stories and walk toward it. They have eyes other people do not see, they have ears other people do not hear, and they are endowed with unique senses and gutsy stamina that is dormant in others. Heretics are people who never give up, deaf to discouragement, who fight until they get what they want. Heretics are talented innovators who are not afraid to tell people 'I am leading. Follow me.' They do not work to please people; even if no one seems to follow them, they keep on going, listening to their inner convictions."

"How do heretics serve and grow up to live?"

"Heretics serve fairly and justly without racial, gender, or religious bias. Heretics become kings, queens, senators, members of Parliament, cabinet members, presidents, millionaires, scientists, doctors, inventors, and billionaires. Heretics do not settle for less. Powers of isolation and intimidation cannot prevent them from following what they hear, see, and smell. They are history makers doing well in the community, and in return, they get satisfaction by helping others. They may probably live a short life; nevertheless, their impressionable memories shall live forever," explains Hayet.

Grandpa resumes, "I can see that you got the point. If you have not been an intolerant heretic or if you do not choose to be one, you will end up in the University of Wilderness, which is not good for our society."

The Gramps for sure know that the UOW has an exit and a graduation. However, it never happens until the right time. When the time is up, just the way a hatching chick exits from an eggshell, the UOW sends out the most convenient intern in the field of service. Although a student has the right to choose where to work, the UOW is the largest entity in the world that assigns interns to the field for the best results.

There, in the midst of the excruciating and painful training of the UOW, one's ears and eyes open and function as they should. However, by the time one learns the life lesson the hard way, it might be too late to undo the wrongs of life.

Bernard is so angry about Hayet's senseless as well as uncomprehending rationale and that Hayet cannot see what everybody else in the house sees. Then he asserts, "Two wrongs will not make a right. You do not have a rational argument."

"What is wrong one?" asks Hayet, waving one thumb.

"You got drunk and disrupted the lives of many people."

"What is wrong two?" he asks, waving a pointer finger.

"Not admitting the wrong you made and wanting to go out for what you call work, disobeying your parents," replies Bernard.

"Are you jealous of me?"

"I was until you dropped us at the club yesterday; no more. However, I wish that you would admit your deficiency so that you may fix it by having a new perception."

"What deficiency do I have?"

"Ignorance and inability to know that you do not know, which leads you into actions where you act in foolish ways without realizing that you are being one," explains Bernard.

How am I ignorant and unable to know that I do not know? Hayet freezes as he contemplates. *The trios have been to clubs and know inside out of such places more than I do. The Gramps from experience know what is beneficial, telling me from their experience. I should be the ignorant one.* Although Hayet is unlikely to admit it openly, he will obviously choose either to listen to his friends' and adoptive parents' advice not to go to Piccolo or ignore their advice and go. Whichever way he chooses, a reward or a punishment of the University of Wilderness await him. The sooner he makes good choices, the better it becomes.

Chapter 32

I have got to say no to the good so I can say yes to the best.

— *Zig Ziglar*

Family and friends discourage Hayet from returning to Piccolo, yet he turns a deaf ear and jaywalks through the perilous way that decides his destiny.

He grabs the car keys. Grandpa proclaims gutsily, "Put the keys back where they belong. The bridge is out. Do not ignore our warning, sin is crouching at your door, desiring to have you. However, you must rule over it. If you are obedient, you will enjoy the blessings of the earth. Nevertheless, if you disobey by doing what God would not want you to do, you will die in vain." Hayet bought the car on a credit. Yet he obeys Grandpa.

"Here we go again," Hayet fires back. "You will not stop me from doing what I want to do."

"If you refuse to stop by our courteous pleading, God will hand you over to people and condition that will put you in trouble; perhaps police officers will get to stop you. You will understand when it gets fulfilled."

"Whenever a person refuses to comply with your way of life, you condemn that person forever. Please do not be overprotective and worry about me. I am a man. Let me enjoy my life! Learn to be tolerant."

"Son, who is tolerant and who is not? In fact, want you to tell us who is tolerant. Give us one example of a tolerant person. I want you to tell us today to find out whether that person is tolerant or not."

"An American president."

"Example."

"He signed an executive order requiring every public-school district in the United States to allow transgender students to use the bathrooms that match the gender identity they have chosen. Grandpa, also do not support Religious Liberty Bill."

"What are the consequences for not accommodating bathroom wants and supporting Religious Liberty Bill?"

"Business people would stop employing, operating from our cities and relocate to other tolerant places. That would be bad for our economy."

"God established our nation, reared our children and brought them up, but we have rebelled against Him compromising the family and identity values one should not compromise. The ox knows its master, the donkey its owner's manger, but we do not know how to distinguish a male gender from a female. If we keep silent at a time such as this, scripture's 'they are blind guides. If the blind lead the blind, both will fall into a ditch' gets fulfilled on us."

"Son, the business people live for themselves; we pay for the services we get. For years, we have lived without such threat and we can still live regardless of all sorts of threats. When their source of money boycotts, refuses to do business with them, they will come to where they belong. What else, Hayet?"

"It would be considered a hate crime and the president would pull of billions of dollars in federal education funding for public schools."

"That is an impeachable offense, which could cause some leaders of states to sell their birthright for the sake of funds. The more we accept the unacceptable liberal ideology neglecting our religious conviction for money, accepting the unacceptable becomes the norm of our time. The Europeans walked such walk long before us and look how socially and spiritually in a hopeless stage they are in, almost becoming Europistan. The more we give in to liberalism, the more liberals demand. By sympathizing with to people who do ungodly practices we do not help them. One has to stand tall and say no, where no is due. That is what the passengers of Flight 93 did, sacrificing their lives averted further catastrophe that could have happened."

"So, what do you expect the Europeans to do?"

"Have a great godly awakening. The more a society devalues family and morality, the worse it gets. Therefore, they should diverge and return to the God of their forefathers, just as we should be, identify and say no to the slow killing political correctness once and for all. Besides, by withholding funds from educating our children and imposing un-American values on poor nations refusing to give aid for not supporting his views, is he being tolerant?"

"No, he is being intolerant himself."

"Thank you for speaking the truth. The champion of tolerance is intolerant, and so are we."

"Take a note, son. Giving and receiving money for a wicked gain it brings a curse on the giver and the receiver. That is what the money that has been given and received for selling Jesus did."

"Son and honey, I have good news for you. Not anymore."

What not anymore? thought Hayet.

"The days whereby people get disinvited from making a scheduled presentation for invoking the name of Jesus, for speaking personal and religious conviction that marriage should be between one man and one woman, for teaching showing the religious differences are numbered and the hours is near. I see a day and it has already come, out of the march of the great improbable, emerging movement, there came a mighty uproar such a great shout that the ground shook. I see an awakening movement such as nothing like this has happened before. It feels like a round loaf of barley bread came rolling in a slow motion into the camp of liberals. It struck the tent with such force that the tent overturned and knocked it flat, causing the inhabitants to be in disarray and making them unable to reason judiciously; and may it never rise again."

"Thank you!" At the same time, Hayet opens the squeaky door and lets it slam shut behind him.

He leans against the door with his eyes closed, thinking about his choices. Then he makes his way to the highway. Suddenly, multiple, violent screeches echo on the busy road, the sounds of an accident. Right after the accident, emergency vehicles swarm over the scene.

It is good that I did not rush into the street. I might have been a victim, Hayet notes, and he starts to question the wisdom of his outing.

Instantaneously, more emergency personnel arrive with blaring sirens and flashing strobe lights as Hayet walks cautiously. Victims whimper, "Help, help." Yellow tape encircles the scene from one parking meter to another. Passing through the bloody and deadly accident scene is slow and difficult.

Abruptly, thicker foggy clouds swirl, making it difficult to see the next step. The fog is so thick that the emergency lights and the sporadic streetlights hardly light the roadways.

Hayet leans by an old yellow phone booth, staring at the warm and hazy mist hovering around him. Emergency vehicles park on the boulevards and pedestrians wait for the moon to shine through the fog.

Hayet is waiting for a gusty wind to blow. He is waiting for bright lightning and thunderous rain showers to come down and dissolve the haze. The waiting does not help; in fact, it becomes darker. Such clouds usually turn into rain. However, this one never seems to produce rain or even drizzling showers, yet he still has to wait.

He is being unrealistic about his own chances of traveling safely. *I wish I had a bat's echolocation navigation system to make it through the cloudy haze safely. Go to Piccolo to make the customers love the entertainment, attain recognition, and earn easy flowing cash.* Nonetheless, daydreams or fantasies cannot override the weather challenge. Working on the reality of the here and now is the only solution.

The clouds never clear, yet he continues walking watchfully. While walking, less than half a mile to Piccolo, he bumps into a curb, falls, and hits a broken parking meter.

"Why is it that hurdles hinder my way?" he cries aloud. In such conditions, Emily would usually say *Porque Dios te ama*. Grandpa would say because God loves you.

Nevertheless, he thinks, *I do not understand a lover who blocks every move I make*.

Although Hayet is not aware of it, an extraordinary hindrance is happening. He has a hard time getting to Piccolo. He is unable to do what he wants, whereas everybody else enjoys a free and flowing life. The hindrances force him to think, *Perhaps God is saying I should return home.*

Against all odds, Hayet finally makes it to Piccolo. Earning money is a priority. Right away, he recognizes a man walking back and forth in front of the main entrance; it is Morris. He is still in the outfit that he wore in the hospital.

"Hi, Morris," greets Hayet.

"Is that you? What makes you come now instead of recovering at home after experiencing such trauma? Yesterday, you humiliated me and let me down in front of my revered customers," shouts Morris.

"Morris, I did not mean to humiliate you. *It just happened.*"

"Whether you meant it or not, there is no excuse for what you did. Nothing like what you did just happens unless someone willfully allows it. Besides, nobody ever has inflicted damage to my business reputation the way you did. I would rather stay without a musician than repeat yesterday's humiliation. Do not expect me to give you an assignment, even if you offer your service for free." Hayet is so disgraced.

"You know, Morris—" begins Hayet, attempting to explain how he can make up the past unfortunate event.

"I do not need any explanation. Go home and recover," yells Morris before Hayet completes his sentence.

In the midst of the discussion, Bernard, Sandy, and Shian arrive and walk toward Morris and Hayet.

Having been refused work now, he thinks, *Perhaps I should have listened to my family and friends and stayed home.* Nevertheless, he pledges, *I will not show any sign of weakness to my friends.*

Bernard probes, "What is going on?"

"Nothing," answers Hayet quickly.

"How could nothing keep two business partners in such intense discussion?" states Sandy.

"Well, I came over for work, and Morris would not give me a job. Perhaps I should have listened to you all," whispers Hayet with a sigh.

"Too late is better than never," replies Shian.

"It might be. However, I am not ready to go home now."

Meanwhile, Shian leads the way inside, and they sit next to the exit door. There is no bustling and live music in the club.

"May I take your orders?" says Delilah with a pretentious smile.

"I will take water," says Shian.

"I am good," says Bernard.

"Not now," replies Sandy.

"Come on, drink what you always order. You cannot go cold turkey in one day," argues Hayet.

"We decided," answers Sandy.

"I do not believe that. You need therapy to give up the drinking habits that you developed over the years. You should ease your alcohol addiction through reduction and replacement medication," asserts Hayet.

"Nope, that is it. The Gramps told us that when God enters in your heart He changes all inside out. We shall see, though, how it works," reiterates Sandy.

"Well, we shall see whether it lasts or not. Tonight, I am going to drink just one on behalf of all of you," says Hayet, turning toward Delilah.

Right then, Delilah's coworker whispers into her ear.

"Delilah, I am ready," calls out Hayet. However, instead of tending to him, she moves to the other side.

"May I take your order?" she asks, facing Sandy for the second time. Hayet follows Delilah with his eyes and then shifts his gazes to the table that has no drink. From the look on Delilah's face, Hayet can tell she has been instructed about him.

"I have already told you, not now," shouts Sandy.

"Sorry for bothering you. I thought you made up your mind. May I take your order?" Delilah says, turning her face toward Hayet.

"Please, bring me just one of what you served me yesterday," Hayet says as he settles into his chair. Delilah frowns and stares at him as if he were saying an awful word.

"Why are you frowning at me?"

"I have been ordered not to serve you drinks."

"Why do you serve the others and refuse to serve me? Is it because I am different?"

"As a man thinks, so he is," Delilah replies. "If you think that you are different, then you are. One bit of information, though, you can choose to use your difference to influence lives for good. Besides, you know the truth. We treat you according to the content of your character, not for who you are."

Bernard speaks to Hayet, "Buddy, cool down—security will boot you out."

"So be it! Why does she treat me differently? I have to speak up for my rights."

"Listen, sir, we do not entertain any favoritism in this facility. Besides, we have the right to refuse service to destructive customers. Even without any orders from the top management, I would not serve you because of how you behaved yesterday."

"Delilah, it is you who pleaded with me to have a drink and served me yesterday. Why do you refuse to serve me today?"

"Yes, I served you. However, I did not force you to become drunk. You are always responsible for your actions."

"I want you to forget what happened yesterday. Just give me one drink for today."

"No, yesterday's action is evidence of what is likely to happen today and tomorrow. Yesterday, you did not behave after you had a couple of drinks. Today, as well. I expect the same. Let me be clear. The club owner is not likely to allow you to drink for several months. You can drink at other places; however, you will not be allowed to have a sip, or even come here drunk."

The absence of lively music makes the conversation the focus of the spacious hall as the drunk and the sober stare. The conversation humiliates Hayet. Yesterday, the servers beseeched him to take a sip. Now that Hayet wants to drink, they are unlikely to give him anything. *It is not fair*; he reflects as he walks away.

"Where are you going?" shouts Bernard.

"I do not know."

"Listen, buddy. If you do not plan and know where you are going, you will end up where you would not want to be and you are not going to like it.

Although I do not have any spiritual knowledge, allow me to repeat what the Grannies told us yesterday when you were asleep at the hospital. I suggest that you 'know where you are going before you start the journey.'"

"Bernard, at home, I indicated it, and let me say it again. You do not have the authority or moral right to confront me on that matter," shouts Hayet.

"I also spoke at home, and let me say it again. Yesterday you were right. However, today I do have the moral stand to challenge you. Besides, one does not have to be a perfect to correct others from going the wrong way," yells Bernard angrily.

Hayet continues toward the door. "Who cares? I am going to do what I want to do."

"Hayet, what you want to do is often what you do not need to do," cries Shian.

"We did not want you to go the way we have been going," offers Sandy.

"Additionally, you used to tell us, come, all you who are thirsty, come to the waters; and you who have no money, come, buy and eat! Come, buy wine and milk without money and without cost. Why spend be it yours or others' money on what is not bread, and your labor on what does not satisfy? Listen, listen to me and eat what is good and you will delight in the richest of fare. What happened to all the friendly lectures that you used to give us, which we vividly remember?"

"Preachers, I can see that you are the best students and know the entire lecture you had at home. Thank you for your sermons. Apply them in your lives," deprecates Hayet. His transformed friends are giving realistic lessons to Hayet. However, it is likely that he will continue to jaywalk.

Chapter 33

Not long after that, the younger son got together all he had, set off for a distant country and there squandered his wealth in wild living.

— *Luke 15:13*

Piccolo, Hayet's hiding place until he finds a purpose for his life, is in a well-known business district of gambling, eating, drinking, gun trading and drug dealing in New York City.

Most of the businesses are operational seven days a week, twenty-four hours a day. It is an ideal area for a GPS-less lifestyle. That is where one will find the lost prodigals loitering.

Outside Piccolo, it is bright under the streetlights. Night owls dressed in light clothing puff on cigars and stroll casually. The highways have no traffic congestion, and most of the vehicles are cabs.

The disgraced musician strolls around Piccolo. At one point, a negative, wishful remark of Grandpa come to mind: *You shall long to fill your stomach with the pods that the pigs eat, but no one will give you anything.*

With his unfulfilled longing for work, and furious anger bubbling within him, he has two options: return home humiliated or go to campus. Hayet does not feel good about going home with no job offer or money to prove the worthiness of his outing. He should realize that he is not a spacecraft that travels in one direction and has a hard time turning around. For a person, it is not bad to admit and return from wrong ways as it is to a spacecraft. Lately, Hayet desperately roams over the streets hungry, angry, lonely, and thirsty, exposing himself to temptation.

After wandering for a while, he meets two fellow students, Emmanuel and Felix. They go to a tavern a couple of blocks from Piccolo. Hayet unintentionally drinks, becomes drunk, passes out, is transported by the same EMS and admitted not only to the same hospital but also to the same room and bed as the night before. Furthermore, the same doctor treats him, and the same visitors greet him when he wakes.

"Welcome back," the nurse who wished to see his return to the hospital salutes him warmly.

Going through the same procedures for discharge, Chenguang, the nurse, wheels him to the shady pickup area. As Hayet enters the car, she says, "Get well." Before she finalizes the speech, Grandma and Hayet thank her in unison. Then, "And see you soon," she adds.

Time flies. A few months pass since the first day Hayet tasted an alcoholic drink. Now he is a habitual drinker. No more choking, teary eyes, throat burning, or irritation— the drinks go down easily, leading him to unforeseen patterns of behavior.

Hayet used to give a ride to his friends to go to clubs on weekends; now he goes by himself, and not only on weekends but also on weekdays. Consequently, while changing drinking places, he lags on his school assignment due dates. Bernard, Sandy, Shian, CU, Corey the resident advisor, and teachers offer Hayet counseling. However, he refuses to diverge; nothing seems to divert him from the new avenue he has chosen. Although Hayet remains friends with the trio on other matters of life, their friendship on drinking and going to club severs.

Hayet commits a sin by forsaking the Lord, the spring of living water, who could gratify him, and digs his own cisterns, broken cisterns that cannot hold water to satisfy his thirst. Eventually, through his rebelliousness, God will lead him to his destiny.

Hayet is supposed to stay purposeful at least until he graduates. However, he will not. He ignores all advice and distances himself from concerned people.

His well-being is in a chasm of the patterns of life that could destroy him. The routine he has fallen into—eat, drink, and sleep, with no time for study—becomes insensible. He spirals downward, as his GPA falls accordingly and he receives two probation warnings. Hayet's inner voice insists, *Greater achievement waits for you once the academic year ends.* Yet he has been unable to perceive that his one day of foolish and impulsive drinking at Piccolo has affected his life and studies extremely and culminates in the loss of his scholarship. What a setback for a formerly ambitious student, his adoptive parents, and the community that he represents!

At the peak of his drinking habit, Hayet goes out to the club one weekday. He decides to drive to campus, but he cannot handle drinking and driving. The moment he takes a curving exit, his head spins badly, causing him to lose control. He slams into a concrete barrier and other motorists.

Within a few hours, he finds himself in jail rather than on campus for driving under the influence. The court orders that he either pays a twenty-one dollar bond, does twenty-one days' community service, or stays in jail for twenty-one days.

After the court hearing, Gramps says, "You wanted it and you got it. We are not going to bail even a penny. We would rather give thousands to needy purposeful people than bond you."

The Gramps generously give thousands to help others make ends meet. However, now they refuse to post bail for Hayet.

"This is cruelty," he argues.

"Cruelty is the act of jaywalking and going where both the old and the young beg you not to go. Cruelty is refusing to save money for the rainy season. When you finish all the punishment that the court orders, you will be welcome home, though on your own, you will have to walk on foot," instructs Grandma.

Hayet does not like being in jail or the Gramps' response. Yet, he does not feel remorse for his actions. The accident results in one fatality, the breadwinner of a family who did not deserve to die. Additionally, Hayet, the one who is responsible for the accident and fatality, emerges from the wreck without a single scratch. *Woe onto the innocent citizens of our city that shall be victims of this drunkard's onslaught,* the statement that he stated to the drunkard woman at Piccolo, gets fulfilled through him.

Hayet manages to find a gift card to trade it to pay the court money. However, the court does not accept such payment. Phone calls to borrow from friends and relatives would not work. The price he has to pay is very high. It includes missing a deadline to hand in projects and assignments. Not long after he is eventually released from prison, he goes into the junkyard on the outskirts of the city to collect some documents from the SUV, accompanied by the campus chaplain, Dr. Michael Olsen.

The moment they enter the office, a junkyard employee asks, "How may I help you?"

"A couple of weeks ago I was involved in an accident. I want to take some stuff from the car," says Hayet as he hands over his school ID, for the police confiscated his driver's license; he can no longer drive.

After confirming Hayet's identity, the man points to a twisted hunk of metal. "It is over there. *Porque Dios te ama*; because God loves you, you survived."

Hayet climbs around and into the twisted metal to retrieve the documents. "How did I survive?" he says and chuckles in astonishment.

"I do not know," replies Dr. Michael. "That is what I am wondering. However, I believe that God is a God who saves. From Him comes escape from death. Possibly, your life was hidden and preserved in Christ by God's hand, for what He has to do through your life in the future."

Hayet is utterly amazed how he survived without a single injury.

"So after such a miraculous escape from death, do you see how God loves you? Are you ready to *diverge*?" Dr. Michael asks, expecting the obvious answer, which is yes. Nevertheless, Hayet chuckles as he maneuvers to retrieve the documents he came to get.

"After such an escape and seeing the death of an innocent person caused by your negligence, are you ready to change and return?" Dr. Michael asks again.

Hayet uncomprehendingly stares at Dr. Michael. Then he declares, "I have nothing to change. Should there be anything to change, I am not ready to do so. However, I am deeply sorry for the accident and fatality that I caused." Hayet is unable to retrieve the items he came or. Finally, they return to campus, Hayet having rejected the indisputable call to *diverge*.

Hayet has blown off his pledge never to have a drink. Even so, he is optimistic that he will not do the same with relationships—that is, he will remain chaste until marriage. In the midst of the optimism, Grandpa's remark, *Once you blow one fuse, all other fuses are most likely to go off*, echoes in his head. Hayet has a choice to make. That is, stop the madness or else face further danger.

Chapter 34

Never lie to your mother. That is like the biggest lesson that I learned, learned throughout my life, you know?

— *Bristol Palin*

Hayet's foolishness has eventually opened a door to unstoppable thoughtlessness and fails his chastity pledge.

A few months after the fatal accident on a late Saturday afternoon, Hayet walks leisurely, feeling handsome. He strolls off campus and in neighborhoods with the soccer fan friends that he met the night the Piccolo owner refused to give him a job assignment. These friends are Emmanuel and Felix. Together with Hayet, they go to participate in a classmate's musical performance about three miles away from campus.

The sun sets on their way back to the campus. The night is warm. Somewhere halfway through the journey, they walk into the neighborhood with bright streetlights and music blaring from the local establishments. Emmanuel and Felix seem to be familiar with every turn of the alleys and byways, searching assertively. They do not explain to Hayet, and Hayet does not bother to ask.

It is a mystery where they head, and this is the first time Hayet has been in such an environment.

After roaming for several minutes, Emmanuel enters an unlocked door. The door shuts and the lights go off inside. In a little while, the light turns on, the door opens, and Emmanuel comes out smiling. Immediately, Felix goes inside. The process repeats, and Felix comes out smiling. Hayet is baffled over his friends' activities. He eagerly waits to be informed what they were up to and how he can partake.

After apprehensive waiting, Emmanuel speaks bluntly about what they were up to and invites Hayet to do the same. Hayet freezes in awe and stares at both. Hayet should say no, yet he does not, because he is caught up in the moment.

Without giving a yes or no answer to the invitation, Hayet hoists his guitar over his shoulder and walks away.

"How many more times do I have to prove to you that I can make it?" he asks.

The survival of others and Corey's bait gives him optimism to play with a fire of immorality and expect to survive. He fails to comprehend that he cannot carry fire against his bosom without burning his clothes or walk over hot coals without burning his feet. It is dangerous to sleep with another man's wife, and it can devastate him.

Hayet has great potential. Regrettably, he treats his life like a tossed pair of dice, which has a probability of one in six of landing on the randomly determined integer that Hayet never guesses beforehand. He does not see the possibility of five-sixths of the integers backfiring on him.

He continues walking. Before he knows it, he is at the doorstep on which a prudent man should not fool around. Swiftly, Ms. JANE JOHN, a pleasant woman, as freshly scented as the Garden of Eden, dressed in ash-colored mini lingerie, comes out to meet him with a crafty smile. She is a person known never to stay at home. She preys on innocent souls in the street and the town square. Immediately, the door shuts, and delicate soft hands grab him by his wrist and snuggle him provocatively. The lights are off behind the vinyl window shades.

Jane takes hold of Hayet, smooches him casually with a shameless adulterous intention. She speaks, "This is your day. Today I fulfilled my vows. I came out to meet you and have found you!"

His pulse rate increases as her persuasive words pile up.

"What am I going to do?" he mumbles.

"Get it over with," replies Jane.

"What will the Gramps and God say?"

"He failed us."

"What will my future spouse say?"

"He is unfaithful."

It is taking longer than it did with Emmanuel and Felix, who are familiar with the transaction. Hayet's chance for survival appears to be slimmer than ever.

"You are a man, no cherry popping to worry. You shall walk out the way you came. What happens in Vegas stays in Vegas."

It makes it worse for Hayet to think that he is new to sensual prowess. He does not know the right moves. He looks for an exit. However, the door shuts, and the lights are out. With relentless and persuasive words, Jane seduces him. Her smooth, graceful talk persuades him to give her what he intended to keep until the day he marries.

After hasty, unreasonable, and incoherent heedfulness, *Just for today*. At the same time, he acts impulsively for fear of the consequence that may come from transgressing.

Jane is experienced in disarming the GPS of chaste young men as well as faithful husbands. Her house is a highway to the grave of promiscuity, leading to the chambers of death.

Physically, Hayet responds to her stimulation. He is unable to let go of her grip and sit cuddled by her warmth, motionless. Jane keeps pestering him. He feels that the only way out is that she attains what she wants so that she will not eventually wear him out with her aggression.

All at once, he utters, *This is my body. I can do whatever I want to do with it. If you have it, flaunt it.* He fails to realize that he is not his own but bought at a price. Therefore, he should honor God with his body. Additionally, he does not know that his body is the temple of the Holy Spirit.

"Go for it, man," whispers Jane.

He follows her like a bird fluttering into a snare. He falls into a bed that is most unlike the bed that he sat on with Corey.

He goes to bed with a woman who is not his wife for an impulsive premarital consummation. In such an unimaginable way, Hayet swaps his V card, not to the one whom he would marry but to Jane. What a terrific bombshell this will be for Hayet, the Gramps, and his faith community that invested limitless time and resources on him to achieve the walk of chastity.

Once Hayet finishes the irreversible and untimely sensual pleasure, he sticks to Jane like a magnet. However, she is done with the transaction and wants nothing to do with him.

"Now, get out. I have got to go somewhere," she yells.

In a false tongue Hayet pleads, "Babe, I love you, so please do not go. Let us stay together a few minutes more," he pleads.

"Huh? You say you love me. What I see on your face is lust, not love. Listen, if you do not go, I will." She turns down the love pleading.

He grabs his guitar and serenades her with KC and the Sunshine Band's "Please Don't Go."

Jane listens attentively. However, she insists that Hayet gets out. Finally, as she did with his friends, the light turns on, the door opens, and he exits, but in confusion.

Hayet has shot himself in the foot in his quest to stay chaste until marriage. He does not comprehend all that has taken place, *It must have been either a dream or a vision.* He walks the length of one block, taking deep breaths. *It is not a dream.* He has discarded his V card so easily with no broken pieces to mend. Yet the psychological part of it, he shall live with.

By the time he reaches campus, he learns that the breaking news has spread quickly by word of mouth. Hayet does not care much about the student body learning of his swapped V card. His main concern is what Corey, Emily, LeAnn, the Gramps, the Grannies, and Tobias and Sanballat will say should they hear the news.

Hayet goes home late at night to avoid any traces of the Grannies. He opens the door slowly and walks softly. To his surprise, what he fears will happen happens. He finds the Grannies and Tobias and Sanballat seated, looking tired, their eyes heavy.

The moment he enters, Grandma comes to meet him. She whirls around him, sniffing, inhaling, and snuffling the way a dog does when it meets a person to identify it as friend or foe.

In the midst of sniffing, Grandma observes a distinct smell. She sniffs to identify the scent. Although not a perfume, a unique scent fills the room and her nostrils, affirming that Hayet has been to a place where he ought not to be.

At the culmination of her sniffing, she asks, "Where have you been and what have you done?"

"Nowhere, and nothing," he offers carelessly for an answer.

Grandma will not stop there, for she knows that Hayet's *nowhere* is a prelude to somewhere; his *nothing* is a prelude to something.

"I want you to tell me where the nowhere is and what the nothing is," she interrogates. Grandma smells an odor that men give off after they happen to sleep with a woman for the first time. He feels ashamed to tell her. Nevertheless, he has to be honest and tell them that he has blown off his chastity fuse.

"Tell us where you have been!" she repeats.

In order to be relieved from her grueling questioning, he replies, "You know where I have been, I am guessing. Why do you ask me? I did it," he pronounces.

"Please say it clearly so that the Grannies may hear it," commands Grandma.

"I blew my chastity fuse, swapping my V card before marriage. Here is my chastity ring, I am no longer chaste," he says blankly, taking off the ring from his finger while attempting to run away from their presence.

Upon hearing Hayet's reply, Grandma tore her clothes and cries, "That is what you yearned and poked for prematurely, and that is what you got. Trust me, you are going down the wrong road." She sits, dazed, with teary eyes.

The news is a significant blow to the Gramps, who have poured all they have into helping Hayet attain academic excellence and a life of chastity. After a moment or so, Grandma puts her hands on her head and walks around, wailing and weeping aloud the way a virgin girl cries for her unjustly taken V card.

"He lost his GPS. He broke his promise to himself, to the future spouse, to the community, and to God," she utters, and then she shrieks wildly.

The news utterly and completely devastates Grandma's being. The Grannies and Grandpa came to comfort her, but she refused to be comforted and wept for Hayet.

Out of anguish, in a choked and coarse voice she says, "God anointed you to be a light to the dark world. He delivered and covered you with his feathers, He commanded His angels concerning you to guard you in all your ways, and they lifted you up in their hands so that you would not step your foot against a landmine, an enemy that you dread most."

That is right, Grandma.

"In the wilderness as well, He shut the mouth of the devouring beasts and murderous thugs to lead you to a place of safety because of God's favor on you."

Yes, Grandma.

As she weeps more, "Son, you did not fear the terror of night, nor the arrow that flies by day, nor the pestilence that stalks in the darkness, nor the plague that destroys at midday. Your very eyes have seen thousands fall at your side, ten thousand at your right hand, killed by dictators, eaten by wild animals, perished in the wilderness or submerged in the sea while escaping to safety; nevertheless, no harm has come near you."

Yes, Grandma.

"In the country of your refuge, He fed you manna for which you did not work until you started eating the fruit of the inherited land, the United States of America. If I am wrong, tell me that I am wrong!"

"You are right, Grandma," responds Hayet, reflecting God's goodness in his life journey.

She starts again: "The Lord gave you the world as your inheritance. If all this had been too little, He would have given you even more. Why did you despise the commandment of the Lord by doing what is evil in His eyes?" She pauses for an answer. Yet Hayet keeps silent.

"As a result of disobedience, you showed contempt for God in the presence of His enemies. Consequently, you will see all hell breaking loose on you, whatever you do shall not prosper, and you will be a restless vagabond on the earth until you return to where you belong, to God."

After hearing Grandma's wailing, Hayet regrets having himself fail in the presence of the Gramps, God, and his future spouse beyond anything possible to explain in human terms. He wishes the earth would open its mouth and swallow him. The moment feels as terrible as when Judas saw the Jesus that he had betrayed condemned; remorse seizes him. Judas returns the thirty pieces of silver to the chief priests and the elders.

"What is that to us?" they reply, stating, "That is your responsibility." They have no compassion for Judas, as if they did not use him. Hayet as well desires to reverse the wrong. However, that is impossible with virginity; all sales are final.

"We did not hear what you just said as a thing that you would like to achieve when we welcomed you from the airport. Was failure part of the achievement that you would like to have? This is the second big failure in a couple of months. There could be other undisclosed failures too," scoff Tobias and Sanballat. The duo's scorn is merciless. There is no legitimate reason Hayet can offer to explain what he did and why he did it.

In order to avoid further grilling interrogation, he rushes to his room, placing the ring on a zebra-colored stool. As Grandma cries in the living room, the Grannies follow him and stand by his bedside, giving him a silent punishment. The silence of the talkative Grannies is worse than a physical beating. Silence is uncommon for the noisy, ultraconservative, Jesus loving, and Fox News–watching Grannies. He tucks himself into bed and tries to ignore their presence. While resting, he is reprocessing all that took place and cannot sleep. Eventually, the Grannies walk out one by one, and Hayet gets some relief. Yet they continue to pray so vigorously that Hayet can hear every word.

"Like an eagle that shakes stirs up its nest, hovers over its young, spreads its wings to catch them, and carries them on its feathers, the Lord will cause a discomforting shake-up in Hayet's life to bring the best out of him," affirm Mrs. Jackson and Mrs. Baldwin.

"What if he dies because of the discomfort?" asks Mrs. Klein.

"Discomfort always refines, shapes, crushes, presses, and removes the chaff," replies Grandma. "It never kills anybody; comfort does. He shall not die, but live, and will proclaim what God has done in his life in the presence of an audience of millions. My father repeatedly told me that I should train my children in the way they should go, and when they are old, they will not depart from it. We have done our share and it is up to the Lord to awaken him. So be it the only one-time mistake."

The following morning, although it is time to go to church, Hayet is troubled to face Grandma and the fear of being struck dead in the manner of the biblical Ananias and Sapphira. Worse, he fears that Elton, whose position in the church has been reinstated, will expose him in the midst of the congregation the way he did with Corey, which turned out for her good.

Hayet grudgingly goes with Grandma. What he finds is worse than what he expected. The first people that he encounters happen to be Tobias and Sanballat. They stare at him with unfriendly looks, as usual. Hayet hopes not to see the same from others.

Nevertheless, it appears that everybody is kept at a distance from him and staring at him wildly. At one point he asks, "Why is it that everybody runs away and stares at me in such a manner?"

"Nobody runs away from you and stares at you in a wrong manner. For me, all is the same," declares Grandma. "Perhaps examine your heart. You might be running away from yourself and hiding from the presence of people and God. The wicked man flees dreary apprehension though no one pursues, but the righteous are as bold as a lion."

"So, are you calling me wicked?"

"Not I; the most reliable maker's manual, the Bible, does."

Hayet's face turns ashen as he considers the truth of the Grannies' remarks. If he were to do what is right, everybody would accept him. However, for going his own way, he suffers in social isolation.

The door of wickedness that he only slightly opened is wide enough to accommodate a multitude of evils. Since he cannot reverse the mistake he has made, his only option is to admit it and *diverge* to save his life from further devastation. However, Hayet is unlikely to do so.

Later in the afternoon, he goes to meet Jane to have more of what he has tasted less than twenty-four hours ago.

Eventually, Hayet's one-day misstep becomes his daily habit that he cannot live without, drinking, promiscuity, larceny, taking narcotics, and the complete abandonment of his GPS. Shortly after his deviance becomes public, he earns the nickname *Son*—a short form of the Prodigal Son. The name goes viral, spreading even beyond campus.

At one point, as Hayet is visiting with Corey and Grandma, "How do you like your new nickname?" questions, Grandma.

"What new name?"

"The Prodigal Son."

"You know it, too?" inquires Corey while staring at Grandma.

"Everybody knows, even Grandpa, the Grannies, Tobias and Sanballat," she replies, glaring at Hayet.

"I do not like it. How did Tobias and Sanballat get to know it?" wonders Hayet.

"The way everybody else did," answers Grandma.

Years after Corey graduated, her nickname still lingers. Before the transformation of Corey, the students used to say, "Angel saved Demon, but she could not save herself."

Now they say, "The Son saved Angel, but he could not save himself."

In the meantime, the academic year is ending, with less than a couple of months left to end the year. The commencement program is set. Most fourth-year students, including Hayet, are getting ready for graduation. Soon the class will disperse to graduate studies or work in diverse fields of service at home as well as around the globe. Just like all the graduating candidates, Hayet has several career and graduate studies options in mind. Since academically most of the assignments are completed at this point in the year, it is improbable for students to drop out due to academic failure. Yet nobody knows what tomorrow holds. Indeed, it was only a couple of months before graduation that Corey and Rahab changed their lifestyles. Hayet could possibly have a shifting experience if he is not careful to keep the first things first.

Chapter 35

Though the world has come a long way, we still dare to imagine a better world. Free of poverty, free of corruption, free of social ills, free of debilitating disease, and free of man's inhumanity to man.

— *Betsegaw Tadele, Valedictorian Speaker morehouse College, 2013*

In the midst of graduation anticipation, Hayet writes his final project for Dr. Tracy Travis, who instigates a lie-synthesis for the college to suspend Hayet.

Dr. Travis is the most unprofessional professor, who grades students based on her personal interest rather than honest service. She comes from a family with a long lineage of having served humanity generously, justly, and fairly. She lives in a gated mansion with her six dogs, six cats, and six birds.

Dr. Travis embraces a misguided attitude in the way she serves that contributes to lie-synthesis, the notion of which is contrary to her upbringing. She helps humanity with a partial GPS, in a point of selfish interest rather than just service, thus undermining the goodness of God. Consequently, she lags in the favor of God. Dr. Travis and most her compatriots fail terribly by God's set standard which determines right from wrong; good from bad.

In the meantime, ADELE HAILE, a classmate, asks Hayet to show her his project so that she may see how to structure her own. Hayet entrusts the project to her, believing that she will return it to the owner. Sometime later, instead of returning it, Adele declares herself the rightful owner without Hayet's consent. Then she rallies the decision makers to be supportive of her cause.

Adele admits that the project does not belong to her. However, Dr. Travis and her friends, based on a lie-synthesis, and their interests commend Adele to legalize the possession. A few students and teachers protest the injustice vocally, yet the authorities ignore them.

Dr. Travis knows Hayet as the rightful owner. Accordingly, during a private interview she says, "From the point of view of justice, Hayet deserves to have his project. Nevertheless, because of our personal interests in the project, it should be given to Adele."

Knowing Dr. Travis's intention and learning that he will not bow down to any intimidation, Hayet opposes the injustice and keeps asking that the project be given to its rightful owner. Yet, the official arbiters intentionally ignore the case.

Hayet's father used to tell him, "Hear the cases between your brothers and judge rightly between a man and his brother or a foreign resident. Do not show partiality when deciding a case; listen to small and great alike. Do not be intimidated by anyone, for judgment belongs to God." The unfair judgment infuriates Hayet.

In a system where money, power, and an invention of a lie-synthesis override the law, the College Security Council awards Adele legal ownership of Hayet's project. What is worse, the college suspends Hayet for one academic year, a mere few months before he is to graduate.

Per the unfair and unjust verdict, Hayet packs his belongings and leaves for a condition he has never faced. What a sad day for Hayet and his loved ones, witnessing unfairness that they cannot see rectified. Instead of heading to graduation and prosperity, rough terrain and an unmarked road await Hayet.

Hayet's soul is overwhelmed with humiliation. How he manages the first few difficult days ahead will determine how soon he gets on a course. Rivers can sweep over him, raging fires can set him ablaze, and he can face steep mountains to climb and valleys of death that are infested with ravaging beasts. Hayet has challenging times ahead that could drain his personhood, leaving him with no strength for positive action. He wishes he had white angelic wings to soar high as well as far away so that he might settle on some solace seashore. Not only that, perhaps he would bury his head in the sand like an ostrich until the great, powerful, and demeaning wind of shame passes. Little does he know that the difficult days ahead will shape, purge, and sift him, to bring forth a person purer and more desirable than diamond.

This is not what Hayet expected in his life. Perhaps the humiliation will lead to a terrific accomplishment that Hayet might learn to embrace and teach future generations. Ostracism and isolation are the first hurdles. Being alone and ostracized is the most horrible effect that requires endurance for one who grew up in a communal culture of Africa. What will Hayet do about his isolation in New York?

Soon some of Hayet's peers will usher in the dot-com boom. However, Hayet has no training for the bumpy roads of life. Nevertheless, he must either submit to the unfairness and injustice and retain a victim mentality or work hard and reorganize his priorities until the truth exonerates him.

Hayet begins to think about what to do and where to go. He does not want to face the Gramps and tell them that the college suspended him at a time when loved ones assume he is going to graduate. Grandpa has made plans to attend the commencement. Hayet is troubled about telling them; the Gramps might have heart attacks and die. What should he do? An unusual thought came into his mind. Nothing is worse than the unjust and unfair treatment imposed on him, besides the shame that he brings to himself and his family.

Hayet sits on a dirty bench, watching through tear-blurred eyes as white and grayish seagulls land and take off across the river. He thinks of one plan after another. Contrary to his loved ones' predictions, *In all conditions God works for your good,* nothing seems to work for his good. *The only option I see is to end my life.* He walks a few meters and then sits again. He fails to perceive that hurting himself would cut short not only his life but his ability to become what he is meant to be. He is meant to be a husband, a father, a friend, a helper, a voice to the voiceless, and an encourager to the multitudes that pass through the same condition.

Why is it that everything and everybody turn against me? Who sinned, my parents or I, that hurdles consistently hinder me? He cries out bitterly before placing both hands on his head and his elbows on his knees. His culture brought him up to believe that a man should never cry. Yet the overwhelming pressure makes him cry.

Life for everybody is easy. However, for Hayet, no matter what he tries, all ends in despair. Whatever others try, through Hayet's help, they prosper easily. In contrast, whatever Hayet tries fails, with the doors shutting like iron gates right in his face. *Perhaps Tobias and Sanballat were right in their prediction of my failures,* he frequently mutters.

In the midst of Hayet's brokenness, he feels a shadow cover him, though not a tree, a cloud, or a flying object that passes quickly. Immediately, a voice speaks that Hayet has never asked for or heard before.

"Neither you nor your parents sinned. This brokenness happened so that God may display His work in you."

Hayet becomes frightened. He sees an elderly man standing right in front of him. "What do you want from me?" Hayet cries at the top of his voice.

"Nothing," replies the elderly man as he sits by Hayet's side, giving him a tender touch to his shoulder.

"Son, I know what is going on with you. Whatever happened shall be for your good, to refine you. Go home and tell your family the truth, and do not do any harm to yourself or others."

Amid the discussion, Hayet pulls out his yellow handkerchief to blow his nose and wipe his teary eyes. Right away, he turns to the elderly man seeking more help. However, the man has disappeared, leaving no trace of his existence.

Where did he go? asks Hayet as he looks in all directions. *He cannot vanish. It should have taken someone as old as him at least a minute to walk out of my sight.*

The startling revelation terrifies Hayet, and he wonders what it might mean.

Then he comes to his senses. *If I make evil decisions that cut my life short, it is a whole family that suffers. The best thing is to see what good would come out of this impassable experience.* He heads for home.

A convoy set on the right path eventually reaches its destination. Hayet walks at a snail's pace; he reaches home and meets Grandpa seated on a wooden recliner. "You did not inform us that you were to come today. Why did you come with your luggage? By the way, your custom-made graduation suit and shoes are ready for pickup. You could go and bring them up. Furthermore, you look depressed. What is going on with you?" Grandpa says.

Hayet tells his adoptive parents bluntly, "The College Security Council has suspended me for the year." The breaking news devastates his parents.

After minutes of numbness and bitter crying, Grandpa utters in a remarkably trembling voice, "I just want to tell you that as long as you are not dead, all is possible. You can still be somebody."

The Gramps encourage Hayet not to give up. Their loving and gracious behavior is contrary to what Hayet expects and deserves.

"So, honey, what are we going to do?" questions Grandma anxiously.

"I don't know. We shall live it day by day, the way we did with the other children. However, facing Hayet, until you start school next year, listen to what I want you to do," replies Grandpa.

Grandpa, I know you are going to say be responsible, work, pay car insurance and rental.

"Since you will be off school, to teach you responsibility I want you to work and pay $1,000 for rental. Then, when you start school I will give you back all the rental that you paid. However, if you choose not to go to school by next year, you cannot get the money back."

Rental in this area is $2,200 X 12 months equals $26,400 a year. Saving twelve hundred dollars every month is a good deal. Moreover, getting the money back at the end of the year, thought Hayet. "What other options do I have?"

"You have two options. Either accept my way or find your own way."

Your way is just ten hundred dollars per month; if I find my own way including bills it could be about thirty-five hundred dollars per month.

After intentional thoughtfulness, "Grandpa, thank you so much for your offer. However, I choose to find my own way."

"Are you serious? If you choose Grandpa's way you would be investing $12,000 on you. However, if you choose your own way you would be dumping over forty thousand by the end of the year. Can you afford?" cries Grandma in disbelief.

In the reality, without a reliable professional job, even if he works twenty-four hours a day, Hayet cannot afford to live in New York. Nevertheless, he replies, "Yes, I am aware of that and I can afford."

The Gramps keep silent for seven minutes. They are not happy over Hayet's unhinged choice. However, they support his choice.

More than anything else, Hayet is not happy about the unfairness and unjust verdict. In the subsequent weeks and months, he decides to wait and see what good will come out of the situation as he works jobs that barely cover his expenses.

Eventually, the year that the college suspended him ends. Registration for the new academic year is right around the corner. Hayet is wavering between bravely registering or cowardly applying for a deferral for one more year. He irrationally feels it would be shameful to attend classes with students who were juniors before. Hayet decides to apply for a deferral to start the following year. He receives immediate approval.

A year later, the deferral comes to an end, and another academic year starts. Still, Hayet feels he is a pathetic example, refuses to study with students that know he should have graduated, and he applies for a deferral until all the students that know him graduate. How long will he wait until his friends graduate with MA or Ph.D.?

The year gives birth to another year, and more than a decade has gone by since Hayet's suspension from the college. He walks through the UOW and abandons his GPS. He wants to go back to college; nonetheless, the financial difficulties because of incurred debt and his other responsibilities appear to make it unlikely for him to improve his life through education any time soon.

Chapter 36

Death is not the greatest loss in life. The greatest loss is what dies inside us while we live.

— Norman Cousins

Life is indeed hard for Hayet after the college suspends him, yet he anticipates there will come a day of refreshment, in spite of Jezebel and her minions who wish to see his downfall beyond repair.

Will there be a day when all his sufferings will end? Yes, of course, there will be a day. However, until then, compartmentalized against his will, where God would bring out the best of him, he works earnestly, rising as early as 3:45 a.m. and staying up past midnight. He labors for bread while his former colleagues who have prioritized their lives have the best jobs working few hours per week, enjoying the fruit of their dedication. Others also achieve well with little or no effort at all. He frequently huffs, *Why is it that every door shuts on my face? What have I not done that successful people do? I wish I listened to the Gramps.*

He makes lots of effort in diverse places working to emerge victoriously. Nevertheless, Hayet appears to be endlessly sinking. There is no solid rock or firm place on which for him to stand. The world appears to collapse around him, and he sees nowhere to escape. All that he tries and everyone that knows him seem to turn against him. He has reached his limit, is at his breaking point, and is at a dead end, betrayed by friends and relatives. Some of his relatives—those he foresaw would support him in his days of trouble—turn out to be the most aggravating enemies. The reason is that they choose to embody Jezebel and thus shut a potential door of progress, voting against him and desiring to crush his personhood beyond restoration. *Persecution for doing wrong is at least acceptable.* Hayet is honest and loyal, desires to see just proceedings; he has done nothing wrong for which he deserves persecution.

Out of anguish under the immense persecution, Hayet cries, "Grandpa, I feel that I have no strength to continue life. My family is the worst tormentor. I feel like surrendering to my persecutors."

"Even if you comply and surrender to the persecuting the Tobias and the Jezebel embodied, you still will not be free from persecution until you get aborted destiny. That is the ultimate goal of they that who want to see your destruction. You have to keep on fighting and walking by faith until you win, and for sure you will. I remember one time my father told me, 'Be alert and of sober mind. Your enemy, the devil, prowls around like a roaring lion looking for someone to devour.'"

"Grandpa, I am about to be swallowed alive. I have no strength to continue."

"I understand. Let me tell you one secret. Whenever a live lion or the enemy of your good comes charging at you, stand still. holding on to your ground and trusting in God, who is able to do immeasurably more than all you ask or imagine, and the roaring lion will never harm you."

"When a roaring lion charges at me, I better run as fast as I can."

"Trust me! You cannot outrun the lion sprinting fifty miles per hour. When the adversary shall come in like a flood, the Spirit of the Lord shall lift up a standard against him. Take the stand, do not get intimidated. Although a lot of times the enemy grows and snarls without attacking you; sometimes you may have to engage in a battle whereby you will come out with scars, yet with a victory. However, if you try to flee, the enemy will catch you alive and destroy you. Stand firm and you will see the salvation of the Lord. You have been raised up to make a difference. You do not have to be likable by your enemies to achieve your goal in life. By your perseverance a little longer and *diverging* to where you belong, to God, you can make things better through your talents. Just stand firm and you will win."

"How long should I stand in such condition, Grandpa?"

"I do not know. Suppose Mahatma Gandhi, Martin Luther King, Nelson Mandela, and so forth had stopped fighting because of persecution by their own family and their oppressors. What would have happened?"

"There would have been no change to what they were fighting for or working on."

"The same principle applies to you. You have a life and a purpose worth fighting and living for. The first thing is, identify your enemy the way Corey told you at the Hospital years back. Do you remember what she said?"

"How could I forget?" *None of us has turned against you. Perhaps you should examine yourself. It is you who turned against yourself, and you need to diverge.*

"Thank you for remembering. Additionally, beginning seeds, visions, and aspirations of all great successes do not look like their blossoming endings. The same guidelines apply in the business world too. For example, Walmart's vision did not start with about 11,000 retail stores—employing nearly two million people. Instead, on July 2, 1962, Sam Walton opened the first store in Rogers, Arkansas. In the same way, McDonald's did not start with about 36,000 restaurants and employing about two million workers. It evolved from Ray Kroc's endeavor's humble beginning in 1940 in California. The rest of these two businesses is history."

"That is for the rich business people, and their families probably were supportive of them."

"No, son. In every family as well as in life in general, there are always spoilers, and one has to persevere. These business inventors did not start big. They started small, persevering all kinds of persecution, and as a result, their projects are still growing. In the same manner, your beginning may seem small, but your ending will be prosperous. Therefore, you should not give in to the disparaging voices of Tobias and Sanballat and the threat as well as intimidations of the Jezebel-embodied minions that do not want to see your success. Keep on walking."

"How can I walk without clarity and not knowing what to anticipate in my future? How would you do if it were you?"

"I do not have to know what tomorrow holds for me. Nevertheless, I trust in God, who holds my future. I keep on walking, trusting in Him, that He would never do anything harmful to me. Though He slay me, yet will I trust in Him. What you need is to trust that in all things God works for your good. Until then, hold fast to the seed of greatness that is within you to be able to see the prosperous ending. Besides, persecution by a family is not a new thing; it brings the persecuted right to the divinely appointed place where one fits in."

"Example."

"Joseph experienced it when his own brothers sold him into slavery. Moses experienced the same from his jealous brother and sister as well as the whole of his country's people. David experienced the same persecution by King Saul and his own brothers, undermining by his father, and a threat by his own son. Jesus experienced the same persecution by his own family and people to the point of crucifixion. Their own people sold your African ancestors into slavery. Tell me if the persecution that you have been experiencing is distinct from than the ones that I have mentioned," says Grandpa.

"Of course, I have not experienced such persecution. Nevertheless, I guess each life journey is unique."

"Based on the persecution that you are going through, I would say that you are getting closer to the Promised Land of your destiny. I would like to sing Lauren Daigle's 'Trust In You.' The song tells about living your life in the face of adversity knowing that God knows all that you go through, for He had been there; keep walking, trusting in Him."

Right after the song, he resumes, "Son, by the way, do you know why people experience persecution by their own family?"

"I do not know. Why?"

"To search out a matter is the glory of kings; it is the glory of God to conceal a matter. The reason why God allows persecution by one's family is that the family is the one that you cannot fight. A family will not kill one another, yet push one another along one's journey to expedite reaching their destiny. The family may hit hard but cannot defeat one. It is not others' persecution that determines fate. Rather, it is how you adjust using life's shock absorber to the persecution and how you treat yourself that portends your end. You are the only enemy that can defeat you. The world will dump all kinds of dirt on you. The best escape route is to focus on Jesus, the source and goal of our faith from all that distracts you. He saw the joy ahead of him on setting the sinner free on his account, so he tolerated death on the cross and passed over the disgrace it brought Him. Now He holds the honored position—the one next to God the Father on the heavenly throne after completing His work on earth. So shall it be with you, once you pass the test victorious."

God uses a lie-synthesis by merciless relatives that Hayet cannot fight to persecute him with the worst kind of intimidation, perhaps without them even knowing it.

Eventually, the persecution ushers Hayet further toward his destiny.

One Sunday late afternoon, a deadly and suicidal persecution that threatens his existence arises at a time and place that he did not expect.

The devil whispers, "What are you going to do now?" overwhelming his being. Hayet has a choice to make. If he makes the wrong choice that would be his last day. In order to live, Hayet has nowhere to turn to but to the Lord. Out of the anguish impulsively his soul calls out, *Lord, what am I going to do?*

A powerful voice flows through his soul. *Hayet, the harder the persecution, the more glorious the triumph. Do not fear, and do not be dismayed, for I am your God. I will strengthen you and help you; I will uphold you with my righteous right hand. The enemy will tell you what you do not want to hear. Nevertheless, you tell him what he does not want to hear, that I am with you.*

Though he has nothing to show for his comeback, he wishes to see Rehoboth, a season of the enlargement against opposition that comes to slow down or far worse to quell his advancement. He is one brain work away from his breakthrough, should he persevere and work within lawful parameters, poking all new doors. God will obviously bless him lavishly in front of the people that do not want to see his blessings.

At one point while Hayet is downcast and slouching in his seat, Grandma says, "My son, you do not look sick. Yet your face appears blue. What is going on?"

After a brief stillness, "Why should not I look blue? I am living a meaningless life from hand to mouth. Will there be a day when my suffering will end?" Hayet cries.

"To begin with my son, it is not what you make, but what you keep and how you manage it that matters. Yes, there will be a day, and it is right now if you are willing to align with God's purpose for your life. The main lesson that you should learn is that every storm that you have been through is not wasted and will bring you closer to God's destiny for your life. If it were not for the hardship and practical training that you are passing through, you would not be able to handle the great responsibility that is ahead of you."

"I like your optimism."

"Grandpa, give me an example of one that perseveres and the rewards earned."

"When the going gets tough, only the tough get going. Honey Badger personifies such. What are Honey Badger's extravagant rewards?"

Grandpa, I know what you are going to say, bringing up this tough and fearless predator. "Snakes and honey."

"How does the honey badger earn them?"

"Tell me."

"Through a vigorous fight, enduring venomous stings and bites."

"But Honey Badger is designed to bear and endure for that."

"So are you, my son. No temptation has overtaken you except what is common to mankind. Realize that God is faithful; He will not let you be tempted beyond what you can bear. When you are faced with multiple hardships, He will also provide grace and a way out so that you can endure it."

"But it is painful."

"Of course. The snake is not going to give its life for free; neither will a bee seeing the hive invaded by an intruding enemy. Honey Badger keeps on going in the face of adversity. Frequently, the venom and the stings of a fierce fight causes them to pass out and get knocked out. When spectators count them out, they never give up. A little while later, step by step they get right back up and continue pushing forward to fight until they finish the job. Whenever a Honey Badger wants to eat, perseverance and endurance of a bee stings and cobra bites are a must. The best of all is that their endurance becomes a blessing to birds and jackals to have their pieces. So shall it be with you, my son. Your victory shall be a blessing to a multitude that are waiting upon you."

"Grandpa, I am nobody. I do not even have enough for myself. How could I be useful to others?"

"Son, you have what it takes. For it is God who works in you to will and to act in order to fulfill His good purpose. By diverging, with God it is possible to shine among the warped and crooked generation like stars in the sky as you hold firmly to the word of life which can make you wise for salvation through faith in Christ Jesus."

"I understand what you mean, Grandpa. But I wish I could live as a free man and with a smooth life without going through the hardship that I have been facing."

"You are not the only one that goes through such practical training so that you may be prepared for what is to come. Moses had two distinct practical training in life. The first was training in Pharaoh's house, learning all the language and etiquette of approaching the king. The second was life in the wilderness, where the route he would lead his people to the Promised Land. Your experience will help you to help others that go through the same situation because you have been there for yourself. In all stages of your life, God will use you for His good, for others' good, and for your own good. Take note that no temptation will overtake you except what is common to humankind. God is faithful; He will not tempt or test you beyond what you can bear. When you are tempted, He will also provide a way out so that you can endure it."

As Hayet listens, he realizes he may be experiencing an overwhelmingly crushing, pivotal, defining moment that could make or break him.

Furthermore, Grandpa says, "It is never too late to begin again. God is waiting for you to be ready."

Grandpa appears to have more to say. "Son, the moment you acknowledge the Lord, all shall be far better beyond your perceptions. Once you give Him first place in your life, you shall not be in want the way you have been. He will make you lie down in green pastures, lead you beside quiet waters, and restore your soul. Even though you walk through the valley of the shadow of death, you will fear no evil, for He will be with you. He shall prepare a table before you in the presence of the people that do not like you. He will anoint your head with the oil of His Holy Spirit, to the point of plenty overflowing from your life. Surely, His goodness and mercy will follow you all the days of your life, and you shall dwell in the house of the Lord forever. Also, make sure to give God one-tenth of your income and time. Additionally, out of the twenty-four hours in a day, two hours and a half belong to God; give them to Him."

"Grandpa, I like your optimism. However, I have two problems with putting your suggestion into practice. The first one is that I have no time to pray and I cannot stand doing so, because I consistently run from one commitment to another, sleeping less than four hours a day. Second, the income that I have is too little for me. I cannot give. Before I make the minimum payments all my money is gone. Therefore, giving out money is not possible."

"Spending hours doing exercise, that is okay; wasting hours listening to music is okay, playing and watching sports for hours is okay; spending hours eating, that is okay; having fun for hours is okay, spending hours talking over useless stuff on the phone is okay; spending the whole night gambling, surfing on the Internet, Facebook is okay, too. However, spending just one hour of prayer is unbearable and nerve racking. In fact, tarrying a couple of hours a day is all that you need to unlock that entire concern you have that has you stuck in your life journey to fall in the right place at the right time," challenges Grandpa.

Furthermore, "To begin with, you have been forcefully trying to grab what God is withholding from you. God wants to teach you to trust him and live by faith the way you did in the country of your refuge. During those years, did you lack anything?"

"I lacked nothing. Yet, life is different in Africa than in America."

"I do know that. Nevertheless, God is the same no matter where one is, and we all have a transcending, unifying, as well as binding biblical culture. God would want you to give to Him before you make any payment. When you first give to God from the little that you have, He blesses the rest. That is what He did with the widow at Zarephath in the Bible. She offers a handful of flour in a bowl and a bit of olive oil in a jar; that will be their last meal, and then they would starve to death. Because of her obedience in putting God's word first, she receives an abundant blessing that never ends. God can do the same to you, too."

"I like the blessing part, but giving before making any payment appears to be madness."

"Giving God from what He gave you is all an investment. However, not giving God from what He gave you is a waste. Choose which way you want to go."

"Grandpa, one time you told me that you would rather fall into the hand of God rather than into the hand of man. However, I do not have faith, and I choose to disobey the creator rather than the merciless credit card companies," refutes Hayet.

"Truly I tell you, if you have faith as small as a mustard seed, you can say to this mountain, 'Move from here to there,' and it will. Nothing will be impossible for you. It is faith and trust that you need more than anything, which pleases God."

Hayet has always wished for all to be as easy as the Gramps trust would be. He desires to see an abundance, which appears to be unreachable. He is fed up seeing his direct deposit pay land in his account and then quickly dissolve like sugar in a fluid. The fifty dollars' cash back reward fools him into borrowing thousands, which he cannot pay. He anticipates a day when a bright new sun will shine to enlighten his darkness, leading him to plenty. The more he longs for it, the more it appears far-fetched. He expects a day that will wipe away all his tears and replace his unfortunate circumstances with abundance, not for himself but for service to others. "I wish I was born during the good old days."

"Why are you saying this? I have heard the same statement repetitively."

"The reason is that I would not have to go through the struggles and temptations that the current generation goes through."

"You think so?"

"Yes."

"My son, the good old days are yet to happen. Additionally, every generation has its struggles and temptations. In fact, if one goes back to the beginning of time, Adam and Eve had their temptation. They were in a perfect place, the Garden of Eden. However, they fell to the temptation of the snake, the devil."

"I am saying so in a sense that people of the old good days had little temptation compared to the one click away alluring baits of my generation. Besides, what you just stated about the fall of the two people is not true. There is nothing like a talking snake."

"Regarding the fall of two people, you cannot understand and will not make sense to your intellectual understanding until God opens your blind eyes."

"You know that I am not a blind man. My eyes are faultless, and I always score perfectly on eyesight tests," Hayet says with a chuckle.

"I am talking about a spiritual eye, the eye of faith, not the physical eyes. Right now, you are foolish and senseless. You have eyes, but you do not see; you have ears, but you do not hear; you have the heart, but you do not perceive until the Lord opens them all."

Additionally, Grandpa says, "Again, there is no excuse for failing to meet the expectation, no matter which generation one may live. The key is in each person's hand. This key opens the door and lets in anyone who would like to enter. It can lead one to success or failure. This key is the choice, which leads to a wise or foolish decision," he jeers, opposing Hayet's reasoning.

"It is understandable that all can go wrong in your life, son. However, no matter what, you should be able to get on the course. You are a person, not a space shuttle; when you fail in life or get lost you can turn around and find your real direction. Failure is not the end of the world and it is never too late to begin again. Return to the Lord and He will restore what you lost."

"Grandpa, I guess Tobias and Sanballat were accurate in their predictions of my failure."

Grandpa gives a horselaugh and says, "Would you rather hear the voice of the successful who says, 'Greater is He that is in you than that which is in the world' or the voice of failed fellows who cannot distinguish right from wrong?"

"I would rather hear the voice of the people that I know who have gone through a lot than a voice written on a paper."

"As for me, I would rather trust the words written on paper. The Word on paper is not like any ordinary word; it is a person, which Jesus embodied. The problem is that, for indeed you have had good news preached to you, just as we also; but the word you heard did not profit you, because it was not united by faith in your heart when you heard it. Additionally, I do not have a high priest who is unable to empathize with my weaknesses, but I have one who has been tempted in every way, just as I am, yet He did not sin. Therefore, listen to God and all shall be well with you," says Grandpa.

In order to help Hayet resurge from despair, Grandma as well speaks. "When we were in high school, Grandpa and I got suspended due to negligent choices."

"Are you ready to tell him? If you are, I have no objection," Grandpa shouts, having previously protested.

Grandma pauses. "Yes, I am ready. Too late is better than never," she declares. "When we were high school students, we got suspended from school," she repeats. "It was the darkest moment in my life. For my parents, family, and the church community, it was like breaking news. I cannot tell you what a shameful daughter I was to my parents."

Hayet can see that clearly, Grandma feels remorse. Hayet deeply wants to know what happened to them so that he may compare it with his own case and find a solution for it. "Why did you get suspended?" he asks, staring at the Gramps.

"You know, sometimes peer pressure can prompt you to make bad choices," says Grandma. "Likewise, the moment one surrounds oneself with immature and foolish friends, one can make a lot of wrong choices when driven by a group mentality."

In the story Grandma tells, one Friday before lunchtime, she walks in the hallway feeling pretty. She grabs a piece of chewing gum from her pocket and chews it. At the same time, Grandpa walks from the opposite direction and put on a cowboy hat. The assistant principal catches them standing together. He takes them to his office and suspends them for violating a school rule.

"What happened then?"

"I told you, we got suspended."

"Why were you suspended?"

"For chewing gum, and for putting on a hat in the schoolyard," she replies.

"Grandma, wait a minute. You got suspended just for that?"

"Precisely. Those were the worst crimes of our days in the school."

"For how many years were you suspended?"

"Son, you are talking about years. It was only until Monday."

The Gramps want to encourage Hayet to *diverge* to the Light. They are unquestionably optimistic that God will bring him back. They see a day and the season of restoration. Freedom and blessings are nearer than Hayet thinks. In fact, they are right here with him. If he can *diverge* and make some adjustments.

The discussion cools off.

"My son," says Grandpa convincingly, "I understand the frustration and disappointments that you have. Trust my words. One day, all shall be far better, beyond anything you thought possible. Be still, and know that the Lord is God; He will be exalted among the nations, in the earth, and in your life."

"How can I be still while everybody is fighting against me? My adversaries are about to swallow me alive."

"In vain," says Grandpa. "You rise up early and stay up late, past midnight, toiling for food to eat. For God grants sleep to those He loves. All that you have to do is be still, come to the Lord, who gives rest to all that are weary and burdened, and He will give you rest. Take His yoke upon you and learn from Him, for He is gentle and humble in heart, and you will find rest for your soul. For His yoke is easy and His burden is light."

Right here, Grandpa sings Casting Crown's "There Will Be a Day," which tells about a bright new day when God gets involved in one's life.

"Thanks for the song and I like your optimism," Hayet pronounces.

So many years have gone by since Hayet got out of college. He wishes and works for a better living.

"I hope to see the outcome of the 2016 presidential election flood America with lots of jobs," he mentions.

Grandpa sits at the edge of his chair. "My son," he says as he stretches, "what you call optimism, we call it faith. No matter who becomes the president, God changes times and seasons; He deposes kings and raises up others. He gives wisdom to the wise and knowledge to the discerning. Besides, a president is as mortal as any human being is. A person should never depend upon another person. My father once told me to put my trust not in a human being but in God."

Hayet grabs a few pistachios and eats bit by bit in nervousness.

"Hayet, you trust economists more than you do God. Economists predict that the hardship we are in will grow worse before it becomes better; expect that. The shake-up of unemployment that people are experiencing is not at its climax. We will see more economic turbulence affecting many lives. Nevertheless, when we take one dose of Rx: RE, only then shall we come out of deadbeat America, bringing healing to the ailing economy. At the same time, we need to lower spending by reducing unnecessary expenses as individuals as well as a nation and discontinuing unbeneficial Trade deals. That is what people did during the Great Depression when unemployment was as high as 25 percent."

Hayet is not comfortable with the notion of the prescription that the Gramps customarily speak of.

"Here you mention Rx: RE. I wish somebody would explain Rx: RE. Then, depending on its veracity, I would take a double dose if it helps."

Almost totally broken, Hayet is forgetting his own uniqueness. Now is the best time his adoptive parents will have to explain the lesson that he most needs to hear. Rx: RE, he learns, is a matchless dose, given in just one dose per person. However, once a person receives the dose, he or she has the right to multiply, increase, grow, and share, making it contagious. Hayet should encourage himself to overcome the worst enemy that can defeat him, which is himself. He ought to look for new windows of better openings. He should be able to see the light beyond the tunnel, using the obstacles that he faces as opportunities for growth. He should look within himself to see embedded deep within him what he feels he can do to help himself and the community.

"Son, until a wide door opens, perhaps volunteering, education or a paradigm shift could be a way out. Besides, if you want to get what you left, go back to where you left and you will find what you left" suggests Grandpa.

"I left purposeful living the day I went to Piccolo night club. If I go there, what I will find is other prodigal children."

"Although physically going to where you left may be necessary sometimes, the kind of going that I am asking is a mental preparation, by your thinking returning to where you belong."

"Returning and volunteering mainly with churches is not going to work, I tried it several times."

"God needs your life than your service."

"Grandpa, I am talking about the old good days."

Several times after reading announcements Hayet applies to volunteer for duties that he can handle comfortably. The volunteer opening call stays for months after Hayet has applied, and sometimes the position gets given to newcomers based on lie-synthesis. Yet, no position avails for him.

Since no door has opened for me, it could mean I must start my own project. Ingenious ideas keep on hammering his imagination. Consequently, he starts his own volunteering project, which eventually could possibly give birth to book writing.

It is never too late to begin again. Perhaps the underemployed Hayet should persistently try new projects. Along the way, the persistence shall ultimately lead him to a twinkling light that he should never lose sight of. He should do all that is possible to chase the twinkling light, and in the end, it will lead to what he is meant to be. Nevertheless, Hayet does not imagine pursuing a twinkling light. Instead, he expects to see the light that outshines the sun. He should work hard, pursuing openings that come along. A twinkling light will lead him to the overflowing abundance. Until Hayet realizes the mystery of the comeback, he will remain in an unbearable psychological and physical torment of sleepless days and nights.

For ages, Hayet has been going without having sufficient sleep, haunted by terrorizing nightmares that are not easy to explain. He finds it hard to sleep. *I wish I were a kid. I would cling to my parents and to their bed to avoid the torment I am going through.*

Before going to bed, he ensures all the doors and windows are shut. The moment he goes to bed and is about to fall sleep, he feels an unexplainable extremely crushing heavy load fall on him, with tons of pressure. After minutes of struggle to open up his mouth, "Uh-ah, help, help, uh-ah, help" he screams at the top of his lungs. The sleep terror happens during his daytime naps as well as at night. He attempts to move or yell for help so that the crushing pressure may go away but in vain.

The heavy pressure causing sleeplessness torments him for a good number of years. Frequently, he sleeps in a churchyard during the day as well as turning on lights during the night. Yet the pressures persist. Subsequently, he visits all available specialists, looking for relief from involuntary insomnia. *In such cases, Grandma would say a spiritual problem needs a spiritual answer.*

At last, he shares his sleeplessness problem with the Gramps. "Whenever I try to sleep, an unexplainable, extremely heavy load pins me down to my bed."

"When the crushing pressure comes upon you, say 'in Jesus's name' and it will vanish promptly," Grandma says authoritatively. She continues writing the weekly menu on the old faded blackboard with a broken piece of chalk without giving him a second glance as if what she has said is an easy task.

Hayet stares at her back blankly while she keeps on writing. Then he walks to her side and, leaning on the new refrigerator, says, "Grandma, I want you to look straight to my face."

Lowering her eyeglasses to her fleshy nose by three fingers of her left hand, while holding the chalk and the menu draft in her right hand, "Yes sir!" she responds.

"Grandma, you cannot be serious. You have got to be kidding. I said that I am going through sleepless days and nights. I anticipate you would suggest a real solution that would require some activities on my side that would alleviate the torment."

"I am serious and you know that I say what I mean to say. My son, if I had told you to pay thousands of dollars, do one hundred pushups or do some other great, costly and demanding procedure, would you not have done it?"

"Yes, I would have done it." *In fact, I spent over two thousand dollars and nothing helped.*

"How much more, then, when I tell you, 'say in Jesus's name and be relieved?' My suggestion is a real solution and that is what I would suggest to myself too."

Hayet needs a scientifically proven prescription. Yet he asks, "You use just a simple three words?"

"Indeed!"

"Words alone cannot make a difference," Hayet argues, ignoring Grandma's advice.

"The word *Jesus* is not like any other word. It is *just words*. 'Get up! Pick up your mat and walk'—that caused the thirty-eight-year-old invalid to be healed. It is *just words*. 'Lazarus, come out.' That caused the man dead for four days to come back to life. It is *just words*. 'Your faith has healed you'; that a woman who had suffered from severe bleeding for twelve years, who had spent all she had on doctors, nonetheless no one had been able to cure her. The moment she touched the edge of Jesus's garment and her bleeding stopped at once. The Word is the one that became flesh and makes His dwelling among us. The name Jesus has a power and it is a name above all other names to which every knee bows, the demons, including the one that torment you with sleeplessness; the winds and the waves of the sea obey."

"I still do not believe that three simple words would make a difference. Besides, I do not have tormenting demons."

"Your unbelief does not change the reality. Your unbelief shows the level of your ignorance. Since you are possessed and do not have a discerning spirit, you cannot understand the spiritual warfare going on inside of you. *A spiritual problem needs a spiritual solution*. Visiting with psychologists, psychiatrists, and insomnia specialist doctors will consume your money and no one will heal you. All that you need is the doctor of doctors. His name is Jesus."

Hayet marvels how she knew that his visits to doctors had not helped. "So, are you saying that I am an ignorant?"

"I did not say that. The Bible does for the unbelief that you display. What I would say is that you must open your heart to the Lord and save yourself from being part of a corrupt generation."

What would it cost me if I accept Grandma's suggestion? Nothing!

"So, son, would you like to be relieved from the tormenting pressure you have?"

"Precisely!"

"Then say 'in Jesus's name'! *A spiritual problem needs a spiritual solution.*"

"I do not think I want to."

"If you do not, then you will not be relieved. I wish you knew the Lord. He could be your refuge and your fortress, your God, in whom you trust. When you put your trust in Him, He will save you from the fowler's snare and from the deadly pestilence. He will cover you with His feathers, and under His wings, you will find refuge. His faithfulness will be your shield and rampart. You will not fear the terror of night that pin you to your bed, nor the arrow that flies by day, nor the epidemic that stalks in the darkness, nor the plague that destroys at midday."

"Grandma, your suggestion is hard to believe."

"Son, if you say, 'The Lord is my refuge,' and you make the Most High your dwelling, no harm will overtake you; no disaster will come near your tent. For He will command His angels concerning you to guard you in all your ways; they will lift you up in their hands, so that you will not strike your foot against a stone. You will tread on the lion and the cobra; you will trample the great lion and the serpent. Because when you love Him, God will rescue and protect you. You will call on Him, and He will answer, be with you in trouble, deliver, honor, with long life satisfy you and show you His salvation," restates Grandma.

Applying the Gramps' information might not be a bad idea. Concurrently, since he knows that the pressure would make him sleepless during the night, he goes to all-night prayer, accompanying a friend for the first time. As usual, the pressure comes the following night. After moments of struggle, "In Jesus's name!" he shouts, and the heavy pressure vanishes instantly. The disappearance of the pressure at the mention of the name of Jesus marvels Hayet. Anyway, that was the last time he experienced the pressure.

Hayet is not at peace with God. Nevertheless, in the time of need, he calls upon the name of Jesus, and God intervenes irrespective of his deviated life.

The Gramps dearly want to see Hayet return and then eventually become who God wants him to be. They keep on poking Hayet in every encounter. In one encounter, "Son, all that you need is Jesus," Grandpa informs him.

"All I need, to be who I was meant to be, is to hit the lottery jackpot."

"What if you do not hit the jackpot, which eats up the poor's money, destroying the individuals and families that strive to win it and those that won it?" asks Grandpa.

"Then I will have to start with something that propels me to a higher speed," replies Hayet.

Grandpa gets excited. "That is what I have been talking about for years. Behold, my son, in every encounter you have, you can choose to either speak to make your life or someone's life better or say negative things to make it worse."

Grandpa desires to see Hayet's good emerge soon, and very soon. Until then, Hayet has to keep on working, poking, starting new projects, and identifying the right path. Because when he is on the right path, the rest will fall into place.

Hayet should enter through the open door, speak life into it, keep on working hard and serving others. By doing good, there is an achievement to be remembered by when he is gone forever. The Gramps so desire to see Hayet come back, and at a cost as simple as "Lord, I come back to you," yet which could have a significant effect in his life that would enable him to see the fulfillment of his mother's wishes.

Chapter 37

God never hurries. There are no deadlines against which he must work. Only to know this is to quiet our spirits and relax our nerves.

— A. W. Toser, The Power of God

Hayet's biological parents prayed God to bless them with purposeful children who would serve the people and God.

Answering prayers, God created Hayet for a purpose of making an impact on people's lives by putting God first, prioritizing his life, and serving others fairly and justly. However, he is not living up to the expectation.

Hayet consistently feels the pain for failing his father and cries sensing his father telling him, *What happened to you my son? You have become less than who you were meant to be.*

Whenever he feels his father's whisper and cries, he becomes exhausted from crying for help; his throat is parched, eyes are swollen with weeping, waiting for deliverance from where he would not want to be.

In general, to fulfill the purpose of one's existence, one ought to live according to the expectations and within permissible bounds. Should a person fail to achieve his or her God-given purpose in life, there may be an atonement.

Hayet has behaved with a little foolishness and has some character flaws. He does not do his best to avoid wrong choices. At the times of his failure, he never realizes that his character failings and doing what he is not supposed to be doing will dampen his bright future. No sacrifice can reverse the shame and guilt. The guilt has been haunting him throughout the wasted years in the University of Wilderness.

It is good to remember that whatever happens in Vegas, Access Hollywood or another place does not remain there. A person does not attain satisfaction in life by mere material gathering, by taking advantage of the weak, having fun, or chasing cool stuff. It is not with substances that destroy the body, which is the temple of God. The Gramps have not wanted to see Hayet stuck forever. They bring up one example after another to propel him. Although their support is necessary, the key person to determine to create success out of the person within him is Hayet.

"My son, life without service is meaningless," says Grandpa, for he knows that Hayet has been running after worthless pursuits that deplete his heart, just living for himself. Not only that but also it has now been a good number of years since Hayet gave up on school. His adoptive parents have grown older than ever. Although they do have faith in seeing Hayet's transformation, as the years go by, the deferred hope makes their hearts sick and heavy.

During one of those hopeless days, Grandpa relaxes on a swivel rocking chair, rocking gently and steadily. At one despairing moment, he asks Hayet, "What is the greatest thing that you would like to achieve?"

Of course, Hayet does have a lot that he would like to achieve.

"More than anything else, I would like to be cool, great, powerful, and rich, caring what I eat, what I drink, what I wear, and where I live and have fun," he states concisely.

His adoptive parents' definitions of greatness, coolness, power, and riches differ from Hayet's current definitions. Hayet has grown so quickly since the first pledge he made back in Africa: to serve righteously, kindly, justly, and fairly. His growth is negative right now, though.

His adoptive parents understand that greatness, coolness, and riches are using whatever one has for the betterment of others.

The discussion progresses and Grandpa speaks. "In order to be great, cool, rich, and powerful, you ought to serve others in humility. That is how Dr. Martin Luther King Jr. and many others that came before us served."

Hayet argues, "Grandpa, thanks for bringing up Dr. King. However, you have got to mention that despite his selfless service to his community, they assassinated him. Where was God at that time?"

"God was at the same place as He was when His figurative son, Jesus Christ, died. Sometimes God allows bad to happen to prudent people so that they may grab better revelation. In life, the "*they*" opponents will do all they can to hinder you from achieving the highest goal in life. Nevertheless, the "*He*" can see you through, circumventing all the invented hindrances and lie-synthesis."

"Who are the 'They' and the 'He'?"

"'They' are the opposing forces and 'He' is God.

"So, son, if being rich and powerful makes you fulfilled, and then go ahead. However, remember that 'Precious in the sight of the Lord is the death of his faithful servants.' Dr. King and his counterparts paid a price for you. Because of what others paid, you have a right to be elected as much as a vice president, if you can make use of it. Also, remember, Dr. King is the only American citizen who has never held public office, yet in whose name we have a public holiday today. If you do not understand what I am saying, then you need a lesson from Psalm 37, on how God functions silently. Further, if you do not serve righteously and honestly with what you are blessed with, the blessings can choke your life from having long days in the land that the Lord your God has given you. Look at the common people, celebrity millionaires, and billionaires in the world."

"Yes, Grandpa, they who serve with little acts of kindness live a longer and happier life. On the contrary, the people who spend what they have just on themselves without serving others die worthless. Commonly, they have overdose deaths in less than half of a man's age, abandoning all that they toiled and built for someone who did not work for it," notes Hayet.

"Thank you for understanding my intention! No matter how rich and powerful one may be, if one does not live fully serving by what God has blessed one with, one-day God replaces him or her with somebody else who can. Take note that the Lord your God is supreme over all gods and powers. He is great and mighty. Always obey him. He does not show partiality, and He does not accept bribes. He makes sure that people treat orphans and widows fairly; He loves the foreigners who live with our people and gives them food and clothes. So then, show love for those foreigners, because you were once a foreigner. By doing what is right in the eyes of the Lord, you remain at the top no matter who and how many people and nations oppose you."

"You think so?"

"Yes!"

Hayet declares, "As I have mentioned before, all that you need to survive in this unfair world is money, power, and a lie-synthesis. If you have these, you can do whatever you want to do and get away with it. I remember how my father suffered because of people who had those things in excess."

"Truly, I tell you son, unless a grain of wheat falls to the ground and dies, it remains only a single seed. However, if it dies, it produces many seeds. Simultaneously, sometimes God allows evil to happen to good people so that He may break them, bless them, and make them a blessing to others. Know that His eye is on the sparrow, and He watches on your father. Who knows that your father might be leaving a good legacy for you to be proud to call him your father, guaranteed to have better peace than the people that mistreated him."

"Grandpa, that is not all; look at the current situation that goes on in the world. A proud president made an incursion in Ukraine, and his erratic actions in Europe go unpunished because he has the power and money. The underlying cause to the external manifestation of this problem could either be his refusal to submit and comply with the demands of the superpowers or economic or political reasons that are disguised from the public." Grandpa listens thoughtfully.

"Here at home as well, an American president, without the authorization of the American people, just discussing with the Arab League and the European Union leaders, authorizes a war on Libya. The rule of law says, 'Everyone must follow the law. Leaders must obey the law. The Government must obey the law, and no one is above the law (including the president).' Nobody says anything to the lawbreaker. On the other hand, when a weak person or nation breaks the law, there are consequences orchestrated by lie-synthesis. Did you get my point?"

"Yes, son, go ahead."

"A lie-synthesis facilitates the murder of a Libyan leader because of a threat, *to avoid the bloodbath genocide like that of Rwanda and Burundi.* On the contrary, we have a real bloodbath consuming over two hundred thousand civilians and displacing nearly ten million in and out of the country. However, because of a lie-synthesis for and against, no tangible help has come forth to the suffering civilians in Syria. That is related to the saying, 'When two elephants fight, the grass is the casualty'; civilians are suffering. Therefore, Grandpa, behold the power, money, and a lie-synthesis. You can even commit unspeakable atrocities; a lie-synthesis allows the assailant to get away without appropriate punishment."

"Do you want to be like the people that use a lie-synthesis for personal advantages?"

"Of course, not. I want to see those illegal procedures get fixed."

"Behold, my son; God has created and perfectly positioned one person who sees the issues that you repeatedly advocate for to make a difference. When that person wakes up from conformity's slumber to hold his place in life, some worldviews could change and raise an army of world changers. Martin Luther, the reformer, nailed his ninety-five theses to the doors of a church, shaking the foundation of the religious operations. In the same manner, the current world system that operates with a lie-synthesis will shift when the person who fixes it, a change agent, chooses to be himself and inscribes his theses in a book."

"Who could that person be?"

"You are the one. God loves you dearly to give you lesser tasks."

"I like your optimism. However, that is impossible. Tobias and Sanballat already have said it. The world cannot bear to hear to an infamous poor immigrant with language and financial limitations. An unknown person cannot hire a global publicist to appear in Los Angeles Times, and give interviews to the *New York Times*, on national TV, in *Reader's Digest*, and at national and international book-signing functions."

Counters Grandpa, "Son, when God is in control, circumstances do not matter. Victims say it is impossible; victors say, with God all is possible. Victims say I cannot; victors say I can do all through Christ, who gives me strength. Believe in God, who makes the impossible possible. He can create something out of nothing, and He can bring an impeccably best out of something good. It takes only one command, '*Let there be*.' God does not see you the way you see yourself. Besides, on the day God works through your life, with all your imperfections and limitations, you shall be His treasured possession. Your life is not about you. It is about Him who works through you for your good, for His good, and for others' good. Additionally, you already have a publicist and an endorsement of every year internationally best-selling author."

"I like your optimism. It is hilarious. Tell me, how does the creator see me? What does He say about me, and who is the best-selling author?" he says in sarcasm.

"God says to you, 'Here is my servant whom I have chosen, the one I love, in whom I delight; I will put my Spirit on him, and he will proclaim justice to the nations.' The bestselling book is the Bible, and its author is God. Cast your net by faith, and you will have a great catch far beyond what you thought could be achievable. Just look and watch and be amazed. God is going to do great and marvelous achievements in and through your life that you would not believe, even if others tell you. God loves you so much that He will not let you settle for less. He will make people uncomfortable to you like a thorn in the flesh until you come to where you belong. There is a saying, '*Ed shena-hit tsena-hit*,' meaning 'The hand that hits others also get hit.' Whosoever does wrong, in one way or another, reaps what one sows."

Grandpa wants to ensure Hayet understands that lie-synthesis, power and money do not allow one to escape from God's judgment. He clarifies, "Please allow me to repeat a few statements that my father once told me. The first one is, 'The wicked are overthrown through their evildoing, but the righteous find refuge in death.' The second one is, 'As a partridge that hatches eggs that it has not laid, so is he who makes wealth, but unjustly. In the midst of his days, it will forsake him, and in the end, he will be a fool.' Lastly, 'For all who draw the sword will die by the sword.'"

Having seen Hayet's unresponsiveness, he adds, "My son, one day you shall die."

Hayet knows that every living being is mortal. He needs more explanations. "So will you, Grandpa. In fact, when it comes to age, you are nearer to death than I am. Besides, what makes my death distinct from any other person's death that you mention it with such a concern?"

"The difference is that when I die, I shall fly away and go to a place no eye has seen. No ear has heard and no mind has conceived what the Lord has prepared for me."

"How do you know that a place no eye has seen exists?"

"By faith and the Bible says so."

"Also, if you go to that place, so will I. Wherever you go, I also will go. Remember what you stated years ago: 'Wherever I go, be it Yale, the capitol, the hospital, or jail, you will go, too.' You have seen the fulfillment of some of them. The same principle should apply in reverse. In addition, I deserve the best because I am good."

"Only God is good. Take one dose of Rx: RE, and God will credit His goodness to you so that you may be acceptable. Then you will go to where we will go. Nevertheless, that is not what I wanted to say right now. What I am trying to say is that when your day has come, you will no longer be on this earth. What will your legacy be for future generations? What will the reader of your eulogy say to the people that attend your funeral?"

"I will have neither a eulogy reader nor a funeral ceremony."

"Why? Are you an exception?"

"Yes, I am. You remember what you told me about the rapture. I will be raptured with all the saints."

"Only the watchful that are ready every day will get raptured," Grandpa replies.

"When you die, what do you think people will say at your funeral?"

"If rapture does not happen by the time I die, people will say, 'A man died with his potential untapped.'" Hayet has admitted the truth.

"So how would you feel, leaving such a legacy?"

"I would feel defeated, ashamed, useless, weak, worthless, confused, powerless, and disappointed. Is this what you wanted to hear?"

"No! I am sorry, though, that you will have such an intangible legacy. However, that is not what I wanted to hear," says Grandpa apologetically. He is eager to help foster the transformation of the real Hayet who'll serve humanity.

Hayet has been living unpredictably just for himself, forgetting the only way to achieve greatness is to serve humankind fairly and justly. His foster parents desire to see Hayet's goodness before their days are over.

After a moment, Grandpa grabs his banjo and sings Wayburn Dean and Doug Beiden's "What Will Be Your Legacy?"

Hayet's face darkens upon hearing Grandpa's remark and considers what it would be like to leave a legacy of nothing to the future generation. Later that day, he identifies a promising and fulfilling job opening posted in the local newspaper, by an enterprise Yes We Certainly Can, abbreviated, YWCC.

Chapter 38

Losers live in the past. Winners learn from the past and enjoy working in the present toward the future.

— DENIS WAITLEY

It has been nearly a decade and a half since Hayet started working unfulfilling jobs and spending endless years in financial scarcity, and he desires one day to come out victorious.

Hayet's friends that remained purposeful with their priorities through college now enjoy earning between three and four figures per hour, while he earns just one figure per hour.

Recurrently he thinks, *What kind of son would I be to my parents and what a shameful father I will be to my descendants if I cannot leave an inheritance to the future generation?*

Hayet works earnestly and trades his vacation and sick days for money instead of enjoying them. During the busy season, he works as much as eighty plus hours a week while his friends work less than forty hours per week making thousands. However, before the next pay period, all the money that he earns is gone, leaving him with the option of swiping credit cards. He also consistently ends up maxing out all his credit cards, paying as much as thirty-five dollars per transaction for an overdraft protection fee and the same percent interest. Meanwhile, he vigorously searches for openings to improve himself. He looks for better-paying jobs without having matching educational requirements.

Hayet attempts to secure one position after another to reorganize his life for a better future, which never seems to come. Will he be able to secure a job for which he qualifies? No matter the outcome, he remains uncertain.

Simultaneously, a company called YWCC Enterprise, Yes We Certainly Can, advertises a position with qualifications that Hayet can handle comfortably. He is attracted to the advertisement, which requires a minimum of a high school diploma. It is a well-known company located in Manhattan. That is where everybody wishes to work.

Hayet has nearly four years of college studies, and he is optimistic that he will secure the position. Given that the advertisement requires one to apply in person, Hayet enters the office. The office is appealing, not only as a workplace, even just for a visit.

Hayet waits for the receptionist to get off the phone. Dozens of applicants line up in the waiting room, each one wanting to hand in the job application form.

A man who looks to be in his thirties, dressed in a perfectly ironed sapphire shirt, with a blue and black tie, walks toward the receptionist holding an envelope in his left hand. He has a familiar face. However, due to self-pride, Hayet says, *I will never greet him.* The man hands over the envelope and goes into a briefly inaudible conversation with the receptionist.

The man soon turns toward the door from which he emerged. He opens the yellowish door with his left hand and takes a couple of steps.

Finally, Hayet decides, *It would not hurt. I better learn to forgive myself. Besides, this could be the best opening for growth.* He yells, "Gupta Gandhi, is that you?" The man turns his head, showing a puckered furrowed brow.

"Who are you?" he asks.

"It is I, Hayet," Hayet replies joyously.

Gupta smiles and looks at Hayet from head to toe. "Look at you! How did you come here? I am surprised to see you alive!"

It has been years since they last communicated. "Good to see you, too. I am still alive," Hayet responds with a hearty grin.

"How has life been going on with you? You did not change much. In fact, you look ten years younger than your age. How did it happen?"

"Yes, people say that I look younger than my age. I beat the system by prioritizing my life; I settled, achieved my goals, and have nothing to worry about. I have peace and more than enough money and time to spend with the family. Besides, when one works for YWCC Enterprises, it should show in one's life."

Gupta then looks at everyone in the waiting area. "Sorry for being too emotional. Please excuse us for a moment. Hayet is my best friend and college mate."

Upon hearing Gupta's statements, one can see the unhappiness on the faces of some of the applicants. They have all come to apply for a single position.

"Come on inside," says Gupta while leading the way.

"Is this where you work?"

"Yes."

"You have not yet changed the way you nod," Hayet notes.

"I have been created to be who I am meant to be unless I adopt somebody else's lifestyle. That is what you did, and you ended up being the person that you became," Gupta utters ironically.

"Tell me, how are Paula and Lee doing?" Hayet probes, reprocessing Gupta's disgracing statement.

"They are doing well. In fact, I am expecting them in the next few minutes." Right after graduation, each one of them went their respective ways. However, after repeated discussion, they agreed to work together. Finally, they decide to join hands and set up YWCC Enterprises.

As Hayet and Gupta talk, the side door opens. The man opens the door and lets a woman enter first.

"Oops! Sorry for the interruption," apologizes the woman who wears a long-sleeved rose-flower-adorned kimono as she retreats.

The moment Hayet sees the duo, he knows who they are. He cannot contain his joy.

"Come on in, Paula and Lee," he shouts.

He rises from the silk-upholstered sofa, stretching both arms widely as he walks toward the door.

Upon hearing the visitor's voice, Lee rushes to stand by Paula. Hayet has grown as wide as a hippo, and he does not blame them for not recognizing him.

Meanwhile, he gives loving hugs to both, one at a time. They are bewildered at who he is and stare at him in surprise. "It is Hayet!" states Gupta as he smiles.

"Oh my goodness, is it truly you, Hayet?" Paula says, widening her eyes in disbelief, putting her right hand over her mouth.

"Wow, how did you come here?" Lee inquires.

"It does not matter how I got here. What matters is that I am alive." The friends echo cheering, shouting, and rejoicing in the office.

"I cannot believe it. Is this a dream?" Paula asks, placing her right hand on Lee's shoulder.

Hayet says, "It is not a dream. It is real. None of you have changed physically! You are the same as the days of our college years. Paula's freckles have not yet gone." Hayet smiles as he looks at each of them.

"Regarding our physical bodies, we have been training clients for years to watch their weight and exercise regularly and suggesting what they should and should not eat to stay healthier. Should not we take care of ourselves first?" Paula walks toward a framed oil portrait, looking like a supermodel.

"You look as good as Miss World," Hayet says.

"Thanks!"

Lee admits, "I do not think I would have recognized you if we were to meet on the street."

"Neither would I," says Gupta as he takes off Hayet's hat.

"I neither," says Paula. "You have grown a bit flabby; you need to exercise a bit."

"Yeah, I gained a little weight," Hayet replies in self-pity.

"Tell us how life has been going with you? You detested our advice, chasing what God was trying to take away from you. I have no doubt that you remember all that we said. An intellectual youth makes hay while the sun shines, but what a shame to see a lad who sleeps away his opportune hour," says Paula.

Paula's words hit Hayet like a missile, and he stands lifeless. His whole body feels like deflating. He is lonely, rejected, abandoned, useless, disgraced, and helpless fellow.

He wipes a trickle of sweat off his forehead with the back of his arm.

Hayet cannot tell them about the shameful ways in which he has failed. *I have to leave without telling them.* He was smarter than the entire bunch in college, and now he is seeking employment; because he did not show his smartness practically on a paper, his smartness is useless. His vision blurs, and he cannot see clearly.

"Here you go," says Lee as he hands Hayet a box of tissue paper.

"Thanks, Lee," Hayet says as he pulls out some and wipes away his sweat.

"Sorry. We did not mean to hurt your feelings by talking about old times and the faculty that suspended you from school," Paula states.

If Hayet had lived to make someone happy as his father instructed him many years ago, or at least listened to the advice to put God first, prioritize his life, and decided to serve fairly and justly, he would have been the person he was meant to be. That is what his family and the college community expected. Even now, late is better than never. Additionally, it is never too late to begin again. The trio want to help him, should he take the first step toward surviving the disgrace.

Paula's consolation appears to be tormenting and humiliating. Hayet regrets all the worthless decisions he has made. He feels jealous of seeing the successes of his former classmates.

It is my fault. I deserve to reap all these shame, he says, fiddling and tearing up the wet tissues in his hands. It is too late to undo the foolishness. However, it is possible to have a fresh start, as behind every cloud there is an unseen benefit.

Paula stands on Hayet's left side and puts her hand on his shoulder. Gupta stands by Hayet's right side and touches Hayet's chest gently with his right hand while patting his shoulder with his left hand.

Lee says, "We understand the situation. Please do not cry over past mistakes; instead, learn from them. It took us about twenty years to reach this stage. It can take the same or a little more for you, too, to reach such a stage. No major achievement happens instantly. The time we retire, you will start.

Until then, go to where you lost, pick what you lost, diverge, reposition, and make up your mind; do not yearn for the choices that ruined your educational journey. Take note, if you do what we did, you will get what we got. You can still make it to your dream goal and be of great help to your community. It is never too late to begin again. Keep on knocking, poking, and inventing until you reach your destiny."

I wish I could, but I cannot.

A few minutes later, Hayet gains his serenity and turns toward his friends. It is difficult to open up and articulate a word. Memories of his wasted years come to his mind as fresh as a nauseating stench. He shuts his eyes, and more tears gush down his face.

He appears to be shaking, talking about the past. After several attempts to speak, finally he utters, "Life has been terrible, treating me harshly and abandoning me."

"Hold on! Hayet, is it you or life who left?" opposes Paula.

"Whatever," Hayet dodges instead of giving the accurate answer.

"You got to answer. Don't blame others for your wrong choices. If you go back to what and where you left, you will get what you left."

Hayet does not want to give an honest answer, blaming himself. Then he resumes, "The difficulties that happened at the college, you all know, it is not a secret. I have come to apply for an open position that you have advertised. I want you to consider me for the position."

Gupta looks at his watch and says, "We have other business to take care of."

"Oh, yeah," affirms Lee. "Please excuse us."

"Sure," Hayet replies while bidding his final farewell."

"By the way, next week we have a company retreat at our vacation home. Would you like to join us at Martha's Vineyard?" Gupta asks.

"I would love to, but I have no money for such a luxurious resort. In addition, I have come here looking for a job. The only thing I need from you is to guarantee me of securing the vacant job," he pushes.

"Hey, buddy; regarding the job, we shall inform you formally, via mail. All expenses for the resort shall be covered by our company; let us all have an enjoyable time," assures Gupta.

"Make sure to reply to our phone calls and e-mails. Do not hide from us the way you did all those years," comments Lee.

"I will not. Thanks for all your kindness," replies Hayet as he exits. Meanwhile, Hayet wonders, *Why would they inform me via mail while they can call or tell me to my face?*

The receptionist looks at him in astonishment. "You mean you know Dr. Paula, Dr. Lee, and Dr. Gupta?"

"Yes, we were college mates."

"Why are you applying for this low-paying job, then?" the receptionist spouts.

"Miss, an intellectual youth makes hay while the sun shines, but what a shame to see a lad who sleeps away his hour of prospect. I outpaced my classmates, deviated from purposeful living, and wasted my precious years with wrong choices."

"Come closer," she demands. He approaches in apprehension. "You are not alone, so am I. That is why I am an employee instead of being an employer. Perhaps we have to set up a team of deplorable, despicable, all those who are in distress, in debt, discontented, with aborted purpose gather them around us, and let us became their leaders and tell them not to walk our walk."

"How did it happen?"

"I did not prioritize my life while chasing fun, refusing to listen to my father's advice who still has structured and disciplined parenting style. I hate him."

"Why?"

"He told me to prioritize my life and no kissing before marriage. To tell the truth, my younger sister followed all his directions. She earned 100% scholarship, up to Ph.D., is married, has four children and nice husband. But I am nowhere. Although I am responsible for my mess, my mother should be blamed. Whenever my father tells me to do what I am supposed to do, my mother who is a militant, radical liberal, interferes and says 'Leave her alone, let her be free to do what she wants to do.' My mother's approval gave me leeway to do what ought not to be done. I dated and partied more than anybody else, not caring about my school. Ultimately, I graduated from high school, but with 1.8 GPA that could take me nowhere. I regretted, but it was too late to undo the damage. If I were to do it again, I would do it my father's way."

"Sorry to hear that," says Hayet consoling her.

"You shouldn't say sorry; I deserve to reap the result of my foolishness."

"My mother's side, grandma, Mrs. Celine Klein is also a disciplined woman. She used to tell me a lot of stories of how doing what I am supposed to do at a time when I am supposed to do could prepare me for a better life."

I know your grandma. "Would you please tell me one of the stories that your grandma told you?"

"Yes, I will. Life will be like ten virgins who took their lamps and went out to meet the bridegroom. Five of them were foolish and five were wise. The foolish ones took their lamps but did not take any surplus oil with them. The wise ones, however, took oil in jars along with their lamps. The bridegroom was a long time in coming, and they all became dozy and fell asleep.

At a time when nobody expected the cry rang out: 'Behold, here is the bridegroom! Come out to meet him!'

Then all the virgins arose and trimmed their lamps. The foolish ones said to the wise, 'Please give us some of your oil; our lamps are going out.'

'No,' they replied, 'there may not be enough for both us and you. Instead, go to those who sell oil and buy some for yourselves.'

While they were on their way to buy the oil, the bridegroom arrived. The virgins who were ready went in with him to the wedding banquet. And the door was shut leaving the foolish out."

"So what did you learn from your grandma's story?"

"If I am not willing to work hard when I am supposed to, then I should not expect a harvest when the hard-working harvest a bountiful of harvest."

"Sorry sir, for taking your time. YWCC is a good place to work, but I am stuck doing a receptionist job. By the way, we have over three thousand applicants for just one open position. The way I see it, you seem to be the best candidate. Although it is too early to predict, I would like to say congratulations in advance for obtaining the job."

Her good wishes and his friendship with the business owners give Hayet a positive affirmation that he will secure the vacant job.

Meanwhile, on his way back home he wonders, *Should I accept the Martha's Vineyard invitation? It is a once-in-a-lifetime event, and it would not hurt to go and have fun with old college mates at their expense.*

Hayet arrives home on a sunny early afternoon. "I applied for a job at one of my former classmate's business. I am hopeful to obtain it," he tells the Gramps.

"I do not agree with it," Grandpa declares, opposing Hayet's wish to accept the job.

"You do not want me to obtain a better job?"

"My son, you are more than what you have become. You are worth more than the job you are hoping for. Besides, the job you are talking about at your friend's firm will be humiliating. Even if you were to obtain it, you would quit. You have to create your own new project."

Hayet understands that Grandpa is right. However, this is the best job offer he is seen in the decade since leaving college early. At the same time, the notion of the vacation expenses bothers him. Should he go to Martha's Vineyard, introducing himself to one and all as a former college mate without any achievements to discuss? *The retreat would be tormenting rather than healing.* He picks up the phone. "I will not attend the retreat for personal reasons," he informs the receptionist. The receptionist accepts his excuse, causing Hayet to expectantly wait for a letter from YWCC Enterprises.

Chapter 39

I have learned that success is to be measured not so much by the position that one has reached in life as by the obstacles which he has overcome while trying to succeed.

— *Booker T. Washington*

Hayet anticipates his friends' return from the lavish and affluent resort and the offer of the vacant job, which did not go in his favor.

He eagerly waits for a reply on his job application. He opens the mailbox a couple of times a day. On the day of their supposed departure, a piece of mail comes from YWCC. The stamped date is the day of his encounter with the trio. He opens it confidently. It is a formal letter, appreciating Hayet's interest in the business. However, it states that another person got the job. There are many reasons.

"We thank you for applying for this job. However, we have not accepted you into this position because of the following reasons:

* You are overqualified.
* You failed yourself, your family, and your friends at college. We are afraid that you could do the same upon receipt of the position.

* You should have been part of our team, not our employee.
* We do believe in second chances. However, hiring you for this position will give us some discomfort.
* Offering you a job in our company will make you settle for less."

Upon reading the letter Hayet emphatically cries to himself, *I knew it. I should have listened to my inner voice that urged me not to apply the moment I saw Gupta.*

He is mad at his former friends. *How could they do that?* he says while pacing on the patio, puffing a cigar. Much worse, he is mad at himself. *Hayet, you deserve such humiliation for not staying intentional, giving priority where priority is due.*

He regains his serenity and accepts the letter, neither downcast nor disappointed. He replies to them, appreciating their considerations.

A couple of hours later, at nightfall, Gramps walk into Hayet's residence. Hayet is not in the mood to talk; he sits slumped on the floor like a withered flower.

"Hayet, how did your application go?" Grandpa asks cautiously.

"Well, you predicted the outcome."

"You got it?"

"No! You know, Grandpa, I do not understand the value of friendship. They use my past failures to determine my future," he cries, pursing his lips.

"That is great. Your friends should be visionary leaders that love you immensely for refusing to offer you the job."

"I suppose I said that I did not get the job offer."

"Yes, you certainly did."

"How come then you are happy and sound to congratulate me over the denial of the job offer?"

"You are a peculiar one. You could fit in only at one impeccable place. Until you find that place where you click in, I am afraid to say you will waste even more years of your life. If you abandon purposeful living for a temporal joy, you will keep on losing until you return to what you lost."

"Grandpa, nobody has ever said the kind of words that you always say to me."

"It is because I love you. Furthermore, because of your uniqueness, the people around you unintentionally will misunderstand and perhaps push you to the limits or will try to restrain you to places and accomplishments that cannot contain you. Being uncomfortable or feeling disconnected even from harmless friends, relatives, and employers can be the normal way of life to channel you to where you belong."

"Life does not make sense. Why do I have to suffer so at the hands of people for things that are beyond my control?"

"Life does make sense. Please be aware that in all occurrences, including all that you do not like to happen, God will work for your good. In addition, open your heart and mind to seize a new door opening because every cloud has a silver lining. I hope you do remember that whatever happens in Vegas does not remain in Vegas. Your character flaws will trail you wherever you go, even in the life after death. Also, that is not all—"

"That is enough! What more do you want to add, Grandpa?"

"That is not enough. Do not be deceived: no one can mock God, for whatever one sows will he also reap. Your yesterday shall haunt you wherever you go. You shall see less-qualified candidates becoming your supervisors, managers, CEOs, and perhaps have supervisors and leaders who have not completed high school. The less-qualified leader shall demean you with nerve-racking intimidation. Then shall you look for an exit from the misfit-wasted life. The only exit is by taking one dose of Rx: RE. Taking shortcuts and changing places will make the process longer and worse." Hayet is not happy with Grandpa's remarks.

"Thank you. The failures that I have are the fulfillment of your ill wishes for me. If you were to have wished me well, I would have gotten the job."

"You know that we always think and wish well for you!" Grandpa cries insistently.

"Yes, of course. However, I want you always to *say well* for me."

His adoptive parents never sugarcoat speech; they speak the truth in love. On issues that they do not approve, they do speak up openly. Much of the time what they say causes discomfort in Hayet's inner being. However, they do not regret it. It is understandable what they say may hurt him, yet the unbearable discomfort and sorrow could cause him to seek one dose of the necessary prescription. Nevertheless, until then he will feel like all fights are against him.

"Until you walk by your God-given purpose, it will feel like all and everybody is fighting against you. Resolve to *diverge* and align your existence with God's intention for your life, which is God's Positioning System. Then, 'Surely you will call people you know not, and people you do not know will come running to you. People that you call for help will help you, because of the Lord your God will bestow favor upon you. Then, all the people and conditions that withhold and hinder your progress will urge you to hurry and leave their territory for advancement. If you refuse to leave, they will kick and fire you from lesser to greater achievement, where you ought to be.'"

"I like your optimism."

"Thank you! In the Disney movie, *The Lion King*, do you remember Simba?" Grandpa asks.

"Yes, I surely do. His jealous uncle chases him and passes through a carefree, purposeless life with a warthog and a meerkat, eating what lions are not supposed to eat. He forgets who he is preordained to be, a king until he wakes up and forcefully takes hold of his position in life."

"I need some explanation in simple terms when you say, 'until he wakes up and forcefully takes hold of his position in life.'"

"If Simba wants to be the king he was meant to be, he should go to where he left and get what he left, meaning his rightful kingship."

"You have stated it perfectly. You have become just like Simba, running away from your true self and living like a loser. Wake up and arise from motivational mediocrity and death, and Christ will shine on you."

Hayet's head spins from the overdose of reproach from the Gramps; having been denied the job by his former classmates makes it worse. He gazes at Grandma. She is busy preparing ginger tea. The discussion has become too hot to bear.

"Grandma, are you hearing what Grandpa is saying?" Hayet asks, seeking her support, who usually supports him.

Grandma comes near Hayet and stares at him eyeball to eyeball. As she wipes her wet hands on a paper towel, she says, "My son, I heard every word of the conversation. I do totally agree with Grandpa. Unless you want me to add to his thoughts, I have nothing to oppose."

"If you have the same view, then that is enough," Hayet says. At the same time, Hayet walks away in despair and tells them, "I have been thinking of relocating to another state."

Upon hearing this, they are not so surprised. They expect such moves could corner him into a painful crushing condition of wilderness that would lead him to his destiny.

"Changing dwellings will not bring a change of the heart. You are relocating with the same Hayet to another state and you will still find the same Hayet with an additional stressful pressure of the enemies that you always try to avoid; the Jezebel's and your brothers. New life comes from choosing a new way of life, not from changing to new places. What you will have to do is renew your mind to the likeness of Christ, submit to God, and be at peace with Him. In this way, prosperity will come to you. Accept instruction from His mouth, and lay up His words in your heart. If you return to God, He will restore you. If you remove wickedness from your heart, then God will be your gold, the choicest silver for you. Surely then you will find delight in the Almighty and will lift up your face to God. You will pray to Him, and He will hear you, and you will fulfill the vows you made years back," mentions Grandpa.

"Do not worry about me. I am hearing all sorts of machines and people making construction noises; the job has started. I will get some job and be successful."

The Gramps reluctantly support the move. They believe that God will have his way in Hayet's life and corner him into a no-exit situation. There, reaching a dead end will cause him to diverge.

Hayet bids farewell to the Gramps. The following day at nightfall, he packs up the little he has and drives away, plowing through the deep snow of January, looking for a better life. After about fifteen hours of traveling, early in the evening he finally drives through Old Peachtree Street, settles in Peachtree Apartments, a rental unit he randomly found by making a phone call. It is not far from Peachtree Hotel, between Peachtree Avenue and Peachtree Corners, in the Peach State of Georgia.

Hayet is in confusion, not well prepared for the move financially or psychologically. All that he wanted was to get away from the humiliation that he encountered with his former college friends and the nagging of the Gramps pushing him to organize his life. Upon his arrival, he is dead tired and falls on the wooden couch, not minding how the room looks and not knowing what the future holds for him.

Chapter 40

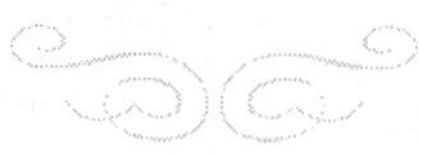

I do not know what my tomorrow holds, but
I do know who holds my future.

— *Tim Tebow*

Hayet has left New York seeking the opening to a better life, and he ends up in a pressing condition that will test him before leading him toward his destiny.

The first morning he encounters two girls. "Welcome to Georgia. We are called the Jezebel sisters," the girls announce, welcoming him as they giggle.

Oh my God, this cannot be true. I thought I left the Jezebel's family in New York and have run away to where I would not find them again.

"We are all over; the ones in Georgia are somehow milder than the ones that you previously encountered. Just be at peace with us and you will have no problem," declare the duo.

Hayet is so confused to find the Jezebel family in Georgia, too. *Besides, what do they mean when they say "be at peace with us and you will have no problem?" God is the only one that can make such declarations.* The only choice he has is to face the fact and see what comes up.

Hayet finds, in Georgia, many names appear to be associated with peaches. Almost every road, business, and neighborhood appears to have the word *peach* in it. At various stores, he comes across distinct types and sizes of peaches. *No wonder it is nicknamed the "Peach State,"* he thought, though he has never seen a live peach tree.

Hayet applies for a job for which he has experience and some training. However, "We are not going to give him the job," declares one who smiles on the outside yet on the inside is a ravaging wolf controlled by Jezebel.

Again, Hayet spices up his résumé and applies for every job he believes he can do. Nevertheless, it appears as if every employer once again turns down his résumé. He becomes extremely frustrated, exasperated, and dejected.

He wants to work in an area where he can help people. However, he never fulfills his life passion. He hopes to achieve the highest possible prestige for himself and his community by working his way up.

At last, the job search lands him a position in a warehouse, presumably until he obtains a better one though he is not sure what it would cost, and how long he may stay there. It is with the Procurement Investment Group, abbreviated PIG.

PIG is a media supplying company that supplies Walmart, Sam's Club, Best Buy, and the US Army and Air Force Exchange Service. PIG has the organizational structure to monopolize the world if the company desires to do so.

PIG is a true American company that is sensitive to community needs and serves willfully. It is well air-conditioned all year long and is family friendly. PIG is one of the unique American-owned businesses, which supports other American businesses. The company rewards hardworking associates in the form of incentives. Hayet benefits and has gone to a few fun places because of the incentives. PIG also offers college scholarships for an associate or a family member taking full-time media-related studies.

On the first day of work, Hayet casually pledges, *By the time I end my employment with PIG, I should be able to write a book. Should I fail to do so, it is a curse.*

The same words that Hayet articulates will chase him until he achieves what he said he should. Doing what he said, he should test his faithfulness to his pledge. Writing an English-language book for English-speaking consumers is not an easy task for an immigrant who speaks English as a second language.

During those early years of employment, knowing his great potential and ability, Hayet is worked to the bone and suffers aching pains. *Lord, when will you deliver me from this kind of work?* he intently prays. In response, a message overwhelms his being. *The only way to get from where you are to where you ought to be is for you to write a book.* At the same time, the Tobias and Sanballat's discouragement crescendo rings loud and clear in his head, and he always feels that he is going to fail long before he starts anything.

At PIG, during the busy season, employees can work as much as fifteen hours a day until the team completes the job. Associates frequently work six or seven days a week. Hayet joyously works voluntary overtime to have enough to cover his expenses and some to save. The good thing is that no matter how many hours and days he works, every day he has an excellent attitude. For he knows that in order to pass to the next level, he should survive and pass the current level with gratitude.

In some learning institutions, the school may push unqualified students to the next level as a social promotion. In some jobs as well, an employer may have offered a job to an underqualified employee in a current position because of lie-synthesis. In the eyes of God, where there is no favoritism, each candidate gets an achievable task and must pass the current level before promotion to the next level.

The duties at PIG include loading and unloading supplies either by a machine or manually, order picking, display building, merchandising and induction, scanning, taping, wrapping pallets, printing paperwork, and shipping. The shift work requires that each employee walk or stand for the entire shift. PIG has no jobs done while seated unless one has an injury. *My back, arms, shoulders, neck, and feet are in excruciating pain all the time*, Hayet frequently utters to himself when he wakes early in the morning. He never tells anybody about the discomfort. Each time, he speaks of the unbearable pain, saying, *Lord, when will you deliver me from such unfulfilling jobs?* the inner voice whispers, *The only way to get from where you are to where you ought to be is to write a book.*

Working for PIG is not all bad. He makes good money during the busy season and runs out during the dry season. Frequently, he uses a hassle-free credit card during the seasons that are not busy. He still does not perceive that credit cards require paying off or understand how he will ever do so.

He yearns for a day of plenty where he will not have to wake up with such excruciating pain. *How many of my college mates have plenty to spend, vacations to plan, and money to save while I languish in scarcity? When will my sufferings end?* he wonders as he tears up. The tears from his brokenness are not so bad; they show that he is on the verge of finding happiness.

Seldom has he admitted, *I am responsible for my mess. I never put the most important thing first, preferring fun over fulfillment.* Nevertheless, he gradually embraces the Gramps' optimism that one day all will change for his benefit, beyond anything he could ever imagine, thou not knowing when and how.

Chapter 41

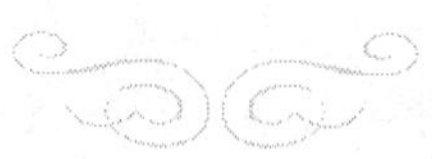

Faith is taking the first step even when you do not see the whole staircase.

— Rev. Dr. Martin Luther King Jr.

As conservatives in matters of faith, the Gramps say, "The Bible says it, and that settles it," and many times, Hayet does not go along with them.

The Gramps state, "What God has done for our forefathers in the past keeps us walking in the present and carries us into the future."

According to Hayet, the Gramps' conservative beliefs are different than the existential, philosophical understandings that give emphasis to the individual's freedom and choice. Hayet lives for the here and now. He is responsible for his decisions and relies on his mere human understanding.

"We are what we can become, and our being has nothing to do with our ancestors' teachings," Hayet expresses what he believes.

In the midst of a heated discussion, during one of Hayet's frequent visits to the Gramps, Grandma cries, "Honey, do not be surprised by what is been stated. We are in the last days. What Hayet is saying is a fulfillment. The Spirit clearly speaks that in later times, some will abandon the faith and follow cleverly devised stories, deceiving spirits and teachings taught by demons. That is what has been going on with the current generation."

As Hayet ponders the Gramps' old-school religious understanding, the phone rings, disrupting the discussion. Grandpa walks to pick up the phone.

"It is Dr. BEN JOHANNES, the company CEO," he whispers, seeing the caller ID. He clears his voice, picks up the phone, and talks while leaning against the wall.

Once he hangs up the phone Grandma asks, "Honey, what is it? Are you okay, and what did he say?"

"It is fine," he replies—just three words. He pauses and sits uncomfortably.

"Tell us what he said," Grandma maintains.

"As we commemorate the greatest gift to humanity, Christmas, he wants me to personally take food and medicine to Somalia, which is one of the most dangerous places in the world."

"Is that what makes you look sad? It is your duty that you pledged to put God first, prioritize your life, and serve others."

"I am aware of that! However, I am somewhat concerned over the security, and piracy. Piracy has been hampering the flow of goods and services in that part of the world. That is not all; a couple of hundred merchant ship workers still remain in the hands of their captors," Grandpa says nervously. Then he turns to Hayet. "Since I am urgently needed, stand by; we shall continue our discussion when I return. I hope you will not mess up and be taken to jail or get killed by somebody."

"You think so, Grandpa?" Hayet scoffs. "Who knows? You might find me transformed. It takes just one troublesome shaking-up shifting situation to change all."

"What troublesome situation do you expect that is worse than being suspended from college and living a defeated and unfulfilled life without notable achievement? You cannot keep your life on hold until a troublesome situation causes life's challenge to change. Whatever you should do, you must do it now while there is still a possibility for growth, or else when the time comes, you cannot stop the train and the rain. Besides, when shall it be? It took eighty years for Moses to figure out his identity. I am afraid to say that it could take you half of that to do the same."

Despite the harsh words, Hayet confidently replies, "If not today, it shall be someday. If it does not happen here, it shall take place somewhere. When that happens, both of you shall live in my house enjoying the fruit of your son."

Grandpa nods his head in disbelief, picks up his banjo. He sits down in his favorite chair. Ponting a yellow guitar pick toward Hayet, he says, "If you help yourself and others that are in need, speaking life into their darkness, that is all what we need from you." Then he sings Toby Mac's "City on Our Knees": "If you gotta start somewhere why not here? If you gotta start sometime why not now.'

After the song, Grandpa says, "My son, if you want to be the real you, the present moment is the right time, and today is the opportune day. It feels you are being a square peg trying to force your way untimely into a circular hole, which can affect your life negatively. When you realize you are at a point that you cannot help yourself, then you cannot fight it out. At that time, call the name of Jesus, surrender your life to God by taking Rx: RE. Then activate the dormant power within you, which has been inactive for years, by plugging yourself into the source of lasting energies, which is God. If not, the only thing you will gain is hurt. Whichever way you may try shall lead you to bad situations as well as conditions where overwhelming problems will press you close to the wall, with no room to turn. At that point, the only option that you will have is to surrender willfully. Should you refuse, He shall spit you out of His mouth, and you shall be a restless wanderer on the earth. I want you to remember before it happens. In the end, after wasting resources and years of your life, eventually, you will do what is right, diverge and return to God."

Hayet understands that the Gramps' advice is loving. However, he does not know what to do. He finds himself doing what he hates. Although he wants to do well, the temptation causes a war to rage within him that he is unable to rise above.

It has now been ages since Hayet became a low achiever.

"Grandpa, I understand what you are saying. Nevertheless, life does not add up. It is cyclic: eat, drink, sleep, work every day."

"Life does add up; there is always cause and effect. One gives birth to the other, eventually leading to culmination."

"I do not like the life journey path that I am on."

"If you do not like the path that you are on, then create one that you need, not one that you want."

"I wish I could, but I cannot."

"Just as in the case of the man who was crippled for thirty-eight years, the Ancient of Days Master has come and is saying to you, arise from the narrow-mindedness that has kept you from reaching for your bursting potential. See what the Lord can do, not what you cannot. Cast your cares on Him and He will carry them for you. Just believe and obey what He says immediately. Because deferred obedience and partial obedience are considered as disobedience."

Hayet mutely twiddles his fingers.

"How old are you now?"

"You know the answer."

"Okay, let me say it this way. If you commit yourself to your true purpose for the next ten years what could you achieve and how old will you be after ten years?"

"Age-wise, add ten years to my current age; I could earn a Ph.D."

"How about if you do nothing for the next ten years how old will you be and what could you achieve after ten years?"

"You just add ten years to my current age; achieve nothing."

"The conclusion is that, whether you do something fruitful or not for the next ten years, ten years will be added to your age. So, would you rather decide to be fruitful or wasteful?"

"Grandpa, what you are saying is so enlightening. But, I am powerless to decide."

"Son, it feels that these are the days of distress and rebuke and disgrace, as when children come to the moment of birth and there is no strength to deliver them. However, trust me; shall the Lord bring the child to the point of birth and not give delivery? He will surely carry you through. God's wings will provide you with safety and refuge, protecting you from a danger that continually attacks you with fears, despair, discouragement, and numerous other negative thoughts. Take the first bold step to diverge to God's call for your life."

The linear time of Hayet's story is winding toward its end. Time is passing. Corey and Elton's son, as well as LeAnn and Springer's daughter, have become grownups. They have graduated from college with BA and MA, are working professional jobs, and are married. That is not all. Even the least expected to graduate, Hayet's previously party crazy friends Bernard Tim, Sandy Shakur, and Shian Carson earned Ph.D.'s, got good jobs, married, and are blessed with children, while Hayet is still stuck in the same old life.

Every morning when Hayet arises, his bones scream for deliverance from the job that he cannot leave. What is more, whenever he counsels people, the counselees succeed. The hurt that Hayet suffers from is not necessarily for the pain he is in; it is what is to be born out of the pain, as commonly pain precedes birth. However, his life appears to be in a shamble, while his internal voice echoes, *There are truly great achievements in life, which are worth working for, waiting for me.*

Hayet has no doubt that he is worth more than what he earns and what he has become. How many more years will he be in such a failed state? Should he continue the way he is walking, a way that seems right, yet eventually ends in death? He will die without achieving what he and others wish to see achievement-wise. The only option that remains is to take the prescribed dose, Rx: RE, and see its effectiveness. However, he still does not know where to start. He needs a motivational booster, perhaps his father's '*what happened to you my son admonition*' or some sort of personal encounter that would propel him.

Chapter 42

You are good when you walk your goal firmly and with bold steps. Yet, you are not even when you go thither limping. Even those who limp go not backward.

— *Khalil Gibran, The Prophet*

It has been years since Hayet thought of his biological parents, he takes a visit which would be a turning point.

He is delighted to learn of a reunion with his parents after decades of separation caused by political instability in his home country.

They currently live in California. He wants to see them; however, he is concerned that his success-obsessed family will question his hand-to-mouth living conditions and underachieving living condition. He presumes that the encounter might be as frustrating as those early years, when his father would come home a couple of days a month and sit on the sofa in darkness. The family provides the airplane ticket. Therefore, Hayet excitedly decides to go to California to meet his parents and other family members.

When Hayet left his home country a few decades back, he had an Afro; he used a wooden pick to comb his hair. However, due to some physical changes, now Hayet uses neither a pick nor a comb because he does not have an Afro anymore.

Early on Saturday, Hayet leaves the Peach State for the Golden State. First, he goes through a harassing and provocative pat down during the airport security check. He is so confused about the nature of the search. *Is this searching, massaging, caressing, or beating up?* If he protests the nature of the search he knows that it would be worse on him than to the men and women behind or in front of him. Perhaps they will take him to prison or disqualify from taking the flight, which would be hard to bear. His unique Semitic color aggravates the search. Once he passes the security check, he hears, "Hayet Africa, please come to the security check," as the officers call him a second time. A brave young woman behind Hayet, with a sense of justice and fairness, says, "I will go with you."

"Why do you have to single out and call him for the second time?"

"It is just standard procedure, ma'am. These checks are totally random." *Honestly, if I tell you the reason why him, you will kill me.*

"That is not right. You have to treat him like everybody else."

Hayet goes through more intensive same interrogation all over again. He does not object to the disgusting and provocative search as long as it keeps passengers safe from terrorists.

"I am going to see my parents after years of separation," Hayet tells people that are near him at the airport.

"Lucky you; I never saw my parents. However, I promised myself to be a good father to my children," says a Falcon shoe–wearing man. After a couple of hours of waiting, Hayet boards the plane that takes off from Hartsfield-Jackson International Airport and lands at Los Angeles International Airport before noon.

Hayet first happens to meet ASHER, the companion with whom he fled home. He also meets another relative with an Afro for the first time.

"We are glad to see that God brought you to your family; congratulations," say the duo while giving Hayet jasmine garlands.

Hayet's big brother, We-ha-thee, and parents are still looking for a parking spot. At first glance upon arriving at the airline gate, his mother, Wa-euro, seeing her prodigal son, cries, "Thank you, Lord, that you kept us alive to see the face of our son."

She has grown old, yet she jumps and shouts joyously, "*Essay, essay, essay,* Hayet, *we-day*," in her language.

Essay is an exclamation of extreme joy, while *we-day* means my son. She acts like a toddler, despite her age, displaying a loving mirth of joy accompanied with laughter and tears.

Sheden, who has grown old, uses a walker and smiles from ear to ear. We-ha-thee also displays a happy face; he does not show any physical change for all those years. What a happy family reunion!

Onlookers stare at the jubilant family reunion in the passenger pickup area, away from the sliding doors. Police officers order the driving by onlookers, "Keep moving." The family laughs joyfully.

"Oh my God, what happened to your Afro?" asks his mother frequently, in hilarity and bewilderment. She laughs ceaselessly as she massages his bald head accompanied with kisses to the lost and found son.

During all the years of separation, Hayet has been struggling with an identity crisis. He has never really known who he is. For years, he wished to meet his parents so that they might help him answer his identity question. In his homeland, his parents either did not explain their identity or else he did not understand the point. Now Hayet has the chance to know his identity, and he does not want to let go of it. At home, the phone rings often to congratulate his parents, and a few people manage to come over to celebrate the reunion with bottles of drink, bouquets, and bunches of flowers.

After lunch, in the late afternoon, Wa-euro roasts coffee beans on an old-style charcoal stove, using a coffee pan known as *men-kesh-kesh*. The roasted coffee smog makes the house look as if it is on fire. The smoke detector goes off. We-ha-thee hurriedly reaches up and disables it.

Once the beans are roasted, and while still rattling, steaming, and sizzling, Hayet's mother takes the roasting coffee and wafts it around about for the visitors. The visitors sniff the aroma and say, "Thank you," as they waft the smell toward them. Then she takes the coffee roasting pan in every room while wafting. A coffee odor is better than any scent that a house may have. The coffee aroma is so powerful that it replaces all other odors. Hayet takes a deep breath and smiles in the memories.

Shortly after, Wa-euro pours the roasted coffee beans on another interlaced ventilator, a *mesh-re-fete*, that people use to ventilate the fire; the coffee beans chill down. After it cools, she pounds the beans with a mortar and a wooden pestle, which can pulverize the coffee finely enough. Then she pours the pulverized, fine coffee powder into a coffee clay pot known as a *jebena*. She mixes the coffee with water and shakes it up, waits until it boils and is ready to drink. A *jebena* has three parts. These are the *me-a-core,* meaning the butt, which stores and boils the coffee with water; the *key-sad,* meaning the neck, the only outlet where a sieve, known as a *leaf*, is put; and the *is-nee*, meaning the ear, a curvy handle that connects with the butt.

At the same time, Wa-euro roasts American flower (popcorn), on a sizzling, oily pan and drizzles salt over it. Once the popcorn stops popping, it is ready. Mother takes and pours it onto a finely woven interlaced, handmade traditional tray called a *safé*. A *safé* is one of the household items that young girls make in preparation for a wedding. It is obvious that Hayet's sister-in-law either made it or bought it. The celebrants scoop it up by the handful from the *safé*.

As the coffee ceremony continues, Hayet anticipates hearing of his identity as well as information on how his parents managed their early life.

The first round of coffee is ready, and Wa-euro fills the little porcelain coffee cups, known as *finjal,* until they overflow, which is a must, to receive blessings such as "May God give you an overflowing blessing." A *finjal* is a small, multicolored or star striped porcelain cup that contains 25–35 milliliters, which one can drink with one chug. However, for coffee etiquette, people drink one sip at a time, taking an average of twenty minutes per stage. The stages are *a-well*, meaning first, which is a must-drink stage; *dereja*, meaning second; and *baracka,* meaning blessings or the third. Nevertheless, some people drink up to seven stages.

Mother, Wa-euro, pours the brewed coffee into as many porcelain cups as are available, which is most likely enough for all visitors. As soon as the cups are full, she says to the young visitor, "Please come and *adele* while it is still hot."

Adele means, dispense without charge-free. The nephew dispenses the coffee starting with the older people. The tallest visitor, seated next to the circular brown table, pronounces, "It is so tasty." By saying it is tasty, the coffee drinkers save Mother from doing the lengthy procedure again.

"May God give you *tasty*," replies Mother, which is the tradition for anyone that brews coffee.

In the early evening, the sunlight dwindles, and the family turns on the house lights.

Hayet's father, Sheden makes an unexpected announcement that nobody has expected.

"God sets the lonely in families. He leads out the prisoners into prosperity, but the rebellious dwell in a parched land. Now that I have seen my son, if the Lord takes me home, it is acceptable."

Sheden pronounces so because he has no possibility of returning to his homeland. After hearing all the wishes of his mother, Hayet declares, "I do not think that is what I feel my heart is saying. You shall not die before we see the fulfillment of Mother's wishes. We shall all go home for the fulfillment of Mother's wishes and then after that, your day shall come."

For Hayet, it is risky to make such a prediction at a time when his parents' health is uncertain. Besides, there may not be an important reason that would take the whole family to Africa. Furthermore, even if a reason that would take them to Africa arises, financially, it is not affordable. In addition, the family is scattered to the west and to the east. Nevertheless, deep down, in his inner soul, that is what he feels. What is more, the promise "God has said: I am with you, and I will protect you wherever you go. One day, I will bring you back to this land" has gone forth.

Many years ago, while she was a childless bride, Wa-euro, also made a wish of going into exile and returning home after a long time. She always talks of her wish. Nevertheless, it is unlikely for the family to return to Africa given the factual impossibilities.

Sheden's life history entrances every listener.

"Please tell us how you became a born-again believer," Hayet requests.

Sheden worked for a Swedish organization, and Hayet expects it is a Swedish person that initiated Sheden's life change.

Sheden gives his life account. It is the first time that Hayet hears it. As an early teenager, Sheden became gravely ill. One afternoon he took a nap and dreamed an unbelievable dream. He dreamed of coming to a city called Lancaster. While riding on a white horse, *God does a miracle such as this, giving life to the dead soul*, he proclaims.

"I saw all the lavish houses that stand in America," Sheden tells.

However, in the physical world, it is unlikely for the poor young boy to make it to a country and people that he never knew existed. The moment he wakes up, the sickness instantly vanishes, and he receives miraculous healing.

In the midst of the life history, Mother whispers, "Excuse me, more coffee of the *awell* is available. Pass me your *finjal* should you want more."

A couple of the visitors reply, "The coffee is so strong that we shall take from the second stage."

A few visitors take more. Hayet and the youngest visitor hand over the empty coffee cups to Wa-euro.

Then Hayet asks, "What about education? I used to hear people asking me whether I am as smart as my father. They used to tell me that my father skipped double grades every year."

"I am coming to it," Sheden says as he sips the sugarless black coffee, which has gone cold while he talks.

Sheden describes having no formal education when he meets the American missionaries. He has no educational credit, only informal lessons given by the Orthodox Church. The Orthodox Church usually teaches the people that have a call to serve how to read and write. Thus, in the whole village the people who know how to read and write obviously start the learning process at the church. Sheden first requests the American missionaries to open for him educational opening, yet they would not. Then he goes to Asmara and asks the same favor of a Swedish missionary.

The missionary declares, "You are too old to go to school. However, I will give you a trial of one year, a first grader at the age of thirty-five."

The first year of his school, he skips through first to fourth. The second year, he skips the fifth and sixth grade and earns a promotion to seventh grade. He takes a year each for the seventh and eighth grade, and then he takes teacher training and eventually becomes a teacher.

Through his persistence, the innovative Sheden creates his educational breakthrough and studies heavily. After surviving biases due to his southern heritage in the central region, which created a purpose of lining in Hayet's life. A few years later, he takes college studies, gains his diploma, and becomes an ordained minister. By the time he finishes telling about his education, Wa-euro has dispensed the second stage coffee.

"This one is not as strong as the first one," announces Wa-euro, who sits on a cushioned wooden stool.

Hayet is excited to hear the true account that explains the quest of his identity. "*Abo*, I have one more question," calls out Hayet apprehensively while seated on one of the brown hardwood stairs leading to the living room.

"Many years ago, I came across a letter that stated the family must vacate the house by June 30 and go to the village where you work. I want to know what happened to that. I expected us to vacate the house, and it did not happen." Sheden is old; nevertheless, his memory is still fresh.

"Yes, I remember that, too," he replies. Prior to the eviction notice, the administration has handpicked who works where with bias. They have favoritism. Thus, Sheden goes to the high-rise brick and black stone headquarters. He enters into a conversation with the decision makers.

"The duty assignment that we have been told of, is it for life or should we expect a rotation?"

"I do not know how people are assigned," replies a leader that has a servanthood spirit.

In the meantime, Sheden decides, until a solution presents itself, to keep working to support his family. At the same time, he writes multiple applications seeking fairness and justice. However, no solution arises.

Meanwhile, the general assembly of the entire organization comes together for a meeting. That is the time when representatives from the whole province attend. The organization provides food, drink, and bedding for those that come from afar. That is when the employees discuss matters of the organization and when the president and other key officers' election takes place.

The villager participants are easily identified by their huddled *gabby* and their walking rods. The rod is a sign of manhood and authority. The attendants are easy to spot; they gather in groups after the daily meeting at cool twilight.

During the course of the year, one of the educational department employees takes up grievances for governmental intervention. Mr. Chekan Yehuda, the moderator, speaks from the platform. "It is wrong to take cases to the government."

The moderator clears the stage for open discussion and a possible solution. The villagers hoist their hands to seek time to speak; the attendants from the city lift their hands for the same reason. Sheden happens to be one of the people who want to give a suggestion for a possible solution. Sheden gets his turn to speak. He knows that what he speaks of may backfire on him should he use words that are not pleasing the key players seated on the platform. It is obvious any challenging statement could endanger the educational well-being of his children, some of whom are in high school, a few more in elementary, and the remaining not yet at school age. He believes that his idea can heal the cause of the problem rather than the external manifestation, and so he speaks boldly.

Sheden describes standing among the long, connected brown wooden pews. Villagers whom he knows surround him. Although he huddles in a *gabby* when he goes to the village for work when he is in the city, he usually dresses up in suits. He clears his voice so that the attendants, as well as the leaders, may hear his point.

The third stage of coffee becomes ready, and We-ha-thee, who has been listening rather than talking, dispenses it. It is lighter than the previous ones. Sheden accepts the cup.

"Tell us what happened next," Hayet says worriedly.

Sheden resumes unfolding the issue that caused the eviction letter. He speaks out, "If the people from one of the departments went seeking governmental intervention, bypassing the organizational chain of leadership, it is totally wrong. However, if these people sought help because the administration would not listen to their repeated cries, then they are right."

"Do we have people that do not listen to the cry of their employees? I believe we do not have unfair and unjust leaders," replies the moderator.

"Yes, we sure do have unfair and unjust authorities. You are one such person. I wrote multiple letters for years seeking fairness and justice, and I did not receive a reply. Should I seek governmental intervention, which I am not going to do unless it touches the well-being of my children; I do not think it is out of order." Sheden strengthens his position. The council covers up and proceeds to other discussion points.

Shortly after, the meeting ends for the day, and the moderator comes up to Sheden.

"Just wait—I will show you!" he threatens as the villagers hear. The threat of the youngest moderator to an old man in African culture is punishable and unacceptable no matter the reason. One ought not rebuke an older man harshly but exhort him as if he were your father and do the same to older women as mothers. Treat younger men as brothers and younger women as sisters, with absolute purity.

Mr. Chekan Yehuda violates the respect norm and does it because he has the power. Upon hearing the threat, Sheden stands still, yet he knows that he is in trouble. The reason is that the moderator has the influential power to make a lie-synthesis to fire Sheden. Although unquestionably Sheden knows a result will come, he is not certain what it might be.

The subsequent days before Sheden go back to the village to work, the mail carrier hands him a typed letter. His firm hands open it. The letter needs divine intervention. The words are so shocking that they could jeopardize the educational well-being of his children. Sheden must do all that is possible to overcome his fears.

Sheden is the only known southerner in the organization. He has no relative that can speak up to intervene in the moderator's onslaught unless someone with a sense of justice comes up, which is unlikely to happen. It is the kind of letter that makes a loving father have sleepless nights, have gastritis, and sit in darkness.

The letter says, "Vacate the house by June 30 and go to the place you have been assigned to work."

Immediately, Sheden writes an appeal, stating, "I never got a good education. Please let my children stay within the city, the way I have been doing so that they may have an education," he pleads.

The reason is that, school is not available where the administration assigned him to work. The nearest high school is about twenty kilometers away. Additionally, there is no adequate transportation, the roads are rough and landmine infested and it is also in the rebel-controlled area. Regardless of the appeal, Mr. Chekan Yehuda under the cover of lie-synthesis of the administration remains firm that the family must vacate.

In the situation Sheden describes, he is helpless and has come into a state of fight or flight. He has to fight wisely to win, or he must take his family to the village. The latter could jeopardize the education of his aspiring children.

"How did you escape the unjust and unfair verdict?" Hayet asks his father while he fidgets with the remaining fragments of popcorn. Sheden for the first time tells Hayet the price he paid and his desire to be with his family every day including Sundays and holidays.

Forgive me, Father, I never perceived that you always wished to be with your family.

That is why I said, "When I grow up, I shall always be present for my family." Upon hearing of the unfair treatment of a defenseless old man, wrath and rage simmer within Hayet.

"What happened then?"

"I am coming to it," replies Sheden confidently as he takes one sip coffee.

Sheden loves the organization dearly and does not want to leave. The organization is one that feeds the hungry, gives water to the thirsty, educates the uneducated, speaks on behalf of the voiceless, and provides medical services to the sick. Nevertheless, the appeal and pleading will not let his children stay within the city. As a last resort, Sheden seeks government intervention. He writes an injunction appeal to the local communist administration authority.

During the in-person hearing Sheden says, "I already lost a son who became a rebel and joined the Eritrean Liberation Fighters. Now I still have a few more teenagers. The moderator is threatening me to go to the rebel-controlled area, and I am troubled that my teenage children will also join the rebel army just as my firstborn son did, and he died in action."

The local authorities warn the moderator. "Never again bother the old man," orders the chairperson. Because of the intervention, Sheden breathes a sigh of relief, and nobody bothers him. His children and grandchildren still live on the premises.

"On the day when God works, even the communists will be His treasured possession. God intervened and spared me, just as a father has compassion and spares his child who serves him."

Nevertheless, the Jezebel-embodied Mr. Chekan Yehuda's threat persists in another form. At one point, Mr. Yehuda summons the old man into his office, shuts the door, and rolls up his sleeves to assault Sheden.

Seeing the seriousness of the threat, Sheden declares boldly, "I am not going to start a fight. You start, and you will see." Mr. Chekan Yehuda fears any repercussions and lets Sheden go, opening the door.

"The unfair treatment of an old man will devastate your life. You will be a restless wanderer on the earth. Besides, remember that '*Ed shena-hit tsena-hit*,'" (The hand that hits others also get hit), says Sheden. He then exits through the granite staircase.

After Sheden finished telling the story, he says, "We are happy and still serving in the house of God. However, the people that treated us unfairly and unjustly are miserable."

Upon hearing the injustice as well as unfairness his father endured, Hayet smiles on the outside, yet internally, ravaging anger boils as a volcano in his being. *I would like to go and meet Mr. Yehuda wherever he may be so that I can take a revenge.*

The anger that pushes Hayet to want to take revenge is not necessarily for the unfair and unjust treatment of his father but of an old man. In Africa, the older a person is, the more respect one gains. Any sensible African, Asian, perhaps any human being would have the same feeling if one treats an older person disrespectfully. Hayet is thankful for the price his father paid, which is so immense that his descendants got an educational prospect of earning degrees up to a doctorate level.

Once I return to the Peach State, I will never be the same again, Hayet resolves. His father's story has ignited a desire to work and achieve deep within.

Additionally, he pledges to *diverge* and take the prescription the Gramps want him to take. The visit with his natural family turns out to be a motivational booster for him to begin to redeem his wasted years.

Once Sheden completes his story, he makes some final remarks. "If a ruler's anger upsurges against you, do not leave your post; calmness can lay great offenses to rest. Injustice and unfairness of others backed by a lie-synthesis may slow or block your advancement. Put God first, prioritize your life, and serve others while fighting wisely. The enemy comes only to steal, destroy, and kill, making you give up and die wastefully; Jesus has come that you may have life to the fullest. Be still, and know that God is God in your hardships, too. God has blessings and abundance for whosoever waits upon Him.

Remember that the pain of injustice and unfairness is temporary; however, quitting lasts forever. For whosoever endures, one day the truth shines, bringing light to the darkness. Rest assured that behind all that happens, and that does not, God's signature is available at every turn of your life. He works all things together for your good, for His good, and for others' good."

Hayet's father survives threats, injustice, and unfairness under Mr. Chekan Yehuda's leadership. Once Mr. Yehuda leaves the organization, Sheden's wish, which is a rotation to duty allocation, comes into effect. Thus, he first works in another village, then in the city, at the place that the British built, until the day he moves to his dreamland, the United States of America. Sheden concludes the gathering reading Psalms 37 and saying a prayer.

At last, congratulating the family over the reunion, the visitors leave one after another. Thank God, you bring the lonely to the family. If it were not for America's kindness through the United Nations High Commissioner for Refugees, Hayet would not have known his parents and his identity. Finally, after serving all the visitors silently,

Wa-euro also says, "Praise be to the Lord, to God our Savior, who daily bears our burdens. He kept my son safe and brought him to the family."

Afterward, the family travels to the Bay Area to meet another sibling. The following morning, We-ha-thee and Hayet go for a hike along Aborn Road, which branches from the Capitol Expressway, which also exits from Interstate 101.

The morning dew and fresh, cool morning breeze make hiking appealing. They walk side by side at a snail's pace, through the hilly, narrow, undivided road that barely accommodates two passing vehicles. The hiking saps one's strength. Alongside the road, cows and horses graze near the blooming chrysanthemum flowers; dogs viciously bark at the brownish hikers from the fenced yards.

It is the beginning of a new day on earth. The high grayish soft-woven winter haze is closed off by the surrounding valleys and rests on the palm tree–adorned city, separating it from the sky and the rest of the Bay Area. The nearby mountain tops are cloudy, and it gives a foggy view of smoggy San Jose. Airplanes eclipsed by the fog often rumble softly across the horizon. The vicinity over the peaks is hazy. The hikers are unable to see the actual airplanes.

In the midst of hiking, We-ha-thee frequently stops and does aerobic exercises along the twisty hairpin road. They approach a second curved turn. We-ha-thee, standing a couple of feet behind and facing Hayet and the hilly terrain, cautiously says, "You have heard how our father survived injustice and unfairness. I want you to know that he is in far much better condition than those people are. What are you going to do?"

"Brother, you did not see his suffering and anguish, see him seated in darkness. I was there and saw it with my own eyes. I know what I am going to do."

We-ha-thee knows Hayet as a stubborn and militant child who could do damage and wants to defuse the situation.

As they talk, they hike higher, and it becomes colder. Eventually, they return downhill before making it to the dead end, where Aborn Road winds. Hayet enjoys a few more days with his family and then returns to Georgia with a pledge to repay his parents for the price they paid on behalf of their children. The visit turns out to be best days in Hayet's life and a turning point that the Gramps wished to see. He eventually takes the long-awaited Rx: RE prescription, which stands for *return*. Hayet embraces the forgotten virtues and makes them part of his life. He also reacquires and embraces his abandoned God's Positioning System, GPS, which also stands for "God, Prioritize, and Serve." That is to say, put God first, prioritize your life, and serve others; yet he does not know where to start or how to achieve his long-life goal.

Chapter 43

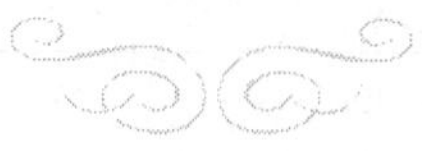

God has an appointment with your breakthrough.

— *Joyce Myer*

Hayet returns from the Golden State awakened to work for the most tangible achievement, not knowing which one it may be or how to attain it.

He frequently tears up over his inability to achieve his goal. Many immigrants, as well as American-born citizens, achieve the American dream, whereas for Hayet, every door shuts on him, no matter how hard he works. The more he longs for life, liberty, and the pursuit of happiness, the more unachievable it seems to be. He has many questions to ask about why life for others is smooth while his life seems rougher than anybody else's does, yet who will answer?

The worst challenge he faces is quitting an addictive habit that he has developed and whose cravings he cannot spend a night without quenching. His eyes turn red and he yawns excessively, sensing the aroma of his addiction from as far as miles away. As the deer pants for stream water, so Hayet's soul pants to meet the unmet addiction that makes him restless and unable to concentrate. Hayet hopes not to take anything to quench the yearning. In order to break the addiction, he reasons, *I have to start a new project, discontinue associating with my old friends such as Emmanuel and Felix, start gymnastics, avoid going to notorious places, and get busy.*

A couple of days after Hayet's return from California, the Gramps come to visit in the Peach State. They exchange greetings and Grampa says, "We have good news for you. Your brothers have diverged from their wayward ways, embracing purposeful living. Some of their scars, however, are irreversible. Thank God they are back. Tell us, how was the visit with your parents and family?"

"It was transforming. This month is a great month for our family. We have to celebrate greatly. You must bring the best robe and put it on each of us. You should put rings on our fingers. Let us have an exquisite banquet feast, rejoice, enjoy choice food and sweet drinks, and send some to those who have nothing prepared. This day is holy to our Lord. Do not grieve, Grandpa, over our past failures, for the joy of the Lord is your strength. For the children of yours were dead and are alive again; they were lost and are found. Besides, I have one song for you as you enjoy the return of all your prodigal children. It is 'I am Not Who I Was,' by Brandon Heath," says Hayet. The song tells about a person transformed by the power of the Gospel.

Right after Hayet sings the song, Grandpa says, "We are glad to see that God caught you by surprise. You cannot outrun Him; He can outrun the most rebellious person. By the way," he says, dropping a bombshell, "I know your father; I was one of the missionaries involved throughout his life."

"How could this possibly be?" cries Hayet in bafflement for a long moment. After gaining his composure, "Thank you for your sacrificial service. However, if you knew my background, why did you let me waste my life in wrongdoing? You should have forced me to stay in the race," Hayet shrieks in a crackly drawl.

"We could not force you because it would be another form of lie-synthesis, helping an undeserving person. Sometimes, one has to let nature take its course. Occasionally, one observes the rich, the powerful, and even some world leaders, based on friendship, racial and gender favoritism, or bias partake in some form of lie-synthesis, which is hurtful, not beneficial for the doer and the recipient. Although we were in pain every time we saw you take a wrong turn, we wanted you to figure out a life for yourself. This is a kind of lie-synthesis that you would like to eradicate from the face of the earth. Achievement through offering help to a help-deserving person fairly and justly is worth doing. Also, success, per one's ability being free from lie-synthesis makes the accomplishment permanent."

"Grandpa, give me an example."

"The Allied forces that defeated the threat and invasion by the Axis powers were a perfect example of help that portrays freedom from lie-synthesis. That is why the enemy got defeated; reconciliation and peace prevail because of fair and just intervention provided. On the contrary, helping undeserving interference and intervention is costing us trillions of dollars, our precious sons and daughters."

Further, says Grandpa, "At the same time, we wanted to wait patiently so that we might give you what we did not give your father, that is, educational openings."

"Grandpa, you should have nothing to regret. Nothing happens without God's will. You sow with tears and reap with songs of joy. You have given my father the best gift of all: life through Jesus. Had my father been part of your team without any struggle, I may not have acquired the serving mentality that I have now. Thank you for your sacrificial service."

Several weeks passed since Hayet pledged to *diverge*. He stands by his decision faithfully, without doing or taking part in activities that destroy his health and character. He is accountable for himself and enjoys a breath of clean air, giving up the contaminated and awful years of his life. He evades going to the dishonorable tempting street of town at all costs. When he does go to town, he travels one of the two parallel streets, circumventing the main one.

After coming to a complete halt in his addictive habit, he thinks, *Then, I can grit the other crucial decisions that stall my progress.* However, he needs somewhere and some reasons from which to start.

Meanwhile, he seeks all life-improving positions. Of course, he believes education is the best. Nonetheless, due to long hours of work and an unpredictable schedule of PIG, he is unlikely to pursue education.

Additionally, the physical pain and the psychological torment of achievement failures force him to seek other positions. Hayet seeks management and loss prevention jobs. Nonetheless, none seems to work.

During one of the interviews, "We have a lot of emergencies and non-emergency related phone calls every day. Would you feel comfortable dealing with the phone calls, given that you have an accent?" asks one of the managers.

"My accent is part of my identity. Just because I speak with an accent, it does not mean that I think with an accent. I have business experience handling property, have worked as a freelancer in a radio broadcasting show, and I have specialized college training on emergency management and loss prevention. I am reliable and honest. Having me could be a great help to the company," Hayet speaks of his qualification.

Anyway, the company offers one LP job to an employee who is within the ninety-day probation period. A couple months later, the company offers other LP position to another employee who has worked for PIG a few years less than Hayet. Nevertheless, PIG fires both the favored and the yet unqualified fluent English-speakers within a couple of months.

Hayet is capable of great achievements, yet he misses a way to secure a progressive position within the company, and it drives him crazy. He fails to realize that God is the one behind shutting the door so that he may not settle for less along the way before he reaches the divinely appointed destiny. At one point he thinks, *This stuff does not work; I am wasting my time here. I better leave this company.*

At the same time, he applies for a job with another company, which supplies high-performance flat panel units for airborne and other ground electronic applications to customers. The work pays lower, four figures a week. It happens to have more benefits in the form of the 401(k) it offers. That is not all. The company also gives paid holidays the Friday after Thanksgiving as well as a paid holiday for the days between Christmas and New Year. He gives his two weeks' notice to PIG, then leaves.

Right away, Hayet makes a phone call and informs the Gramps that he has left PIG for another job. Grandma cries, "My son, it feels that you left the company prematurely. Mark my words, you will return and restart not where you left off, but all over again."

Grandma is right, and the reason is that he has not achieved the pledge of writing a book that he made when PIG hired him. The project has not materialized. However, to defend his actions, he says, "Grandma, what other proof do I need other than securing a job with better benefits and pay?"

"You know the time when it is an opportune moment."

The new electronics company work is pleasing to Hayet. Although the pay is rewarding, he thinks, *I know this is not where I am meant to be.*

The long hours interfere with his volunteering and other responsibilities to which he has committed. However, he keeps on working faithfully, not knowing how long it will last.

Suddenly, an economic wind that has the potential to shake up the whole world blows gently in California. It initially affects the housing industry. The homeowners that have unreliable finances, fewer savings, risky jobs, and perhaps others with mysterious reasons are the first casualties of the economic turmoil.

The shakeup displaces well-established families from their dream homes, and the job market becomes shaky. For some of the affected people, the shakeup works out for good, causing them to launch deep into education, reinvent into real estate, and venture into the stock market with other new business openings. Others fail to fathom the doings of God, which in all occurrences He works for good, and became casualties. They crash into failed self-esteem, divorce, alcohol, drugs, depression, and a few suicides. The news agencies spend many hours talking about the affected families.

The unaffected people consider the shakeup as indigenous to California, and they speak their ideas about what Californians should and could do to protect their homes and jobs. They never realize that they could be victims, too. Nevertheless, slowly and surely the wind blows steadily toward all corners of the United States, and South America as well as Canada.

The widening and increasing momentum hops across the Atlantic and eventually reaches Europe, causing default and austerity measures and setting a policy of cutting deficits by lowering spending. The wind continues to blow, affecting Africa, Australia, and Asia.

Monday morning, July 2, 2007, two days before American Independence Day, Hayet is ready to celebrate the holiday at home after seven days of long hours at work. Suddenly, the HR manager who hired him comes at an unusual time. The atmosphere turns tense. The employees grumble, "Why is it that the HR manager has come to the site so early from the head office?" First, he summons a couple of employees to the office one at a time. The employees never return to their post; instead, the HR manager comes out for the third time all alone.

While Hayet is doing his duties, the HR manager says, "Hayet, I want to see you."

Hayet follows apprehensively through the shadowy corridor. The office has three chairs and one table, nothing else. No computer accessories, no phone, no folders, no pictures; it is as empty as a new establishment. Of course, the building is a newly acquired property in the remodeling process to be suitable for the company.

"We are at a crucial time for the survival of the company," the HR manager says and hands Hayet a separation notice. It is the first time he has received such a letter. Hayet needs an explanation as to what the separation notice is, and the manager clarifies.

"So what do you want me to do with the letter?"

"You take it to the Department of Labor, and you will receive unemployment benefits for six months."

"If you know that you are to lay me off so quickly, why would you hire me, to displace me from my former job and the benefits that I earned?"

"We thought our company would be good when we hired you. However, before it becomes too late for our company, the best thing is to lay off some of you."

The worst part is that some employees with tardiness stay, whereas Hayet, with perfect attendance, is let go. He is neither hopeless nor disillusioned over what has unfolded. *A separation notice is not the end of the world. This place is not where I belong for my future life.* Hayet remains optimistic. *A door never shuts without leading to an open door.* However, he is not sure which door may open and what it will cost him.

Hayet immediately makes phone calls to family and friends, seeking counsel on how to handle the situation. He expects one family member to go ballistic and say something like, *Did not we tell you to go back to school?* instead, he often hears, "You come home. It is for your own good," though he does not know what good would come out of this bad situation.

At the same time, he makes phone calls and informs his biological parents, "I have been separated from my work."

"Fine, *Christos alo*, meaning Christ is present. It is for your good. Now, come to California. Even people that do not have what you have are making it to the top at a time when it seems hard going to school. You can live with us until you graduate from college and obtain a good job," his mother replies.

His father also says, "Listen, my son, many years from now you shall thank the person that laid you off, because, without the layoff, you would be lost and wandering in minor achievement. God will bring greater out of you and lead you to where you belong."

"Father, I lost a job, and how could I thank the person who made me jobless?"

"It is not about now; it will be about tomorrow; what God is going to do as a result of this firing."

"Well, I shall see how it goes."

Hayet wants to live with his parents for as long as they are alive; nevertheless, he is unlikely to do so now. The reason is that he believes that they should live with him, resting and enjoying their son's achievement, not vice versa.

The following day, Hayet begins to apply to college to pick up where he left off. In the meantime, he takes the separation notice to the Department of Labor. He passes an interview, attends orientation for how to deal with unemployment, and they approve him for the weekly benefits should he keep on trying at least two jobs per week. The orientation includes information on how to reduce spending and how to get subsidized services, including food stamps.

After the holiday, Hayet applies to more colleges, one of which happens to request a reactivation of his deferral application. Thanks to quick e-mail communication, he receives a consent form and some other requirements. He completes all the requirements right away and e-mails them back.

Soon, a new department head sends him an acceptance letter. "You must first pay your unpaid school fee, and you must start not where you left off but start all over again." Hayet welcomes the letter joyously. Nevertheless, as the day to travel to the Empire State for readmission draws nearer, he thinks, *I have no money to travel or pay my old-school fee.* Thus, he requests another deferral. The college understands the economic problem and grants his request.

Within the first couple of months of unemployment, he receives two stunning letters without a sender's address. The letters arrive on separate days and have cash in them. Although Hayet does not know the sender, he thinks, *Thank you, Lord, for reaching out to me at the time of my need.* At the same time, he plans to make three achievements: apply for multiple jobs, volunteer, and start working on a book project in order to achieve the pledge he made.

He applies for over a hundred positions. Nevertheless, it results only in a couple of unsuccessful interviews. Meanwhile, he volunteers for an organization that helps immigrants settle in the United States as well as other community related involvement such as writing, training, and mentoring. Soon he exhausts the six months of unemployment benefits, and no employment opening comes. The unemployment percentage lurks higher with the possibility that credit-rating agencies could downgrade US debt. The sluggish economy will default, and US debt may hit over $20 trillion. With no prospect of employment, he cries to himself, *I hate my life, my existence, and blame the poor decision I made in leaving PIG.*

During the early days of layoff, he utters to himself, *Let me do the book writing that I always wanted to do until another job opens.*

Hayet begins to volunteer a good number of hours every week, reaching out in his community. *To be accountable, I must write all the services that I provide,* he thinks, which happen to be about five pages a week.

A young Californian leader who loved Hayet's services comments and asks, "We greatly love and appreciate your services. Would you allow us to post it on our website so that many more may benefit from it?"

"If people can benefit from it, that would be a great idea," replies Hayet, not knowing what would be born out of the volunteer service.

Upon the completion of the set volunteer service, Hayet gathers tens of thousands of words.

Then, a couple of months later, "You have good exposure through our website. If you could make a book out of the services that you provided, that would be great," suggests the same young man.

For years, Hayet struggles within himself, realizing that he is not worthy to write about such matters because he has not been a good example, saying, *Let somebody else do it*. Yet nobody avails. Nevertheless, the urge to do so grows so strong that he has to accept and surrender in order to transfer to the next phase in life. Finally, he thinks, *As an imperfect man, if I tell others to avoid the wrongs of life I made, that would be great*. Then he starts to compile his presentation with the intention of writing about family issues in his mother tongue. He does not have much time to add such a huge project to his busy schedule. It would cost him to discipline himself to manage a full-time job and volunteer services that he has committed himself to.

Hayet expects the writing project to contribute to fixing the foundation of the national base that is the family. He believes if the family is weak, so is the nation, and if the family is strong, so is the nation. He wants to serve and cause change by fixing the prevailing family problem. Concurrently Hayet assumes the project through shows to alleviate the stated problem. He also hopes the project will ease his current and future struggles, setting him on solid ground to navigate life as he continues applying for jobs. Nevertheless, even securing temporary jobs through staffing agencies proves to be difficult.

The day he submits his writing project for printing, he secures his first job assignment through a staffing agency. It is exactly ten months after he got his separation notice and he has survived without receiving food stamps, yet at a cost of going to lower five-figure credit card debt. A few weeks later, he receives the printed project, and he is happy and excited.

At the peak of the excitement, "How many books do you expect to sell?" asks the all-time demeaning Jezebel.

"A few tens of thousands," Hayet replies confidently.

"I guess if you sell twenty, that would be great."

"All I want to do is God's will in and through my life. Even if one person gets the book and gives birth to others who would implement all that I desire to see, that is a great achievement."

The day he put his project on the market, the job assignment ends. What a poor man; his tribulations never end, and one problem comes after another. Not only that but also the sale on his printed book withers before it blossoms.

Having seen the failure of the book sale, "I told you," declares Jezebel.

Hayet is very unhappy about the result of the book, which did not go as what he had anticipated and becomes mad.

"Grandpa, did not I say before I started the project that I am not good at it and let somebody else do it? Did I not tell you, 'Do not raise my hopes of becoming successful through writing?' I did my best, and regardless of how hard I endeavor, nothing seems to pay off. What is the meaning of my existence?"

Hayet is so mortified. "I am better off dead than alive, just as my brethren who perished in the wilderness. Additionally, I made several appearances and speeches; yet nothing seems to work," Hayet cries as his tears cascade.

Perhaps Tobias and Sanballat were right when they admonished me from speaking of big dreams. I will never get through to potential clients; people do not want to hear a bubbler.

Grandpa is an excellent artist and knows how to apply the five W's and one H artistically. Without saying a word, he unbuttons the shirt cuff and gauntlet buttons. Then he flips the cuff back inside out. Next, he folds back, using the cuff to set the width and rolls up his sleeves. Last, he puts on man's artificial hair, wears sunglasses as well as a silver pendant necklace, and puts on his hat backward. The way he is dressed, he appears to be as a young boy. Grandpa wants to portray himself as somebody; Hayet is not sure, though, who. Hooking up the microphone to the black musician's mic stand, he grabs his banjo. As Grandma plays tambourine, declaring, "Never say never, because there is a great person within you," he sings Justin Bieber's "Never Say Never."

Right after the song, Hayet hilariously laughs and gives Grandpa a big hug. "This is an amazing expression."

After singing each word of the song, while standing with the banjo strapped on his shoulder, he asks, "Tell me where would JB be had he said 'never' and stopped further endeavors?"

"Probably in London, Ontario."

"Thank you. He refused to be silenced by the factual giant impossibilities; he stepped it up, and the rest is history. So shall it be with you when you learn the mystery of 'Never Say Never.' Until then, maximize your potential; take bold risks to create an incredible future. When all said is done, you shall clearly sing the song of the redeemed; I have escaped like a bird from a hunter's trap; the trap is broken, and I am free, witnessing "Never Say Never." Obviously, it is understandable that you have worked hard on the book project in your mother tongue. Perhaps that may not be the one God expects of you," says Grandma hesitantly.

"I have had enough of it. Now I quit."

"Quitters never win; likewise, winners never quit. The ones that do not quit are those that succeed. Additionally, you have come too far not to go a little further, walking, crawling, and persevering to your destiny. If you quit, God will not let go of you, because He has said, *I will not leave you nor forsake you until I have done what I have promised you.* Moreover, He is not done with you yet," adds Grandma.

"I have made numerous appearances and nothing seems to work for a breakthrough. I do not know how to talk; nothing like that is for me," all night long Hayet cries out in distress. *It would have been better to die in the wilderness before I made it to the America. I want to avoid the torment that I am undergoing.*

The following morning, Grandpa says, "Son, we understand your dilemma. However, you are the best candidate for what God called you to do."

"No, Grandpa, speaking to people is not for me. I tried and it did not work; neither will it work. I have never been a good speaker, and I have not become one, be it in Africa or in America. I am a poor speaker."

"You sound like Moses, who spoke the same words of discouragement. If God sees it is necessary, He will send Aaron as unto Moses, Barnabas as unto Paul's life. In fact, it is often such as you, reluctant people who make great achievements."

"Instead of sending people like Aaron or Barnabas into my life, it would be easier and better to send those people; they are teachers and can do the project very well."

"Each one of us has unique callings. I cannot perfectly make your calling; neither can you do my calling. The people that come to help you, that is their call. God expects you as well to pass along what you received to others who would do the same to others. Embrace the call and you will reach your destiny within a short period. Additionally, God used a donkey to rebuke a rebellious prophet, Balaam. You are far much more valuable than a donkey and He can use you, too."

Furthermore, Grandpa says, "I have one more story to tell you. One unknown boy left his country at a young age. Wherever he goes, he influences people. One day, he tells a wealthy, influential man, 'If you live just for yourself, one time you shall die. People will say a great man died and your story will end in the grave. However, if you serve others by what you have, you will still be remembered when you are gone, and God will bless you. Life is not about living for you or about the mere material fullness. It is about living to serve and affect the community for good, being equipped with three fundamental life principles that sum up the purpose of human existence. These are put God first, prioritize your life, and serve others."

"'Well, I would like to be remembered when my time is up and I am gone,' the man says and embraces the young boy's invitation, accepting Jesus Christ into his life. The influential man shows a radical change and decides to serve his community by his profession like never before. Thus, he chooses to be God's ambassador and humanitarian helper. That is not all; he has been able also to serve his community as much as hundreds of thousands, or perhaps even millions every year. The transformed man opens the door for another internationally known author, speaker, and entrepreneur; both continue to reach out to the multitude."

"How could an unknown boy make such a great impact?"

"To your surprise, the young boy does not know the ripple effect that he initiated that is benefiting humanity. Instead, he considers himself a loser without a notable achievement."

"Somebody needs to sit down and tell him the truth until he recognizes and appreciates the great person within him."

"That is what I am doing. The young boy I am talking about is Hayet. You have opened a door for Bishop T. D. Jakes to set foot in Kenya, who is involved helping communities."

"Grandpa—" Hayet begins to pile up excuses of his failures.

"Son, it is too sad to see you appreciate the small achievements of others while undermining your own impeccable contribution," Grandpa rebukes Hayet.

Hayet is not convinced of the Gramps lecture, yet he listens. In order to achieve the American dream, he has to keep on poking and starting projects that will lead him to his destiny. He should poke all the openings that he believes he can follow until the poke unleashes an unstoppable flood of blessings that shower him and his community, eventually achieving what God wants him to do. The more he keeps on poking, the better it will be. Education could be one of those avenues.

To finance his education, he searches for employment openings. Yet nothing comes up. Some family members advise him to return to PIG. However, he thinks, *Returning to PIG will depict me as a defeated and humiliated person.* The reason is that previously, he left PIG for a better-paying job.

Finally, since nothing opens, returning to PIG is the only option. Therefore, he swallows his pride, reapplies, and makes a phone call to the head of the HR department, asking, "Would you like to rehire me?"

"I will first ask the general manager if I am authorized to rehire you," the HR manager says. After a day or so, she replies: "I am authorized to rehire you. You have come at a time when we needed you most. Nevertheless, it is a precondition for you to accept a base pay, not the rate that you had before you left," she says.

Hayet agrees and starts over, not knowing what contribution the rehiring will make in his life.

Chapter 44

It is not where you came from; it is where you are going that counts.

— Ella Fitzgerald

Hayet helps others to attain purpose in life, bringing forgiveness and reconciliation. Tyler Taylor is one example, but he is unable to help himself.

Hayet returns to PIG, and he finds out that the company has grown deeper and wider, securing more business openings, and hopes some better opening will come for him. The company assigns him to work on a humongous, roller coaster–like induction machine that was in the initial stage of design at the time he left. Now it is operational. He adjusts quickly to the new system. He works as much voluntary overtime as available. However, he barely makes it to the next biweekly payday, let alone having a surplus to save for college. Usually, the first two weeks' salary barely covers utilities and house rent, while the second two weeks' income covers food and unnecessarily incurred credit card debts.

As usual, his back, arms, shoulders, neck, and feet are in unbearable pain when he wakes up in the morning. Yet he works with dedication and a good attitude. Due to the severe pain he habitually suffers, he prays, *Lord, when will you deliver me from this kind of job?* The answer, as is customary, is, *The only way to get from where you are to where you ought to be is for you to write a book*. However, he does not know when, where, or how to start an English project, fulfilling Grandpas comment, *Perhaps that may not be the one God expects of you*, that he previously said after the completion of Hayet's book in his mother tongue.

Hayet is insightful, has tenacious potential, and is talented in doing extraordinary duties. He instructs and counsels others what to do; the counselees follow Hayet's instructions and come out productive and prosperous.

Sensitive coworkers such as Tyler Taylor say, "Why do you look depressed while you do not seem sick? You must be deeply disappointed."

"Why should I not look depressed? I am stuck and unable to achieve the American dream, while everybody else does."

"You are not alone. So am I," Tyler admits. In a little while, Tyler comes back and says, "Thanks for sharing your desire to achieve more. It is a wake-up call and means a lot to me. I never thought about such stuff, because I am comfortable where I am at."

The following day, Tyler displays a gloomy face as he scans the incoming mound of boxes that are rolling onto the conveyor.

"Why is your face unhappy? You do not look sick. The unhappiness on your face is nothing but blues of the heart," Hayet comments.

"Why should I not look blue? I am middle-aged without any achievements, and I have nothing to give to my children and grandchildren. Furthermore, my best friend was shot and killed in California, and I have no money to attend the funeral. I am troubled that I might die one day without giving a good legacy to my descendants," says Tyler desperately.

"Brother, the situation that you are in is understandable. Never give up! Keep on poking around for whatever your hand can reach. Be optimistic and maximize your potential; start new projects and one day the sun will shine on you. Obviously, the life journey that you have fallen into has a bright destination, although you are not aware of it. Someday in your journey, you will tally up the bits and pieces, the threads of your life, and you shall see God bringing something good out your messes. God is in control. Who knows, America might even have President Tyler in the future."

"I cannot vote, let alone to be a president."

"Aren't you an American-born citizen, with the privilege of holding the highest position on earth?"

"Yes, I am American born. However, I have made multiple terrible choices. Whenever one searches my name, a lot of filthy baggage—DUI, mugshot, possession of drugs—pop out of the screen, barring me from voting."

"It is comprehensible, brother. We all make mistakes. The thing you need to do is learn from them and avoid making the same mistake again. Even a couple of the presidents had filthy reports. However, they *diverged* and braced for a fresh start. That is not all, a couple of 2016 Presidential candidates also have multiple bad rumors yet they chose to step up for the presidency. For you, depending on the severity of the crime, once the probation years are gone, you can have a grace period."

"Brother, the rich and the politician have a lie-synthesis to circumvent justice, but I cannot. In my case, God may forgive you; however, when your name appears in the criminal record, no forgiveness and atonement are available."

"Perhaps go back to school or start poking and doing a new project that you have never done before. It is not too late to begin again."

"I hate school," blurts Tyler.

"Then, maybe start poking and doing something else new that does not require education."

On the last day of the week, right after the kickoff meeting, Tyler comes up to Hayet tersely.

"The words '*Start poking and doing something new that you have never done before,*' have been tormenting me like a thorn in my flesh, giving me sleepless days and nights. Each moment, the words ring through my head, and I become motivated to think of doing all that I have never done before."

"You have a sensitive heart, and the same words that torment you will lead you to a situation where you will experience the full revelation," assures Hayet.

"I am here to tell you what happened today." Tyler's mother, Mrs. Tully Taylor, walks into his room.

"Son, we have to visit your dad in the prison tomorrow. I have set up an appointment," she announces authoritatively.

"Why would you want me to visit the person responsible for all the mess this family is in? Had he been a loving father, I would not be where I am today. I hate to see, talk to, or think of him. He did not care about me, so why should I care to visit him?"

"Son, he did not care about you, but God did, which matters most."

"Let him stay where he belongs. He does not deserve a visit. Our family is in confusion because he was selfish, caring only about his pleasure. Had he been a good father, we would have been safe from the turmoil that we are in."

Mrs. Taylor understands Tyler's words are sincere. "Son, I understand what you mean! It hurts me as much as it does you. I told him repeatedly the very words I have said to you. However, he would not listen and ends up in the state he is in now. The more I harbor bitterness about him, the more hurt the bitterness inflicts me with. In order to have peace of mind, I forgave him."

Upon hearing the idea of giving forgiveness to the undeserving, Tyler freezes in disbelief.

"Mother, how could you forgive the one responsible for jeopardizing our family, including burdening you? He deserves neither forgiveness nor a visit. His wrongdoing should punish him the way he punished this family. Forget about him and get married to another one the way all our relatives suggest. How many more years will you wait?"

"Son, what God has joined together, let no one put asunder. Divorce is not an option. Moreover, forgiveness is given to one who does not deserve, in the way our heavenly Father did to us."

"If the heavenly Father you are talking about is like my father, then I do not want Him."

"The heavenly Father is far better than all excellent fathers combined. Besides, keep in mind also that no matter what, he is your father. Also, remember that a person who does not learn from the mistakes of others is more likely to repeat the same."

"What do you mean?" Tyler asks, seeking clarification.

"If you do not learn from the mistakes of your father, you are likely to repeat the same mistakes that he did. Besides, just this week, you have heard of the death of your best friend. If you do not turn your life around to do the most important thing a man ought to do, which is to provide, serve, and protect, you also could die unjustly."

"You have got a good point, Mother. Perhaps I am the walking dead."

"Son, it will not hurt to visit him for a few minutes. I promise we will come right back. I strongly feel this is the day that you have to see your father."

"Why are you pushing me so hard?" shouts Tyler. His mother leaves the room.

After a minute of silence, Tyler contemplates doing what he has never done before, visiting his father. Then he calls out, "Mother, where are you?"

"Here I am," Mrs. Taylor replies, standing by the door.

"Maybe we can go and visit *just for today*."

Mrs. Taylor gives him a tender hug. Early the next morning, Tyler dresses up and is ready to visit his dad. His mother comes into his room and finds him seated on his messy bed, with socks, plates, books, and other items spread everywhere. Tyler is so concerned about what he will say to his dad and what his dad will say in return. The visit is Tyler's first encounter with his father.

Mrs. Taylor says, "You are so anxious to see your dad, huh? He knows all that you have been. I appreciate your willingness, and I promise it will be all right."

"It is my pleasure, Mother."

As planned, they take a speedy subway ride, walk a few blocks, and make it to the prison. It is concrete, with a high wall, fenced by a barbed wire. Guards walk back and forth on top of the wall.

Once they enter the compound, passing through multiple checkpoints, Tyler's eyes wander through the group of inmates standing on the other side of the lobby. Tyler and his mother happen to be the first visitors.

"The tall one is your dad," whispers Mrs. Taylor. He is graceful, as tall as Tyler is, and appears dejected.

"Mrs. Taylor, you may come now," the warden summons them after an interval to see the prisoner. While seated in person and with a bulletproof window between them, Mr. Taylor picks up the phone. "I am sorry for all the wrong choices that I have made. Will you forgive me?" he apologizes for the first time.

Abruptly, Hayet's *"Start poking and doing something new that you have never done before"* remark overwhelms Tyler's imagination.

His dad continues intently, "I wish I could have a second chance. I would do all right, be the best husband and father that you could have. However, I do not think it will happen. Recently, the prison injected and killed Mr. David Davis. Regardless of his innocence declaration and the outcry of humanity from home as well as abroad, the prison denied clemency. Each time the prison kills one person, I get closer to being the next. Besides, I want you to know that I did not do what the prison accuses me of, though I was present with the wrong crowd, which is responsible for my imprisonment. Son, watch out and do not associate with an inappropriate crowd. I shall not be able to achieve anything more in this life and I have nothing to give you for remembrance. Be who you are meant to be, a winner, by putting God first, prioritizing your life, and serving others fairly and justly."

Mr. Taylor pours out supportive statements in the apology. *Start poking and doing something new that you have never done,* mumbles Tyler, to the point he cannot take it anymore. Finally, he chooses to do something that he has never done before.

"I forgive you," he declares.

"Will you forgive me for all the wrong attitude and blame I have placed on you, too?" asks Tyler. Mr. Taylor accepts and gives forgiveness with gratitude. In such a simple act, the family reconciles.

Right after the exchange of forgiveness, "My dear, time and time again, I have stated it. Let me say it once more. Since you have admitted, God will do now a miracle. I have been waiting for you faithfully for all those decades. Even before the imprisonment, I told you that I saw in my dream your release from prison."

"What dream did you tell him, Mother?"

"God said in my dream, 'You were like an abandoned wife, devastated with grief, and I welcomed you back, like a woman married young and then left. I left you, but only for a moment. Now, with enormous compassion, I am bringing you back. In an outburst of anger, I turned my back on you but only for a moment. It is with lasting love that I am tenderly caring for you.'

Therefore, I will stand at my watch and set myself on the ramparts; I look forward to seeing the release of my husband that God showed me. I may see neither wind nor rain, yet water shall fill this valley. When the context applied to my current situation, it could mean, I may not have a justifiable reason to say, nevertheless I believe that the prison will release my husband. This is an easy thing in the eyes of the Lord; he will also make you what you were meant to be, God fearing a good father and a great husband" declares Mrs. Taylor convincingly.

"If I ever come to see the miracle you are talking about, then I shall believe that God is for real," says Tyler.

"Nothing is impossible with God," replies Mrs. Taylor. The following morning, "It is finished," a gentle whisper comes. However, Mrs. Taylor does not understand what it means and goes to work. The words came up in her mind recurrently for the whole day.

Late in the afternoon, Tyler and his mother reach home from work at about the same time. They continue discussing at the cool of the day, standing by the dilapidated porch and leaning on the faded railing. Suddenly, an unexpected familiar face, dressed up in 1960s blue jeans, love beads, and an embellished T-shirt appears. *This outfit looks like the one that I bought for my husband for our first-year wedding anniversary.*

Mrs. Taylor walks toward the visitor. It is Mr. Taylor. The moment Mrs. Taylor sees her husband, "I told you," she yells hysterically. Filled with compassion, she runs to her husband, throws her arms around him, and kisses him. The first kiss ever each has shared in decades.

"Thank you, Lord. You have come to proclaim freedom for the prisoners and recovery of sight for the blind, to set the oppressed free," cries Mrs. Taylor, wiping tears of joy.

"A person who committed the act that took me to prison wrote a letter one would open the day he dies. The prison received the letter and ordered that I have an expedited release," discloses Mr. Taylor.

"With God all things are possible," restates Mrs. Taylor.

In the meantime, the insightful discussion of Hayet's inability to achieve the American dream ignites Tyler to venture into a new perspective on life. As a result, Tyler undertakes and starts a tailoring business that his school-hating brain can handle. From the get-go, Tyler makes hundreds of dollars in profits.

In order to concentrate on his budding business full time, he resigns from PIG and moves back to his birthplace, Tyler City. The business blossoms and brings in thousands, then tens of thousands of dollars. Tyler names his business Tyler Taylor Tailors in Tyler. From such a humble and insignificant beginning, Tyler flourishes. Consequently, he dedicates his life to serving his community as never before.

Tyler often tells Hayet, "You should have given me the wake-up Rx: RE dose when we first met."

"Previously, it was not time. Now it is time. You have always had what it takes. You never knew what you were capable of," retorts Hayet.

"Forgiveness unlocks God's blessings. I am amazed to see how God beautifully arranged the forgiveness and reconciliation. It is because of the reconciliation and forgiveness we had at the prison that I let my father in the house. Having seen the fulfillment of my mother's dream, I accepted God into my life and feel having peace in my life."

Meanwhile, Tyler's "Forgiveness unlocks God's blessings," speech hits Hayet as powerfully as lightning, raising hope to reach his unfulfilled dreams and wishes. Hayet's lasting life's lesson that cannot be taken away from him that he will learn are from deep wounds, unforgettable scars, terrible mistakes, and irredeemable failures, not from success.

Chapter 45

Change is good. Yeah, but it is not easy.

— *The Lion King*

Through multiple trial and errors, Hayet pokes at his destiny, which leads to a shower of abundance for himself and the community.

For decades, he has not been able to unlock himself from where he does not want to be. He is the driver behind the wheel of a car going down an allegedly easily flowing freeway of existence, yet he has been stuck, unable to move to breakthrough.

He wishes and dreams of serving others exponentially, giving a good name to his family, bringing justice and fairness, being a provider for many, and a voice for the voiceless. Hayet has been just one step away from becoming the person he ought to be. One backlogging issue is that he cannot fix a problem unless he understands who the problem is, which is himself. To be able to un-backlog, he should continue poking seriously and bravely enough examine and reroute his map, as well as get rid of things that are not working in his life journey. Thus, eventually he adjusts, changes his life circumstances, and rewrites history.

He has the opportunity of the immediate moment to write a manual. Current and future generations can follow it before the door shuts on him, which can happen at any time. In order to fit the opportune moment that does not wait on him, one option of survival he has is to reposition himself to face the assailant that tampered with his untapped potential. Multiple voices of a wake-up call to where he ought to be descends on him relentlessly from family and loved ones. The urgency to move on hammers him via electronic means, the physical pain of his current job, and memories of unachieved pledges made while in Africa and here in America. The Tobias brothers, the Jezebel daughters and their parents as well, who never get satisfied no matter what, they keep on poking him to be restless until he is motivationally crushed and dead.

Perhaps he must poke more and dig deeper in the mud and water, spewing writing services that he has abandoned that could determine his destiny. Hayet should vigorously poke until he hits the writing bedrock, which underlies the black gold that transforms and would enable him to serve. Nevertheless, his ESL status to the Anglo clients stands as an impediment between his personal, incompetent dread and the possibility of striking the writing foundation, where healing, restoring and encouraging messages gush exponentially, reaching out all over the world. Besides, he has no topic to write about when addressing the eloquent, English-speaking consumers. However, still it is possible that every cloud has a silver lining.

The months of deferral have gone. It is nearly time to go back to college.

A new US president is elected in November 2016. In January 2017, President Barack Hussein Obama exits the White House after eight years of service; President Donald John Trump replaces him. Again, the economy is sluggish, and Hayet is unable to gather enough funds to take him back to college. It is a couple of weeks before the inauguration of the new president. Hayet sits in despair, knowing that he is not going to make it to college again. He watches a TV station that the anchors refer to as the "most trusted cable news network, CNN."

One of the anchors, who migrated to the United States of America when he was a toddler and grew up dealing with prejudice, makes a speech. The speech hits Hayet like a defibrillator, giving him a wake-up shock. Once his mind becomes pregnant with a writing idea from the anchor, he requests an indefinite deferral until he completes the proposed book project.

Eventually, the historic inauguration comes and goes. Each time Hayet tries to distance himself from the book-writing responsibility, an unexplainable urgency pulls him toward it. In the meantime, Hayet endures nostalgic pangs and then starts the writing, breaking ground. It will fulfill his pledge and is what he loves doing, serving.

Shortly after the start of the project, the company fires the anchor. Nevertheless, Hayet continues with the project. An internal urgency consistently tells him, *This is the only way out to be of great use to yourself and to cause a change in people's lives.* At last, the physical pain persists, yet, Hayet stops praying about the deliverance from the job he does, for he knows the answer. Consequently, he keeps on writing, utilizing every minute, sleeping two to four hours every day. He needs good sleep and does not have enough transition time from one obligation to another, yet he consistently rushes to make it on time.

One of those days, he works second shift and sets up an alarm to sleep just for four minutes before the clock in time at the compound of PIG. As little as a one- to five-minute nap could be enough to keep him awake for the whole night. Eventually, the alarm sets for a.m. because Hayet did not remember to set the p.m. He wakes up at the wrong time and is about ten minutes late, which happens to be his second tardy in years.

A year or so later, on a warm summer early dawn, the worn-out Hayet drives home from work. About one hundred feet ahead, he recognizes the traffic light is red. He falls asleep and travels another hundred feet past the traffic light.

Suddenly, a wailing police siren and flashing blue light wake Hayet as he makes a right turn toward his house, which is about a couple of hundred feet away.

"License and proof of insurance. Are you drunk or on drugs? You ran the red traffic light," says the officer.

"I did not recognize that I ran the red light, sorry. I am coming from work," replies Hayet apologetically. He is ready to accept whatever punishment the officer may hand out without excuse.

After returning to his vehicle for a few minutes, the officer comes right back, "Watch your driving. Do not make the same mistake," he warns and let Hayet go without any penalty.

A couple of days later, Hayet tells Tobias, who loves playing the racial game, "I ran a red traffic light; the policeman pulled me over. Nevertheless, he let me go with a warning."

"Was the officer black?"

"No!"

"White?"

"No! He is a color- and race-blind true American who serves with compassion," replies Hayet.

At that very moment, his Father tells him, "You may fall asleep and slumber, but God will not let your foot slip. He who watches over you will not slumber; indeed, He who watches over Israel will neither slumber nor sleep."

In the meantime, during the Christmas season, Hayet returns to California.

"Move to California and work for me," invites his brother. As a result, Hayet takes the training for real estate–related business. Hayet does so, not to disappoint his family because they always talk about helping him to stand on his own. However, deep in his heart, *You did not complete the book-writing project*, his soul screams with unpassable nags. The training goes on well; the job is easy; Hayet loves it. Moreover, regarding money, it pays three times more than what he earned working for PIG. Hayet has to make a decision. *If I choose to move to California now because of getting a better-paying job, that may not be what God has in store for me at this moment.*

After careful consideration, he says, "Brother, I thank you for opening the door for employment for me. I know that I can handle the job. However, my soul cries out, '*You have to complete the book project that you have started.*' The impatient person within me would have given up writing many years ago. However, in one way or the other, I find myself thinking or doing some book writing. Please allow me to publish a book, and after that, I will come to California." We-ha-thee graciously accepts Hayet's proposal.

Hayet believes in his soul that writing will enable him to serve tremendously. However, personal anxiety and insecurity make it hard to carry out the task. The internal conflicts include his concern over the unlikeliness of an unknown immigrant with a funny name being able to reach the English speaking and reading public. Months and years have gone by since the proposed completion of the project. His bones still ache worse than ever. *When will I deliver myself from such pain?*

Hayet should take a moment to realize that the greater the pain, the greater the gain. The hotter the fire, the purer the gold; the higher he wants to go, the deeper he needs to dig; the greater the tribulation, the higher the exaltation; the more he survives through pressing sowing conditions, the greater the harvest. Hayet excruciatingly cries out of pain; the internal voice repeatedly laments, *The only way out from where you are to where you ought to be is to write a book.*

The voices of "Yes, you certainly can" from his adoptive and his biological parents as well, saying, "Move to California; we are praying for you," keep him relentless all the time.

The hurricane waves of persecution and hardship seem never to end. One tallies up after the other. The worst of all is that he has had to survive his most nerve-racking and bothersome Jezebel-embodied relatives who are not only marginalizing him but also mobilizing people against him. In the midst of the unfavorable discomforting conditions, *Why is it that my worst rejecting enemy happens to be my relative, an enemy that I cannot fight?* he wonders. Although Hayet is not aware, every now and then exaltation to destiny could come through rejection. He is capable of fighting and winning any battle.

The underemployed and misfit Hayet goes to visit the Gramps. "Son, so how is a settlement in camping, and how long do you intend to stay there?" Grandpa asks.

"Campers never settle at camping. Camping is always temporary. After a brief or sometimes long stay, campers align their GPS, break up camp, and advance into the hill country. They go to all the neighboring territories and reach higher achievements and abundance that they have never had before. What do you intend to say?"

"Yes, I understand that. However, some talented people, when the adversity of insecurity and fear hammers them, do camp and settle for less."

"So, are you saying that I am settling for less?"

"Yes," says Grandpa.

"It is because I am afraid."

"You have to break settlement and set yourself free from your doubts and fears of failure. Not doing what you are supposed to do because of fear of failure is far worse than trying and failing. If you do what you are supposed to do, you have the possibility of gaining confidence and adjusting your failures into triumphs. However, if you do not try, you never get opened for growth. Moreover, we have always been in the 'Yes, We Certainly Can' generation. Besides, the United States of America is one of the places where anybody can be somebody. We have confidence in you. You are a trailblazer, having what it takes, and can make it. Not only will you survive and thrive but fly and soar high as an eagle."

"I wish I could, but I cannot. I like your optimism, though. The Jezebel family, Tobias, and Sanballat count me out. They have said it a long time ago, that I cannot have great achievements. Besides, I tried and failed in all. I am not cut out for what you expect of me."

"As intelligent as you are, how could you echo the voices of devil's minions?"

"Grandpa, I wish you could walk in my shoes."

"Son, you walk in your shoes and I walk in my shoes. You cannot fit in mine and neither can I fit in yours. Everybody should carry his own burdens until he or she finds rest in God."

Honestly, the Gramps' burden is much worse than mine.

"Son, the question is not, am I able or is it possible for me to make great achievements. The question you have to ask yourself is, will I choose to accomplish great achievements? If you are willing to lead, you can, and if you are not willing, then you cannot. You are valuable to yourself and to the world surrounding you, and you have what it takes. Nothing that you have been through shall be in vain; keep on poking until your destiny floods you with showers of abundance. Who knows? The service that comes out through you might help you reach a green pasture that spreads throughout the world. I am certain that you know how an anxious man became a commander in chief, shaking off his insecurity as he served his community."

Grandpa continues to encourage Hayet. "A son is born to parents at a place and time where birth certificates are easy to forge. Although there is no reliable documented birth certificate to prove or disprove the place of his birth, trustworthy eyewitnesses, authors, and historians say that he is foreign born, in Africa, to be specific."

Grandpa, who are you going to talk about?

"Before he is elevated into the commander in chief position without much experience, he faithfully serves his community. That is the time the electorate knew him for his rhetoric, 'Yes, we certainly can,' silencing even the most doubtful compatriot. During the early years of his service, his academic years and birth, documents were not important. However, the time he holds the vacated commander in chief's office, then people begins to question his identity."

"Regardless of the opposition, the man grows stronger, to the point of melting the hearts of his nation's enemies across the sea. The man completes tasks that his predecessor left incomplete, and he leads the people to the Promised Land."

Hayet goes into deep thinking about how the person got into the high position without proving and identity verification. "I guess I know who you are talking about," interjects Hayet.

"Of course, you should," affirms Grandpa. "His humble beginning and service to the community propelled him to the highest position the nation offers. The man I am talking about is Joshua, the son of Nun, of the Bible."

"I knew it," exclaims Hayet.

"Good, my son. Even if it does not pay now, keep on serving fairly, justly, and wholeheartedly. Whatever you do to others is not about them. It is about Him, God. Your deed shows who you are and what you do. Eventually, your good work to others reciprocates for you and you get the best reward from the Lord. Thus, one day, you shall be pleased with your humble service taking you to lofty places you never thought possible."

"I like your optimism. I also would like to inform you that lightning struck my computer and it no longer works. I quit the book-writing project because I lost over fifty thousand words. I will not redo it. In fact, from the very beginning I said that I do not qualify for such duties," says Hayet, using the data loss as an excuse to evade the responsibility.

"God will not let that happen. We are going to say a prayer for the restoration of the disappeared data," Mrs. Lionel, who has just arrived with the Grannies, informs them.

"Prayer will not restore the lost data; a computer technician does," objects Hayet.

"Have you not heard that God fills, selects, trains, and gives understanding, skill, and the ability for every kind of artistically skilled work? God equips one gift for planning skillful designs and techniques working in the medical and technical fields in gold, silver, and bronze; for cutting jewels to be set; for carving wood; and for every other kind of artistic work. God enables people so that they can make all work for the good of His people," Mrs. Lionel supports her argument.

"What I mean is that computers got invented a few years back, probably—uh—"

"It is obvious what you want to say. Before the creation of the computers and after as well, God was, God is, and God will still be present in the future. God is behind all inventions and knows countless times more than the computer prodigy. God is an inventor and creator; He creates new inventions through His sons and daughters who would subdue the earth. Though some inventors hate Him, He still loves them."

"Well, we shall see if He can restore the data; that would be great. I do not have time for prayer, though, now." Hayet says so because he knows that they customarily take hours to shake the heavens and turn every stone upside down until they find what they lost.

"Real quick, Lord, as you have made the lost donkeys of King Saul's father found, we pray that the lost data be found, in Jesus's name," Mrs. Lionel prays.

"That is the shortest prayer I have ever heard," notes Hayet.

"The earnest prayer of a righteous person has great power and produces wonderful results. The effect of short prayer comes because of spending mornings, days, and nights in commune with the Lord. Watch and pray so that you will not fall into temptation. If Jesus had to pray for hours, you too must pray behind the curtain for the result to reveal itself in front of the curtain," says Grandma.

"The spirit is willing, but the flesh is weak," replies Hayet.

In the meantime, Hayet takes the computer to a technician to have a look at it. After changing few parts, the computer is back on, with all the lost data restored; he resumes writing.

Hayet has no ample time to serve and write, yet he does it. While exploiting every minute, he manages to keep going on with his writing project, making use of words while hoping to see the fulfillment of the dreams of his father and the wishes of his mother.

Chapter 46

I am with you and will watch over you wherever you go,
and I will bring you back to this land. I will not leave
you until I have done what I have promised you.

— Genesis 28:15

Mr. and Mrs. Sheden and their children and grandchildren return to Africa for the fulfillment of Mrs. Sheden, Wa-euro's, wishes.

It has been over six decades since Sheden left his home village. Wa-euro incredibly believes in God that He can do the impossible. She goes into exile. First within the country, then, to the dreamland of her husband, the United States of America.

Meanwhile, during one of their family reunions, a phone call comes from the youngest sibling, who lives in Asmara.

"I am going to have a rite of passage and I invite the whole family to join me for the celebration."

The phone call could lead to the fulfillment of Wa-euro's wishes and Hayet's earlier prediction to his father: *You shall not die before we see the fulfillment of Mother's wishes. We shall all go home for the fulfillment of Mother's wishes and then after that, your day shall come.*

Countless reasons make travel to Africa impossible. It is costly. They have no place to stay once they go, and several days of one-way travel will be tiresome for Hayet's aged parents.

The family has multiple hindrances. However, the whole family agrees to go to their homeland to witness the rite of passage—not only the ones that are in the United States of America, but also other family, relatives, and friends that live in Europe, Canada, and in Saudi Arabia. It is the first time the family has returned to Africa. Against all odds, the family prepares to travel, obtaining all the necessary documentation.

Their homeland faces all sorts of sanctions based on a lie-synthesis because the country's desire to live as a free nation comes under attack. Thus, getting a flight is another challenge. After months of searching and waiting, the family finds a deal and travels in three groups.

After many tiresome days of journey, the flights touch down one after the other. It is raining on the ground; nevertheless, the perfect drainage makes the puddles of rain disappear fast.

"Welcome to Asmara International Airport," announces a woman in a drawling voice via the PA system. It is cloudy, rainy, and dark in the early dawn. The family walks out of the airport after going through customs and other procedures. In the meantime, Hayet counts for the kids that are on board.

"They are all present. However, six more pieces of luggage are still missing," he announces.

The family heads to their dwelling place. A couple of kilometers from the airport, right by the black stonewalled Expo gate, a car stalls by one of the columns of palm trees. "An accident," calls out Mr. Abishai Abby, the driver who happens to be one of the villagers that witnessed the injustice and unfair treatment Sheden endured.

Less than a couple of hours into their arrival, they witness an accident. *What is going to happen during the next days during our stay?* Hayet wonders.

Mr. Abishai pulls to the red soil, rocky shoulder and rushes to the aid of an accident victim. The accident occurred on the driver's side, and so Mr. Abishai moves around to the passenger side. He opens the door, and the door light turns on. Mr. Abishai, who lived for all those years in Asmara, instantly recognize who the person involved in the accident is, as do Sheden and Hayet.

Why was he coming to the airport at this time? wonders Hayet.

Big sister, WE-HA-THEE-T, hurries to the scene. We-ha-thee-t is a feminine name meaning something that flows ceaselessly.

"I see one unbuckled person."

Immediately, she takes the person's wrist and uses her fingers to test for a pulse.

"He may be alive though it is faint!" she shouts.

Upon hearing the accident survivor is alive, Mr. Abishai whispers, "Today God has delivered the enemy into your hands. Today is the day the Lord spoke of when He stated in His holy word, 'I will give your enemy into your hands for you to deal with as you wish.'"

Sheden goes into flashbacks, leaning against the stalled car boot. He remembers how the man threatened to beat him up, intimidated and denigrated him, and spoke all evil, mobilizing others for injustice using a lie-synthesis. Perhaps Mr. Abishai is right: this is the perfect day to deal with his enemy. There has never been or ever shall be such a convenient day.

After a few more minutes of waiting, Mr. Abishai probes, "What are you going to do? I suggest that you order your children to enter into the cars and drive. None of your family shall pin him to the ground with a thrust of a spear. You let him stay the way he is and come in the morning; he shall have a long sleep, because it is most likely he will not find other emergency help," Mr. Abishai whispers as he glances.

Mr. Abishai is right. Meanwhile, Hayet helps We-ha-thee-t pull the survivor out of the car and into the shade of a palm tree. It is still raining. We-ha-thee-t attempts to wake the victim up.

"He is not responding," she calls out. Then she begins chest compressions, administering CPR. "One, two, and three . . ." she counts.

"The victim is still not breathing," she announces.

Meanwhile, "So what is your decision?" Mr. Abishai asks.

"I will not return evil for evil. You do not win by killing your enemy, but by bringing them to your precepts. I learned a lesson that if your enemy is hungry, feed him; if he is thirsty, give him a drink. In doing this, you will heap burning coals on his head," Sheden responds.

"It is up to you. However, if I were you, I would leave him and drive," replies Mr. Abishai.

Sheden makes a good decision by not accepting Mr. Abishai's suggestion. Even if he were to accept the suggestion, Hayet would agree; however, We-ha-thee-t would not have agreed with it. She made an oath, "I will serve in purity, and practice my profession faithfully. I will abstain from whatever is harmful and mischievous, and I will not neglect or knowingly administer anything injurious to people."

We-ha-thee-t begins mouth-to-mouth resuscitation. She opens the victim's airway to make the breath flow easily. She gives a powerful enough breath to make his chest rise. She lets the chest fall and then repeats the process, about twelve breaths per minute. At last, the victim chokes and coughs more frequently.

"He is breathing; good news; he has a higher possibility of survival," she affirms. The family chooses to take the victim to a hospital not far from Cinema Capitol. Sheden pays the deposit. "Take care of this person and I will reimburse you for any extra expense you may have," he says.

The grandkids' eyes are heavy; they slept through the intervention. Meanwhile, the family makes it to their destination, about half a kilometer from Radio Marina, which houses the black stone-gated American embassy and the worship center that the British built. The family travels for five days due to some delays. Uninvited loved ones come in and go out of the house consistently. What a joy!

Late in the evening, the phone rings from the hospital, requiring the financially responsible person to come. The grownups hastily rush to the hospital.

A blonde nurse says, "The victim that you brought to the hospital miraculously survived and wants to see you." She leads the way and knocks at the wooden brown door.

"Come on in," pronounces a feeble voice.

The nurse and the whole family enter the room. "These are the people that brought you here," she introduces them graciously.

Immediately, the patient recognizes Sheden. "*Be-Shim-AB*"—meaning in the name of God the father— "How can this be?" he yells uncontrollably.

"Is that you?" The survivor, Mr. Chekan Yehuda, asks and weeps aloud. "You are more righteous than I. You have treated me well, but I have treated you badly. The workers have just now told me about the good you did to me, instead of letting me die without intervention. May the Lord reward you well for the way you treated me today. I am kindly requesting you to forgive me for all the intentional wrongs that I have done to you."

To the family, especially to Hayet and Sheden, it is at a crucial moment. Do they choose forgiveness to bring reconciliation or harbor a grudge? Sheden looks at the face of his wife and children, one by one, seeking an affirmation of forgiveness. Except for Hayet, the rest nod their head affirming forgiveness.

It is hard for Hayet, who witnessed his father's suffering, to forgive. Right then, 'Forgiveness unlocks God's blessings,' overwhelms his being. In order to unlock God's blessings through forgiveness, Hayet instantly chooses to forgive not only Mr. Chekan Yehuda but also others that intentionally persecuted him.

As Sheden waits for Hayet to give his forgiveness affirmation, We-ha-thee elbows Hayet.

"Oh, yes, forgiveness affirmed," utters Hayet.

Then Sheden says, "I have held your life in my hands. However, I gave it back to you. You intended to harm me, but God intended it for good. Seeing the goodness of God in my life, I forgive you," he announces.

"I do not deserve forgiveness. However, thank you for forgiving me," the survivor says hysterically.

Eventually, the reconciliation ushers in a great day of relief for Hayet! At that instant he thinks, *Praise be to the Lord, who has kept me from harming Mr. Chekan Yehuda for treating my father with disrespect. God has kept me from bloodshed and has brought Yehuda's wrongdoing down on his head.* Moreover, Hayet is thankful to Sheden, who did not tell him what Hayet needed to hear at a time Hayet wanted to hear it. Had his father told him what he wanted to hear at the time he wanted to hear it, Hayet probably would have completed the revenge a long time ago. Nevertheless, because of the injustice and unfairness Sheden endures, Hayet embraces a life of service to humanity. Without the unfairness and injustice of his father's endurance, it is unclear how Hayet may have turned out.

The next morning, the family travels to their home village. The stratus clouds blanket the horizon. Tethered donkeys and mules safe from landmine graze graciously. On some of the open farms wheat seedlings sprout. Aloe that women use to wean a child, cactus, and eucalyptus fill the mountain terrains.

After a long journey through winding roads that had only one roadblock, which does not look like a war zone, the family makes it through the main cities, the birthplaces of Wa-euro, Sheden, as well as the older siblings.

Wherever the family stops, "Who are these people?" ask the villagers.

Others reply, "These are the children and grandchildren of the man and woman who believed uncommon beliefs from us. They return to us with a multitude." A gray-haired old man sits on a sundeck and strokes his beard.

"How can this be? The blessings from one person to many descendants resembles the fulfillment of what prophet Isaiah spoke, 'Look to Abraham, your father, and to Sarah, who gave you birth. When I called him, he was but one and I blessed him and made him many.' The barren has become a mother and grandmother," he says.

The family walks, drives, and rides in a carriage. The visit to the parents' birthplace seals about a seventy-year-old fulfillment of Mother's wishes. What a fabulous day! The parents walk proudly in the very streets where the community isolated them because of their acceptance of the gospel of salvation.

At one point, Sheden speaks. "Lord, I am not worthy of all the unfailing love and faithfulness you have shown to me, your servant. When I left home about six decades ago, I owned nothing except a walking stick. Now my household is overflowing the large house in which we live."

Sheden gives thanks and concludes with a word of prayer.

Enjoying the rite of passage, walking through the streets of his parents birth places, drinking from the well they drank water from, eating the cactus they ate from, and the street they walked, he returned to America. Upon his return, PIG fires Hayet, saying, "You have no-call, no-shows for August 7 and 8."

The senseless case does not mention the off days that Hayet took up to August 11 before the departure.

Frankly speaking, the manager admits that Hayet is the most reliable person if not in PIG, at least in the department. The manager fires him mysteriously, causing shifting to move Hayet from his comfort zone. The firing from the job brings to mind what the German theologian Martin Niemöller has written. Martin Niemöller was a pastor of the Lutheran Church, initially a supporter of Adolf Hitler. Until the time he experienced imprisonment by the Nazis, which he narrowly escaped death, he did not oppose the system that targeted certain peaceful citizens. However, after his imprisonment, he expressed his deep regret about not having done enough to help the victims of the Nazis. Thus, he made the following remarks:

"First, they came for the Socialists, and I did not speak out because I was not a Socialist.

Then they came for the Trade Unionists, and I did not speak out because I was not a Trade Unionist.

Then they came for the Jews, and I did not speak out because I was not a Jew.

Then they came for the Catholics, and I did not speak out because I was not a Catholic.

Then they came for me, and there was no one left to speak for me."

The firing is unjust. However, it works out for his good, as his parents, Emily and Gramps, consistently say. He manages to secure a better job that could enable him to be with his prospective dependents in the evenings, on weekends, and on holidays. The job fulfills Hayet's four-decades-old pledge, *When I grow up, I shall always be present for my family.* Also, he submits the book project to a publisher, fulfilling a pledge he made when he was at PIG.

"Grandpa, I have done what you wanted me to do. What next?" Hayet asks during the book release ceremony.

"Son, do not do what we want you to do, because it could turn you into another person. Please make every effort to do and conform to God's calling for your life. For if you do this, you will never stumble into being a person who God did not intend you to be, and so that you may not go where you do not belong. Be at peace with God; humble yourself under His mighty hand, so that he may lift you up in due time far beyond your wildest dreams."

"I am already feeling the change since I gave forgiveness, I turned my face to the Lord, and started giving God one-tenth of my first income, as you told me."

"Son, please refrain from including us in the doings of God. Our instruction could mislead you. We want you to do as God tells you."

"Well, okay. I have been giving one-tenth as God's word instructs me. For the first time in years, I have surplus money before the next pay period, unlike the previous years when the shark-like creditors called Mr. and Mrs. Bill consumed my money the day the direct deposit landed in my account."

"Blessings happen only when God prevents the devouring pests from consuming your crops, and the vines in your fields from dropping their fruit before it is ripe," speaks Grandpa.

"One more thing, Grandpa. Monday, March 17, 2014, at exactly at 5:00 a.m. before the alarm went off, in my dream, God gave me Deuteronomy 6:10."

"Wait, I am going to read it," says Grandma. For the first time without putting on her reading glasses, she reads, "The Lord your God made a promise to your ancestors, Abraham, Isaac, and Jacob. He promised to give you this land, and He will give it to you. He will give you great and rich cities that you did not build."

"Son, the Scripture that you mentioned is not a new revelation. Your father, about seventy years ago in his dream, saw the prosperous cities that he reaffirms to give you. Glory be to God!"

"So, what is next, Grandpa?"

"I do not know. You just follow His guidance and see what He does with and through you."

Because of his obedience to God's word, Hayet becomes an agent for change to the unjust systems of the world. God perfectly positions him at a place, in a time that fulfills his innate feelings and talent within him, where he makes life easier and satisfying for himself as well as for others.

God touches Hayet through conditions that he did not anticipate. The creator withholds good from Hayet, so that he may learn to trust in Him who brings somebody great out of nobody. Had Hayet gotten economic stability and a passport when he wanted to get them, he would have left the United States many years ago. Instead, God withheld things that would let him do so, yet giving him barely enough to survive. Moreover, God wants to teach Hayet to trust in Him and gives Hayet the passion and urge of keep on moving in the midst of adversity.

The Lord makes stable the steps of the one who pleases in Him; though he may stagger, he will not fall, for the Lord upholds him with His hand. The purpose is to prove that Hayet's faith is genuine. Even as fire destroys and tests gold, to separate gold from the chaff, so his faith, which is much more precious than gold, must also be tested so that it may endure. Then he will receive praise and glory and honor on the day God works through his life. He is no longer a fish out of a water. Where God places him, he literally shines being himself. He uses his difference as an attraction while he swims in his and others' territory, adapts accordingly, finding fish out of water and reconciling them to themselves and God. Thus, God makes His appeal through Hayet and implores others on behalf of Christ to be reconciled to God.

Hayet puts God first in his life. As a result, God blesses him beyond measure. After decades of service, the university promotes Corey to another position.

"The best person to take over the RA role, whom Rahab and I have been waiting for, is Hayet," recommends Corey.

The first day Hayet comes to the campus for the job assignment he gets to see from afar the bane of his existence, Emily.

Oh my gosh, how am I going to face her? Perhaps she may spare her sickening words through some divine revelations because I have become the kind of person she wanted me to be.

Truly speaking, Emily is an unconditional and sincere friend, who wiped Hayet's tears at the hospital and desires to see his best. *I wish I had listened to all that she used to say; I would have avoided nearly thirty wasted years.*

In the first encounter, excitedly, the way she used to do, she asks, "Do you want to go away again?"

Hayet answers, "Emily, to whom shall I go? Jesus is and has the word of eternal life; I believe and have come to know that He is the Holy One of God."

"Now that you have returned, I accept you as a brother. My nearly thirty years' prayer and wish fulfillment happen. No more waiting."

"Thank you for your prayers. I am home now." Additionally, and hesitantly, he asks,

"How is your family and children?"

"I have none. You may probably remember at college that I told you, 'Only the blessed one will legally take me to be a wedded wife at the right time.'"

"Is he ready now?"

"His return and homecoming make him valid and the blessed one to take me to be his wedded wife."

For sure, blessed is the one that takes Emily.

Hayet glances at his surroundings. "May I have the honor of knowing who the valid returned one is?" inquires Hayet.

"His name is," Emily pauses, giving a sigh of bliss, "his name is Hayet Africa," she says, causing shock and awe in Hayet's being.

"This cannot be true. I do not deserve to have you; you deserve somebody as clean as you."

"Apart from the grace of God that covers me, I am as weak as you are. Remember that God has forgiven you. Besides, I have learned that if a man is in Christ, he is a new creation: the old has gone, the new is here. I see you not for where you have been but for where you are going. If you are willing to be mine and mine only, staying in the house of God, I am willing and ready to be yours and yours only," says Emily excitedly.

On Thanksgiving Day, the Gramps and the Grannies are together to celebrate the holiday.

"I have good news for you," Hayet tells them. "I discussed the marriage issue with one woman and I need your advice. I want to do all right and should start and end with you."

"It should be the girl that wiped your tears at the hospital all those years ago, Emily," shouts Mrs. Lionel.

"Yes, she is, but how did you know?" asks Hayet.

"We knew it and we have been praying for it. We thank God; go for it and our blessings are with you," assures Grandpa.

Eventually, Hayet gets married to Emily, the noble kind of woman a blessed man would have. As she had previously predicted, for the very thing that he hated her, he loves her now. That is not all. He becomes the RA and does it wonderfully, starts his own streaming show, does some projects that make him a voice to the voiceless, and fulfills his full living passion with nothing to slow him, influencing the multitude. At last, Hayet materializes the innate feeling that told him that there is a seed of greatness in his life, not waiting, begging, compromising others to recognize, or to reveal to him his identity, but by walking to his destiny through purposeful living.

Hayet believes in doing what he is supposed to do, and all that are beyond his ability, he commits into God's hand to do as He wishes.

"After all those wasted years, what is your message to the current and future generations?" asks Grandpa.

"Your parents are your teammates, not your enemies. Listen to whatever they tell you and obey them even if you do not like or agree to what they want you to do. They have been through the same or worse situations and listening to them could save you from repeating the same mistakes they did."

"What about confessions to make to God who patiently waited for you?"

"Grandpa, Natalie Grant's 'King of the world' song sums it up beyond all available words," and Hayet sings the song. The song tells that how God is greater, wiser, faster, richer, stronger, loving, forgiving beyond anything possible one could think or imagine. Hayet is so happy that the Gramps, the Grannies, and his mother to see his return to God and embracing purposeful living, but his father who waited for so long.

Glory be to God, who makes the impossible possible. There are no limits with Him. Thank you and God bless you for reading Hayet's story. Hayet hopes to see your story too, because everybody has a story to tell to bring hope and healing on others' lives!

Songs used in the manuscript

1. Tenth Avenue North's Healing Begins
2. Laura Story's Blessings
3. KC and the Sunshine Band's Please Do not Go
4. Lauren Diagle's Trust In you
5. Casting Crown's There Will Be a Day
6. Wayburn Dean and Doug Bieden's What Will Be Your Legacy.
7. Toby Mac's City on Our Knees
8. Brandon Heath's I am Not Who I Was
9. Casting Crown's Slow Fade
10. Mercy Me's Greater
11. Justin Bieber's Never Say Never
12. Natalie Grant's King of the world

It was good for me to be afflicted
so that i might learn your decrees

— Psalms 119:71

GLOSSARY

What you know today can affect what you do tomorrow. But what you know today cannot affect what you did yesterday.

— Condoleezza Rice

The following are Tigrigna words pronounced in English, as well as their meaning.

N.B. — Some of these words may not be in this book. However, they are helpful to learn about the language and the culture where Hayet is from. There is no formal way of writing English words in Tigrigna, and so when Tigrigna speakers write a word, there can be a small difference as to the spelling. For example, for Abby, one can write it as *aby*, and for cough one can write it as it as *cof* or *kof.* Additionally, there may be some difference when other language speakers say the word. The author has made it easy to remember and say them. For example, the easy way for saying a donkey is add-gee; while the hard way, which is correct is *adgi*. These Tigrigna words may probably mean the same in Italian due to the colony there; they can mean the same in Arabic and Hebrew because they come from the same language family, which is Semitic.

The English word *you* can refer to a male or female, the old or the young, plural or singular, the respected or a common person. However, in Tigrigna each of the abovementioned categories has its word. That is why the glossary lists by gender, age, status and plural/singular. Note also the letter 'A' at the beginning of a word is always pronounced as 'A' in apple.

1. A, A, A—a sound people make when crying over the death of loved ones
2. Aba-Ha-bash—(Father of Ha-bash, Abyssinian people) name of a popular granite built apartment named after an Arab owner
3. Aba—father, religious father (leader) (God)
4. Aba-ha-go—grandpa
5. Aba-ha-go-y—my grandpa

6. A-bay—big, old, great (feminine), grandma
7. A-bay-e-y—my grandma
8. Abbey—where?
9. Abby—big, old, great (masculine)
10. Abby-ingera—big ingera, abundant blessings
11. Abet—yes sir/madam
12. Abishai—my best friend. It is a title given to a married woman in southern Eritrea.
13. Abo—father
14. Abo-Na—our father
15. A-boy-Abby—is a respectful way of addressing a man that you do not know his name, which could be your father (age wise). If you know the name then, you would say A-boy plus the name. It means my big father.
16. A-boy—my father
17. Acer—footsteps
18. Adam—mankind
19. A-day-A-bay—respectful ways of addressing a woman that you do not know her name, which could be your mother (age wise). If you know the name then, you would say A-day plus the name. It means big mother
20. A-day—my mother
21. Add-gay—my donkey
22. Add-gee—donkey
23. Add-gen—their donkey to older, plural, respected women/woman
24. Add-goo—his donkey, belonging to a male age mate or younger (MAMOY)
25. Adele—dispense without charging, MAMOY doing
26. Adele-lee—dispense without charging, (FAMOY) female age mate or younger doing
27. A-de—mother
28. Afar—one of the nine tribes and one of the nine languages of Eritrea
29. Ally—one who protects, provides, and takes care of people that are not able to do so for themselves.
30. A-met—year
31. A-Mel—habit (negative way)
32. A-mill—customer

33. Amy—last year
34. Ann-Be-sa—lion
35. An-dome—their pole, support
36. Andy—a pole that supports an item
37. Angle—continuously feed the hungry until they are satisfied
38. Anne—I
39. Anne-e-ye—it is I
40. An-so-la—bed shit
41. Arabia—wheelbarrow
42. A-ran-she—orange
43. Arbate—four
44. Arby—Friday
45. Are-K—my friend
46. Are-key—friend
47. Asmara—the act of creating unity and oneness by feminine genders.
48. Ass-car-baa—shoe
49. Ass-hit—Flint stone
50. Ass-tea—telling someone to give a drink to a person, animal, plant
51. Ass-tea-yea—telling someone to give a drink to FAMOY
52. Atal—goats
53. A-tea—you, for an FAMOY, disrespectful way of calling an older and respectful woman
54. A-to—Mister
55. Atta—you, for a MAMOY, disrespectful way of calling an older and respectful man
56. At-yea—entered FAMOY, entered for feminine
57. At-yen—entered for respectful, older female or plural female
58. At-Yom—they entered for older, respectful man or plural men
59. At-you—he entered MAMOY, entered for masculine
60. Audi—a place for treading out the grains
61. Audrey—mustard seed
62. Aura—main
63. A-well—the first stage of coffee
64. Baal—holiday or word used when mentioning list of names

65. Bah-tea—first day of a month
66. Ban-dear-a—flag
67. Bara—to fire somebody from a position
68. Bared—ice
69. Bark—bless; a MAMOY saying or doing the blessing.
70. Bark-e-nee—bless me, requesting to be blessed by MAMOY, God or your father
71. Bark-u-nee—requesting to be blessed by highly respected older male (plural)
72. Barnett—slavery
73. Ba-rote—slaves
74. Bar-yea—slave
75. Bear-K—my knee
76. Bear-key—knee
77. Belen—say or hit to more than one woman, and to the same age or older and respected female
78. Bella—to say or hit for a FAMOY
79. Belle—he said for MAMOY
80. Belles—cactus
81. Bell—say, for MAMOY
82. Belly—say, for FAMOY
83. Be-Shem-AB—in the name of the Father (God)
84. Beth—house (of); a prefix that comes before the noun: Beth-Christian, Beth-prison, Beth-school
85. Beth-ma-sir-tea—prison
86. Beth-Tim-hear-tea—school
87. Bet-tree—staff weapon
88. Betty—that way
89. Be-thee—this way
90. Bib—honk
91. Bleach—extremely marvelous light that goes on and off
92. Blush—a wasted thing
93. Brkti—Blessed
94. Brook—blessed or merciful male
95. B-S-rat—good news

96. Bun—coffee
97. Bunny—bread
98. Burr—to suddenly wake up from sleep
99. Bush—a glass cup; when a liquid pours out uncontrollably, you say bush-bush
100. Cabana—from us
101. Can—saying or doing something, never to turn back or regret
102. Can-za—pain
103. Casa-Kenisha—house of protestants
104. Cd—spoiled (person)
105. Celeste—three
106. Cell-Dee—money n
107. Chaff—edge
108. Cha-ma—shoe
109. Cha-quit—chick (tiny)
110. Cha—sayings go, go ahead to a donkey. While for horse one would say sue
111. Chat—a narcotic shrub leaf (drug) used for the stimulant effect
112. Chekan—cruel
113. Chief-luck—squashed thing
114. Chi-nook—worrisome masculine, any age
115. Christos—Christ
116. Ciao—bye
117. Co-me-de-re—tomato
118. Congo—a popular factory made rubber shoe
119. Coo-at—dig, MAMOY
120. Coo-bay-yea—a cup
121. Coo-bo—dried cattle dung collected from the field
122. Co-bore-ta—blanket
123. Cool-fee—belt
124. Core-bet—skin
125. Core-did—a tick. It could also refer to a person who sticks to another person to gain what he/she did not labor for
126. Corey—Be unhappy, be mad, get annoyed over somebody or something to MAMOY

127. Co-sham—flirtatious
128. Cough—sit
129. Cough-bell—sit down to a MAMOY
130. Cough-belly—sit down to a FAMOY
131. Coy-ne—I became
132. Cub—from
133. Curry—cold
134. Danny—judge, act of judging MAMOY
135. Dan-ye—judge, act of judging done by the first-person singular
136. Dan-you—judge, the act of judging saying to older or respected male
137. Dee-coo-an—a shop
138. Dembe—a pen where cattle sleep/feed/sleep
139. Dem—blood
140. Die—be extremely fast at doing or saying something.
141. D-Nish—potato
142. Dodge—converse shoe
143. Dude—when fire burns out of control
144. Due—is it? Word used as a suffix showing whether somebody or something is it or not
145. Easy/EZ—this/these
146. Easy-atom—these people
147. E-bay—to refuse or say no, MAMOY
148. Ed shena-hit tsena-hit— The hand that hits others also get hit (the saying originates from a donkey or any animal kicking people)
149. E-day—my hand
150. Eden—their hand, to plural, older or to respected women
151. Ed—hand
152. Edna—our hand
153. E-do—his hand, MAMOY
154. Edom—their hand for plural, older male, or for a male of a highly-respected status
155. Eh—sympathetic feeling or invoking a curse
156. E-Leal-ta—a chant or a unique joyful sound that usually women make
157. E-let—date

158. Elf—thousand
159. Ella—she said for a FAMOY
160. Elle—I said
161. Ellen—she said for an older female, plural women, or a respected woman
162. E-manna—have faith, trust, believe for plural female, older, respected woman
163. Em-bill-ta—folk windpipe instrument
164. E-men—have faith, believe for a MAMOY
165. E-menu—have faith, believe for plural males, older males, respected males
166. Essay—extreme joy or happiness, when getting a victory; also, defeat of an enemy
167. E-toe—saying enter into something to MAMOY
168. E-toe-we—enter into something saying to FAMOY
169. E-toe-woo—saying enter to male respected or older one
170. E-yea—is for masculine gender/thing
171. Eye-nay—my eye
172. Eye-nee—an eye
173. E-you—is for the feminine gender/thing
174. Feet-he—justice
175. Fidel—alphabets used by Tigrigna and other Afro-Asiatic Semitic languages
176. Fill-fill—water that springs from a source
177. Fin-fin-tea—despised, refuse, unacceptable person or thing (feminine)
178. Fin-fun—despised, refuse, unacceptable person or thing (masculine)
179. Fin-j-al—a coffee cup (porcelain)
180. Focus—easygoing, restless, hyper FAMOY
181. Foe-kiss—easygoing, restless, hyper MAMOY
182. Foe—stinking smell or something that is not pleasing
183. Full—peanut
184. Fully—separated, detached, exceptionally perfect; for males
185. Fuss—an ax
186. Gabby—a white knitted shawl made up of woven cotton
187. Game—hairstyle braid of an unmarried woman

188. Geez—Language of the Orthodox priests as Latin is to Catholic
189. Geisha—she went to out of town, perhaps out of country or state
190. Geza—a prefix meaning house, the same as the Spanish casa
191. GMAT—vein
192. Go-go—local bread that is the hardest to eat and break
193. Go-huff—garbage
194. Good—something terribly unheard of, bad news or unpleasant happening
195. Good-gad—a hole or pothole on the ground
196. Good-goo-doe—dried cattle dung, it is personally prepared
197. Gray—left handed
198. Groom—fantastic
199. Ha-bee—ordering to give, for a FAMOY
200. Ha-das—new (feminine)
201. Ha-dish—new (masculine)
202. Hager—country
203. Haggai—dry season; one of the four seasons
204. Ha-goes—joy/happiness
205. Haile—power/strength
206. Ha-Kim—physician
207. Ham-bees—swim, MAMOY
208. Ham-be-sue—swim, MAMOY doing,
209. Ham-b-see—swim, FAMOY
210. Hammed—a soil
211. Ha-ram—something culturally which should not be done or said
212. Haram-be—homemade shoe utilizing worn-out tire.
213. Harass—one that gave birth recently
214. Ha-r-net—deliverance
215. Harry-com—they are angry, older, respected male
216. Harry-coo—he is angry MAMOY
217. Harsh—an ox that plows
218. Ha-tea-at—sin
219. Ha-then—bereavement
220. Hawaii—a wound that gets healed easily
221. Ha-way—my brother

222. Ha-well-tea—statue
223. Hawk—disturb for a MAMOY
224. Ha-yet—a cub lion
225. Hayley—my power, my strength
226. Hazy—hold, saying to a FAMOY
227. Hear-can—anger
228. He-bay—monkey
229. He-boo—he gave, for a MAMOY
230. He-boo-nee—he gave me, for a MAMOY
231. He-dem—flee, MAMOY
232. He-mam—sickness
233. Hewett—life
234. Hid-at—calmness
235. Hill-me—dream
236. Hi-ma-note—religion
237. Hiram—battered
238. How—a brother
239. Hub—ordering to give, for a MAMOY
240. Hub-Rome—clever, smart
241. Hub-tea—wealth
242. Hub-Tom—their wealth, for plural males or older/respected male
243. Hub-too—his wealth, for a MAMOY
244. Huff—to stand up from a sitting position
245. Huff-tea—sister
246. Huh—opening wide (mouth or sinkhole) to swallow all that is there
247. Humus—Thursday
248. Hurry—poop
249. I—a prefix that makes a word negative
250. In-je-ra—traditional bread, also known as ingera. It could also mean anything edible, the same as bread in English.
251. In-key—giving something to, for a FAMOY
252. Is-nee—ear
253. In-tie—what?
254. Juba—pocket

255. Kahn—a priest
256. Kara—knife
257. K-do—he went, he left, for a MAMOY
258. K-dome—they went, they left, for older men or a respected man
259. Keen-at—jealousy
260. Keen-day—how much or how many?
261. Keen-fee—a wing,
262. Keen-teat—feather
263. Kenisha—protestant
264. Kenny—stay few more days, for a MAMOY
265. Ken-sha-be—male circumcizer
266. Ken-sha-beat—female circumcizer
267. Key-cha—local bread
268. Key-sad—neck
269. Keshi—priest
270. Kiddy—ordering to go, for a FAMOY
271. Kid—ordering to go, for a MAMOY
272. Kirar—five/six-stringed musical instrument
273. Kitten—get skinny or be a skinny, for a MAMOY
274. Kobo-roe—timbrel, (drum)
275. Kreme—stay summer season MAMOY
276. Kreme-tea—summer, rainy season
277. Kudus—holy
278. Kun—be (MAMOY). Kun also be used as in God said let there be (Kun) light, and it was so.
279. Ku-nee—be (FAMOY)
280. Lad-yea—used to in a negative way, (overused) if something becomes Lad-yea then it is useless (feminine) example, teeth less chain ring
281. Lad-you—used to in a negative way, (overused) if something becomes Lad-you then it is useless (masculine) example, teeth less chain ring
282. Lam—cow
283. Lay-tea—night
284. Leaf—a sieve used to filter coffee
285. Le-date —birth (Christmas)

286. Lee-mad—habit (negative way)
287. Le-mean—lemon
288. Libby—heart
289. Lie-synthesis—It is a process whereby you do not punish an ally over punishable offenses, but you punish an enemy over an unpunishable offense. It perpetuates the interests of the powerful, the ruling class as well as the rich. It is also a way of legalizing the illegal using the law. Lie-synthesis covers up the wrongs of an ally to evade punishment. It also paralyzes and forces one to muzzle up from speaking what is just and fair. Should one speak against Lie-synthesis, one it libels on as an antagonist or and other names. Lie-synthesis illegally makes fortune out of the weak and the poor.
290. Mallet—meaning
291. Man-goose—mango
292. Manta—twin
293. Mark—make your enemies surrender, do not kill enemy combatants
294. Marsha—gear of an automobile
295. Mass-tea-ca—chewing gum
296. Maya—her water, for a FAMOY
297. Me-a-core—butt
298. Me-a-D—dinner table (where people eat together from one tray)
299. Me-al-tea—day
300. Mean-ass—younger, comparing older and younger
301. Mean-Sue-Sue-lie—squirrel
302. Me-an-ta—intestine
303. Mel-AK—an angel
304. Melissa—she answered a question, she returned (something borrowed),
305. FAMOY
306. Men-deal—handkerchief or head cover
307. Men-fess-kudus—Holy Spirit
308. Men-fess-say-tan—spirit of the devil
309. Men-fess—spirit
310. Men-gees-tea—government
311. Men-gees-to—his government, MAMOY
312. Men-ke-sh-ke-sh—coffee roasting pan

313. Men-she-ma—What is her name? FAMOY
314. Men-she-moo—What is his name? MAMOY
315. Men-shim-key—What is your name? FAMOY
316. Men—who?
317. Mere-at—bride
318. Mere-A—wedding
319. Mere-A-we—groom
320. Merit—rusted
321. Me-rough—chapter
322. Mesmer—a measuring ruler
323. Mess-Kreme—September (first month of the year)
324. Mess-you—it is a late night
325. Me-tea—hundred
326. Me-than—weight, scale
327. Mid-Han—salvation
328. Miss-am—the act of kissing
329. Miss—with
330. Miss-men—with who?
331. Mo-go-go—clay pan for baking tie-ta/injera
332. Mott—death
333. My—water
334. N—for (N, as in Ken)
335. Nab—to
336. Nag-ram—problematic, one who fights with everybody pointlessly
337. Nay—for belonging to someone
338. Nay-men—whose?
339. N-E—come, FAMOY
340. Ne-a—come, MAMOY
341. Ne-bee—prophet
342. Nee-D—a platform mattress-less bed made up of clay and stones
343. Nee-gees-tea—queen
344. Nee-goose—king
345. NH-bee—a bee
346. Nigger-Renée—tell me, to a MAMOY

347. Nigger-Rome—tell them, to tell to plural or to respected males or a
348. MAMOY
349. Nigger—tell, for a MAMOY
350. No-no-E—no
351. Nora—White paint that is dusty
352. Quack—raven
353. Ray—to look at, saying to a MAMOY
354. Reggie—bra
355. Riesa—coffin
356. Safe—sword
357. Safé—traditional interlace handmade tray
358. Salaam—peace, hello, hi, greetings, rest, free from agitation or discord, bid farewell, completeness, wholeness, safety, absence of war, good-bye
359. Say-tan—devil
360. Seal-tan—authority
361. See-nee—teeth
362. Seldom—their money, for older male or male of high status
363. Semen—north
364. Se-may—heaven
365. Shah-he—black tea
366. She-all—hell (hyper person)
367. She-core—sugar
368. She-den (Sheden)—a lion, leader of the pride
369. Sheen-tea—urine
370. Sheen—urinate, for a MAMOY
371. Sheet—sale, saying to MAMOY
372. She-ha-nee—a tray for washing feet, for eating injera
373. Sheila—one that snatches and disappears (e.g., an eagle)
374. She-ma—her name to FAMOY
375. She-may—my name
376. She-nee—to urinate, for a FAMOY
377. Sheriff—loose tooth
378. She-shy—abundant blessing of something
379. Shim—name

380. Shook—market
381. Shush—small cotton fabric shawl
382. Sly—for my sake
383. Sony—Monday
384. Sue—horse rider says Sue to horse to make it go ahead; for a donkey—cha
385. Sue-wa—a traditional drink
386. Sunday—my best friend. It is a title given to a woman when addressing another woman in southern Eritrea.
387. Susa—sixty
388. Talk-see—shooting
389. Tara—queue, turn to do or say something
390. Ta-Rick—history
391. T-beat—pride
392. Ten-Cole—intentional craftiness to attack someone
393. Tess-me—butter
394. Than-ta—storytelling
395. The-Kerr—remember, saying to MAMOY
396. The-my—brother or sister in law
397. The-men—century
398. There-E—seed
399. There-om—their seed
400. They—not; a prefix used to show a negative
401. They-tea—oil
402. Tiel—goat
403. Tie-ta—traditional bread, also known as injera
404. Tim-bell—be silent, ordering to MAMOY (shut up)
405. Tim-belly—be silent, ordering to FAMOY (shut up)
406. Tim—ordering to be silent
407. Tin-beat —prophesy
408. Tipsy—roasted, meat or corn
409. Toby—if someone is eating and you want him to give you some for free, you say toby
410. Toe-leash—woven mat

411. Tom-back—heavy smoker
412. Tough/tuff—Millet–like, small, seeded crop; used for tie-ta/injera
413. T-rat—fart
414. Tree—January
415. Tse-bell—holy water that people drink/wash
416. Tub—Breast
417. Wa-euro—lioness
418. Way—or
419. Way-the-rite—title of an unmarried, yet matured woman
420. Way-the-roe—title of a married woman
421. We-day—my son
422. Weds—give praise
423. We-ha-thee—meaning ceaselessly flowing something, perhaps a river, a masculine
424. We-ha-thee-t—meaning ceaselessly flowing something, perhaps a river, a feminine
425. Wencho—an itchy blanket, also known as a blanket of shame
426. Were-he—month
427. When-char—unkempt hair of a female
428. Win—extreme desire to get something you crave, such as a cake
429. Yee-A-kill—that is enough
430. Ye-sues—Jesus
431. Za-gua-lay— Z is a short form of (EZ or easy, referring to (this), the word means 'Oh my daughter
432. Zig-nee—red hot, chilly stew
433. Z-we-day —Z is a short form of (EZ or easy, referring to (this), the word means 'Oh, my son')